Civilizing
Torture

Civilizing Torture

An American Tradition

W. FITZHUGH BRUNDAGE

THE BELKNAP PRESS OF
HARVARD UNIVERSITY PRESS

Cambridge, Massachusetts

London, England

2018

First printing

Library of Congress Cataloging-in-Publication Data

Names: Brundage, W. Fitzhugh (William Fitzhugh), 1959– author.
Title: Civilizing torture : an American tradition / W. Fitzhugh
 Brundage.
Description: Cambridge, Massachusetts : The Belknap Press of
 Harvard University Press, 2018.
Identifiers: LCCN 2018017055 | ISBN 9780674737662 (alk. paper)
Subjects: LCSH: Torture—United States—History. | Torture—
 Moral and ethical aspects—United States. | Justification (Ethics)
Classification: LCC HV8599.U6 B78 2018 | DDC 363.25/4—dc23
LC record available at https://lccn.loc.gov/2018017055

For S. E. J.

Irás, iremos juntos por las aguas del tiempo.
Ninguna viajará por la sombra conmigo . . .
                              —Pablo Neruda, *Sonnet 81*

Contents

A Question of Civilization

IN DECEMBER 1858 *Harper's Weekly,* one of the most popular American magazines of the day, published a gruesome article entitled "Torture and Homicide in an American State Prison." Accompanied by graphic illustrations, the article dwelled on the so-called water cure. In this punishment, an inmate was stripped and seated in a stall with his feet and arms fastened in stocks and his head extended up into a tank that fit snugly around his neck. The prisoner's head was drenched with freezing water that cascaded down from a height of a foot or more for several minutes at a time. The tank that encircled the prisoner's neck emptied slowly, inducing a sensation of drowning while the prisoner struggled to keep his mouth and nose above the pool of draining water.[1]

About thirty years later, an investigation at Elmira Reformatory, the most acclaimed American penal institution of the day, revealed that the staff continued to douse prisoners with cold water in addition to confining them in darkened cells for weeks on end, shackling and hoisting them until their toes barely touched the floor, and "paddling" them with specially made boards.[2] In 1899 American soldiers occupying the Philippines after the Spanish-American War sent home letters boasting of their routine application of a variant of the water cure to coerce information from Filipino guerrillas. To apply the "cure," soldiers pinned their victim to the ground by his legs and arms and partially raised his head "so as to make pouring in the water an easier matter." If he refused to keep his mouth open, his tormentors pinched his nose closed and used a rifle barrel or bamboo stick to pry his jaws apart. Then they poured water into his overextended mouth until he looked like "a pregnant woman."[3] According to witnesses, a few applications of the water cure usually elicited a flood of information.

A century later, the outlines of the "enhanced interrogation" methods adopted by the Central Intelligence Agency and military interrogators during the so-called War on Terror became public. Americans learned that between 2003 and 2006 at least eighty-nine Middle Eastern detainees in CIA custody had been slapped, slammed against walls, deprived of sleep, stuffed into coffins, and threatened with violent death. The most severe method used was "waterboarding," a modern-day variant of the technique applied a century and a half earlier in American prisons. Waterboarding entailed pouring water over a cloth covering the face and breathing passages of an immobilized detainee, which produced an acute sensation of drowning. One detainee endured more than 180 waterboarding sessions.[4]

Torture in the United States has been in plain sight, at least for those who have looked for it. To acknowledge this history is not to suggest that it is equivalent to that of societies in which state-sponsored torture and terror have been endemic, such as Germany during the Nazi regime, Argentina during its "dirty war," Guatemala during the late twentieth century, or Zimbabwe since its independence. Only some Americans have been subjected to torture, while most have been able to live in denial or ignorance of the practice taking place in the nation.

The "American tradition" in this book's subtitle is not a particular method of tormenting the body. It refers instead to the debates that Americans have waged regarding torture. Like a minuet in which the dancers change fashions over time yet the steps remain the same, these debates have unfolded in predictable fashion. When Americans have debated torture, they invariably have invoked the nation's utopian ambitions to serve as the exemplar of modern democratic civilization. Since the nation's founding, Americans have boasted that the United States is a unique nation with uniquely humane laws and principles.

The roots of this certainty in American exceptionalism can be traced to the earliest days of the European conquest of North America. Champions of European ambitions in the New World insisted that they were transplanting the rule of law and civilization to a continent gripped by the savage and cruel violence of Indians. For civilization to survive and thrive in North America, savagery had to be eradicated. Thus the torture and violence of the New World became a mirror in which Europeans looked most often for confirmation of their righteousness and civility and less often for evidence of their regression. Europeans excused their complicity in the cycle of violence by insisting that their violence was retaliatory and necessary for the creation and preservation of civilization. In time, the generation of colonists who waged the American War of Independence and presided over the young republic would congratulate themselves for consigning torture and other relics of savagery to a past that no longer retained a hold over the new nation. Henceforth torture would be synonymous with tyrants and savages. Where torture persisted in the New World and beyond, it did so only because American institutions and civilization had yet to fulfill their destiny.

Undergirding this presumption of American exceptionalism is a widely held conviction that the nation's founders bequeathed a constitution that codified the Enlightenment principle that rational laws, rather than superstition or tradition, would secure the greatest justice and best government. Enshrined in the nation's constitution is a prohibition on torture and "cruel and unusual punishments." Americans during the nineteenth century heaped scorn on autocratic regimes elsewhere in the world for their fealty to inhumane traditions, including torture. During the past century, Americans found further confirmation of the singular virtues of their institutions and principles as Fascist and Communist regimes in Europe, Russia, and Asia employed torture as an essential tool of statecraft. Both defenders and opponents of torture have staked out their positions, confident that they were citizens of a modern, civilized nation that was, in Abraham Lincoln's words, mankind's best hope.

Stretching across the past century and a half, the instances of simulated drowning that open this book seem to confirm the Argentine torturer Julio Héctor Simón's claim that "torture is eternal." Pressed to explain his actions in Argentina's "dirty war" during the 1970s, Simón responded that torture "has always existed and it always will. It is an essential part of the human being."[5] In his mind, his conduct was little more than a complement to the relentless cycle of the seasons. His self-serving insistence that torture is inherent in the human condition should not discourage us from appreciating the crucial importance of historical context to understanding his acts during the Argentine junta of the 1970s or those of Americans during the 1850s, 1890s, or 2000s. His apparent intent was to mitigate the import of his historical agency and the particular acts of torture that he carried out on particular people, in particular places, for particular reasons.

More often, torturers have dwelled on the exceptional circumstances that they claim provoked their conduct. Whereas Simón preferred to see his actions as swallowed up in the long record of human history, others have pointed to allegedly unprecedented threats and extraordinary conditions that compelled them to act in ways they otherwise might never have contemplated. Cofer Black, the head of the CIA's counterterrorist operations during the War on Terror, voiced this perspective when he testified before Congress in 2002: "All I want to say is that there was 'before' 9 / 11 and 'after' 9 / 11. After 9 / 11 the gloves come off."[6]

Neither Simón's contention that torture is a historical inevitability nor the claim that each instance of torture is historically unique will enable us to make sense of the simulated drownings and other tortures that have punctuated American history. Both of these explanations of torture pose obstacles to historical understanding. Simón's perspective is fundamentally ahistorical; torture cannot be explained by appeals to metaphysical destiny. The other perspective, with its exaggerated emphasis on unique historical circumstances that excuse specific uses of torture, is no less ahistorical. It discourages, indeed precludes, any recognition that torture has been both a recurring practice and a subject of debate since the arrival of Europeans on the shores of the present-day United States.

The history of American torture reminds us of Montaigne's wisdom that "each man calls barbarism whatever is not his own practice."[7] Torture, like other forms of cruelty, is in the eye of the beholder. There is no unambiguous threshold that separates cruelty from torture. In common usage, cruelty includes the wanton, unnecessary, outrageous, and inhumane infliction of suffering on the body or mind. Cruelty may be a spontaneous expression of anger, frustration, or contempt, or it can take the form of the deliberate and extended infliction of pain. Torture, in common understanding, is purposeful and entails the infliction of suffering as punishment or a means of interrogation. The ambiguous boundary that separates cruelty and torture has been the battleground where defenders and opponents of torture have repeatedly clashed.

Every significant debate about the ethics and efficacy of torture in the United States has been accompanied by strenuous jousting over definitions of and euphemisms for torture. In each instance of water punishments described earlier, some Americans recoiled in disgust and dismay at what they viewed as indefensible acts of torture. But others defended the controversial practices by dismissing any suggestion that they were equivalent to torture. A proponent of "hydropathic punishment" during the 1850s insisted that simulated drowning was a "perfectly proper method of compulsion" that illustrated the "good, though melancholy, uses to which cold water may be applied."[8] A half century later, the superintendent of the Elmira Reformatory responsible for the punishment regime there described the water cure and other punishments as analogous to "harmless parental discipline."[9] Champions of the American occupation of the Philippines went so far as to stage mock applications of the water cure to willing subjects to demonstrate that accounts of the interrogation method greatly exaggerated its severity. Indeed, some apologists went so far as to claim that the water cure had salutary health effects.[10] When controversy arose over waterboarding during the Bush administration, defenders of the practice asserted that it did not meet the definition of torture because it induces fear, by simulating drowning, but does not inflict pain. An administration spokesperson repeatedly declared that "there's no extreme pain" caused by waterboarding.[11]

Torture cannot be disentangled from the discourse surrounding it. The historical study of American torture necessarily catalogs not only acts of violence but also the explanations, justifications, and denunciations of them. While this book undoubtedly betrays the vantage point of its twenty-first-century author, it does not impose a present-day definition of torture on the past. Instead, it traces debates over forms of violence and coercion that at least some contemporaries labeled as torture. Throughout the book I acknowledge that other historical actors adopted euphemisms for the violence they condoned while flatly rejecting the use of the word "torture" to label the practices they sanctioned. Bush administration officials, for example, pointedly avoided the use of the word "torture" and instead referred to "enhanced interrogation." Their use of language was of a piece with their intent to devise the severest possible techniques of interrogation that stopped just short of meeting the narrowest possible definition of torture. When they did so they clearly had in mind the definition of torture adopted by the United Nations in 1984, which provides the basis for present-day prosecutions of human rights violators. Torture "means any act by which severe pain or suffering, whether physical or mental, is intentionally inflicted on a person for such purposes as obtaining from him, or a third person, information or a confession, punishing him for an act he or a third person has committed or is suspected of having committed, or intimidating or coercing him or a third person, or for any reason based on discrimination of any kind, when such pain or suffering is inflicted by or at the instigation of or with the consent or acquiescence of a public official or other person acting in an official capacity. It does not include pain or suffering arising only from, inherent in, or incidental to, lawful sanctions."[12]

Although of undoubted usefulness in the contemporary campaign to limit torture and punish torturers, this definition is less useful as a basis for historical analysis. It requires careful and extensive qualification when applied to the practices labeled as torture by past generations, from ancient Greece to the early twentieth-century United States. The meaning attached to the word "torture" has varied substantially over time and from society to society. Moreover, since at least the fifteenth century, Europeans and Americans have used the word expansively and promiscuously. In addition to applying the word to formal torture as defined in contemporary law, they used it to describe the physical and spiritual torment endured by Christ and saints as well as the banal discomforts of everyday life, ranging from delayed gratification to wretched food. Consequently, any history of torture needs to be attentive to the evolution of the language used to define, describe, and debate torture.

Debates about torture have flared episodically when substantial numbers of Americans have concluded that practices of violent coercion by Americans acting in the name of the state (or with powers granted to them by the state) transgress both national principles and modern norms of civilization. That torture carried out by agents of the American state has been a focal point of these debates is testament to the deeply rooted presumption that the nation's laws and constitutional principles should serve as a bulwark against torture. The founders of the republic looked to the beneficent influence of modern civilization to tamp down private violence but to the nation's legal traditions and democratic institutions to inhibit any tyrannical tendencies by the state.

Despite the Founders' care to inhibit the establishment of an oppressive central state, the nation's democratic institutions and traditions have proved far more hospitable to torture than many Americans assume. Bedrock elements of American democracy have arguably both fostered torture and hindered efforts to curtail it. The dispersal of authority across multiple layers of local, state, and federal government, combined with a potent tradition of popular democracy and localism, may have protected the liberty of the citizenry from the tyranny of the national government, but that same decentralized power gave license to countless legal and self-declared agents of the state to wield the power of petty despots.

The choreography of participants in debates regarding American torture follows a strikingly consistent pattern, reflecting the imperative for defenders and opponents alike to square themselves with the nation's professed principles and with the dictates of modern civilization.

When accusations of torture are first broached, implicated officials are certain to issue categorical denials of any systematic and inhumane violence. Intentional violations of sacred American principles are unthinkable, as Secretary of War Elihu Root implied in 1901 when he proclaimed that the occupation of the Philippines had been conducted "with scrupulous regard for the rules of civilized warfare" and "with self-restraint, and with humanity never surpassed."[13] Such categorical denials prompt opponents of the controversial practices to ferret out more evidence of wrongdoing, which in turn goads apologists to concede that a few lamentable transgressions may have occurred even if their incidence and character were grossly exaggerated by critics. A prominent national spokesman for police superintendents adopted this stance in 1910 in response to quiet grumblings about cruel police interrogation techniques; he assured Americans that "rough usage" of suspected criminals had once occurred but that "such procedure does not obtain at large nowadays."[14] Defenders of controversial practices are also likely to dismiss the victims of alleged torture as neither credible nor deserving of sympathy. Torture victims invariably are portrayed as loathsome, depraved, and violent. The lawyer representing a Chicago policeman accused of torturing scores of suspects during the 1980s, for example, exemplified this response when he denounced his client's accusers as "the scum of the earth" while lauding his client for decorated service in the military and as a police officer.[15] Anyone who takes up the defense of odious criminals, groups, or enemies of the nation risks guilt by association. When unassailable evidence surfaced in 1969 that American troops had committed torture, rape, and other atrocities in Vietnam, Governor Ronald Reagan of California complained that the exaggerated attention on atrocities gave "comfort and aid to our enemies."

These denunciations of alleged torture victims and their champions are often accompanied by claims that the controversial practices are justifiable and effective in the specific circumstances in which they are used. Without the judicious application of stern measures, the argument goes, American civilization will succumb to attacks by vicious enemies unrestrained by respect for our civilization and institutions. Thus at the outset of the War on Terrorism, while President George W. Bush warned the nation that it would wage "a war unlike any other,"

Vice President Dick Cheney explained, "It's going to be vital for us to use any means at our disposal basically to achieve our objectives."[16] The "enhanced interrogation" methods that the administration subsequently adopted were wholly consistent with its stance that the president had carte blanche to respond to the extraordinary provocation of the terrorist attacks of September 2001.

In this and other instances, opponents are likely to counter that stern measures are at once counterproductive and immoral. Equally important, the nation's principles should not be bent to circumstances. Any concession to expediency risks undermining institutions and principles that are themselves the nation's greatest protection. Senator John McCain made precisely this argument in 2014 when he denounced the interrogation methods employed in Guantánamo and Iraq and pledged that all Americans "are obliged by history, by our nation's highest ideals and the many terrible sacrifices made to protect them, by our respect for human dignity to make clear we need not risk our national honor to prevail in this or any war. We need only remember in the worst of times, through the chaos and terror of war, when facing cruelty, suffering and loss, that we are always Americans, and different, stronger, and better than those who would destroy us."[17]

When the offending practices are halted, either because the circumstances that gave rise to them ease or because the controversy that they aroused prompts it, the substance of debate shifts to the significance that should be attached to the practices. Defenders are sure to insist that they were effective and therefore no hand-wringing over them is warranted. And in those instances of exceptional violations carried out by a "few bad apples," they will say, it is counterproductive to assign broader responsibility or to implicate the larger cause with which they were associated. In 1903, for instance, Senator Henry Cabot Lodge batted away demands for further congressional investigations of American atrocities in the Philippines by disparaging the accusations as hackneyed and baseless persecutions of soldiers who defended the nation's interests while in harm's way.[18]

A common thread in these rival perspectives is the presumption that Americans should exist in a state of national innocence, with torture held at arm's length. Americans have been at best complacent and at worst willful in presuming that torture is something that other people do elsewhere. This predilection was evident in the newsrooms of the *New York Times* during 2003 when a correspondent in Afghanistan filed a story revealing that two Afghani detainees had died while undergoing interrogation by Americans. Despite thorough confirmation, many of the newspaper's editorial staff were reluctant to print the story because it seemed inconceivable that Americans might willfully beat, freeze, and suffocate detainees to death. A member of the *Times* staff recalled that some editors "insisted that it was improbable; it was just hard to get their mind around." The newspaper eventually ran the story, buried on page 14, leading its author to conclude that the editors had been reluctant to "believe bad things of Americans."[19]

Torture poses a particular challenge in democracies because the extreme inequality that is a precondition for torture cannot easily be reconciled with democratic practices. Torture does not occur when the torturer and the torture victim possess equal power; the abject powerlessness of the victim is a precondition for torture. If we accept the proposition that torture is most likely to occur in any context in which there is a severe disparity of power, we can reconstruct where and when it was most likely to have been employed in the past (and can anticipate where and when it may be employed in the present or future). The condition of individual autonomy that is the presumptive basis of American political and legal traditions would seem to preclude the severe asymmetries of power necessary for torture. Yet throughout the nation's history, inequality and democratic practices have coexisted. Torture is likely to occur in severely hierarchical and enclosed institutions or in settings that resemble the "total institutions" described by the sociologist Erving Goffman or the "disciplinary institutions" described by the social theorist Michel Foucault, such as religious communes, prisons, or fraternal organizations.[20] Torture also is likely where extreme inequality pervades labor relations, such as factories that employ child workers or convict laborers. Torture is a tragic reality within those families in which neither tradition nor law circumscribes parental power. In all of these instances, inequality has been tolerated, even defended, in the name of the public good, tradition, or the inexorable consequence of nature.

The disparity in the comparative power of torturers and their victims not only shapes the practice of torture itself but also distorts the historical record of torture. Perhaps no historical silence is more profound than that of the victims of torture. Although some torturers keep copious and surprisingly revealing records of their actions, most intentionally shield their activities from prying eyes. Torturers and their defenders labor to ensure that surviving historical records present their conduct in the most favorable light. With this aim in mind, they usually exclude whenever possible the voices of their victims from their records. Any protests by torture victims heard beyond the walls of the torture chambers are routinely dismissed as groundless, defamatory, or unworthy of recognition. Because the tortured can seldom successfully rebut these charges, the combination of their imposed silence and ostracism facilitates an eventual amnesia about the torments they endured.

The extreme disparities in power that empowered torturers and muted their victims inform the circular reasoning that has enabled many Americans to retain their faith in the nation's innate innocence. When the reviled, abject, and downtrodden who were deemed unworthy of the protections accorded to citizens and who were most at risk of torture—Indians, the enslaved, prisoners, and suspected criminals—did suffer torture and other cruelties, apologists were sure to insist that they had violated societal norms and had brought their misery on themselves. In the abstract, no one should be tortured, but if people were tortured, they must somehow have deserved their fate. Consequently, the torture itself did not represent a chronic violation of national principles because its victims were undeserving of public concern.

The most marginalized in our midst remain at the greatest risk of being tortured. But the gradual expansion of rights over the course of the nineteenth and twentieth centuries has substantially reduced this portion of the nation's population. However, we should not assume that the seemingly inexorable expansion of rights will eradicate torture. Widening inequality in American society, which has accelerated since the end of the twentieth century, and escalating rhetoric and policies intended to cleanse American society of the undeserving and unwelcome augurs ill for those Americans consigned to these groups. Simultaneously, experiments in "nation building" far beyond the American shores during the past century, from the Philippines to Vietnam and Iraq, have created new frontiers where vast populations have experienced the imposition of American power. Americans have typically regarded these international subjects as apprentices of American democracy even while their tutelage has been nearly invisible to most Americans and they have enjoyed few if any of the protections offered by American law or traditions. As such, they have joined the ranks of those most at risk of torture.

ONE

The Manners of Barbarians

B EFORE PÁNFILO DE NARVÁEZ stepped ashore near present-day Tampa in April 1528, Tocobaga Indians were already leery of Spaniards. Lore about Spanish marauders, who for two decades had absconded with captives and had plundered the Florida coast, had reached the Tocobaga. While the Indians kept their distance from the Spanish, Narváez and his entourage sought out the village where Hirrihigua, the local cacique, presided. Nothing in the Indians' previous experience was likely to have prepared them for the encounter. Using methods of intimidation mastered during earlier campaigns in Cuba, Jamaica, and Mexico, Narváez terrorized the Indians. Without provocation he ordered his troops to set fire to the village's charnel house and to unleash snarling mastiffs, which fatally mauled the cacique's mother. Compounding the horror and humiliation, Narváez amputated the chief's nose, a disfigurement that was a mark of extreme dishonor in early modern Spain.[1]

The Tocobaga, like the Spanish invaders, were adept at using violence to subdue foes. Stunned by the Spaniards' dogs, weapons, and brutality, Hirrihigua and his people waited for several months until an opportunity for vengeance arose. Then they captured a small search party sent from Cuba to locate Narváez's expedition. Hirrihigua ordered the captives stripped and forced them to sprint naked through the village plaza while archers methodically shot them. All of the prisoners, except for Juan Ortiz, a young nobleman from Seville, succumbed in the fusillade of arrows. Ortiz's endurance afforded him no protection against further torment, however. His captors flayed him over flames for hours until he was "half baked" and his body was scarred with "blisters that looked like halves of oranges had formed on one of his sides." But before this agony killed him, women in the village appealed for his reprieve. Ortiz recovered from his ordeal, escaped, and eventually found safe haven in another village with one of Hirrihigua's rivals. (A decade later, in 1539, he was rescued by Hernando de Soto's ill-fated expedition.)[2]

Narváez's unprovoked violence and Hirrihigua's persecution of his Spanish captives must have been among the earliest instances of torture involving both North American Indians and Europeans. It is tempting to assume that this tragic sequence of events in Florida was predictable. After all, both the Indians and the Spanish possessed robust traditions of violence and torture. Henceforth, along with fumbling attempts to master each other's languages and to barter, Indians and Europeans would teach each other about themselves through acts of violence. Extravagant violence against European and Indian bodies became a means of communication, complementing the broader negotiation, exploitation, violence, and theft that accompanied the European conquest of North America. Torture became one of the most emphatic forms of cultural exchange between these wary interlocutors.

However influential and enduring the proclaimed distinction between European civilization and Indian barbarism, in practice Europeans had to adjust their behavior and beliefs to the circumstances they confronted in the New World. Many Europeans came to understand that Indians were not so exotic as to defy comprehension. In many fundamental regards, Europeans and Indians could recognize aspects of themselves and their cultures in the other. Their differences did not render Indians and Europeans incapable of acknowledging one another's humanity. Yet their cultural similarities, at least as much as their alleged cultural incompatibility, generated friction and misunderstanding.[3] As one scholar has pointed out, "Indian and English similarities enabled them to see their differences in sharp relief," differences that both Indians and Europeans exaggerated over time.[4] The practice of torture by Indians and Europeans in North America was an especially conspicuous example of cultural similarity fostering cultural distance.

A brutal logic dictated the torture that Juan Ortiz endured as a captive of the Tocobaga. Torture was long established and widespread among the Indian nations of North America, including those along the Gulf Coast and the Eastern Seaboard. Wherever Indians practiced torture, they did so according to traditions that were as coherent as any that regulated it in Europe. For all of the cruelty inherent in Indian torture, Indian culture did not license wanton violence, and torture's conventions were well understood from one Indian nation to another. Rather than an act of primitive bloodlust, as many Europeans presumed, it was both an extension of Indian spirituality and an important facet of Indian warfare.[5]

Indian warfare and torture were corollaries of each Indian's obligations to family and nation. In the wake of a serious act of violence, customary Indian law sanctioned the defense of clan honor. When an Indian was killed, his male blood relatives were duty bound to punish either the killer or a member of the killer's lineage. Unpunished wrongs impugned the honor of the victim's blood relatives, threatened to destroy amity, and, equally important, thwarted the journey of the souls of the unavenged to the afterlife. Trapped in the world of the living, these tormented souls would harass their surviving relations and clan. To assuage the "craving ghost of their deceased relations," Indians were obliged to secure either retribution or compensation.[6]

This most fundamental obligation to kin and nation seldom translated into simple revenge. Indians drew fine distinctions between death at the hands of kin, of allies, and of enemies. The appropriate response to each was carefully calibrated. If an Indian murdered a member of his family or village, his kinsmen and village might decide that his deed had somehow been justified. If no punishment was demanded by the kin of the dead Indians, no one else had the right to demand punishment. If the murderer was from another clan or village, a payment in lieu of blood revenge might mollify the victim's kin and restore peace. But if the murder was committed by someone from a "foreign country," the French Jesuit missionary Joseph-François Lafitau observed, "this grievous death is a matter of concern to a whole people" and might be grounds for war.[7]

The obligation to vengeance could fuel ongoing cycles of retribution that spanned generations and shaped the daily lives of Indian nations. European observers often had difficulty making sense of the endemic conflict that endured between some Indian nations along the Atlantic Seaboard. William Strachey, an early chronicler of the Jamestown settlement, marveled that "they seldom make warrs for landes or goodes" but instead "principally for revendge, so vindicative and jelous they be, to be made derision of, and to be insulted upon by an enemy."[8] Writing a century later and summarizing his experience among the Indians of North Carolina, John Lawson concurred: "The Indians ground their Wars on Enmity, not on Interest as the Europeans generally do."[9] These early ethnographers, however, failed to recognize that Indian vengeance between nations, just as between clans, could be tempered. As long as the warring parties abided by the traditions surrounding vengeance and exacted retribution commensurate with their losses, cycles of violence could be contained or even halted.

Of immediate relevance to Juan Ortiz and his fellow captives was the manner of retribution that the Tocobaga law dictated for them. The violence precipitated by Narváez's expedition revealed many facets of that law in practice. In the eyes of the Tocobaga, the conquistadors' brutality warranted the severest retaliation. Beyond Hirrihigua's wounded dignity, familial duty obliged the cacique and his relatives to revenge the murder of clan members by outsiders. According to the logic of the Tocobaga, Ortiz and any other Spaniards were as culpable in Narváez's transgressions as were the conquistador himself and his men. That Ortiz was not even in Florida at the time of the outrages was irrelevant. Individual culpability mattered little because each captured Spaniard shared collective guilt for Narváez's crimes.

Ortiz and his companions were unlikely to have appreciated the subtleties of the traditions that guided their fates. Not all captives in Indian wars were tortured to death, or even tortured at all. The incidence of torture by Indians is difficult to determine, especially because many Europeans exaggerated its frequency. The perception among Europeans that Indians were habitual torturers seems to have been sustained by European lore rather than by the actual extent of the practice. In seventeenth- and early eighteenth-century New France, for example, where Jesuit missionaries closely chronicled Indian affairs, the Iroquois and Huron apparently tortured a small minority of their prisoners. More often Indian raiding parties dispatched their enemies on the battlefield or captured them with the intent of adopting or enslaving them. Torture most likely was an exceptional ritual.[10]

The fate of captives in Indian wars typically rested with their battlefield captors and the surviving relatives of warriors killed in battle. A raiding party that achieved the requisite vengeance by killing and scalping a sufficient number of the enemy might elect to spare the lives of captives. Clan members instead might adopt captives as surrogates for relatives who had died in combat. The Iroquois, in particular, engaged in "mourning wars" to symbolically replace members lost to disease or warfare. One mid-eighteenth-century observer noted that "it has been a constant maxim with the Five Nations [the Iroquois], to save children and young men of the people they conquer, to adopt them into their own Nation."[11] Likewise, among the Indian nations of the Southeast, women and children were often adopted. Yet among the Huron, captured women and children were killed summarily on the battlefield or, less often, tortured soon thereafter.[12] Even then, captives condemned to undergo torture might escape death. For instance, a prisoner who could satisfy his captors that he had never killed a member of his captors' nation might be spared. But according to the Baron de Lahontan, a French officer stationed in New France at the end of the eighteenth century, "If evidence be brought that the poor prisoner has kill'd either Women or Children in his lifetime, his Executioners lead him to a Woodpile, where he is forc'd to undergo the dismal Torments."[13]

The rituals of torture that Ortiz experienced would have been familiar to Indians along the Atlantic coast of North America. When raiding parties returned to their villages, they typically compelled their captives to run a gauntlet. The severity of the violence varied according to the aims of the captors. When the intent was to adopt the prisoners,

FIGURE 1.1. *The Death of John Lawson.* Baron Christoph Von Graffenried depicted himself, his slave, and John Lawson, an English colonist, being held captive by Tuscarora Indians shortly before Lawson's execution in 1711. Europeans interpreted such torture and execution as barbarism, ignoring the elaborate rituals that circumscribed Indian torture and warfare.

the gauntlet served as an initiation ritual that erased the captives' former identity and ushered them into their adoptive clan. In other instances, as in Ortiz's case, the gauntlet provided for collective participation in the ritual of vengeance. Among some Indian nations, prisoners had their fingernails ripped off, fingers severed, and gashes made in their necks and bodies while they ran the gauntlet. Women no less than men joined in inflicting these torments. Perhaps reflecting their influence in many Indian polities, women often had an outsized role at each stage of the rites of torture. Among the Cherokee, Shawnee, and several other Indian nations, women determined which captives were condemned to die, which were adopted, and which were enslaved.[14] Adults also encouraged children to participate in the torture of captives. As part of some Iroquois ceremonies, the blood of torture victims was rubbed on children. In another instance, Iroquois children were tasked with throwing burning cinders on the stomach and chest of captives while they were staked to the ground.[15]

In a practice that Europeans found utterly baffling, captives who survived the gauntlet and were destined for subsequent torture were sometimes treated with meticulous politeness prior to their execution. A Huron explained, "We have nothing but caresses for them a day before their death, even when our minds are filled with cruelties, the severity of which we afterward find all our pleasure in making them feel."[16] European observers failed to understand that such decorum was in keeping with the profound religious and ceremonial significance that Indians attached to the rituals of torture and execution.

Throughout these proceedings, both the Indian torturers and the tortured Indians understood their respective roles. Similar expectations of behavior applied to both captors and captives, despite their different circumstances, during ritualized torture. It provided the occasion for both the torturers and the tortured to demonstrate command of their emotional and rational faculties. The goal of the torturers was to vent sufficient emotional fury to avenge their dead kin while simultaneously restraining themselves from killing the captive until the appropriate moment dictated by Indian spiritual beliefs. Torturers who completed their work prematurely risked enabling the soul of their victim to linger and torment their community. Captives undergoing torture also needed to maintain the proper equilibrium between their intellect and their emotions; if they managed to do so, they would simultaneously ensure that, after death, part of their soul would travel to its resting place while their emotional soul would linger to haunt their tormentors.[17]

The aim of the torturers was to stage a cathartic spectacle of extended and carefully modulated suffering. A methodical and public execution of a captive provided the occasion to unleash their anger for a wrongful death and to revel in their victory over a bitter enemy. Equally important, to violate the body of an enemy was to capture a portion of his soul and to inhibit its journey to the afterlife. By destroying the physical corpse of a tortured captive, the torturers ensured that their community would be protected against the soul of their victim, which would no longer have an anchor in the physical world.[18] Like the practice of scalping, rituals of torture were a symbolic means of seizing and consuming the spiritual strength of foes.[19] The future fate of the captors, moreover, was at stake when they tortured their victims. The

Huron, for instance, believed that if they failed to break the spirit of a torture victim and to goad him into pleading for mercy, they would subsequently suffer misfortune on the battlefield.[20]

Tradition called for torture victims to display fortitude and stoicism while defying their torturers. William Douglass, a contemporary historian, confessed wonder at Indians' "great fortitude in enduring torture and death."[21] In the act of enduring torture, captives embodied their tribe's character. As Henry Lewis Morgan, an uncommonly perceptive nineteenth-century ethnographer, explained, "They considered the character of their nation" in "the manner of their death."[22] Among Indian warriors, for whom physical and spiritual trials were prerequisites to full manhood, the endurance of pain was perhaps the paramount test of bravery and manliness.[23] Nicholas Perrot, a fur trader in New France during the late eighteenth century, observed that the motivating "passion" of Indian warriors was "to attract praises to themselves, either during life or after death."[24] Displays of stoic fearlessness in the face of death gave the captive an opportunity to redeem the honor he lost by being captured and to win lasting praise for his valor.[25]

Captives did so by mocking their torturers and goading them to administer harsher torments. A brutal symbiosis between the torturers and the tortured often developed, with each egging the other on. "During all these torments," one mid-eighteenth-century traveler reported, "the captive takes care to show a constant undaunted courage, to rebuke his enemies as cowardly and womanish people for inflicting on him such a womanish death, that he only laughs at all these torments, that nothing better has previously happened to him."[26] A French colonist was similarly flabbergasted: "They even taunt their executioners by saying that they are not suffering enough. If things were reversed, the victims would know how to make the executioners suffer even greater torment."[27] Torture victims who failed to display the proper resolve garnered unqualified contempt, as when Massachusetts warrior Wituwamat mocked the cowardice of Englishmen who, when facing death, "died crying, making sowre faces, more like children than men."[28]

Many facets of the ritual that Ortiz experienced at the dawn of the European conquest of North America became familiar to Europeans in subsequent decades and centuries. Indian traditions of torture proved as enduring as those of their European counterparts. Nevertheless, Indian torture was neither timeless nor unchanging. As Indian nations gained access to European technology, such as gunpowder and iron goods, they altered their techniques of torture accordingly. It became commonplace for torturers to pack gunpowder into the open wounds of their captives before they were placed on burning pyres. As the flames rose around the victims, the gunpowder would periodically ignite, intensifying the captives' agony. Similarly, Indian torturers quickly grasped the limitless possibilities of red hot iron metal when applied to the bodies of captives.[29]

The ebb and flow of conflict and warfare among Indians resulted in a corresponding ebb and flow in the frequency of torture. European technology made Indian warfare more lethal, which increased the violent deaths that demanded revenge and consequently increased the circumstances that led to ritualized executions through torture.[30] This sequence at least partially explained the long-running and often brutal conflict that the Iroquois and Huron waged during the seventeenth century. A similar dynamic between Indians and Europeans developed by the mid-seventeenth century. At least initially, English settlers in Virginia and New England seldom were victims of Indian torture. But as tensions over land, resources, and power mounted and violence flared, Indians responded by adopting harsh methods of warfare and retribution that they had previously reserved for their Indian enemies. By 1637, when the Pequot War erupted in present-day Connecticut, English settlers there experienced the full horror of Indian torture.[31] Four decades later, during King Philip's War, Indians would again employ torture in a desperate campaign of terror intended to expel their English adversaries from the region.[32]

Indian torture also evolved under the influence of European culture. As Christian missionaries made inroads in some Indian nations, some Indians were tolerant of and even embraced the new faith. Missionaries typically discouraged indigenous traditions of torture, scalping, and other violence among their converts, and some Christianized Indians did abstain. During the seventeenth century, for example, the deepening influence of Catholicism among the Indians of New France led to widely divergent attitudes toward torture. Some Catholic Algonquians proclaimed that "their old cruelties must be abandoned" and began executing captives quickly and without torture.[33] Perhaps the most striking recasting of Indian torture was by Catherine Tekakwitha, a Mohawk convert at the Jesuit mission village of Kahnawake, south of Montreal. Drawing on both Indian traditions of torture and Christian traditions of the mortification of flesh, Tekakwitha resorted to fasting, flogging, cutting, sleeping on a bed of thorns, and burning herself with hot coals to make the suffering of Christ palpable to herself and the other Mohawk women whom she converted. Even many Iroquois who persisted in torturing captives incorporated Christianity into their rituals. They encouraged Jesuit missionaries to baptize captives while they were undergoing torture and in at least one instance they beseeched a priest to continue to comfort a convert while they burned him alive.[34]

Other Indians revised rituals of torture to display their scorn for Christianity. Iroquois during the eighteenth century, for instance, mocked Christian ritual when they "baptized" Jesuits with boiling water, a form of torture they reserved for French missionaries.[35] Some Huron and Iroquois took to cutting off the hands of converts to prevent them from praying while undergoing torture. When a Jesuit missionary asked some Huron about their extreme cruelty to a group of Iroquois captives, the Huron answered that they wanted the recently baptized captives to feel the torments of hell as the priest had described them. In 1649 when Iroquois tortured Father Jean de Brébeuf, who would be sainted for his martyrdom, they taunted him, "Thou hast told others that, the more one suffers in this life, the greater is his reward in the next; therefore, thank us, because we increase thy crown." Two decades later, when the Onondaga prepared to burn several captives, they attempted to stop a Jesuit priest from baptizing their captives so that they would burn in this life and for eternity.[36]

Indian traditions of torture arguably were even more profoundly altered by deepening trade and diplomatic alliances with competing European powers during the late seventeenth and early eighteenth centuries. The advent of the European slave economy transformed Indian captivity by giving new value to captives. Once a thriving market for enslaved Indians developed among the European colonies, Indian captives became valuable commodities. Indian captors might chose to torture some captives and to adopt others to repopulate their community, while trading the remainder for European goods. This innovation benefited Indian nations by removing or reducing their enemies, and Europeans welcomed it because it provided a source of labor while shrinking the number of independent Indians. The slave trade in Indians was especially brisk in the Southeast, where perhaps as many as fifty thousand Indians were traded between 1670 and 1715.[37] Almost certainly some of this human chattel would have been ritually tortured had the Indian slave trade not come into existence.

Diplomatic and military alliances with the various European powers further altered Indian war customs, including torture. Don Joseph de Zuñiga, the Spanish governor of Florida at the dawn of the eighteenth century, pressured Chacato and Timucua Indians to desist from the "diabolical custom" of scalping and other atrocities.[38] A half century later, British officers and agents, notably William Johnson, the British superintendent of Indian affairs during the Seven Years' War (1754–1763), lobbied to curtail the cruelties that accompanied the military tactics of their Indian allies. In the aftermath of the Battle of Lake George in 1755, Johnson "with Great Difficulty" managed to prevent Indians from scalping and killing a captured French general (a scene that artist Benjamin West would immortalize in his painting *General Johnson Saving a Wounded French Officer from the Tomahawk of a North American Indian*, circa 1764–68). Johnson and his officers satisfied Indian demands for captives and scalps by offering them material rewards instead.[39] Similarly, three years later during the assault on Fort Frontenac, a French fort on the shores of the St. Lawrence River, Lieutenant-Colonel John Bradstreet prevented his Indian allies from harming prisoners by encouraging them to plunder instead.[40] But in other instances, Europeans deliberately sought to exploit Indian warfare and violence as a potent weapon against their Indian enemies and imperial rivals.

For Hirrihigua and the Indians of North America, the violence of the European invaders must have been shocking and inexplicable. Narváez displayed no regard for the conventions of Indian diplomacy and dispensed unprovoked cruelty. From the outset, the Spanish invaders conducted themselves as if they were waging war on the Tocobaga even while Narváez ignored (or was ignorant of) the norms of Indian warfare. As the Tocobaga and other Indians would come to understand, the European invaders had their own traditions of torture and warfare.

Torture was enmeshed in European statecraft, warfare, and culture. It had been employed by the ancient Greeks, codified in law by the ancient Romans, and widely adopted, with church endorsement, during the Middle Ages. Lawbreakers then were publicly flogged, chained in iron collars, and tormented in stocks; they suffered having their hands and ears cut off, and their bodies racked, burned, flayed, and pulled apart. Churches were adorned with depictions of saints enduring horrific torments by knife, spears, arrows, and fire. And everywhere were graphic reminders of the torture that Christ had endured—nails, spears, thorns, whips, and, especially, the Savior's blood. While the struggle for mastery of North America unfolded, learned jurists in Europe continued to parse the circumstances in which torture was appropriate, and manuals cataloged, in meticulous detail, accumulated wisdom about effective torture techniques. Meanwhile contemporary playwrights, most especially William Shakespeare in *Titus Andronicus* and *King Lear*, displayed a macabre virtuosity while enthralling audiences with dramatic renderings of torture.

The pervasiveness of torture after the twelfth century was one consequence of a profound reorientation of government and criminal justice in Europe. Previously, similar to the systems of law that prevailed among North American Indians, most crimes in western Europe, including even murder, had been understood as private conflicts between individuals or families that were resolved through negotiated compensation. During the twelfth century, a more expansive idea of public order and state authority took root, transforming private disputes into threats to the public welfare. Now culprits could be prosecuted at the behest of the public good even when their victims failed to press charges. Simultaneously, expanding formal authority discouraged hasty resort to personal vengeance. For the rulers of Europe, this redefinition of crime as a matter of public order provided both a rationale for and the means to augment their authority. From the perspective of Europe's monarchs, the widespread use of torture and capital punishment bolstered their power and burnished their legitimacy as protectors of public order.[41]

The starkest manifestation of the use of torture to demonstrate state power in early modern Europe was the punishment of treason. Since the Roman era, treason had been considered an especially vile crime against one's community that warranted torture. Treason was comparable to patricide; both were intolerable affronts to the majesty and authority of the proper rulers of the nation and the family, respectively. The escalating severity of the punishment for treason during the later centuries of the Roman Empire legitimated the application of torture to classes of citizens who previously had been protected against it. Germanic law subsequently incorporated these and other aspects of Roman torture, and the practice persisted until it was strengthened and codified during the so-called legal revolution of the twelfth and thirteenth centuries. Henceforth, the application of torture in cases of treason was virtually universal in Europe, including England, where the constraints on the use of torture were stricter than anywhere else in the region.[42]

The 1605 torture of Guy Fawkes, a member of a group of conspirators who schemed to restore Catholicism in England, was a case study of the use of torture to punish treason. When Fawkes was arrested and a storehouse of gunpowder was discovered under the House of Parliament, King James gave orders that the would-be bomber be tortured. The monarch spelled out a program of escalating torture to be used on the prisoner: "The gentler Tortures are to be first used unto him *et sic per gradus ad ima tenditur* [and so by degrees proceeding to the worst]." Over the course of three days of torture, beginning with Fawkes's suspension in manacles and probably culminating with time on the rack, supervised by royal officials, Fawkes revealed the plans of the plot and named his fellow conspirators. His torment, like that of many accused of treason, did not end with his confession. He subsequently was condemned to be executed in a protracted and gruesome spectacle of public punishment.[43]

Such executions, which flamboyantly humiliated the treasonous and prolonged their intense suffering, demonstrated through spectacle both the sovereign's resolve to monopolize violence and the ferocious majesty of the law. Whereas torture to elicit a confession or information was conducted outside of the public gaze, the torment that accompanied some executions was conspicuously staged before the public.

During the High Middle Ages, for example, those found guilty of treason were hanged, disemboweled, burned, beheaded, and quartered.[44] All of these torments were imposed on William Wallace, a leader of the Scottish Wars of Independence during the fourteenth century; he was strangled by hanging but released while he was still alive, castrated, eviscerated and his bowels burned before him, beheaded, and finally cut into four parts.[45]

Torture occupied an equally prominent role in the Roman church's evolving campaign against heresy. Prompted by an apparent eruption of heresy during the twelfth and thirteenth centuries, the church initiated an Inquisition to quash it. The ecclesiastical adoption of torture followed in the wake of this newly articulated authority as well as religious leaders' willingness to adapt torture to complement new inquisitorial procedures. Milestones in this chain of events were Pope Innocent II's condemnation of heretics as traitors to God in 1129, Pope Innocent III's equating of heresy with treason in 1199, and Pope Innocent IV's 1252 papal bull authorizing the use of torture by church inquisitors.[46]

By the middle of the thirteenth century, torture had become part of the ordinary criminal procedure of the Roman church and would remain so for another four centuries. Although church inquisitors were forbidden from permanently harming suspects or drawing blood, they still devised effective methods of torture, including the rack, the strappado, and simulated drowning to determine the guilt of heretics. In practice, Inquisition courts did not pronounce sentences but instead handed over confessed heretics to secular authorities, who oversaw their punishment. Church authorities, who were proscribed from taking human lives, thereby avoided having a direct hand in condemning and executing heretics, and the authority of the state was harnessed to the church's needs. Even so, church inquisitors could have had no doubt about the fate of any alleged heretic they remanded to secular authorities.[47]

If the legal revolution of the twelfth century precipitated the institutionalization of torture in medieval Europe, the religious and political turmoil in early modern Europe led to its proliferation. Across Europe, torture figured prominently in the struggle between orthodoxy and heresy, including the campaigns against witchcraft in both Protestant and Catholic regions. Although secular and church authorities had previously been attentive to sorcery and witchcraft, not until the middle of the fifteenth century, in what are now the borderlands of Switzerland and France, did the pursuit of witchcraft reach a flash point.[48] The torture of witches increased after 1468, when Pope Paul II declared witchcraft to be *crimen exeptum* and thereby removed all legal limits on the application of torture in cases where evidence against witches was otherwise difficult to glean. Accused witches were subject to the customary tortures used by civil and clerical courts, as well as extreme sleep deprivation and forms of sexual humiliation.[49] Like those found guilty of treason, convicted witches who may have avoided torture during their trials were often subjected to it during their executions. Across most of Europe, witches were burned, often alive and in groups, which magnified the horror of the proceedings. How many alleged witches were executed between the fifteenth and eighteenth centuries is unknown, with estimates ranging from forty

FIGURE 1.2. *Several Modes of Inflicting Pain during the Inquisition.* This engraving by Bernard Picart (1722) depicts inquisitors extracting confessions while a scribe records them. Such depictions of interrogation techniques, including simulated drowning and rope and pulley systems used to lift victims by their wrists, fed the "black legend" among Protestants about the innate barbarism of Old World Catholic tyranny.

thousand to sixty-five thousand.[50] Many, perhaps most, had endured torture.

That Europeans resorted to torture when confronted with especially heinous alleged provocations—treason and heresy—is perhaps predictable. But the application of torture was explained only partially by the severity of the alleged criminals' offenses. Even in cases involving lesser transgressions, Europeans relied on torture to identify truth. Torture, in short, became an established component of continental law. Lacking any investigatory capabilities, state and clerical authorities necessarily looked to witness testimony and confessions to arrive at truth and impose justice. But clerical and secular jurists faced a quandary when confronted with cases in which there were neither witnesses nor voluntary confessions. During the early Middle Ages, communities had resolved such cases with judicial ordeals during which the guilt or innocence of the accused was determined by subjecting them to bodily torment. By observing how the accused endured the ordeal or the extent of their injuries, courts claimed to be able to discern God's judgment as to their guilt. After the Roman church withdrew its sanction for trials by ordeal in 1215 and banned priestly participation in them, jurists experimented with new judicial procedures to determine truth. They gradually settled on an elaborate method to secure proof through confessions, with torture providing a means of eliciting them. Torture also was a sanctioned method to wrest the names of accomplices from the guilty. The transition to an emphasis on strict definition of proof, and the resort to torture to secure it, was of a piece with the accumulation of new power and authority by public authorities.[51]

Simultaneously, the growing importance attached to confession in church practice and doctrine heightened the cultural significance of confession more generally. Early modern ideas about confession, pain, and truth undergirded the new understanding that confessions, complemented by torture, revealed truth. Beyond holding that physical suffering was a path to redemption, Christian dogma located truth in the body, not the mind. The pain of torture made "spontaneous truth" accessible by eliciting testimony from the body rather than the "composed truth" of the mind.[52] The application of torture encouraged the body to confess what the mind sought to withhold or deny.[53]

In important ways, England deviated from the broader European embrace of torture. After the Roman church condemned the use of judicial ordeal, Henry III directed English justices in 1216 to develop a substitute for it.[54] For complex (and much debated) reasons, the English crown and jurists settled on trial by jury rather than judicial torture to discern truth and assign guilt. Torture consequently did not become a systematic part of English criminal procedure. The long-term implications of this distinctive facet of English law were evident, for instance, in the differences between the English and continental witch-hunting traditions. The checks and balances inherent in the English jury system, which required a grand jury to indict and a petit jury to convict, seem to have slowed, if not always prevented, the rush to judgment against accused witches. The number of witchcraft prosecutions in England was smaller than in many European countries; so too the number of executions.[55] Most important, as eighteenth-century jurist William Blackstone put it, torture was strictly "an engine of state, not of law," used principally against those accused of treason and heresy rather than a standard judicial procedure to elicit confessions.[56] England formally permitted it only when authorized by the monarch, and comparatively few torture warrants were issued throughout English history.[57]

The closest that English law came to routine judicial torture was the *peine forte et dure* (strong and harsh punishment), a method used to coerce defendants who refused to enter pleas seeking judgment from the court. Under English law, courts could not proceed with a trial until defendants voluntarily offered a plea. Jurists recognized that it was folly to restrict punishment solely to those criminals who consented to a jury trial. The need for some means of coercing obstinate defendants became apparent during the thirteenth century. Some judges ordered juries to deliver verdicts even in cases when defendants refused to enter a plea. More often, judges remanded the accused to prison, where they endured horrific conditions until they agreed to plead. But in cases involving especially uncooperative indicted criminals, the solution was *peine forte,* during which heavier and heavier stones were placed on "mute" defendants' chests until they relented and entered a plea, or, as happened with lamentable frequency, they suffocated or were crushed to death. The threat of *peine forte* apparently was effective in compelling most English defendants to enter a plea when brought before the court. Although it had a different aim than the judicial torture common on the Continent—to coerce a plea rather than discover the truth—its existence underscores that everywhere in Europe, including England, bodily torment was viewed as an essential tool for the discovery of truth and the suppression of crime.[58]

Torture, then, was a well-established complement to religious and state authority in early modern Europe by the time Europeans encountered the New World. But nowhere in North America was this tradition of torture fully replicated. While the laws regulating the use of torture were recorded in the statute books of all the European colonies, in practice authorities only rarely applied them to Europeans in the New World. However marked the differences in imperial methods and culture that distinguished New France, New Spain, New Netherlands, and the British colonies in North America, nowhere did imperial officials or church leaders routinely resort to torture against their own.[59] Not until the hysteria surrounding the Salem witch trials in 1692, for example, did Massachusetts authorities impose *peine forte et dure* to coerce a recalcitrant suspect into entering a plea. In New Netherlands, the harshest torments were applied exclusively to Indian and African residents; otherwise, the Dutch authorities punished most offenses by Europeans with fines or banishment. Likewise, in New France, torture procedures were codified yet virtually never applied. Even in New Spain, where colonial authorities had been accused of promiscuous cruelty since its founding, extant evidence suggests that neither religious nor imperial officials regularly employed torture on Europeans. Drawing a firm line between *gente de razón* and *indios bárbaros*, between rational Europeans and savage Indians, Spanish authorities resorted to torture when threatened by Indian resistance, as happened after an Indian uprising near San Diego in 1775, for example. *Gente de razón*, in contrast, apparently had no cause to fear the torturer's art. In more than seven thousand legal cases in Mexico during the mid- to late eighteenth century, not a single instance of torture was recorded.[60]

The rarity of the torture of European settlers during the early years of settlement almost certainly is explained by both expediency and principle. Given that colonial authorities throughout North America were desperate to lure new settlers and to retain those who were

already resident, there were compelling grounds to refrain from punishments that would discourage settlement. So desperate were Dutch
authorities in the Hudson River valley to retain settlers that they tolerated in their midst all but the hopelessly incorrigible. At the same
time, colonial administrators saw themselves as extending the rule of
law to North America. Because formal, modern law purportedly was
an essential prerequisite for civilizing the New World, colonial authorities could be meticulous about enforcing the letter of the law. Strict
observance of the law with regard to torture almost inevitably worked
against its use in the New World. Colonial authorities apparently had
little difficulty securing competent executioners, but trained torturers
were exceptionally rare even in Europe, let alone North America. And
even autocratic administrators were loath to arouse local opposition
and provoke interference from the imperial officials by engaging an
amateur torturer. Colonial administrators and local officials, then, did
not explicitly renounce the torture of their fellow settlers so much as
they found that circumstances in the New World rendered it of little
immediate value to their task of transplanting European civilization.

Juan Ortiz had the great misfortune to learn firsthand about Indian
traditions of torture. He and the European colonists who followed were
familiar with the time-honored practice of torture in Europe, which
enjoyed broad legitimacy until the eighteenth century. But many
Europeans condemned Indian torture as alien and repellant. In doing
so, Europeans differentiated between the two traditions so as to insist
on the incompatibility of the torture practiced by Indians and the
"civilization" that Europeans brought to the New World. What Indians
thought of European traditions of torture is difficult to reconstruct.

In September 1637 a revealing colloquy took place in New France
between a Jesuit missionary intent on demonstrating the superiority
of European civilization and Huron warriors mystified by European behavior. The Huron had captured an Iroquois and brought him to the
village of Onnentisati to torture him. Grasping an opportunity to baptize the prisoner and to proselytize to his captors, Jesuit missionaries
attended the execution. During the subsequent day and a half of the
prisoner's torture, the missionaries debated with the gathered Huron

about Christian concepts of sin, heaven, French treatment of prisoners of war, and French methods of torture and execution. At one point, a Huron asked, "Why are thou sorry that we tormented him?" To which the priest replied that he did not disapprove of the execution of the captive but the manner of execution. The warrior queried: "How do you French do [it]?" The priest explained that his people executed criminals, "but not with this cruelty." "What! Do you never burn any?" the Huron asked. "Not often," responded the priest, "and even then fire is only for enormous crimes, and there is only one person to whom this kind of execution belongs by right; and besides, they are not made to linger so long,—often they are first strangled, and generally they are thrown at once into the fire, where they are immediately smothered and consumed." In this exchange, we can observe the Jesuit father as he made the case that Christian and European traditions were not only distinct from but also superior to the Indian practice of torture. But even in this account, which was reported by a Jesuit observer, we are left with the impression that the priest was grasping for distinctions with which to distance French torture from its Indian counterpart.[61]

Early in the conquest of the New World, some Europeans voiced skepticism about the alleged barbarity of Indians and the contrasting civility of Europeans. Had Jean de Léry, a sixteenth-century Frenchman who joined a colony of Protestant settlers in Brazil, participated in the dialogue in New France, he almost certainly would have chided both the Jesuits and the Huron for their tolerance of cruelty and torture. Drawing on his experience in South America, Léry ruminated on the similarities and differences between the violence of New World Indians and that of their Old World adversaries and concluded that they were not so much different in kind as in order of magnitude. He devoted a chapter in his book *Histoire d'un Voyage Fait en la Terre du Brésil* (1578) to cataloging the cruelties that the Brazilian natives inflicted on their captives and their penchant for cannibalism. Although his disgust at such behavior was evident, he did not fix his gaze exclusively on it. He gave even more prominence to Old World perpetrators of violence, entitling a portion of his book "On the cruelties exercised by the Turks and other people: and namely by the Spaniards, much more barbarous than even the savages [of the New World]." Léry singled out the Spanish for reproach not only because of the scale of their violence but also because of their apparent intent to dehumanize the natives. After taking stock of the cruelty in the New and Old Worlds, his conclusion was decidedly in the favor of the Indians he had observed in Brazil.[62]

Léry's scorn for European cruelty was in many regards idiosyncratic, but his comparison of the motivations behind and the scale of violence in the New and Old Worlds was prescient. It was hardly coincidence that both the European conquest of the New World and the European wars of religion coincided with a heightened preoccupation with torture and cruelty in western Europe. A keen interest in cruelty and violence was altogether understandable in an age when wars of faith racked the whole of western Europe and the violence that accompanied the conquest of the New World pressed on the consciousness of Europeans. One consequence of this concern was a new attention to variations in the severity and extent of violence. To make sense of contemporary violence, it was no longer sufficient to divide peoples into opposing categories of cruel or not cruel, violent or peaceful. Instead, Europeans calibrated which groups were crueler or more violent than others. On this basis, Europeans could then compare the violence perpetrated and endured by Protestants and Catholics, by New World Indians and their European conquerors, by Spaniards and English.[63]

Léry engaged in precisely such a comparison when he drew attention to the cruelty of the Spanish conquistadors. His tallying of Spanish crimes was consistent with the broader politicization of cruelty during the political and religious strife of the sixteenth and seventeenth centuries. As Europeans splintered and aligned themselves along religious, regional, and national lines, they marshaled the charge of cruelty to undermine the legitimacy of opposing rulers, minorities, or religions. Protestants and Catholics alike threw themselves into a massive propaganda effort, hurling the charge of cruelty against their adversaries with the intent of discrediting them, rallying their own supporters to avenge past affronts, and justifying their own violence. In Léry's case, he added his denunciations of Spanish barbarism to remarkably effective campaigns by fellow French, English, and Dutch Protestants who blackened the reputation of Catholic Spain to such a degree that for centuries it was a byword for tyranny, cruelty, and intolerance.[64]

When the Jesuit interlocutor in New France and other colonists staked out the differences between European and Indian violence, they inevitably tapped into deep-seated notions of barbarism. From ancient Rome onward, violence and cruelty were prominent markers of barbarism in the European imagination. According to Seneca, barbarians committed senseless violence that served no rational end other than to gratify their savage impulses. By the early modern period, Europeans had compiled a long list of people who qualified as barbarians, including the Scythians, Vandals, Saracens, Vikings, and Mongols. Given this cultural patrimony, Europeans needed no intellectual creativity to classify North American Indians as savages. They, after all, were nomadic, lacked formal systems of law and property (that Europeans respected), and engaged in violence that, in the eyes of Europeans, lacked any higher purpose.[65]

The conflation of North American Indians with lawless savages circulated among Europeans from virtually the outset of their conquest of the continent. William Bradford of the Plymouth colony described "savage barbarians" who lived in a "hideous and desolate wilderness, full of wild beasts and wild men." The New England Charter referred to "Savages and brutish people," while the Virginia Charter mentioned "Infidels and savages" who lived an existence of "Darkness and miserable Ignorance" bereft of "human civility." Over the next century, accumulating accounts of Indian culture and traditions, especially torture, enabled European observers to refine their portrait of Indian primitivism.[66]

By the mid-eighteenth century, many Europeans concluded that Indians lacked any capacity for elevated human sociability and instead lived "outside normal morality." So thought Scottish economist Adam Smith, who, in his *Theory of Moral Sentiments*, postulated that Indians' preoccupation with daily survival precluded their development of sophisticated sentiments, including sympathy. Confirming this deficit was the widely reported capacity of stoic Indians to inflict and endure frightful torture. Adam Ferguson, Smith's contemporary and fellow philosopher, concurred, holding that Indians lacked the moral development sufficient to feel either pity or remorse. Indians who witnessed bouts of torture, Ferguson claimed, evinced no pangs of compassion but instead displayed limitless enthusiasm for sadism.[67]

The prominent participation of women and sometimes children in Indian violence elicited particular disgust among Europeans because it exemplified Indians' coarsened sensibilities. From the Jesuit mission-aries in New France, for instance, came an account of the torture of an Iroquois captive. After a gauntlet of Huron women and children had stabbed, cut, and burned the victim's limbs, one woman attempted to bite off his finger, "as a dog would do." As the captive endured further torments, she eventually hacked off his finger, roasted it, and gave it to some children "who continued to suck it for some time." That com-munities tolerated, let alone sanctioned, such violence by Indian women ran contrary to European conceptions of appropriate feminine behavior. Worse yet, any nascent moral sensibilities that Indian children might have possessed were extinguished by their participation in ritu-alized torture and other violent depravity.[68]

By sifting through early ethnographic reports on Indians, Europeans looked for verification of the cultural distance that separated them from North American savages. Significantly, Smith, Ferguson, and many other mid-eighteenth-century European commentators dwelled less on any innate differences between Indians and Europeans than on the divergence in their stages of development. By fitting Indian culture into a history of the progressive evolution of civilization through which all societies could pass, Smith and other commentators acknowledged commonalities in their historical experiences, but they did so to better highlight disparities between contemporary Europeans and Indians. It was ancient Europeans who shared close similarities with con-temporary primitive peoples; present-day "savages" in North America were facsimiles of earlier savages in Europe. The primitive culture of North American Indians confirmed that humankind had passed through stages of development from savagery—or as Alejandro Mala-spina, an explorer in the employ of Spain, put it, "the earliest stages of society"—before reaching the pinnacle of civilization that prevailed in Europe.[69]

Contemporary Indian practices offered a glimpse of the long-abandoned modes of justice and warfare that had been employed by the ancient Gauls, Britons, and Germans. According to the *Universal Magazine*, a London journal, in 1757, North American Indians "form a very striking picture of the most distant antiquity." Adam Ferguson agreed, explaining, "It is in their present condition that we are able to behold, as in a mirror, the features of our own progenitors." To observe contemporary North American Indians, Ferguson and others concluded, was to witness the rudest stage of human development, when perpetual warfare, an absence of property, and a surfeit of bodily torture prevailed. Centuries of gradual development presumably would be required until Indian barbarism would give way to advanced civilization.[70]

The details of Indian torture offered further evidence of the lawless savagery of Indians. Like the Jesuit missionary who conducted the colloquy with the Huron over torture in 1637, many Europeans contrasted the elaborate formal procedures surrounding torture in Europe with the perceived anarchy of Indian torture. In keeping with the oft-cited "rule of law" that Europeans proclaimed to be the prerequisite for civilization, European torture was, by law, the exclusive prerogative of trained state and clerical authorities who professed to act in the interest of society. Only after a prisoner was convicted of high crimes was his ignominy, manifest in his execution, made public. As the Jesuit priest protested, the gruesome spectacles of European public executions differed from the ritualized public torture favored by Indians, because, in theory, European crowds were witnesses, not participants. In fact, on occasion, spectators in Europe did seize the opportunity to torment notorious villains, as when crowds in London in 1305 whipped William Wallace and pelted him with rotten food and waste while he was in transit to his execution. Similarly, Thomas Prichard, a Catholic priest, was so severely abused by the crowd that gathered to witness his execution in Dorchester in 1587 that his executioner was almost deprived of his job.[71]

European officials jealously guarded their monopoly on torture. If that authority was challenged, state and clerical elites were quick to restore it, as events in the Champagne-Ardennes region of France during the late sixteenth century demonstrated. When a witchcraft panic erupted there in 1587, both local judges and residents flaunted normal judicial procedures and restraints. Alleged witches had their fingers smashed with hammers, were hoisted over fires, were repeatedly dunked in cold water, or were summarily executed by villagers. In response, the Parlement of Paris, which had jurisdiction over the area, proclaimed that it alone possessed the authority to review witchcraft sentences. The Parlement's motivation was not to create obstacles to witch trials but rather to restore control over torture and impose judicial uniformity.[72] European observers discerned no comparable restraints on the reported circuses of cruelty that entire Indian communities engaged in.

Differing European and Indian practices regarding war captives also fed Europeans' sense of superiority. Europeans still sometimes condoned the taking and killing of hostages during war, but by the eighteenth century the leading students of international law, especially Emer de Vattel (who was widely read on both sides of the Atlantic), endorsed the humane treatment of captives. During the Middle Ages, rules began to regulate the exchange of captured nobility and knights, and despite the chaotic wars that marred much of the period, prisoner exchanges were fulfilled as often as breached. A significant milestone occurred during Spain's suppression of the Dutch Revolt in the sixteenth century, when the rudimentary protections that had been applied to knights and nobility were extended to all combatants, regardless of their social status. Regular exchanges of prisoners of war subsequently became commonplace. New regulations, which accompanied the tightening control of armies by European states, also began to soften violence against noncombatants. And instead of relying on armies to fund themselves through plunder and ransom, which inevitably devolved into a license for brutality against civilians, European states increasingly supported their troops directly. Thus as Europeans grappled with endemic wars and religious strife during the sixteenth and seventeenth centuries, they looked to fledgling codes of military conduct to temper the violence of war.[73]

To the dismay and disgust of Europeans, Indians had no comparable tradition of prisoner exchange. So different were the conceptions of captivity by Indians and Europeans that prisoner exchanges, along the lines of those carried out during European conflicts, seldom occurred in North America. When captives were "adopted" by their Indian captors, they surrendered their former identity as an enemy. To exchange them would not only have reduced the population of Indian communities that in many cases were struggling to recover from the devastation of epidemics, but also would have wrenched the adopted captives from their new social identities. Moreover, captives were valued spoils of war that accrued to the credit of their captors. Prisoner swaps would have eroded the prestige and honor garnered by victorious warriors. For European statesmen and jurists who were sketching out the rudimentary rules for "just wars," Indian captivity, and the torture that sometimes accompanied it, served as a graphic illustration of the forms of cruelty they pledged to reduce.[74]

The European storehouse of ideas that linked barbarism and lawless violence also affirmed the link between heathenism and cruelty. In the Old Testament and elsewhere, Christians encountered portrayals of violent heathens as agents of divine justice sent by God to murder, plunder, and rape. Persecutions of Christians, during both the faith's founding and more recent past, forged Christians' understanding of violence and torture. Given the prominence of martyrdom in Christian self-understanding, the torture of Christians by "heathen" Indians inevitably prompted analogies with revered Christian martyrs of yore. To interpret Indian violence against Christian Europeans in this manner was to give the violence, suffering, and cruelty theological significance and to transform suffering Christians into virtuous martyrs and Indian persecutors into heathen savages.[75]

Christian priests in the New World were disposed to assign providential importance to the travails of Christians; their understanding of history assured them that God regularly intervened in their daily life to reward their fealty and punish their lapses. Indian cruelty, they presumed, was one of God's tests of their resolve and another manifestation of the minions of Satan thwarting the godly. Thus when English colonists from South Carolina and their Creek Indian allies invaded Spanish Florida in 1704, Catholic priests there interpreted the impending onslaught on their missions in starkly religious terms. They understood that the invasion was one front in the ongoing imperial struggle for North America, but they dwelled on the threat that the invading "pagans" posed to the "law of God" and the sanctity of "Christian lands." The wholesale destruction of Catholic missions and the slaughter of Catholic Indians by the English and Creeks devastated the Spanish colony. But even while Catholic accounts acknowledged the calamitous consequences of the raid for Spanish imperial policy, they lingered on the tenacious piety displayed by Catholic captives, both Indian and Spanish, who were abused by Creek Indians. One captive reportedly taunted his Creek tormenters by boasting that "his body would die but his soul would go to enjoy God eternally." Another persevered in proclaiming his faith throughout more than a day of torture, and yet another ignored the "great ridicule and mirthful mockery" of his pagan torturers, all the while thanking God for the strength to undergo "this martyrdom." The stoicism displayed by these Indians undergoing torture acquired a sacred significance far different from the meaning that Adam Smith and others had ascribed to Indian fortitude; it demonstrated the powerlessness of bodily torment to overwhelm resolute piety and contrasted with the inherent barbarism of their Indian tormenters.[76]

In their accounts of the torture of martyrs in Florida and elsewhere in New France and New Spain, Catholic writers frequently evoked the imagery of Christ's crucifixion. Through careful attention to the details of the suffering of martyrs—the mortification of their flesh, the removal of their clothes, the use of blades and spears to torment them, and the elevation of the victim during torture—New World Catholics aligned their accounts with the conventions of Catholic hagiography. By doing so, they translated episodes of Indian torture on the fringes of the French and Spanish empires into spiritual events that had meaning for European Catholics far removed from the threat of Indian torture. This hagiography of missionary martyrs helped forge a common community among Catholics on both sides of the Atlantic and incorporated Indian torture into that shared identity.[77]

Protestant ministers in North America, like their Catholic rivals, interpreted the torment of Protestant settlers by Indians similarly. Indeed, by the beginning of the eighteenth century, Protestant ministers took the lead in crafting and circulating accounts of Indian torture that figured prominently in the first genre of popular literature in British North America: the Indian captivity narrative. The sensationalism and enduring popularity of these narratives had far-reaching consequences. Their attention to bodily torment spread ideas and images about the ubiquity of Indian torture while providing a template for subsequent accounts of Indian savagery.[78]

These narratives tended to follow a common pattern. A hero was abducted from his or her home, witnessed horrific acts of barbarism by Indians, and endured the ordeal of a long journey through the savage wilderness and subsequent initiation into Indian society, before eventually returning, by escape or ransom, to civilization. A recurring thread was the spiritual benefits of affliction, which, once endured, confirmed God's blessings and mercies. God tested the faith of the captives through suffering before restraining the savagery of the Indians and delivering the Christians from their travail. To help demonstrate the paramount role of the divine, captivity narratives portrayed Indians as so incalculably evil and brutal that only God's intercession enabled Christian captives to survive their ordeal. Captivity narratives, with their often-extended accounts of Indian torture and cruelty and stark distinctions between Christian victims and Indian savages, sharpened the sense of cultural difference that separated Europeans from Indians.

Prejudices about Indian barbarism and heathenism gave a measure of license for Europeans to ignore professed principles of war and justice that otherwise might have circumscribed their conduct. Certainly, early international law offered little protection to barbarians in arms against the civilized. In 1625, Hugo Grotius, a Dutch pioneer of international law, stated, "War is lawful against those who offend against Nature." Vattel, whose much admired *Laws of Nations* was widely read in North America, concurred: "When we are at war with a savage nation, who observe no rules, and never give quarter, we may punish them in the persons of any of their people whom we take." No pretext, other than the inherent depravity of barbarians, was required to wage a just war against them. And the definition of "those who offended against Nature" was sufficiently elastic to include Indians, whose mode of living and beliefs were already cast as shocking inversions of civilized norms.[79]

Even the rules of war codified by Europeans provided generous scope for ruthless brutality. Confronted by the exigencies of war, European foes struggled to consistently comply with the new rules of military conduct and instead periodically engaged in summary slaughter and extravagant cruelty. Much as the conquistador Narváez had done in Florida and elsewhere, commanders sometimes employed exemplary punishment against unyielding populations. The Spanish did so during the Dutch Revolt of the seventeenth century, and Oliver Cromwell's New Army did so against the Irish town of Drogheda in 1649. Contemporary codes of war, after all, condoned such savage retaliation against rebellious subjects. The combination of religious strife and rebellion that sparked conflicts across Europe between 1500 and 1650 fueled the excesses there, since, according to prevailing wisdom, neither rebels nor heretics deserved sympathy. Moreover, European strategists openly acknowledged the utility of brutality, positing that exemplary violence could reduce terrorized foes into submission and thereby dissuade continued or future rebellion. Hence, during the campaign to suppress a rebellion against English rule in Munster, Ireland, in 1569, the English commander absolved his use of deliberate cruelty by insisting that "terror . . . made short wars."[80]

Such tactics were equally appropriate in the New World, where, in the words of a Spaniard, there was a chronic need for violence against a people of "vicious and ferocious habits who know no law but force." A Jesuit with more than a decade of service in Spanish America reached a similar conclusion: "So barbarous" and so "lacking in reason" were Indians, he deplored, that they could not "understand the truth through . . . spiritual means." Violent coercion apparently was the only effective method to compel obedience from Indians.[81]

The newly promulgated restraints on war were inevitably weakest on the margins of European empires, or precisely where violence between Europeans and "barbarians" was most likely to erupt. Most certainly, they had their least influence along the frontiers of imperial expansion, such as in the New World and Africa. There, Europeans confronted adversaries who were pagan, and the circumstances of European colonizers were precarious. Acts of extravagant violence, like Narváez's entrance into Florida, were intended to overawe potential foes who often greatly outnumbered the European invaders and settlers. On this basis, Samuel de Champlain excused French cruelty against the Indians of New France, including torture, as justified to cow the native people. Otherwise, he protested, "I knew them to be people governed by example; that they might accuse the French of lacking courage; that if no further mention of it were made, they would judge that we were in fear and terror of them, and that if we let them off so easily they would become more insolent, bold and unbearable." Joseph-François Lafitau, a Jesuit missionary, conceded that the French answered Indian cruelty in kind. "When, to avenge themselves on the Iroquois, they were permitted to treat their prisoners as the Indians treated ours, they did it with so much ferocity and zeal they were, in no way, inferior to the barbarians but even surpassed them." But he excused his countrymen for their violence, concluding, "The truth is that it was necessary to treat them [Indians] this way."[82]

As Europeans accommodated themselves to the New World, their behavior often made it difficult to discern clear lines between European "civilization" and Indian "savagery." Early evidence of this erosion appeared in the seventeenth- and eighteenth-century reports of Jesuit missionaries to their superiors in Europe. In New France, Jesuits initially boycotted any participation in Indian torture rituals and admonished Indians against them. But they enjoyed little success in changing Indian behavior, and eventually they persuaded themselves that Indian torture rituals were opportunities to proselytize both the perpetrators and victims of torture. Father François-Joseph le Mercier confessed in 1637 that "at first we were horrified at the thought of being present at this spectacle [the torture of an Iroquois]; but, having well considered all, we judged it wise to be there, not despairing of being able to win this soul for God." When the Jesuits attended the torture ritual, they baptized the captive and taught the Huron about the Passion of Christ by drawing comparisons between their captive's torments and those of Christ. Subsequently, missionaries to the Huron and later the Iroquois routinely attended ritual tortures and baptized captives during their drawn-out executions.[83]

Jesuit accommodation to Indian torture continued to evolve and eventually extended to tacit acceptance of it. In December 1639, when Huron in New France returned with more than one hundred Iroquois captives, Jesuits promptly baptized eighty of them. One baptized captive, after suffering through extended torture, attempted unsuccessfully to choke himself to death. Because suicide was a mortal sin, the missionaries chastised him, admonishing him to endure his torment and warning him that if he killed himself he would not enter heaven. They gave him absolution after he acknowledged "his fault." The Huron then resumed his torture until the appointed time of his execution, when they finally killed him. Jesuit attitudes shifted yet further in 1647, when a party of French and Algonquians captured an Iroquois who previously had tortured and killed Father Isaac Jogues, a Jesuit martyr. Missionaries baptized Jogues's murderer (giving him the same name as his victim) and then turned him over to the Algonquians, instructing them to burn him to death in order, in the words of a Jesuit, "to extract Justice from him." Thus by the mid-seventeenth century, Jesuit attitudes in New France had evolved to the point that a missionary who decades before had been outspoken in his opposition to Indian torture now openly condoned the torture and burning of an Iroquois by Huron in Montreal, observing that "he richly deserved" his fate.[84]

Europeans accommodated themselves in other ways to Indian traditions of violence, especially when it advanced their own goals.[85] Colonial authorities on occasion encouraged Indian torture. When the governor of South Carolina led the expedition that routed the Spanish missions of Florida in 1704, he made no effort to discourage the Creek Indians who joined the raid from torturing and executing Spanish missionaries or their Indian allies. Indeed, the English actively fomented the wholesale slaughter that ensued. Similarly, after the Natchez Indians rose against the French in 1729, French authorities welcomed the subsequent torture and execution of Natchez captives by the Choctaw. To the north, beginning in 1712, French authorities repeatedly incited Indian foes of the Meskwaki (Fox) to adopt the harshest possible violence against them during a three-decade-long campaign against the Indian nation. And in 1731, Étienne Périer, the governor of the Louisiana colony, attempted to cajole the Illinois to burn three Chickasaw captives. He hoped the executions would discourage the growing incursions of British slave and fur traders and their Indian allies into the region. By the time of the Seven Years' War, Europeans even began to use the threat of Indian torture against their rivals. Louis-Joseph de Montcalm-Gozon, the commander of French forces in North America during the war, for example, explicitly warned besieged Anglo-American garrisons that his Indian allies would subject them to torture and inflict massacres if they did not surrender.[86]

For Louis de Buade, Comte de Frontenac, the governor-general of New France during the late seventeenth century, torture complemented the other methods he used to protect French interests against British and Indian enemies. He earned a reputation for ruthlessness in part because he tolerated and sometimes even ordered the torture of Indians by their Indian and French captors. On at least one occasion, his policies led to a reversal of the conventional roles in European accounts of torture in the North American hinterlands. During the 1696 invasion of Iroquoia, Frontenac allowed French soldiers to burn an elderly Onondaga man. Indian allies of the French, who had accompanied the campaign, protested against the torture of the Onondaga because he, like the French and the Iroquois, was Catholic. Nevertheless, the French soldiers proceeded to slowly roast their captive until, after an hour of torment, an Iroquois spectator intervened and killed him with a blow to the head.[87] Imperial officers and colonial authorities might publicly profess disapproval of Indian cruelty in the abstract, but they often tempered their criticism when it complemented imperial objectives.

At times the cruelty of colonial settlers and soldiers against convenient Indians was a simple expression of a thirst for revenge and frustration over the evasiveness of Indian adversaries. A few such instances achieved notoriety, such as the wholesale slaughter of the Pequot Indians by English settlers in 1637. But usually these acts of violence passed without comment or record. A campaign journal of a 1695 Spanish expedition against the Pima Indians offers a rare glimpse of officers resorting to ever more desperate measures as their patience and morale waned. Following the murder of a Jesuit missionary by Pimas, the governor of Nueva Vizcaya ordered troops to punish the rebellious Indians along the present-day border of Arizona and Mexico. As the soldiers meandered through the western deserts searching in vain for their Indian adversaries, dissension and exhaustion sapped their health and will. Frantic to locate the rebellious Pima, commanders escalated their harsh treatment of any Indians they captured. Neither violence nor explicit threats of severe torture succeeded in prying information from the captives, however, and the expedition retreated, having accomplished little. On other occasions, soldiers intent on vengeance struck out against Indians far from imperial frontiers. During the mid-eighteenth century in what is now northern Mexico, Spanish soldiers avenged themselves against Apache Indians by carrying out torture and summary executions in jails and public squares.[88]

In this and countless other instances, colonists and imperial agents contended that the depravity of Indians justified their resort to extreme violence. After a 1622 Indian uprising decimated the ranks of the English in the Virginia colony, surviving settlers were uncommonly forthright in expressing their newfound resolution to use every weapon at their disposal against their adversaries. Their hands, "which before were tied with gentlenesse and faire usage," were "now set at liberty by the treacherous violence of the Savages, not untying the Knot, but cutting it." As if through furious words alone, the colonists pledged to crush the Indians "by force, by surprize, by famine in burning their Corne, . . . by destroying and burning their Boats, Canoes, and Houses, by breaking their fishing Weares, by assailing them in their huntings, . . . by pursuing and chasing them with our horses, and blood-Hounds to draw after them, and Mastives to teare them."[89] Three quarters of a century later, Solomon Stoddard, a New England cleric, contended that if the "Indians were as other people are, & did manage their warr fairly," they would be dealt with humanely. But because Indians would not do so, he advocated that all manner of terror against them was justified. A half century later, the *New York Gazette* advanced a similar rationale during the Seven Years' War. Indian cruelty, the newspaper raged, made it necessary to ask, "Will it not be strictly just and absolutely necessary from henceforward that we . . . make some severe examples of our inhuman enemies when they fall into our hands?"[90]

Throughout the colonial era, voices of both colonists and imperial officers periodically were heard counseling against Europeans tolerating or perpetrating violence against Indians that they would not inflict on other Europeans. These voices warned that civilization could not take hold and flourish in the presence of chronic savagery. During the seventeenth and eighteenth centuries, various Spanish and British imperial officials encouraged forbearance and advocated negotiations with Indians, if only on the pragmatic grounds that European violence begat Indian violence, which interrupted valuable trade and dissuaded European immigration to the colonies.[91] Others worried that New World conditions would erode the civilized sensibilities of European settlers. Such concerns prompted Father Le Jeune, a Jesuit in New France, to lament in 1637 the recent torture of an Iroquois warrior by Algonquians near the village of Trois-Rivières. In a report to his superiors, he confessed, "What saddens me is that they give vent to this madness in the presence and in the sight of our French people. I hope however, that in the future they will keep away from our settlements, if they wish to indulge in this mania."[92]

A few voices expressed regret that, when Europeans displayed growing fluency in the barbarous ways of Indians, they were regressing to a state of primitivism. Critics of the settlers' violence against Indians, like Jean de Léry at the dawn of the conquest of the New World and Benjamin Franklin at the end of the colonial era, drew unfavorable comparisons between settlers and North American Indians. They pointed out that in only exceptional instances were Indians accused of sexual violence against Europeans, whereas colonists routinely adopted rape as a tactic of war against Indians.[93]

Instances of the cold-blooded murder of friendly Indians by settlers confirmed the extent of European regression in the backcountry. Perhaps the most egregious example of such transgressions, at least in the eyes of the advocates of restraint and civility, was the massacre of Conestoga Indians near Lancaster, Pennsylvania, in 1764. The pogrom had its origins in the suspicions that land-hungry settlers in western Pennsylvania harbored toward their Indian neighbors after the Seven Years' War. Angered that some Indians had sided with the French, settlers began to foment for the expulsion, and even execution, of all Indians within the colony. Without provocation, a self-appointed militia from the village of Paxton targeted the tiny nation of Conestoga Indians, who had lived peacefully and without controversy among their European neighbors. On December 14, a throng of "Paxton Boys" descended on the small hamlet occupied by the Conestoga Indians, killing and mutilating six while they slept before razing the community. Almost two weeks later, another crowd of Paxton Boys broke into the workhouse in Lancaster where the remaining Conestoga had been sheltered against further violence. The mob attacked the defenseless Indians with tomahawks, hacking off their hands, splitting open their heads, shooting them in the mouth, and scalping them. When they finished, the bodies of fourteen men, women, and children, "shot—scalped—hacked—and cut to pieces," were strewn about the workhouse yard. The marauding settlers were unapologetic about their apparent appropriation and indiscriminate application of traditional Indian violence.[94]

The outrages perpetrated by the self-appointed frontier militia provoked fierce denunciations from Quakers and their allies, including
Benjamin Franklin. Committed to pacifism in principle and to the
creation of a "peaceable kingdom" consonant with their faith, many
Quakers worried that the frontiersmen's violence threatened the colony's existence. In an acrimonious pamphlet war that erupted within
weeks of the slaughter in Lancaster, Philadelphia Quakers depicted
backcountry settlers as more primitive and bloodthirsty than their
Indian adversaries. They blamed uncivilized and vicious Scotch-Irish,
not Indians, for instigating violence along the frontier. So debased were
the frontier settlers that one anti-Paxton pamphlet imagined two of the
mob boasting of their handiwork: "We shot six and a wee ane, that was
in the Squaw's Belly; we sculped three; we tomhawked three; we roasted
three and a wee ane; and three and a wee ane we gave to the Hogs."[95]
Franklin added his voice to those reprimanding the militia responsible
for the massacre, describing them as "barbarous MEN" who defied "all
Laws human and divine." The settlers, as professed Christians, "ought
to exceed Heathens, Turks, Saracens, Moors, Negroes, and Indians, in
the knowledge and Practice of what is right." He asked, "Do we come
to America to learn and practice the Manners of Barbarians?" In his
most stinging accusation, Franklin concluded that the Conestoga Indians "would have been safe in any Part of the known World—except
in the Neighborhood of the CHRISTIAN WHITE SAVAGES" of Paxton.[96]

Like Léry two centuries earlier, those who denounced the Conestoga massacre presumed that Europeans varied in their proclivities for
violence. Many Quaker pamphlet writers marshaled stereotypes of
vicious and primitive Scotch-Irish to draw invidious comparisons
between them and their Indian victims. Franklin vented similar prejudices, confiding privately that "our Frontier People are yet greater
Barbarians than the Indians."[97] Even Arthur St. Clair, a Scot who
himself was not squeamish about waging war against Indians, conceded that "the common people" of western Pennsylvania were "actu-
ated by the most savage cruelty" to "perpetrate crimes that are a dis-
grace to humanity."[98]

Critics of the Paxton militia and their ilk warned that conspicuous lapses in civilized behavior, even those that occurred along the

margins of North American imperial boundaries, would be scrutinized by both friend and foe. Because accusations of cruelty were already routinely levied by opposing powers in Europe intent on dele-
gitimizing their enemies, it was folly to assume that the reputations
of Europeans in North America would remain unblemished if they
waged war unencumbered by the legal and customary strictures that
applied in Europe. Louis de Bougainville, one of Montcalm's senior
officers during the Seven Years' War, acknowledged as much when he
confided in his journal after the capture of Fort William Hurt in 1757
that "all Europe will oblige us to justify ourselves" for the "horrible
violation" of the terms of surrender by the French and their Indian allies.[99] At stake in this instance of cruelty and others was the legitimacy of the European conquest of North America.

But hand-wringing over brutality along the frontiers of Europe's
North American empires was insufficient to quell the impatience of
settlers aggrieved by the perceived timidity of imperial policy and colonial authorities. Defenders of the settlers marshaled all cultural resources at their disposal to brush aside accusations of barbarism.
Throughout the colonial era, a kind of legal limbo, where the "rule of
law" was attenuated and ambiguous, prevailed in the sparsely settled
hinterlands of European colonies. There, the rules that governed contact and relations between Europeans and Indians were not only vague
but also difficult to enforce.[100] For colonists who resided along these
cultural frontiers, whether they were Spanish, Dutch, French, or English, events repeatedly demonstrated both the tenuousness of the rule
of law and the precariousness of imperial authority.

The much publicized exploits of Hannah Duston (or Dunston), a
captive of Indians during King William's War, was a case in point. In
March 1697 Hannah Duston, her husband, and their nine children
came under attack by a group of Abenaki Indians from Quebec.
Duston's husband managed to flee with eight of their children, but
Hannah, her newborn daughter, and her nurse were captured and forced
to march through the wilderness and back to New France. Six weeks
into her ordeal, and after witnessing the murder of her six-day-old infant, Hannah seized an opportunity to attack her captors while they
slept. Brandishing a tomahawk, she killed three adults and six children,
then scalped them (so as to have proof sufficient to collect a bounty

for killing them), before escaping by canoe to Haverhill, Massachusetts, where she was welcomed as a hero.[101]

For Cotton Mather, the noted Puritan cleric and man of letters, Duston's murder and scalping of her captives was beyond reproach. Although her desperate actions, especially the execution of sleeping children and the scalping of their corpses, would seem to have contradicted all civilized norms, especially those that applied to women, Mather condoned her actions. His defense could not disguise that her conduct demonstrated that colonists adopted methods of warfare that they otherwise denounced as savage when carried out by Indians. He excused her because she had been beyond the boundaries where formal law prevailed. "Being where she had not her own life secured by any Law unto her," he explained, "she thought she was not forbidden by any Law, to take away the Life of the Murderers, by whom her Child had been butchered."[102] Rather than evidence of settlers degenerating to the level of the savage, Duston's actions testified to her resolve to protect the foundations of civilization and civil society.

Defenders of Duston, the Paxton Boys, and other frontiersmen accused of wanton violence tirelessly complained that they were beset by savages yet were denounced when they defended themselves. In the case of the Scotch-Irish settlers in western Pennsylvania, Quaker land policies had driven them to the fringes of the colony in search of cheap land and lower taxes. There, when tensions erupted into violence, the Scotch-Irish suffered torture, death, captivity, and destruction of property, while the Quakers in Philadelphia wrung their hands over the unwelcome disruption of their "peaceable kingdom." How, they asked, could Quakers excuse "the horrid Ravages, cruel Murders, and most shocking Barbarities committed by Indians on Her Majesty's Subjects" on the grounds that they were merely the Indians' "Method of making War" while assailing backwoods settlers for resorting to arms in self-defense?[103] The Paxton Boys, in their "Declaration and Remonstrance," depicted themselves as victims of policies that protected savage Indians while leaving the Scotch-Irish defenseless. Members of the Paxton militia, their defenders pointed out, knew Indian cruelty firsthand; during the Seven Years' War they had discovered the mutilated remains of settlers in the Susquehanna valley, including women who "had been roasted" and men who "had Awls thrust in their Eyes, and Spears,

Arrows, Pitchforks, &c. sticking in their Bodies." By pointing to past Indian treachery, defenders of the Paxton Boys recast the attack on the Conestoga as a desperate act of vulnerable settlers beset by Indian barbarism and Quaker indifference.[104] This line of argument not only turned public opinion in favor of the Paxton Boys but also helped forge an ascendant coalition of opponents to the Quakers' domination of the colony's politics. That Franklin and other prominent critics of the Conestoga massacre soon lost their positions of influence and power in the colony was a lesson of the possible consequences of tampering with the categories of "civilized" and "savage."

Pánfilo de Narváez's actions in Florida in 1528 may have been confounding to the Tocobaga, but they were altogether consonant with contemporary European attitudes about war and conquest. The Spanish expedition and other European invaders of the New World took for granted that they were agents of civilization who, as the Virginia Charter put it, would "bring the Infidels and Savages living in these parts to human civility."[105] Because Indians existed beyond the boundaries of human civilization, they were undeserving of the protections that the civilized could claim as a natural right. Encapsulating what civilized beings were not and must not become, Indians seemed to have fallen as far away from their proper state as they could and yet remain human.[106] Some anxious Europeans caught glimpses in Indian culture of what they would become if they failed to live according to their highest nature.

The most prominent advocates and architects of the European conquest of the New World insisted that they were transplanting the rule of law and civilization. At a time when Europe was convulsed by war and religious strife, European rivals in the New World felt an urgent need to justify themselves and their imperial methods to themselves and their rivals. For all the differences in the approaches to Indians adopted by the European competitors in North America, none of the European powers renounced intimidation, violence, dispossession, or conquest. Given the prevailing military, religious, and political values in Europe, and given the stakes for the indigenous peoples of North America, recurring violence was inevitable. But for Europeans to concede fully the violence of their conquest would have called into question the rationale for and the legitimacy of their hard-won gains. The charters on which the colonies in North America rested were silent about the violence that was implicit in them. They depicted the native occupants of the continent as lawless barbarians and the land they moved through as empty space awaiting absorption into European states. Yet Europeans were not so obdurate as to ignore all the violence that accompanied their occupation of North America. To tame the savage and cruel violence of North America, Europeans marshaled rhetoric and force in ways both subtle and harsh. They acknowledged the centrality of violence, but only in a manner that affirmed the justice of their mission. When they engaged in violence against Indians, they professed to do so in defense of civilization. For civilization to survive and thrive in North America, savagery had to be eradicated.

Even stern critics of settler cruelty and violence, such as Jean de Léry and Benjamin Franklin, measured European transgressions against the standard of Indian savagery. And in their eyes, Indians became civilized only to the extent that they abandoned customary violence, including torture. Because they took for granted that torture on the North American frontier was the antithesis of modern civilization, they failed to appreciate the nature and full extent of the violence that undergirded the dispossession of the continent's Indians. Meanwhile, in the eyes of other settlers, their compatriots who adopted or tolerated Indian violence surrendered their place among the civilized only temporarily; apparently they, unlike the Indians, had to overcome their true nature to torture, maim, and murder.

When Léry and other Europeans made sense of Indian traditions of violence, they necessarily did so by reflecting on their own cultural preoccupations and traditions of violence. By accentuating the link between torture and savagery, they simultaneously eroded the legitimacy of the torture of Europeans and European colonists in the New World. During the eighteenth century, European intellectuals, jurists, statesmen, and clerics began to scrutinize inherited ideas about cruelty and punishment, with many concluding that torture was perhaps the most glaring affront to modern human dignity. Whereas in the past, torture, properly conducted, was an essential means to secure public order, now it emerged as an especially offensive manifestation of the ancien régime's tyranny. Against this backdrop, lurid accounts of torture in North America underscored the distance that separated the centers of progress and civility in western Europe from the New World's vulnerable outposts of civilization. By 1770, European torture was fast becoming a relic, while in North America it loomed as a terrifying reality in the struggle for mastery of the continent.

Over time, European colonists in North America rendered much of their violence, especially its most troubling forms, invisible. In the new world that they were creating, they would be free of the threat of torture. To push torture to the periphery of colonial America, to consign it to the past, and to deny that it had a place in the project of wresting the continent from Indians, ennobled settlers by yoking their quotidian struggle for survival to the grand advance of civilization and progress. The generation of colonists who waged the war for American Independence and presided over the young revolutionary republic would complete this process of erasure by consigning torture, as a tool of the state and the law, to a past that no longer retained a hold over the new nation. Henceforth torture would be synonymous with tyrants and savages. Where torture persisted in the New World and beyond, it did so only because American institutions and civilization had yet to fulfill their destiny.

TWO

Discipline in a Young Democracy

W HEN PHILADELPHIA'S GREAT and good gathered to lay the cornerstone of the Eastern State Penitentiary in May 1823, they were also celebrating the culmination of a half-century campaign to transform criminal justice. Roberts Vaux, a Quaker reformer, merchant, and the keynote speaker at the dedication, alerted the assembled crowd that they were witnesses to the dawn of a new era in civilization. "Those cruel and vindictive penalties" that passed for justice for most of human history—the whip, the pillory, and the public gallows—would now give way to "milder correctives" that would "wisely and compassionately . . . secure and reform the criminal." Gentle coercion would replace the physical suffering that had, for too long, familiarized "the mind with cruelty" and "hardened the heart."[1]

With the founding of the republic, Americans comforted themselves that torture would be confined to the contested boundaries of the nation where European civilization abutted Indian primitivism. The threat of Indian torture would remain conspicuous in American popular culture. But where civilization prevailed on the continent, torture was to have no place in the affairs of state. Humane and precisely calibrated correction would replace the sanguinary criminal punishments of yore. Henceforth, incarceration would be the punishment most consonant with the new nation's enlightened spirit and pressing needs.

The promise of incarceration, however, proved elusive. Less than five years after Eastern State opened in 1829, a crisis there demonstrated how difficult it was to mete out punishment so that coercion, in the name of rehabilitation, did not devolve into cruelty that violated the principles of enlightened justice. Rehabilitation required time, restraint, and money, whereas violence was swift and brutal and made manifest the authority to reform prisoners that prison authorities claimed for themselves. In 1834 a joint committee of the Pennsylvania state legislature heard testimony about defiant prisoners being subjected to physical and psychological torture, including being drenched with freezing water outside during winter months, getting strapped into chairs with tight leather restraints and beaten for days on end, being put into a pit called "The Hole" where they had scant food and no light or human contact for as long as two weeks, and having a five-inch device fitted over their tongues and chained to their wrists, which were crossed behind their backs, so that any struggling against their fetters caused their tongues to tear. Rather than acts of spontaneous cruelty, these punishments had been devised to compel obedience and produce intense suffering and in several cases resulted in death.[2]

Vaux and his fellow reformers never anticipated that their work would create environments where such suffering would occur. In their search for a method of "just" punishment, Vaux and his generation did not invent the penitentiary so much as they championed and refined it. In this process, they created institutions where torture often took root. Accusations of torture and abuse arose not only at Eastern State but also at other American prisons, underscoring that torture persisted in some of the very institutions that were acclaimed by Americans and international observers as emblematic of the nation's *novus ordo*. Periodic revelations of conditions in penitentiaries indicated that the new era in civilization that Roberts Vaux had announced in 1823 was as yet still in the future and that efforts to disown harsh forms of coercion in the young republic were uneven and incomplete.

Once acknowledged, these abuses could not be passed off as manifestations of archaic European practices. Nor could they be dismissed as the lamentable effects of Indian savagery on erstwhile civilized settlers. Instead, torture in American penitentiaries was bound up with the contemporary American experiment to replace the "tyrannical" punishments inherited from English law and European custom with a system of criminal punishment appropriate to a modern, enlightened republic. Advocates of the new prisons never accepted either cruelty or torture as inherent to the penitentiary. Instead, they dismissed the periodic revelations about excessive violence and indefensible cruelty by countering that a properly supervised and well run penitentiary was the most humane system of criminal discipline yet devised. Indeed, as often as not, even critics castigated penitentiaries less for the cruelty that occurred within them than for their expense and dubious effectiveness.

Penal reform during the early republic was tightly bound up with Americans' deeply conflicted attitudes toward British law and criminal justice. For all their revolutionary ambitions, Americans remained deeply indebted to English and European thought and institutions. Many Americans of the revolutionary generation simultaneously celebrated and reviled English law. They admired the protections afforded to defendants and citizens by English law but condemned the punishments meted out by English courts as cruel and despotic. Before the Revolution, critics pointed out that the English state imposed death for 165 transgressions, many of them comparatively trivial. (By the end of the eighteenth century, the number would swell to more than two hundred.) Moreover, as unrest in the colonies worsened, anxious colonists detected mounting evidence that the Crown applied capital punishment arbitrarily, even lawlessly, in the colonies.[3]

The critique of English justice went much further. Prevailing punishments under British justice, critics asserted, were both unjust and ineffectual. The capricious application of English justice purportedly bred contempt for the majesty of the law. Often officers of the state and jury members recoiled at the severity of prescribed punishments for crimes and therefore refused to impose severe sentences even when circumstances may have warranted them. Critics scoffed that with-holding justice in this manner nurtured scorn for the law. Detractors also questioned inherited assumptions about the efficacy of prevailing methods of punishment. They rejected the proposition that only fear of pain or death could inhibit the criminal propensities of the multi-tudes. Instead, they contended that all humans were subject to both reason and their consciences. Their optimism about human sensibili-ties found support in the writings of Adam Smith, who posited that even "the greatest ruffian, the most hardened violator of the laws of society," possessed a conscience. Consequently, punishments should exploit each human's advanced faculties, including his conscience and capacity for sympathy, rather than fear and other base instincts.[4]

Critics of English justice held up for particular ridicule the public spectacles that accompanied capital punishment in England and in British North America. Executions, they complained, were a detri-ment to the communities they were intended to protect. Too often, con-demned prisoners failed to display proper contrition or deference to authority during their executions. Their torment before and during their death throes sometimes elicited sympathy from spectators, thereby transforming a ritual intended to demonstrate the grandeur of the state and its authority into a gruesome carnivalesque spectacle.[5]

For Vaux and like-minded reformers during the Revolution, the an-tiquated punishments and unjust laws of the old order were incompat-ible with the principles of the new nation. One of the first steps the revolutionaries took when they began to disentangle the colonies from the Crown was to curb or abolish "tyrannical" punishments. The au-thors of the constitutions in several of the new states, including Ver-mont, Pennsylvania, Virginia, and South Carolina, sharply restricted capital punishment to a few serious crimes. The constitution writers claimed that they were reaffirming a prohibition of "cruel and unusual punishments" that had already been recognized in English law. It had been an important provision in the English Bill of Rights of 1689, in which Parliament declared "that excessive bail ought not to be re-quired, nor excessive fines imposed, nor cruel and unusual punish-ments inflicted." Subsequently, English jurist William Blackstone, whose *Commentaries on the Laws of England* was widely read and ad-mired in the colonies, had bolstered this principle when he wrote that although English courts had vast power, "it is far from being wholly arbitrary." He affirmed that "excessive fines ought not to be imposed, nor cruel and unusual punishments inflicted."[6]

Virginia legislators took Blackstone's prohibitions to heart and explicitly incorporated them into the state's Declaration of Rights of 1776. Twelve years later, the state convention that ratified the federal constitution urged that these same prohibitions be added to that document. George Mason and Patrick Henry, among others, warned that in the absence of an explicit restriction, the federal government might "inflict unusual and severe punishments." In response, the Eighth Amendment to the federal constitution was adopted in 1791.[7]

On its face, the amendment was a milestone in the long campaign to enshrine human rights in the Western legal tradition. It unambiguously pledged the new federal government to refrain from torture or cruel punishments. But at least during the nineteenth century, the Eighth Amendment was practically an abstract pledge that had little bearing on criminal justice in the states. Not until the mid-twentieth century did the Supreme Court conclude that the amendment applied to the states. Thus while the amendment constrained the federal government, it did nothing to protect American citizens from harsh punishments by state or local authorities.[8]

Indeed, the inchoate state of criminal justice after 1775 allowed for wide variation in the punishment of criminals across the young republic. Although quick to renounce "cruel and unusual" punishments, the revolutionary generation failed to settle on a coherent system of justice consonant with republican principles for at least a decade after the nation's independence. Virginia, for example, moderated its capital punishments even while keeping on its books various forms of mutilation and severe physical punishment, including whipping, branding, ear-cropping, and the stocks. The jumble of inherited and new forms of punishment in Massachusetts and many states during the late eighteenth century is apparent in the string of punishments that Stephen Burroughs, a notorious and colorful scofflaw, experienced during a life of crime. For counterfeiting, he was sentenced to the pillory, local jails, and eventually prison. After his release, he was tried for assault with intent to rape, but he pleaded guilty to lesser offenses, for which his sentence included whipping, the pillory, standing in the gallows with a rope around his neck, and three months' imprisonment, as well as bonds for good behavior and the payment of court costs. He thus underwent some punishments that would have been familiar to his ancestors in previous centuries and others that presaged the future of American criminal justice.[9]

The challenge that American critics of inherited systems of punishment faced was that they had no template of modern justice suitable to their needs. Much of English justice was anathema. The existing system of English punishment only rarely imposed incarceration. Heretofore incarceration had been intended to coerce delinquent debtors to pay their debts, to segregate incorrigible criminals from the community, and to prevent accused defendants from taking flight. The occasional prison sentence in colonial America often posed no great hardship on prisoners. Local jails were effectively rustic boarding houses in which jailers served as landlords. A prisoner's comfort depended on his financial means; relatives and friends could supply food, drink, and clothing and were free to socialize with the prisoner. So while Americans were in broad agreement that they ought to renounce the harsh punishments commonplace in Europe, they had almost no experience with anything but the most lenient and informal incarceration.[10]

Only gradually did the rudiments of a system of punishment deemed appropriate for the new nation emerge, inspired by both European and American precedents. Searching for new models of punishment, champions of legal reform fixed on the tradition of English workhouses, in which vagrants were detained until they adopted habits of rectitude and industry. In principle (if less often in practice), the workhouses combined coercive incarceration with the promise of rehabilitation through hard labor. Across the eighteenth century, English jurists and statesmen had expanded the writ of the workhouses to include petty criminals; and by the time of the American Revolution, Parliament was poised to substitute long-term incarceration with hard labor for sanguinary punishments. Colonists and their lawmakers in Massachusetts, New York, and Pennsylvania, who had firsthand experience with workhouses, began to advocate for hard labor as a punishment for a lengthening list of offenses.[11]

The writings of John Howard, an English prison reformer who advocated for imprisonment as the means to encourage penance and redemptive labor, exerted particular influence on American reformers. Appointed high sheriff of Bedfordshire in 1773, Howard visited local jails, where the conditions and the degradation of their occupants appalled him. In *The State of the Prisons*, published in 1777, he touted prison improvements with an eye to promoting both prison order and the well-being of prisoners. He did not advocate the adoption of long-term incarceration, but by making it seem feasible and humane, his proposals encouraged reformers to look to prisons as possible laboratories of rehabilitation. His recommendations were not immediately adopted in England, where conservatives, who were alarmed by the radical innovations of the American and French Revolutions, clamored to retain and even stiffen traditional punishments. But across the Atlantic, his ideas found fertile ground.[12]

Complementing nascent ideas about the potential of long-term incarceration was the conviction that criminal punishments should be commensurate with the gravity of the crime. American reformers had only to look to the writings of Montesquieu, the much-cited French philosopher, and Cesare Beccaria, an Italian jurist whose ideas exerted a broad influence in the young republic, for compelling arguments that retribution failed to deter crime and that capital punishment was a savage relic inconsistent with modern civilization. Beccaria insisted that the certainty, rather than the severity, of "public, prompt, and necessary" punishment was the most effective means to deter criminality. Yet he neither prescribed the punishments that should take the place of those of the ancien régime or repudiated sanguinary punishments that fell short of capital punishment.[13]

Public anxiety over property crime and criminality during the 1780s gave additional urgency to calls for criminal justice reform in the American republic. In the decade following the Revolution, a postwar depression with high levels of unemployment and poverty roiled virtually every state. The incidence of crime may not have increased, but concern about crime unquestionably did. Newspapers regularly reported robberies, burglaries, and murders carried out by "banditti," "gangs of villains," "nefarious wretches," and other "pests of society." Existing sanctions, including harsh sentences in those states that retained colonial-era laws, proved inadequate to suppress this lawlessness. Lawmakers had few obvious choices other than to consider new methods of punishment.[14]

In the short space of a decade and a half, the whole strategy of eighteenth-century punishment had been thrown into question—by a perceived crime wave that refused to respond to the old remedies and by the arguments of reformers that there was a more just and rational way for the new nation to discipline its subjects. Responding to these forces, American reformers in almost every state began experimenting with new schemes to punish and rehabilitate miscreants.

Massachusetts took the lead in 1780 when a state commission revised the state's legal code. The commission's decade-long effort reoriented punishment in the state by reducing the punishments for some crimes, narrowly defining others, and introducing hard labor. That incarceration began to emerge as a common punishment was not altogether surprising at the historical moment when the value of labor was increasingly measured in time and hourly wages. Reformers were keen to instill habits of industry no less than pangs of contrition in convicts, and time could be precisely allocated to advance both. So too the length of punishment was now calibrated to the severity of the crime. The legislature concluded that criminals guilty of property crimes should be detained in a quasi-military facility rather than in-effective local jails. The state's new facility became one of the nation's first large-scale experiments in imprisonment and hard labor. Located in Boston Harbor on Castle Island, the facility simultaneously imposed stern, military-like discipline on inmates, satisfied the public's desire for protection and retribution by isolating prisoners from society, and compelled inmates to work in a blacksmith shop and later in the man-ufacture of nails.[15]

Pennsylvania also began incorporating forced labor into criminal sanctions, but in public rather than isolated settings. In September 1786, the General Assembly transformed state law by moderating many pen-alties and by replacing the scourging and rending of criminals' bodies with enforced labor on public projects. Persuaded that punitive exhi-bitions would chasten criminals and discourage future criminality among spectators, Pennsylvania reformers intentionally sought to create a public spectacle of male convicts, adorned with iron collars around their necks and heavy iron balls attached to their legs, working on the streets of Philadelphia. (Female inmates were to be confined in the city's workhouse, thereby establishing for the first time in the state a clear distinction on the basis of gender in criminal sentencing.) Such work was intended to instill useful habits that would accelerate the criminals' rehabilitation while directly compensating society for the criminals' misdeeds.[16]

Neither the isolated drudgery in Massachusetts nor the public humiliation in Pennsylvania, however, fulfilled expectations. Too many inmates remained unchastened. In Massachusetts, Stephen Burroughs, the recidivist who was also an inmate at Castle Island, rejected incarceration as an improvement over older forms of physical punishment or humiliation. Like recalcitrant prisoners elsewhere, Burroughs and other inmates adopted various stratagems to subvert the prison regime, such as malingering, organizing periodic escapes, and fomenting inmate insurrections. After serving his sentence, Burroughs used his widely republished autobiography to compare imprisonment at Castle Island to slavery and to puncture claims that prisons represented the humanitarian punishment hailed by reformers.[17]

Convicts in Pennsylvania also proved intractable. At least one convict preferred death on the gallows to incarceration and hard labor, while others voiced their vigorous opposition to penal labor in general. Equally worrisome were the confrontations between inmates and the spectators they attracted when they worked in public. Inmates panhandled from, fraternized with, harassed, and even threatened passersby. Moreover, the inmates enjoyed unrestricted opportunities to socialize among themselves. Critics of the practice complained that it failed to remove inmates from the corrupting influences of either the streets or the jailhouse.[18]

The most influential critic of the innovations in Pennsylvania was Benjamin Rush. A man of diverse accomplishments, he was a civic leader, physician, politician, educator, and social reformer. The reforms he advocated were a distillation of ideas that had been circulating on both sides of the Atlantic and that were especially well suited to the intellectual milieu of Philadelphia, where Quaker reformers were receptive to harnessing the consciences of prisoners to rehabilitation. He contended that Pennsylvania's system of public convict labor was ineffective in transforming the criminal and was corrosive of the public good. Instead, he proposed an alternative system of private punishment that would employ the criminal's guilty conscience to rehabilitate him.[19]

Rush's key innovation was to articulate a coherent logic for rehabilitation through private repentance and state-enforced discipline. He made the case that the deprivation of liberty (and of participation in society) was essential to both justice and rehabilitation. As an alternative to the model of public works, Rush proposed the establishment of a large facility "in a remote part of the state," whose accessibility "would be rendered difficult and gloomy by the mountains or morasses." A prison in such a location would prevent the mind of criminals and spectators alike "from accustoming itself to the view of these punishments, so as to destroy its terror by habit." While Rush opposed the public terror displayed at the whipping post, the pillory, and the gallows, he still believed that terror—in this case the terror of imagination—was a crucial element of effective punishment.[20]

Ongoing submission and obedience was Rush's goal. Rush's regime of punishment marked an enduring shift in the locus of punishment from the body to the will of the criminal. Instead of violent and public displays of state power on the body of criminals, now the power of the state would be manifest in its capacity to inculcate habits of industry, personal restraint, and submission to the law. Failure by inmates to display sufficient reformation and submission opened up the possibility of more severe discipline and supervision. Although the state's new power assumed less sanguinary forms, it nevertheless was deeply invasive. Neither pain nor coercion were eliminated from the emerging rehabilitative incarceration. After all, criminals had to be sufficiently intimidated in order to abide by the disciplinary regime that over time would socialize them adequately to rejoin the ranks of free citizens. But in Rush's formulation, the target of the state's power was not the prisoner's body but his soul. No less significant was the shift in the goal of criminal justice that Rush advocated: to discipline the prisoner so that he could be rehabilitated. Penitence, not pain and suffering, was the intended outcome of the new techniques of punishment. Rush's ultimate aim was prisoners who complied with the law in accordance with their awakened consciences rather than out of cynical calculation.[21]

By articulating a program for the systematic control and discipline of criminals that applied punishments proportional to the crimes committed, that promised to both punish and deter crime, and that was couched in the language of science, Rush inspired like-minded reformers to envision penitentiaries as the young republic's humanitarian temples. In Philadelphia, Walnut Street Jail became a laboratory for a trial of his program. Similarly, in New York City, Thomas Eddy, a Quaker reformer, set out to transform the Newgate Prison, the first penitentiary in the state, into a model prison committed to rehabilitation. By 1810, Kentucky, Maryland, Virginia, and eight northern states had adopted the penitential model, and prison sentences had become the predominant punishment for crime.[22]

But within two decades, Newgate, Walnut Street Jail, and many of the other early prisons were widely perceived to be failures. At none of the prisons did authorities isolate prisoners from contact with other inmates or the general public, as Rush and other reformers contended was essential for rehabilitation. While prison staffs struggled to establish the institutional mastery that the idealized prison required, inmates routinely subverted and defied them. Displaying few signs of repentance or obedience, inmates malingered at work, periodically engaged in arson, escaped with regularity, and violently resisted prison authority. If critics were to be believed, instances of successful rehabilitation were the exception rather than the rule. Indeed, even some reformers conceded that the earliest penitentiaries had become "schools of turpitude."[23]

Unwilling to surrender their commitment to the penitentiary in the face of public skepticism, advocates of prisons redoubled their defense of long-term incarceration during the 1820s. They wrung their hands over the expense of prisons, and some even conceded that the sanguinary punishments of earlier times might need to be restored unless more effective methods of incarceration could be developed. Nevertheless, proponents urged, the penitentiary experiment could yet be salvaged. The failings of pioneering prisons in New York, Pennsylvania, and elsewhere, they insisted, were the result of overcrowding, poor administration, and inappropriate design, rather than any inherent flaws of custodial incarceration. Although the purported aim of the penitentiary had been to remove lawbreakers from civil society and sequester them from worldly temptations, prisons instead had housed prisoners in a milieu certain to further corrupt them. Frustration with past failings and anticipation of future success gave urgency to Roberts Vaux's speech at the dedication of Eastern State Penitentiary in 1823. He and his audience recognized that Eastern State and other prisons, either newly established or in planning, would determine the fate of the American experiment with incarceration.

New York and Pennsylvania were at the forefront of the reimagining of the penitentiary. Both states had energetic prison reform advocates who saw themselves as national cultural, intellectual, and philanthropic leaders engaged in an important experiment in social engineering. For these elite reformers, especially in New York City and Philadelphia, rising levels of crime following the Panic of 1819 exposed a dangerous erosion of public virtue that threatened the nation's fledgling democratic experiment. Refining the penitentiary was crucial to the restoration of public order in the young republic.[24]

Reformers in Pennsylvania and New York touted competing models of prison management that demonstrated the continuing influence of Benjamin Rush's model of incarceration. Eastern State Penitentiary, the exemplar of the so-called Pennsylvania system, was not located in the remote wilds of the state, as Rush had proposed. But to a greater extent than any previous prison, Eastern State held prisoners in the perpetual isolation that he had advocated. Confined in individual cells, inmates were to have no contact with fellow prisoners and only minimal contact with keepers and visitors. Inmates no longer undertook public works on the streets of Philadelphia but instead labored alone in their cells on artisanal crafts such as shoemaking and weaving. Sequestered from bad influences and subject to the remorseless work of their consciences, prisoners would have few opportunities to commit transgressions.[25]

At Auburn State Prison in New York, inmates endured a regimen of enforced silence and strict military-like discipline. A monotonous daily schedule required of prisoners lockstep movements, robotic-like gestures, and complete silence, whether they were confined at night in their individual cells or toiling together during the day to produce a wide array of manufactured goods. Expressing amazement that "not a sound is heard" within the prison, visitors presumed that "the very silence mocks [the inmate's] degradation." Whereas work at Eastern State was mainly intended to impart skills and instill diligence, work at Auburn was expected to subsidize the operating costs of the prison.[26]

For at least two decades, these competing penitentiary models stimulated vigorous debate about their merits and defects. In a flood of reports that constituted some of the earliest modern social science research, defenders and detractors parsed statistics regarding inmate mortality rates, incidence of recidivism, and use of physical discipline to confirm their claims about the competing models of prison organization. By the outbreak of the Civil War, state legislators and prison officials across the nation had adopted the Auburn plan on the grounds that it was cheaper than the Philadelphia alternative. But the rivalry between the two prison systems was sustained by debates over which forms of punishment were appropriate and which were cruel. In the starkest terms, antebellum Americans confronted the challenge of calibrating penal punishments and distinguishing legitimate punishments, consonant with American legal and constitutional principles, from forms of cruelty and torture.

The contentious tenor of the debate exaggerated the differences between the competing systems and obscured crucial similarities in penitentiary regimes everywhere in the United States during the first half of the nineteenth century. The differences in the programs were important, especially for the prisoners subject to them. The daily schedules and rigors of existence at Mount Pleasant Prison (aka Sing Sing) in upstate New York and at Eastern State were markedly distinct. Each had its unique hardships. But whether at the state prisons in New Hampshire and New Jersey or at Virginia State Penitentiary, early nineteenth-century prison regimes shared similar aims and underlying assumptions.

Everywhere the penitentiary was intended to be a laboratory of rigorous, coerced rectitude. The goal of nineteenth-century prison discipline was audacious: the complete submission of prisoners. Repeatedly, prison officials employed metaphors of the modern machine age to describe their aims. State commissioners who visited Auburn Prison in 1826 commended prison policies designed to reduce an inmate to "a silent and insulated human working machine." Massachusetts prison officials described an almost identical aim—to compel inmates "to move and act like machines." At Wethersfield Connecticut State Prison, "convicts shall be industrious . . . conduct themselves toward the officers with deference and respect; and cleanliness in their persons, dress and bedding is required. When they go to their meals or labor, they shall proceed in regular order and in silence, marching in lock step." The successful penitentiary would elicit obedience that represented prisoners' tacit consent to their own punishment and rehabilitation. Merely imposing the state's will on the body of the prisoner was insufficient to achieve this end. The body was the means to access the mind of the prisoner, for it was the conscience of the inmate that had to be fully disciplined.[27]

But how was obedience to be assessed, and how much discipline was appropriate to secure it? Could obedience freely given be distinguished from obedience compelled through intimidation? The former was the measure of successful rehabilitation; the latter, a mockery of prison aims. The only sure method to discern evidence of a prisoner's submission was to deprive him of privacy and to parse his every action for signs of his internalization of penitentiary protocols. With this aim in mind, the prison warden at Auburn boasted that prisoners there "were subject to the closest scrutiny." Allegedly, prison keepers in the Massachusetts State Prison were positioned so that they could "hear a whisper from the most distant cell." Staff at Charlestown Prison were tasked with closely observing inmates throughout the day, assessing their "cleanliness, industry, sobriety," and "moral conduct," and stamping out "all insolence and ill language and all obstinate and refractory behavior." An exceptionally broad range of behaviors could be interpreted as willful and intolerable transgressions. At the New Jersey State Prison, prisoners were forbidden "to exchange looks or laugh with each other or make any signs."

Under the Auburn system, in which strict rules and regulations governed every conceivable daily behavior, a prisoner who whispered furtively to another inmate, possessed a pencil in his cell, grinned "darkey fashion," failed to march in precise lockstep, looked a prison

FIGURE 2.1. *Implements of Torture, and Their Dangerous Effects*. This etching by James Akin depicts the gag that contributed to the death of an Eastern State Penitentiary inmate in 1833 and prompted an investigating committee in Pennsylvania to denounce atrocities there. The illustration quotes from the report: "In a Land too, where Tyranny, and Oppression, is held in utter abhorrence, and Liberty, Equality, and just enjoyment of rights, are the constant boasting of the people!!! The Spanish inquisitions, cannot exhibit a more fearful and barbarous mode, beyond all human endurance! It ought to be forever abolished!!!"

keeper in the eyes, or failed to display appropriate industry was, in the eyes of his keepers, engaging in behavior that warranted "every species of vexation which the caprice or malice of their keepers might choose to inflict." Meanwhile, guards at Eastern State were vigilant to ensure that inmates there did not break the stifling silence by whistling, laughing, humming, singing, or playing the crude musical instruments they fashioned out of odds and ends in their cells.[28]

Prison chaplains assumed a crucial role in this intrusive surveillance of prisoners. They became, in historian Michael Ignatieff's apt phrase, the penitentiary's "technicians of guilt." They were among the most ardent champions of the penitentiary because they were optimistic that Protestant piety, nurtured in prisons, would humanely rehabilitate the wretched and corrupt. During the first two decades of the nineteenth century, Rev. John Stanford, a Baptist minister at Newgate Prison in New York, made the case that prisons were unique sites of redemption where the "holy truth" could penetrate the "minds and hearts" of the incarcerated. Beginning in the 1820s, Rev. Louis Dwight of Boston also identified the penitentiary as an especially rich field for mission work. He mustered an impressive list of educators, ministers, church leaders, lawyers, and jurists to join the Prison Discipline Society of Boston, and together they took it upon themselves to inspect prisons from Maine to Louisiana and expose their deficiencies. The society's influence was felt broadly, but especially at Auburn Prison, which Dwight and his allies tirelessly celebrated and defended.[29]

Stanford, Dwight, and other ministers involved in prison reform were by no means uncritical of the administration of prisons, but their endorsement of the value of the "redemptive suffering" of incarceration legitimized the perception of penitentiaries as benevolent institutions committed to the rehabilitation of inmates. By linking suffering, conversion, physical chastisement, and moral rehabilitation, prison ministers endorsed the proposition that corporal punishment, "inflicted in mercy," had redemptive power. The ministers' message of repentance and submission complemented prison officials' program of obedience and order, especially at prisons that operated on the Auburn plan. The collaboration of ministers with prison administrations provided a measure of protection to penitentiaries whenever reports of cruelty or inhumane discipline aroused public concern. Thus when graphic and widely repeated accusations of cruelty were leveled against the Auburn prison staff in 1839, Rev. B. C. Smith, the prison chaplain there, dismissed the charges as baseless, countering that the hardened disposition of some of the inmates warranted their punishment and that the staff had been diligent in promoting their rehabilitation.[30]

At the same time that prisoners were subject to the constant scrutiny of prison authorities, they were on display for visitors. Some prisons, especially Auburn, Sing Sing, and Eastern State, attracted thousands of visitors who were charged $0.25 admission to visit the prison grounds and gape at the prison workshops. During the 1840s, Charleston Prison in Boston attracted nearly three thousand visitors a year, while Auburn hosted more than seven thousand annually. Opening the prisons for inspection by the public was, legislators and prison advocates claimed, crucial to assuaging public anxieties about the unprecedented power that was now invested in penitentiaries. If the public concluded that the penitentiary was "a sort of bastille or in-quisition," "it might occasion such a prejudice against the system as to endanger its stability." In the absence of a semblance of transparency of prison administration and accountability of prison staffs, the peni-tentiary almost certainly could not gain legitimacy in the eyes of the public as a modern and democratic engine of civilization.[31]

Visitors, however, had few opportunities to make a careful firsthand appraisal of prison operations and discipline. Indeed, prison wardens often restricted access out of concern about the prying eyes and deli-cate sensibilities of visitors. Administrators instead preferred the public to learn about prison life and administration from antiseptic annual reports and official documents. Such reports typically presented prisons as orderly and prison staffs as efficient and professional. Replete with tables and statistics that reported the minutiae of prison administra-tion, the reports calculated the productivity of inmates but made no mention of the hardships associated with it, tallied the number of lashes applied but made no notation of the pain that resulted, and reported the instances of binding and gagging of prisoners but acknowl-edged no trauma that prisoners experienced while bound. By design, the penitentiary system effaced the particulars of each inmate, ren-dering them instead as quantifiable attributes, behaviors, and fail-ings that became the measure of the penitentiary's effectiveness. The daily exercise of coercion at the heart of the penitentiary was not easily discerned in the reports of prison inspectors or in the journal articles by prison reformers. Nor could it be easily seen behind prison walls.[32]

Enforced isolation wrested control of the inmates' consciences from all other influences and consigned them to a form of social death in which all meaningful contact with the world beyond the penitentiary ceased. For good reason, visitors Gustave de Beaumont and Alexis de Tocqueville described the somber, sepulchral atmosphere at Auburn as "that of death" and a "desert solitude." Gershom Powers, a warden at Auburn penitentiary during the 1820s, warned new inmates there that they were "literally buried from the world." The silence and regimentation of prisoners marching in lockstep suggested "a military funeral" or "culprits when marching to the gallows."[33]

Admissions procedures at Eastern State made this contrived social death starkly manifest. On admission, each inmate was assigned a number that would take the place of his name; it was sewn on his prison uniform, it hung over his cell door, and prison staff used it to address him. He was then hooded so that he could not see the prison layout or glimpse any other prisoners as he was led to his cell. There his hood was removed. If need arose to transfer the inmate from his cell, he would again don his hood before entering the prison corridors.[34]

Yet for all the efforts of prison authorities and state officials to control public perceptions of the penitentiary and to render inmates mute, they could not suppress exposés by former inmates and local newspapers. A spate of prisoner autobiographies appeared during the 1830s and 1840s testifying to the resolve of former prisoners to lift the veil from the penitentiary. Levi Burr, who served three years in Sing Sing and published a scathing denunciation of the "cruelty and torture" he had experienced there, pointed out that the business of the modern penitentiary, unlike most public institutions in the young republic, remained virtually secret. The public only gained a glimmer of penal practices from "the pen of some unfortunate sufferer" who, like him, "had tenanted the horrid place." John Reynolds hoped that his prison memoirs would "drag iniquity from her dark retreats out into the view of mankind." He decried that the cruelty of prison staff was "screened from the arm of the law and the force of public contempt." Newspapers in the vicinity of penitentiaries also periodically reported accusations of cruelty, malfeasance, and incompetence by prison administrators.[35]

Even while dismissing the prison disclosures as lurid and unfounded, prison authorities periodically conceded that inmates' "wits and contrivance are continualy [sic] at work to circumvent and defeat the objects for which the prison was created." No prohibition of speech was sufficient to prevent inmates from occasionally shouting abusive language, taunting guards and fellow prisoners, or uttering blasphemous comments. No prison regime could preclude intractable convicts from refusing to work. Abraham Pettis, an inmate in the Charlestown Prison, for instance, had to be punished repeatedly in 1815 for "bad weaving and insolent behavior," for "wantonly and maliciously destroying property in cutting a whole web from the loom," and yet again for "malice & destroying property." Unsatisfied with breaking their tools, wasting materials, and producing shoddy work, some stubborn prisoners set their workplaces on fire. Another favored tactic of prisoners was to feign illness. In 1827 Charlestown Prison authorities discovered that inmates furtively consumed digitalis so as to reduce their pulses and thereby avoid work and "obtain the leisure, and attention, and comforts of the hospital."[36]

Prisoner resistance sometimes took the form of overt violence against guards. Inmates rioted against their overseers, demonstrating a degree of coordination and resolve that alarmed prison officials. At Charlestown prison in 1816, inmates threw rocks and brickbats at guards to provide cover for more than twenty prisoners who scaled the prison walls in an attempt at a mass escape. Four years later, inmates working in the stonecutting shed at the same prison refused to work, threatened their keepers with harm, and manifested "a dangerous spirit of insubordination and insurrection." And on yet another occasion when prisoners rioted, officials needed the intercession of soldiers with fixed bayonets to overawe the riotous inmates and regain control of the facility. At Eastern State Penitentiary, prisoners sabotaged their toilets to create opportunities to assault their guards. Order in the New Jersey State Prison was apparently equally precarious in 1830. Prisoners there rioted with alarming frequency, and more than one hundred (or one in twelve) managed to escape.[37]

"Refractory" inmates posed more than just a danger to the prison staff. They also challenged the legitimacy of the penitentiary. Debates about the need for severe discipline in penitentiaries were a tacit acknowledgment that prisoners often needed to be coerced to rehabilitate. Roberts Vaux, Thomas Eddy, and other early champions of the penitentiary had anticipated that the lash and other severe corporal punishments would be outmoded in modern prisons and that discipline would be applied infrequently and only to the most incorrigible inmates. But the persistence of disobedience and violence among prisoners seemed to demand a clear rationale for prison punishments that would distinguish them from the discredited punishments of the colonial era.

Proponents of physical chastisement to coerce obedience and habits of industry insisted that their methods were not cruel and would not devolve into torture. They pointed to the widespread application of corporal punishment by parents, teachers, employers, and the military. Moreover, there was wide acceptance that when the conscience of a prisoner failed to respond to the prison environment, some form of physical coercion was both appropriate and necessary. Many reformers, including Louis Dwight and his allies in the Prison Discipline Society of Boston, advocated a precise and rational calibration of discipline that took into account each prisoner's transgression, character, and degree of rehabilitation. Discipline, they insisted, should be governed by strict rules, routines, and supervision so as not to be distorted by whim, emotion, or prejudice. This purportedly precise calibration would ensure that punishment was meted out by design and so was altogether distinct from cruelty. The ideal balance of stern judgment and measured mercy would preclude "absolute power, unlimited power, despotic power," which should be "entirely inadmissible in the American penitentiary system."[38]

Many prison officials bridled at punctilious discipline and fretted that humanitarians sought to interfere unduly in their application of discipline. Prison authorities argued that violence, when properly directed against an inmate, could be a catalyst for rehabilitation. A warden at Newgate in 1817 justified a free hand with discipline on the grounds that inmates needed to learn that prison "is not to be a place of good living and light punishment, but a place of dread and terror, and that his [the inmate's] turpitude will receive the punishment it merits." A New York legislative commission concurred, concluding that suffering and terror were the most effective means to inspire "a salutary horror of the consequences of criminality." Another oft-repeated justification for corporal punishment was that both the threat and application of violence were essential for the maintenance of order in penitentiaries. Judge Reuben H. Walworth, at the close of the trial of an Auburn guard for beating a prisoner in 1826, tightly aligned the welfare of law-abiding citizens, the degradation of inmates, and the application of corporal punishment. To impose "bodily suffering" on prisoners, who should "feel that they were in reality slaves of the state," was an appropriate means to compel submission and rehabilitation. Equally important, Walworth invoked the common law precedent to establish that prison guards were within their rights to resort to violence to maintain discipline. Such reasoning gave license to prison administrators to exert almost unfettered power over inmates.[39]

While the interpretations of Walworth and the New York legislators gave a measure of legitimacy to the adoption of corporal punishment in penitentiaries, each prison staff still had to work out the regulation of the day-to-day application of discipline. Prison staff had to be inventive to devise "bodily suffering" that was more severe than the unvarying drudgery of daily life in prison, the ubiquity of silence, and the completeness of personal isolation. Explicit incentives for good behavior were often scorned because they were perceived to reward facile compliance with prison rules without instilling true self-discipline and rehabilitation. Instead, prison staffs demonstrated a presumption that a regimen of escalating coercion, especially deprivation and severe physical punishment, was the means by which submission would be compelled.

In one prison after another during the first half of the nineteenth century, prison administrations struggled to resolve the question of what forms of violence were legitimate components of modern, civilized punishment. What was the proper balance between moral suasion and rehabilitation, which were crucial to claims that the penitentiary was virtuous and civilized, and stern coercion, which was justified as an essential complement to the penitentiary's humanitarian aims?

In a recurring sequence, mounting anxiety about lax discipline at a facility would gave rise to demands by legislators and prison administrators for the imposition of harsh discipline. Eventually, concern about reported excessive punishments would prompt renewed expressions of commitment to rehabilitation and the adoption of milder discipline. Then fresh concerns about prisoner insubordination would lead to the reimposition of more stringent discipline, and on and on.

Nowhere was this cycle more pronounced and perhaps nowhere was the challenge of calibrating discipline more apparent than in New York's prisons. Although Auburn prison became synonymous with corporal punishment, especially flogging, it was first the site of an experiment with strict solitary confinement that had not been possible at Newgate or older prisons. On Christmas Day in 1821, eighty-three of the most incorrigible inmates at Auburn were perpetually confined in their cells, where they were "deprived of every enjoyment arising out from social or kindred feelings and affections; of all knowledge of each other, the world, and their connections with it." Within two years, many of the sequestered inmates succumbed to illness and at least one to insanity. One inmate beat his head against his cell wall until he was rendered blind in one eye, while another took the first opportunity to hurl himself off a balcony. The experiment proved so ill-advised that the governor interceded, released some of the surviving prisoners from solitary confinement, and pardoned the remainder.[40]

After this disastrous experiment, the imposition of perpetual isolation was viewed by many penal observers as indefensible torture. Auburn officials concluded that prolonged deprivation and extreme isolation often had catastrophic effects on inmates, ranging from lasting physical ailments to mental trauma and suicidal impulses. The Auburn experiment loomed large in Louis Dwight's and the Prison Discipline Society of Boston's relentless criticism of the application of solitary confinement at Eastern State Penitentiary and a few other prisons. Pointing to the high rate of insanity among prisoners confined in "secluded and gloomy imprisonment," critics contended that unless solitary confinement was restricted to short durations, it devolved into a form of torture. Charles Dickens, in his churlish *American Notes*, which recounted his travels in the United States in 1842, offered an especially devastating denunciation of the solitary confinement he saw practiced at Eastern State. Shocked by its effect on the inmates there, he declared "this slow and daily tampering with the mysteries of the brain to be immeasurably worse than any torture of the body." Dickens's claims infuriated defenders of Eastern State and solitary confinement, but their rebuttals of his charges could not erase the perception that prolonged and extreme isolation was cruel and inhumane.[41]

The lesson that many reformers and prison staffs drew from the criticism of solitary confinement was that corporal punishment, especially flogging, was a superior method of discipline. At the flick of the wrist, the whip produced the "bodily suffering" that compelled obedience. Moreover, it purportedly did not have the debilitating emotional and mental consequences associated with solitary confinement. The New York legislature endorsed the adoption of the lash in 1819 by legalizing flogging at both Auburn and Newgate. (The legislature also approved the use of stocks and irons.) Although the law was a tacit acknowledgment that previous methods of coercion were insufficient to make the penitentiary function as intended, it also revealed that legislators were cautious about granting too much unchecked power to prison staffs. The new law limited whippings to no more than thirty-nine blows delivered on a single occasion and required that keepers carry out the punishment under the supervision of two prison inspectors. Legislators may have intended to prevent abuse of prisoners by restricting the duration of floggings and the authority to inflict them, but this putative safeguard against abuse subsequently proved to be wholly ineffectual.[42]

Captain Elam Lynds, first as prison keeper and then as warden of Auburn Prison, established a severe program of corporal punishment that took full advantage of the license granted by the state legislature. A veteran of the War of 1812 who championed stern military discipline, Lynds "encouraged the use of the whip to maintain a perfect submission to the rules." So extreme were Lynds's methods that local residents, some of whom worked in the prison, eventually denounced them before grand juries called to investigate accusations of cruelty in the prison. Testimony revealed that guards had been given summary authority to inflict corporal punishment immediately after an infraction and without the supervision of higher officials. The jury maintained that such whippings directly contravened the 1819 law, warning that "the inevitable tendency of the system is abuse, oppression and cruelty; and the report to the keeper, after the infliction of the punishment, is a miserable guaranty against barbarity in the infliction of it." The commissioners charged with the prison's oversight nevertheless dismissed the grand jury's warning by reaffirming the authority of wardens to inflict "instant chastisement" whenever an offense was "fresh and flagrant," thought to be "infectious," or likely to impair prison discipline. Not even the death of Rachel Welch, a female convict who died from complications associated with a flogging she had received at Auburn in 1825, was sufficient to end Lynds's career. Her flogging violated the 1819 law, which had explicitly prohibited the whipping of female inmates, and the grand jury that investigated her death uncovered other flagrant violations of the law. Despite, or rather because of, his record at Auburn, state authorities appointed Lynds to serve as the first warden at Sing Sing Prison.[43]

Lynds's successor at Auburn, Gershom Powers, initiated a system of discipline that was strict yet less likely to arouse public opposition. Convicts still lived in silence, moved in lockstep, and were routinely flogged. But Powers moderated the use of extreme discipline and emphasized the importance of prison ministers, whose work with prisoners was intended to "make them better convicts." The presence of a minister at Auburn gave a measure of credibility to Powers's professions of support for the rehabilitation of inmates. His political ambitions ensured that his time at Auburn was comparatively brief, but he was succeeded by several wardens who continued his methods. Then, in 1838, Captain Lynds, who retained influential political allies, secured his reappointment at Auburn. Affirming his reputation for harsh discipline, which had been burnished further during the previous five years as warden at Sing Sing, Lynds set a goal of crushing prisoner disobedience, especially among working-class immigrant and African American inmates who represented, in his mind, the most incorrigible and dangerous criminal element in his prison.[44]

Lynds's program of discipline had reached its apotheosis at Sing Sing, where his successor as warden was his nephew, Robert Wiltse. Wiltse was forthright in his pessimism about the feasibility of "a general and radical reformation" of prisoners. Reformers and citizens, he cautioned, should not expect their appeals to conscience to foment moral rehabilitation among prisoners. Inmates, according to him, "can feel nothing but that which comes through bodily suffering." The main mission of the penitentiary, he insisted, was to demonstrate that "criminals must be made to submit through corporal punishment." At first glance, Wiltse's program of brutal discipline seemed to harken back to the sanguinary punishments of the eighteenth century. But his regime of relentless subordination was fully consonant with the modern penitentiary movement. While it placed little stock in the promise of rehabilitation and dismissed any hand-wringing over "unnecessary severities," Wiltse still presumed that the penitentiary was the most efficient, economical, and fear-inducing machine for humbling and chastising law breakers.[45]

Lynds, Powers, and Wiltse defended their extraordinary power by stressing that the modern "science" of incarceration informed their methods and those of their properly trained staffs, who possessed the requisite wisdom and self-control to inflict corporal punishment. Prison reformers affirmed that the success of the penitentiary in rehabilitating criminals and deterring crime would be determined less by prison regulations than by "the character of the men to whom the government of the prison is entrusted." Thomas Eddy listed the exemplary qualifications prison keepers should possess: patience, perseverance, discretion, "sound understanding, quick discernment," a "cool, equable, and dispassionate" temper, "dignified and commanding" manners, and "a heart warmed by the feeling of benevolence but firm and resolute."[46]

In practice, prisons seldom appear to have been successful at recruiting staff who possessed these rare qualifications. Prison guards typically lacked any meaningful training. They were hired on the basis of political patronage rather than any relevant qualifications. The corrosive effects of political patronage on prison staffing became a major issue at Newgate Prison at the dawn of the nineteenth century, at Eastern State a quarter century later, at Sing Sing in 1840, and at Auburn and the New Jersey State Prison at mid-century. Even at institutions that operated according to regulations that were "as merciful as they were wise," prison inmates complained that staff became "intoxicated with power and claimed the homage of god." They devolved into "cruel and heartless" despots who ignored rules intended to shield prisoners from abuse. Another former inmate dismissed prison staff as "the worst men that society could produce, not possessed of common morality, drunkards, swearers, &, &." Exacerbating the problem were the demands placed on prison staff. Well intentioned or not, prison staff were not qualified to handle many forms of inmate behavior, especially that of inmates who were intellectually deficient or manifested mental disorders. Moreover, many prisons, including Auburn and Sing Sing, were bursting with too many prisoners. Overworked staffs could not be expected to perform all of their assigned duties. Instead of the tightly controlled, carefully calibrated exercise of the authority that legislatures granted to prison administrators, anxious and worn-out prison keepers in practice resorted to arbitrary, erratic, and excessive displays of their power.[47]

With the tacit approval of wardens, prison keepers in New York terrorized prisoners with the cat-o'-nine-tails, which was a stick with nine cords with sharp wire ends attached to each cord, and the cudgel, which was a stout cane used to beat the heads and bodies of inmates. Prison staff often delivered many more blows with the whip than law allowed. A former inmate condemned prison guards at Sing Sing for being as cruel as "the negro drivers of the South." He raged, "It is abominable to think, in a Christian country," that prisoners "should be flogged to death, and their bodies given over to dissection." Levi Burr, another former inmate, denounced the staff at Sing Sing for flaying a prisoner with the cat 133 times on a single occasion. Former inmate James Brice recalled seeing prisoners' backs "as raw as a piece of beef." Periodic investigative commissions launched by the New York legislature corroborated such accusations of excessive use of the whip. In 1839 a civilian contractor testified that he had witnessed a convict stripped naked, bound with ropes, and whipped for three successive days. The same commission heard that a mentally ill convict at Auburn had been flogged to death and the warden had refused to allow a coroner's inquest. After Charles S. Plumb, a mentally ill convict at Auburn, was whipped to death in 1846, the warden insisted that Plumb had received an appropriate punishment of twelve lashes. The postmortem, however, revealed that the dead inmate's back was so badly lacerated that he had been subjected to at least three hundred and perhaps as many as six hundred lashes.[48]

Plumb's death finally prodded the New York legislature in 1847 to prohibit the lash and to restore solitary confinement as the preferred method of severe punishment. Yet even as the lash was banned, state prison inspectors continued to endorse it as a "time honored" and "antiquity hallowed instrument."[49] They insisted that a "judicious system of discipline" required the use of the cat. As had been true in the past, new regulations on severe punishment were ignored, and prison staff quickly devised alternative punishments that were at least as severe as their predecessors. Prison keepers apparently concluded that they were free to apply any methods of discipline that were not explicitly prohibited. H. Wells, warden at Sing Sing in 1849, boasted that his administration had abolished any punishment that "lacerates the body or degrades the mind." He then recounted that during the past eleven months, 351 punishments had been inflicted, including the shower bath, solitary confinement, bread and water diet, and "ball and chain" to the leg or "iron collar around the neck." The warden was especially impressed by the effects of the iron collar; "it inflicts no personal injury upon the offender, enables him to pursue his usual employment, points him out to his fellows, and in every instance has produced a salutary influence," he said. Wells's catalog of "humane" punishments would have been familiar to prison staffs at other penitentiaries across the nation during the 1840s.[50]

Prison staff at Sing Sing and elsewhere adopted punishments that left no permanent scars but produced extreme physical discomfort and mental disorientation. To intensify the isolation that inmates endured daily, guards confined insubordinate inmates in "dark cells" where they were deprived of light, any diversions, and full rations for weeks, even months at a time. In place of the lash, guards adopted the yoke, which was a long and heavy bar with a hole in the center into which the offending prisoner's neck was placed. The prisoner's hands were then tautly chained to either end of the bar. The combination of the weight of the bar pressing down on the prisoner's neck and spine as well as the tightened chains forced prisoners to hunch over for hours at a time. Prison keepers in New York even employed a mechanical apparatus to compel prisoners to stand in excruciating stress positions for hours. While an offending inmate stood on one leg, prison keepers tugged his other limbs up by means of a pulley. (At New Jersey State

Prison, troublesome inmates were "stretched" by chaining their feet to the floor while winching their hands above their heads. Yet other prisoners were subjected to "bucking," which was a punishment commonplace in the American military. A convict would be forced to sit with his knees drawn up to his chest and his arms securely fastened to his legs. A stick, which was inserted between his knee joints and elbows, enabled prison keepers to roll the offender's body across the ground at will. Yoking, the pulley, and bucking all produced nearly unbearable physical torment; when freed from them, prisoners were often incapacitated with swelling, numbness, headaches, acute muscle pain, and "paralyzation" for days thereafter.[51]

The most common method of discipline during the 1840s and 1850s was the so-called shower bath. It was already in use at Eastern State during the early 1830s, but it came into much wider use during the 1840s when flogging fell out of favor. By then the shower bath had become, in the opinion of Auburn's physician, "the most important and valuable means of enforcing prison discipline that was ever devised."[52] An inmate condemned to this punishment was stripped, seated in a stall with his feet and arms fastened in stocks and his head extended up into a tank that fit snugly around his neck. Once shackled in the contraption, the prisoner's head was drenched with a torrent of freezing cold water that cascaded down from a height of a foot or more for several minutes at a time. The tank that encircled the prisoner's neck emptied slowly, inducing a sensation of drowning. According to observers of the procedure, "Its effects are to shock the nervous system and weaken the whole body." The shock and force of frigid water, which was sometimes chilled with ice, and the sensation of drowning often sent victims of the punishment into convulsions and even prolonged states of delirium. Some suffered deafness and lasting mental effects.[53]

Despite the periodic deaths of inmates subjected to the punishment, proponents of the shower bath argued that it was a humane substitute for the whip and that its effects were even therapeutic. Pointing out that the method was applied to mental patients who suffered from "disease of the brain," Louis Dwight and others declared that it was a humanitarian form of discipline. Dorothea Dix, the most famous prison reformer of the age, endorsed the shower bath as preferable to the lash, claiming that prisoners "would yield as readily" to a shower from "a single bucket of water" as to the lash.[54] The editor of the *Fort Edward Ledger* tied himself in knots trying to distinguish civilized punishments, such as flogging, the shower bath, and solitary confinement in the dark cell, from bucking, yoking, and "crucifying," which were "a resuscitating of ancient barbarism that modern ingenuity, not to say mercy, can and should rectify." George Throop, warden at Clinton Prison, insisted that the shower bath was "much less degrading and brutalizing" than the lash. He claimed that he had never heard of an application of the shower bath that was "prejudicial to health" but had witnessed many instances when it was "beneficial to it." An anonymous article in the *New York Evangelist* in 1851 dismissed the suggestion that the shower bath was "barbarous" or "savage." Contrasting the shower bath to the "torture of the lash," the correspondent testified that the shower bath was more effective, less cruel, and less severe than the alternatives.[55]

Other observers were far less sanguine about the beneficial effects of the water torture. Reports that guards at Clinton Prison in New York forced prisoners to stand naked while they were subjected to the procedure roused the editor of the *Plattsburgh Republican* to wonder "which most deserves the prison uniform, the convict or his tormentors." He went on to ask, "Why in the name of reason, of humanity, of civilization and refinement" were prisoners subjected to a punishment that "calls for the reprobation of every friend of humanity." The application of the shower bath was, in the eyes of critics, evidence of a "backwards revolution" in morality and justice. They invoked the ideals of modern civilization and progress to impugn the water torture as a relic of barbarism. A scathing report in the *Independent* in 1860 lamented that the "tortures of Sing Sing exceed by far the punishments of prisoners of Naples or any other country in the world." *Harper's Weekly* concurred, pointing out that "we need no longer, it seems, to travel to China and Japan for illustrations of torture." Even worse, the technique "is a greater barbarity than the scalping knife of the Indian" and perpetuated a torture that had been practiced by the Inquisition. *Harper's* concluded its denunciation of the "tortures" employed at mid-century penitentiaries with a simple appeal: "If the prisons of New York are to be mere modern editions of the dungeons of the Inquisition, it is right that the people should know the fact."[56]

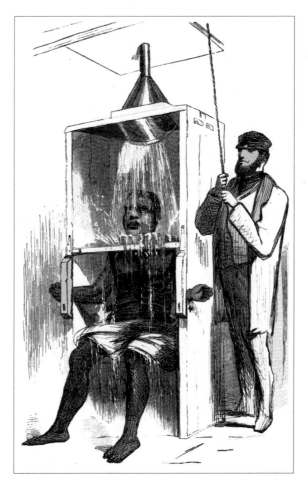

FIGURE 2.2. *The Negro Convict, More, Showered to Death.* After flogging was deemed cruel and excessive, many prisons used the so-called shower bath to punish inmates. After the death of an African American prisoner at Sing Sing Prison in New York, *Harper's Weekly* published an exposé, "Torture and Homicide at an American State Prison." Despite legislative bans on the punishment, it continued in use for the remainder of the nineteenth century.

But not even periodic reports of prisoners who were killed or permanently harmed by the shower bath were sufficient to end the practice. An inmate who was subjected to a constant stream of nearly freezing water for a half hour fell into a "perfectly unconscious state, with convulsive twitchings," and his mouth filled with "frothy saliva." He failed to regain consciousness and died. An eighty-eight-year-old inmate who underwent the shower bath went into convulsions, which lasted thirty minutes, suffered "congestion of the brain," and had to be bled thirty ounces of blood before his "derangement" subsided. Another convict who survived a shower bath emerged from the punishment "with a mind totally destroyed." Chastened by such incidents, the New Jersey legislature prohibited the shower bath after it had been in use for two years. But the New York legislature permitted the continued use of the punishment "under the advice and direction" of a prison physician. This loophole was so widely invoked that the punishment continued to be applied almost as frequently as before the new restriction. At Sing Sing in 1860, it was applied on at least 161 occasions.[57]

More than three decades after Roberts Vaux's christening of a new era in human justice, *Harper's Weekly* published an exposé of the methods of discipline routinely employed at New York prisons. Illustrated with graphic images, the sobering account demonstrated that the systematic infliction of intentional pain and mental suffering had not been excised from American justice. Many of the forms of discipline were variations on time-honored techniques of torture that would have been familiar to any jurist in early modern Europe. But the sites where prisoners experienced violence were distinctly modern, as were the justifications for it. The aim of the violence, its proponents vouched, was not pain but rehabilitation and obedience. Any acute suffering that prisoners endured when subjected to simulated drowning, to the searing pain of brine splashed on scars left by the lash, to the disorientation resulting from weeks confined in complete darkness and silence, and to the other modes of punishment that accompanied modern humanitarian penology was, advocates insisted, never by design. In light of their laudable aims, these modern techniques of penal coercion were neither cruel nor torturous.

During the second half of the nineteenth century, a new generation of prison reformers would renew experiments in rehabilitation and would again renounce violence and torture. New York State prisons were at the forefront of the "new penology." By the end of the century, prisons in the state stopped shaving the heads of inmates and making them march in lockstep; by 1907 prisoners no longer had to maintain continual silence. And after 1899 prisoners could seek redress for acts of brutality by prison staff by sending sealed letters to appropriate state officials. Previously, prisoners could only lodge protests with the permission of the wardens, which, given the complicity of wardens in prison discipline, was a meaningless privilege.

The Elmira Reformatory, established in 1876, quickly became the lodestar for prison reformers across the nation. Just as visitors from around the world had once trekked to Auburn to see enlightened punishment and rehabilitation, they now traveled to Elmira. There they observed an institution that rewarded prisoners for good behavior by offering parole and that provided classes in both basic education and artisanal skills. Havelock Ellis, a pioneering psychologist who also studied "the criminal class," gushed that "in character and results" the methods at Elmira were "very unlike the barbarous and ineffectual code of prison customs" practiced at almost all other contemporary prisons. Zebulon Reed Brockway, who was the superintendent of the facility, was the model prison official that Thomas Eddy had envisioned decades earlier; he had begun his career as a guard in the Connecticut state prison at Wethersfield and by the time of his arrival at Elmira had a national reputation as an innovative and visionary administrator.[58]

But behind the relentless publicity of the marvels of Elmira and other model prisons that Brockway and his peers generated, the elements of the "new penology" would have been familiar to Levi Burr and prisoners a half century earlier. The lash had fallen out of favor; it was too redolent of slavery to retain favor as a tool of discipline in prisons, the military, and other institutions of the North. But prison staffs had no shortage of methods to chasten prisoners. Despite having previously banned such methods, the New York legislature in 1869 yet again was compelled by sensational reports of abuse to prohibit the shower bath, yoking, bucking, and "the crucifix" (an especially excruciating stress position).[59] Another investigation fourteen years later found that prison staffs ignored the ban and continued to douse prisoners with cold water, confine them in the dark cell, and employ pulleys to stretch those who failed to meet work quotas.[60] Yet another investigation in 1890 revealed that guards at Sing Sing and Clinton prisons shackled and hoisted prisoners until their toes barely touched the floor. The investigation also revealed that "paddling," which was a less scarring form of flogging, was commonplace.[61]

Even more damning revelations emerged during an investigation of abuses at Elmira Reformatory in 1893. That the abuses occurred at the shrine of the "new penology" made the charges especially notable. Vexed by the behavior of large numbers of prisoners who failed to comply with prison protocols, guards routinely applied harsh corporal punishment, with Brockway himself commonly meting it out. Brockway justified the punishments with rationales that echoed those by Elam Lynds a half century earlier. When appeals to the best instincts of prisoners failed, Brockway advocated making a "more direct appeal through bodily sensations." Unlike the severe methods of yore, a "simple, altogether harmless physical shock" analogous to "harmless parental discipline" was sufficient to command the obedience of a prisoner.[62]

Brockway's benign description of his aims and methods bore no resemblance to the punishments that prisoners experienced. Between 1889 and 1893, for example, Brockway and the guards conducted 2,578 beatings with rubber hoses and paddles. The incidence of beatings increased each consecutive year, indicating that the violence was routine rather than an exceptional measure necessary to restore order. Those defiant prisoners who were not beaten were shackled in a dark cell where they were deprived of human contact and light for lengthy spells. One prisoner who endured five months in the cell on a bread and water diet went insane and had to be transferred to a mental institution. Despite a mountain of evidence of serial brutality, Brockway remained superintendent with the support of both prominent politicians and prison "reformers" until Governor Theodore Roosevelt forced him out in 1899.[63] Finally, in 1913, a century into the penitentiary experiment, an investigation of Sing Sing Prison brought forth harrowing accounts of prisoners being sequestered in dark cells where they became emaciated, lost their sanity, and in several instances took their own lives.[64]

During the first century after the innovation of the penitentiary, Americans remained conflicted about the success of their experiment with incarceration. They attested to the utility of the penitentiary but were periodically reminded of the gap between its loftiest goals and its evident failings. Reformers and civilians alike periodically confessed a loss of confidence in the rehabilitative capacity of the penitentiary. But no one envisioned or proposed a viable alternative. The enduring legacy of the early nineteenth century was to establish the precedent for state institutions that deprived large numbers of Americans of their liberty and subjected them to continuous and intrusive supervision, pervasive discipline, and, all too frequently, extreme physical and mental coercion.

The recurring challenge was to rid the penitentiary of any associations with tyranny and barbarism. The language of rehabilitation had tempered the harshness of prison life while the isolation of prisoners in penitentiaries hid from public scrutiny and regulation the extraordinary power that agents of the state exercised over inmates. It is a testament to the success of the campaign to legitimate the penitentiary that each exposé regarding torture in prisons was accompanied by an expression of shock and dismay from the seemingly unaware public. Readers of the 1858 *Harper's Weekly* article on abuses at Auburn or the 1883 *New York Times* accounts of cruelty at Sing Sing learned little of the abuses that had previously occurred at these prisons. Instead, each time reports of prison abuse aroused public attention, the same solutions were proposed: greater professionalism in prison staff and tighter regulation by state officials.

While Americans were thought to be exceptionally wary of any institutions that fostered despotic tendencies, they nonetheless came to accept penitentiaries where, by design if not in practice, the power of state agents over inmates was virtually absolute. Nineteenth-century America offered no starker daily display of the state's power than the penitentiary. Beginning with Benjamin Rush, the most optimistic reformers thought that state officials needed vast power over the penal environment to rehabilitate convicts. Less optimistic reformers felt that state officials needed virtually absolute power over convicts to incapacitate, control, and punish them. The ideology of rehabilitation, moreover, drew no clear distinction between moral suasion and coercion.[65] After touring the nation's pioneering prisons in 1831, Gustave de Beaumont and Alexis de Tocqueville were particularly struck by the power that Americans granted to prison staffs: "Whilst society in the United States gives the example of the most extended liberty, the prisons of the same country offer the spectacle of the most complete despotism."[66] The directors of the Massachusetts State Prison pledged to exercise fully that power by striving for prison discipline that would be "as severe as the law of humanity will by any means tolerate."[67] Ample evidence suggests that prison reformers were sincere in their hope to redeem the nation's criminals, but they designed and defended prison practices that perpetuated in a modern democratic society the state's continued assault on the criminal's body.

Neither the founding generation nor its successors established a prison regime that fulfilled the lofty ambitions that Roberts Vaux sketched out in 1823. The expectations voiced at the dawn of the nineteenth century were unrealistic. They nevertheless, both intentionally and unintentionally, urged on the experiments with discipline in nineteenth-century penitentiaries that produced pain and suffering. They legitimated a degree of invasive scrutiny and subordination that was at sharp odds with the prevailing rhetoric of liberty. The language of rehabilitation, however sincere it may have been in some instances, obfuscated the stark principle that underlay the penitentiary experiment. When moral suasion or prevailing mores failed, the state could and would exercise almost unlimited power to compel self-control and social conformity.

THREE

Cruelty and the Paradox
of Slave Property

W HEN FIRE BROKE OUT in their New Orleans mansion on April 10, 1834, Delphine and Louis Lalaurie struggled to save their possessions from the flames. They rescued furniture and other accoutrements of their elegant lifestyle but displayed no evident concern about their nine slaves. As the fire spread, neighbors and Good Samaritans volunteered their assistance. The Lalauries rebuffed appeals to extricate their slaves, berating would-be rescuers for meddling where they were not welcome. Spurred by long-standing rumors about the Lalauries' mistreatment of their slaves, members of the crowd pushed their way into the slave quarters, where they discovered horribly abused slaves. In the kitchen, where the fire had apparently been intentionally started, a badly abused and elderly slave cook was chained to the floor. In another room the searchers found mutilated and emaciated slaves suspended by their necks. One slave was described as "rotten with sores, and in them were found numbers of living creatures."[1] After removing the gagged and manacled slaves, the rescuers incarcerated them in the city jail for their protection.

News of the fire and the gruesome discovery of "barbarous and fiendish atrocities" at the Lalaurie mansion spread quickly, fanning "popular fury." Later that day, a crowd surrounded the mansion, which had been saved from the fire, apparently intent on imposing popular justice on the Lalauries. Delphine escaped harm by fleeing in a carriage, thereafter making her way to Mobile and finally Paris. Her husband disappeared as well, leaving the mob to direct its fury against the mansion, which they gutted, scarring the walls with graffiti, smashing its lavish furnishings, and strewing them along Royal Street.[2]

The scandal of the Lalauries gripped the city in the days after the fire. Decorum as well as the inadequacy of words discouraged newspapers from full disclosure of the horrors the Creole couple had inflicted on their slaves. The *New Orleans Courier* confessed that the scenes in the Lalaurie mansion "inspired in us so much horror that even at the moment of writing this article we shudder from its effects." City residents, however, betrayed few qualms about gawking at the spectacle of the ruined mansion or the Lalauries' traumatized slaves. Thousands of spectators swarmed the jail to inspect an array of manacles, neck rings, and devices of torture collected from the mansion and "to witness the unfortunate wretches who had escaped cruelties that would compare with those of a Domitian, a Nero, a Caligula."[3]

The Lalaurie scandal garnered national and international attention, becoming a flash point in the intensifying debate over slavery.[4] News of the Lalauries' atrocities coincided with a marked shift in the tenor and substance of this debate. Increasingly, critics of slavery abandoned the cause of gradual emancipation and rallied behind a campaign for immediate abolition. In 1829 African American abolitionist David Walker signaled the new stridency when he published his inflammatory *Appeal . . . to the Coloured Citizens of the World*, which mocked white Americans who prattled about the barbarism of Turks, Spaniards, and Indians while ignoring the "barbarous cruelties" of American slavery.[5] He beseeched blacks to assume the leadership of a crusade to destroy the institution. Two years later, Nat Turner's failed slave rebellion in Virginia horrified southern slaveholders, who concluded that their human chattel had fallen under the sway of Walker and other abolitionists. Simultaneously, abolitionists began building organizations to wage a prolonged campaign. In 1831 William Lloyd Garrison launched the *Liberator*, an indefatigable voice for immediate emancipation that had an influence far beyond its modest subscription list. A year later he and his allies established the New-England Anti-slavery Society and, in 1833, the year before the Lalaurie scandal broke, the American Anti-slavery Society.[6] After the British parliament abolished slavery throughout most of the British empire in that same year, American abolitionists took heart that the campaign against slavery was gathering momentum.

Embedded within the national argument over slavery during the three decades before the Civil War was one of the most sustained debates in American history about torture, coercion, and obedience. Although the Lalaurie scandal was only one, albeit sensational, piece of evidence in the litany of slave masters' cruelties compiled by antebellum abolitionists, it provides an apt starting point to consider debates about slave torture in antebellum America. With mounting certainty, opponents of slavery asserted that torture was inherent to slavery. This contention acquired particular resonance at a time when other forms of violent coercion were under scrutiny in the United States. The outrages committed by the Lalauries and other slave owners, slavery's critics protested, could not be reconciled with the principles of enlightened civilization that the American republic should embody. Slavery was a relic of barbarism that should no more be tolerated (or worse, protected) than other archaic practices such as absolutism, polygamy, or human sacrifice. In the words of George Bourne, a Presbyterian minister in Virginia and an early advocate of immediate emancipation, slavery was indeed "the climax of cruelty," a "system of merciless horrors," and "a dungeon of damnation."[7] To level the charge of debased cruelty and torture against slaveholders, as Bourne did, was to associate them in the American imagination with the Spanish Inquisition, Old World autocrats, Oriental despots, and bloodthirsty savages.

Together, black and white abolitionists punctured the notion that torture and callous cruelty were something done exclusively by primitive people. Relentlessly, abolitionists laid bare the sordid reality that people—Americans—who boasted of being benevolent heirs to the most advanced civilization in history carried out acts of callous cruelty that elsewhere in the world would have been denounced as acts of savagery. This indictment transformed the nation, its institutions, and its culture from a harbinger of modern, progressive civilization into a citadel of barbarism and tyranny. Whatever exceptional destiny the United States may have once had was subverted and would remain postponed as long as slavery endured. With an acute urgency inspired by recognition of the suffering endured daily by slaves, abolitionists dismissed any ideas of piecemeal amelioration of slavery. Garrison pointed out that it would be small comfort if "slave-drivers shall apply the lash to the scarred and bleeding backs of their victims somewhat less frequently."[8]

In their campaign against slavery and American hypocrisy, abolitionists proposed an expansive understanding of freedom. They retained a healthy suspicion of the threat that state power could pose to a citizen's freedom; the Fugitive Slave Law of 1850 was one stark illustration of both invasive and abusive state power. But abolitionists also worried about unjust coercion in private relations that the state implicitly protected and that were regulated, if at all, only by community tradition. At a time when both the language and the concept of rights were still immature, abolitionists staked out a position that challenged not only the ownership of human beings but also time-honored patriarchal privilege in American society. They advocated an expansive notion of universal and inviolate freedom that did not reserve one set of rights for the privileged and powerful—patriarchs—while assigning another to their dependents. Individual sovereignty, in simple terms, should not secure the right of some to exercise personal authority over others. As Elizabeth Cady Stanton, who was both an abolitionist and a pioneering suffragist, put it, there can be no "independence where there is subordination to the absolute will of another."[9]

Accordingly, abolitionists insisted on the sanctity of each person's right to self-ownership and freedom from coercion. Although Abraham Lincoln was not an abolitionist during the 1850s, he recognized the starkly divergent definitions of autonomy held by antislavery and proslavery advocates: "With some the word liberty may mean for each man to do as he pleases with himself, and the product of his labor; while with others the same word may mean for some men to do as they please with other men, and the product of other men's labor." At issue, he concluded, were "two, not only different, but incompatible things."[10]

Abolitionists committed themselves to consigning to the dustheap of history those institutions, laws, and folkways that protected the exercise of direct, absolute sovereignty over others. Thereafter, once slavery and patriarchal tyranny were expunged from the nation, two pernicious and long-standing engines of cruelty and torture would be purged as well.

Defenders of slavery, in contrast, dismissed the Lalauries and their ilk as exceptions to the norms of a time-honored patriarchal system, while also defending the absolute authority that masters possessed over their human property. The proslavery riposte to abolitionists recast the slave owner's exercise of discipline and coercion as the patriarch's biblically sanctioned duty to chastise his dependents. Dismissing the emphasis that abolitionists placed on consent as the basis for society, proslavery advocates stressed submission. From the vantage of white southerners, the intimate violence of slavery was the mark of enlightened civilization, not its absence.

The Lalaurie atrocities, of course, were not the first incidence of cruelty to slaves to attract attention. Even before American antislavery advocates ratcheted up their attacks on the institution of slavery, the graphic details of cruelty to slaves were commonplace in abolitionist writings and speeches. British abolitionists during the late eighteenth century had dramatized the immorality of slavery by lavishing attention on the horrors of the transatlantic slave trade. Because slavery was condoned in the Bible, early British abolitionists could not easily assert unassailable theological grounds for their opposition to the institution itself. But the systematic abuse and torture of human beings held in captivity was altogether different. Christian ideas of just warfare and contemporary conventions of international law, in principle, imposed strictures on the treatment of captives. In the eyes of the British abolitionist William Wilberforce and his allies, the trade in African captives made a travesty of Christian morality, natural justice, and the principles of modern civilization. To substantiate their attack on the trade, abolitionists dwelled in detail on the appalling conditions on slave ships and the ordeal of their human cargo, who traversed the Atlantic while stripped naked, bound and shackled, ill-fed and thirsty, exposed to heat and cold, and subject to cruel and arbitrary discipline from slave traders. Even for many contemporaries who retained doubts about the humanity of African slaves, the misery and neglect uncovered by the British abolitionists were the moral equivalent of torture.[11]

Critics of slavery seized on the Lalaurie affair in part because, like the horrors of the slave trade, it seemed certain to evoke a sympathetic response. Abolitionists relied on appeals to both perfectionist strands in nineteenth-century American Protestantism and sentiment to soften the hearts of white Americans to the long-tolerated cruelty of slavery. Central to the sensibility that informed antislavery tactics was the presumption that the visualization of experience, especially physical suffering, was essential to fostering sympathy. Adam Smith, the Scottish philosopher whose ideas about moral sentiment exerted broad influence during the late eighteenth and early nineteenth centuries, explained the connection between the visualization of suffering and sympathy: "By imagination we place ourselves in his [the sufferer's] situation, we conceive ourselves enduring all the same torments, we enter as it were into his body, and become in some measure the same person with him."[12] To see suffering, then, if only through the mind's eye, was to experience and understand it.

When abolitionists placed the details of the scandal in New Orleans before readers, they sought to heighten the immediacy of the pain and suffering of the enslaved and to diminish the seemingly unbridgeable distance that separated the Lalauries' manacled slaves from newspaper readers in Boston, New York, and elsewhere. Abolitionists knew that they had to make visible and immediate the horrors of slavery to white Americans outside the South who lived, according to Garrison, in "exceeding ignorance" of the institution.[13] As the *Haverhill Gazette* conceded when it justified reprinting the Lalaurie story, the realities of the institution of slavery could not be "described or fully known except by observation."[14] As public spectacles of bodily torment became more hidden in the United States, the challenge for slavery's opponents was to make more visible the physical violence of slavery.

The vicarious spectatorship that ran through the reporting of the Lalaurie scandal, and the antislavery campaign in general, placed a premium on the most lurid and horrific examples of slavery's evils. It was these that would animate moral imagination, establish the humanity of slaves, and energize the crusade to destroy the institution. Because "language is powerless and inadequate to give a proper conception" of "details which seem too incredible for human belief," one account of the Lalaurie atrocities averred, "we shall not attempt it but leave it rather to the reader's imagination to picture what it was." Nevertheless, most reports provided sufficiently vivid details to aid readers in visualizing the physical distress of the Lalauries' slaves and to elicit sympathy. Bodies were described "in deplorable condition" and "covered with bruises and wounds from severe floggings." Especially graphic was the description of the condition of one slave who "had a large hole in his head: his body, from head to foot, was scarred and filled with worms!" Also highlighted was the torment endured by a "mulatto boy, who had been chained for five months, being fed daily with only a handful of meal, and receiving every morning the most cruel treatment."[15]

The accounts of the Lalaurie atrocities tutored readers' emotional response by imagining them to be witnesses. As such, they would have recoiled in horror and then been flooded by sympathy. "We saw one of the miserable beings," one account reported. "The sight was so horrible that we could scarce look upon it. . . . The most savage heart could not have witnessed the spectacle unmoved." Many commentators prodded readers to engage in imaginative empathy like that which Adam Smith had described.[16] By mobilizing sympathy and emotion on behalf of their cause, abolitionists aimed to transform their readers and audiences into witnesses against slavery in a national court of public opinion. Employing the conventions of courtroom and church disciplinary proceedings, abolitionists marshaled vivid documentary evidence, especially firsthand testimonials and damning news accounts, to indict slavery and slaveholders. Theodore Dwight Weld was explicit about the task laid before readers of his *American Slavery As It Is:* "Reader, you are empaneled as a juror to try a plain case and bring in an honest verdict. . . . A plainer case never went to a jury. Look at it."[17]

The sordid details of the case could not be dismissed as a fabrication of antislavery zealots. An Ohio newspaper pointed out, "The truth of it cannot be called into question, as substantially the same facts are stated in three different New Orleans papers."[18] Moreover, the accounts of the Lalauries' cruelty were firsthand reports from white southerners, which bolstered claims of their credibility. Had abolitionists eschewed the specifics of the carnage of slavery and instead relied on abstract critiques, they would have left themselves open to charges of sweeping exaggeration and risked fostering doubts that would weaken the sympathetic response they sought. For this reason many editors framed their republication of accounts of the Lalauries' atrocities by alerting their readers to the authenticity and veracity of the reports. As one editor confessed at the bottom of a column devoted to the event, "Any comments of ours on a case so horrible as that described above would only weaken the impression."[19]

In myriad instances far less lurid than the Lalaurie outrages, the deliberate infliction of pain, especially against defenseless humans and animals, provoked controversy because it flouted the purported refinement of the age. Modern liberal societies, above all the United States, required of citizens public virtue and the subordination of destructive impulses through rational self-control and inner moral constraints. The English philosopher John Stuart Mill captured the tenor of the era when he observed that "the spectacle, and even the very idea of pain, is kept more and more out of the sight of those classes who enjoy in their fullness the benefits of civilization."[20] By that measure, a reluctance to inflict cruelty was a mark of civilization, while a disposition toward cruelty placed one beyond the pale of civilized humanity. To surrender to passion, to display insensitivity to suffering, and to cause intentional pain was to mock the code of civilized society.

Evolving understandings of the physiology of pain also influenced ideas about the moral imperative to prevent intentional suffering. By the early nineteenth century, advances in medical theory and practice began to ameliorate the experience of pain and raised the possibility that pain need not be an unavoidable accompaniment of the human condition. Rather than a divinely inflicted punishment or an atonement for sin, pain was increasingly thought to arise from human action or inaction. Pain no longer needed to be endured or ignored because human intervention now could either prevent it or ameliorate it whenever it arose. Once pain was understood as a physical, mechanical sensation without redemptive qualities, then humans had a moral obligation to free others of the conditions that produced it. Reform-minded contemporaries presumed that civilized humankind would be stirred by "an irresistible compassion" to relieve the torment of sufferers, including slaves who were victims of cruelty.[21]

Having activated the moral sense of Americans who opposed the sanguinary criminal punishments of yore, reformers voiced a growing concern about tolerating deliberate pain not just at the hands of the state but wherever it might lurk. They drew attention to harsh physical discipline within private families that destroyed familial harmony and socialized children into cruelty. Antebellum reformers proposed new state powers to protect battered wives and children, pressed for revision of divorce laws to include an expanded definition of marital cruelty, and advocated against corporal punishment of children in schools. Even the entrenched tradition of corporal punishment within the military, especially the navy, came under serious attack. Opponents of flogging, including a former sailor, William McNally, denounced it as a "slavish" form of discipline unsuited to the nation's military. Richard Henry Dana, in his best seller *Two Years before the Mast*, offered chilling depictions of shipboard punishments. To arouse outrage about them, he recounted his captain's tirade aboard ship that made an explicit analogy between the punishment of sailors and slaves: "I'll flog you all, fore and aft, from the boy up! You've got a driver over you! Yes, a slave driver—a negro driver! I'll see who'll tell me that he isn't a negro."[22] Although these antebellum campaigns against cruelty failed to achieve their most ambitious goals, they demonstrated the breadth of the contemporary sensitivity to traditions that were increasingly perceived as wanton, cruel, and archaic.[23]

To the extent that any single tragic event could, the Lalaurie atrocities revealed the "unparalleled barbarity" of slavery wherever it existed, including in New Orleans, one of the nation's richest and most cosmopolitan cities. In the eyes of slavery's opponents, the innate rights that each human possessed had been flagrantly transgressed by the Lalauries. For William Lloyd Garrison and many other commentators, the case illuminated the perverse and almost unlimited prerogatives that slave masters enjoyed. After receiving the initial accounts of the fire, the *Liberator* dwelled on the likely fate of the rescued slaves if the Lalauries were not convicted of some offense. Where in the South, Garrison asked rhetorically, was "the chaining, starving, lacerating, and torturing of slaves" treated as a punishable crime? If it were, the

Lalauries would take their place in a long line of slave masters awaiting sentence in the halls of justice. He predicted that Mme. Lalaurie would not be "molested" by the courts, but instead would have her badly abused slaves restored to "her accursed hands."[24]

Garrison's supposition was well grounded. During her visit to New Orleans two years after the Lalauries were driven from the city, Harriet Martineau, a British author, was told that Mme. Lalaurie's alleged cruelty toward her slaves prior to the fire had prompted an official inquiry and that her nine slaves had been subsequently seized "according to the law" and sold.[25] Louisiana law, in fact, did provide for such action against a cruel master. When the United States had purchased Louisiana in 1803, slaves in the territory enjoyed unique legal protections under prevailing Spanish and French law. The territorial legislature, at slave owners' demand, had abridged those rights soon thereafter when it revised its slave codes. Even so, the revised laws, at least in theory, granted a judge the authority to order a slave owner convicted of cruel treatment to sell his slaves. The statute's definition of cruel punishment, however, was ambiguous and specifically allowed floggings and the placing of slaves in fetters. The standards of evidence required to establish an owner's guilt further restricted the law's scope. If a slave was clearly a victim of abuse and there was no white witness to establish an owner's culpability, the court was to presume the owner's guilt. This provision provided the means to prosecute owners when slaves, who could not testify against whites, were the only witnesses. Yet the practical import of the law was undercut by another provision allowing a slave owner charged with cruelty to clear himself "by his oath." A slave master, in short, could be convicted of cruelty only if he admitted his guilt.[26] In principle Louisiana's laws afforded slaves the promise of protection against cruel treatment, but in practice slave owners, prosecutors, judges, and juries routinely ignored the laws.

It is unlikely that this law was enforced against Mme. Lalaurie. Her slaves could not testify against their master. And whites, especially fellow slave owners, were typically reluctant to curtail even a cruel master's authority over his chattel. The experience of Thomas B. Chaplin, a cotton planter on St. Helena Island, South Carolina, illustrates how hesitant slave owners were to intervene in the affairs of other owners. In February 1849, Chaplin received a summons to serve on a jury of inquest at the neighboring plantation of James H. Sandi-ford. There Chaplin joined eleven other prominent white landowners. Their charge was to determine whether Sandiford should be prosecuted for killing his slave Roger, a cripple who had been choked to death by a chain his owner fastened around his neck before shackling him to the floor of an outbuilding. Chaplin later recorded in his diary his dis-gust over Roger's death. The inquest had heard testimony that Sandi-ford had punished his slave for the "impertinence" of disobeying orders and talking back to his master. His punishment, in Chaplin's words, was to be chained in "a position that none but the most bloodthirsty tyrant could have placed a human being." Chaplin was certain that his neighbor had murdered his slave, but the other members of the jury apparently were unwilling to deny a fellow planter the prerogative to treat his property as he saw fit. Sandiford suffered no legal consequences as a result of his slave's death.[27]

Prosecutions of slave masters for cruelty, whether in South Caro-lina or Louisiana, were exceedingly uncommon and even less often successful. Even in exceptional circumstances when a court compelled a cruel master to sell his slaves, the law's intent was easily subverted. Relatives or friends of the slave master could purchase the forfeited slaves and then sell them back to the former master at a later date.[28] Even after the Lalauries' cruelty had been exposed and the couple had fled the city, they retained ownership of at least some of their slaves, whom they rented out.[29]

As Garrison and others emphasized, the Lalaurie affair underscored the extent to which the formal law of slavery enshrined the property rights of masters while severely circumscribing the appropriate powers of the state and courts. For Garrison, there were few more telling illustrations of the archaic and barbaric nature of slavery. "The master-passion in the bosom of the slaveholder," he explained, "is not gain, but the possession of absolute power, unlimited sovereignty."[30] The institu-tion of slavery, Garrison and others fumed, endured because for two centuries American slave owners had been granted life and death power over their human chattel, including the power to inflict torture.[31]

Keenly aware of the import of this power to the preservation of the institution of slavery, slave masters tolerated no abridgment by the state to their dominion over their slaves. Slave masters and southern jurists alike were convinced of the necessity of so-called plantation justice. In 1846 a court in Alabama summarized the conventional wisdom of slave owners across the South: "The good morals and quiet of the state are not concerned in the prosecution of every slave." "So far as it concerns the public, it is quite as well, perhaps better," the court concluded, "that his punishment should be admeasured by a domestic tribunal."[32] James Henry Hammond, a leading antebellum champion of slavery, offered a similar endorsement, boasting, "On our estates we dispense with the whole machinery of public police and public courts of justice. Thus we try, decide, and execute sentences, in thousands of cases, which in other countries would go to the courts."[33] For most slaves, their masters and overseers were their judge, jury, and punisher.

Colonial and later state lawmakers had not only sanctioned but also encouraged this tradition of private justice. In colonial North Carolina, for example, early statutes granted slave masters the right to inflict virtually unlimited violence on their human chattel. Lawmakers there did not conceive of white violence toward slaves as criminal because they took it to be a routine and necessary feature of slavery.[34] Only masters' self-restraint and self-interest imposed restrictions on the level of violence they could direct against their slaves. Judge Thomas Ruffin of the North Carolina Supreme Court codified this right in 1829 when he wrote in *State v. Mann* that "the power of the master must be absolute, to render the submission of the slave perfect." (Ruffin conceded that slaves did have a legal right of protection from persons other than their owners; otherwise no slave owner's property would be safe.)[35]

As James Henry Hammond made clear, slave owners were comfortable applying "plantation justice" to punish challenges to their authority, petty crimes, thefts, minor affrays, and other intimate forms of misbehavior. Usually, after an impromptu trial of sorts by the planter or his agent, the master or his overseer administered a whipping, beating, or some other form of physical punishment to the errant slave.

In the slave autobiographies and accounts that proliferated at midcentury, such proceedings were so ubiquitous that, in the words of abolitionist Samuel E. Cornish, they would "make the heart to bleed and the ear to burn."[36] Page after page recalled the crack of the whip,

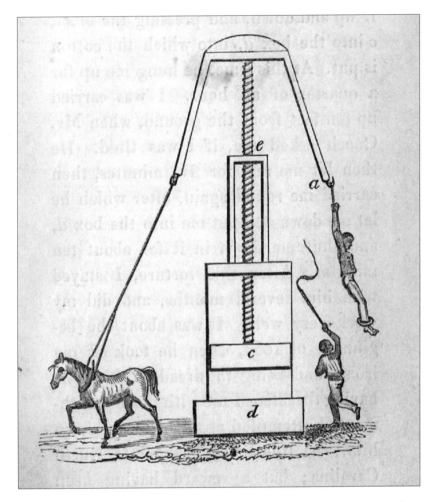

FIGURE 3.1. *The Author Hanging by His Hands Tied to a Cotton Screw.* Ex-slave Moses Roper described elaborate tortures that he had experienced and witnessed. His and other accounts refuted defenders of slavery who dismissed slaves as brutes who were insensitive to pain.

the lashing of flesh, the tearing of skin, the streams of blood, and the shrieks of pain that punctuated the lives of slaves. Former slaves cataloged a staggering array of punishments that demonstrated that masters employed terror no less than pain to impose their will.

Moses Roper, in one of the earliest narratives by a former slave, recalled a South Carolina planter who drove nails into hogsheads, with the points of the nails protruding inside of the containers. He would force slaves selected for punishment into the hogsheads and then roll them down "a very long and steep hill" so that the confined slaves were punctured by the exposed nails. Roper himself experienced a horrific litany of abuses, including undergoing severe lashings and beatings, being forced to wear forty-pound shackles and chains, having his feet and fingers crushed and his fingernails pulled out, having tar poured over his head and then being set on fire, and being suspended by his manacled hands from a cotton press ten feet above the ground.[37] Madison Jefferson recounted being kept shackled in chains for months at a time and being contorted in excruciating positions as punishment.[38] James Smith, a field hand in Virginia, was branded on one side of his face and on his neck with the initials of his master.[39] John Brown, a fugitive slave from Georgia, described slaves being suspended by their hands from beams with sharpened stakes below their dangling feet so that if they tried to reduce the pain in their stretched arms by standing on the stakes, their feet would be pierced to the bone. After flaying the backs of his slaves to "jelly," Brown's master rubbed their wounds with red pepper and salt and water.[40] An anonymous runaway recalled the terrifying array of whips and tools of torture in the incongruously named Sugar House in Charleston, South Carolina, where slave owners could request punishments calibrated to maximize pain, to prevent scarring, or some other objective.[41] William Wells Brown recounted that a Virginia slave owner would tie his slaves up in a smokehouse, whip them, and then build a fire of tobacco stems to "smoke" them.

According to Harriet Jacobs, a former slave from Edenton, North Carolina, the "favorite" punishment of a notorious master there was to tie a rope around a slave's body and suspend him above the ground. Then, "a fire was kindled over him, from which was suspended a piece of fat pork, so that scalding drops of fat continually fell on the bare flesh." Lewis Clarke, a former house slave in Kentucky, listed the array of "instruments of torture" that his slave mistress had wielded, which ranged from rawhide straps and fire-hardened hickory sprouts to brooms, tongs, shovels, shears, knife handles, the heels of shoes, and hefty oak clubs.[42]

Slave masters only turned to the courts to prosecute capital offenses, and only then because the state promised compensation for slaves who were executed for such crimes.[43] When a slave's actions posed a perceived threat to society at large, formal legal institutions replaced the master's informal methods. State-sanctioned punishments imposed on slaves and the violence inflicted by masters differed little in severity. Among the penalties were nailing ears to a pillory or whipping post and then cutting them off, branding, whipping, castration, execution by burning, hanging, hanging then burning, castration then hanging, and hanging then decapitation. The degradation and dehumanization of blacks during their executions were stark. These state-inflicted punishments were intended to heighten the prisoner's agony. A slave in North Carolina, for example, was chained alive to a gibbet to die slowly and in torment. Sometimes courts ordered white authorities to place on public display the severed heads or mangled bodies of executed slaves. The intent of these public spectacles of state-sanctioned violence was clear: to instill terror in slaves.[44]

When threatened by alleged slave insurrections, whites ignored even the modest legal formalities that they observed when handling black defendants. The scale of violence that followed the rout of an army of rebellious slaves marching on New Orleans in January 1811 was exceptional, but the methods used to restore order would have been familiar to slave owners anywhere in the South. While white militiamen set upon captured blacks, an ad hoc tribunal fashioned procedures to deal with the crisis, sift evidence, and punish captured insurrectionists. One alleged leader of the revolt had his hands hacked off and his legs broken before he was shot and his remains thrown into a bonfire. Other captives were summarily executed. Eventually, the bodies and severed heads of as many as one hundred executed slaves lined the roads and riverbanks surrounding New Orleans, serving as warnings to would-be conspirators.[45]

Given these legal traditions regarding the punishment of slaves in the South, it was not clear that the Lalauries had broken any law. The slave master's almost unlimited authority over his human property was enshrined in law. Legal codes, moreover, displayed a very high tolerance for extreme forms of physical punishment of slaves while providing no precise definition of acts of prohibited cruelty. Southern lawmakers and jurists struggled for decades to reconcile the preservation of public order with whites' absolute power over slaves. During the

1830s and thereafter, courts began to circumscribe, in principle, the power of whites over the life and death of black slaves. But such laws were riddled with ambiguities. Extant laws protected slaves "only to the extent that was 'necessary' to protect their property values from wanton white killers and to promote the power and authority of the master class."[46] In scattered instances, courts expressed disapproval of members of slave patrols who exceeded their official charge to monitor slave behavior, as when a Louisiana court concluded that the ferocity of a patroller's discipline of a slave had been unjustifiable and "done in mere wantonness of power."[47] The dockets of southern courts also were stuffed with civil suits brought by slave masters seeking compensation from overzealous overseers and renters who abused slaves. Accusations of cruelty and excessive violence were rife in such cases, but the suits inevitably advanced the slave owners' interests while otherwise leaving slaves virtually defenseless.[48]

A North Carolina Supreme Court decision in 1857 provided a stark measure of the legal protections denied to slaves. The court ruled that a slave had no right to self-defense comparable to that of a freeman, and a slave who resisted his master's assault forfeited whatever protection the law might provide. "Resistance to the master," the court found, "is a species of petit treason, and the master not only has the right but it is his duty to overcome it at all hazards."[49] Given the latitude that whites enjoyed when punishing blacks, only in exceptionally rare circumstances was a white ever subject to criminal prosecution for terrorizing or killing a black.[50] With the Lalaurie outrages in mind and cognizant of the infrequency of the prosecution of slave masters, William Lloyd Garrison observed, "All the southern states have ostensible laws against the murder of slaves." But the laws were acts of "heaven daring hypocrisy" intended "only to put public opinion asleep." Hidden behind a veil of unenforced laws and hollow pledges by slavery's defenders that harmony prevailed on plantations, cruelty and torture went unpunished.[51]

Slaves were acutely aware of how vulnerable they were. As Frederick Douglass explained in his autobiography, the slave's fate was to "stand, listen, and tremble."[52] That the Lalauries' slaves did not cry out for help as the flames advanced around them was, according to Garrison, revelatory. The *Liberator* asked, "Why did they not shriek?"

FIGURE 3.2. *Wilson Chinn, a Branded Slave from Louisiana*, ca. 1863. During the Civil War, images of abused former slaves and implements of torture were widely reproduced in the North. Such images confirmed abolitionists' claims about slavery's inherent cruelty and the barbarous tortures inflicted by slave masters.

There were only two plausible answers, and both exposed the soul-crushing oppression of slavery. Garrison speculated that the Lalauries' slaves had "either welcomed death as a friend . . . or they were accustomed to know that cries of distress from a slave are wont to bring succor or to attract attention."[53]

The horrors of slave torture included the sexual exploitation of female slaves, which, in the eyes of opponents of slavery, exemplified the slaveholders' arrogance, tyranny, and lack of restraint. In the words of one opponent of slavery, the events in New Orleans had exposed "a system that places our fellow beings . . . to be ravished and tortured without the power of resistance by the fiendish lusts, caprice, and malevolence of the worst of men."[54] Henry Ward Beecher, perhaps the most celebrated minister of the era, explicitly invoked the specter of Oriental cruelty and licentiousness when he claimed that, compared to the South, "a Turkish harem is a cradle of virgin purity."[55] Garrison raged against the apathy of Americans who turned their eyes as "more than a half a million of adult females without any protection for their chastity" were "constantly prostituted by their owners."[56] Former slaves were even more forthright about the pervasiveness of sexual violence endured by slaves. William J. Anderson, in his recollections of a quarter century as a slave, described how his former master had "divested a poor female slave of all wearing apparel, tied her down to stakes, and whipped her with a handsaw until he broke it over her naked body," and then subsequently "ravished her person and became the father of a child by her."[57] Solomon Northup recounted the heart-rending predicament of Patsey, "an enslaved victim of lust and hate," who was under constant threat of rape at the hands of her master and of punishment at the hands of her jealous mistress.[58] Harriet Jacobs, who herself had spent years thwarting her owner's efforts to rape her, charged that slavery made "the white fathers cruel and sensual, the sons violent and licentious" while contaminating the daughters and making the wives wretched.[59]

The attention devoted to the cruelties inflicted by owners on their slaves was an indictment of the society that nurtured and harbored such human monsters. Indeed, the vilification of Delphine Lalaurie (and the comparative inattention to her husband's role in the atrocities) was an amplification of the critique of what a Massachusetts newspaper called "the deadening effects of slavery on the sensitivities of our nature." None of the accounts established that Mme. Lalaurie alone was responsible for the condition of the slaves in her household. But her involvement in the abuses, even if only as an accessory, made a mockery of the contemporary idealization of women as acutely sensitive and innately nurturing. She, evidently, was neither. Instead, she was variously described as a "fiend," "a demon in the shape of a woman," "a wretch too base to live in a civilized land," and a "miscreant." Garrison even mocked the convention of referring to her by the formal title of Madame. "How polite in this she tiger," he fumed. So contrary to conventional feminine behavior was Delphine's apparent sadism that the *Providence Patriot* posited that a "hideous transformation" was necessary to turn "one of the softer sex into a monster of cruelty." The editor of the *Connecticut Gazette* reached similar conclusions, lamenting, "We should hardly have believed that such an inhuman wretch could have been found in existence in a civilized community, . . . much less could we have thought that the wretch existed in the form of woman!"[60] That "a demon in the shape of a woman" displayed a taste for sadistic violence was irrefutable evidence of the irrationality, depravity, and barbarism that prevailed under slavery.

That American society not only tolerated but protected the unbounded, arbitrary, and overweening power of slave masters was intolerable for many abolitionists. So riddled with protections for slavery were the constitutional foundations of the American republic that Garrison denounced the Constitution as "an agreement with Hell," and Wendell Phillips complained that the nation's institutions had been rendered tools of the slaveholders. Abolitionists pointed to the Fugitive Slave Law of 1850, which compelled law officers everywhere to arrest anyone suspected of being a runaway slave on as little as a claimant's sworn testimony of ownership, as highlighting the warped priorities of the nation. The act criminalized efforts to aid escaping slaves even while unconscionable acts of cruelty by slaveholders like the Lalauries remained beyond the reach of the law. What further evidence did Americans need that slavery truly was a "relic of barbarity"? Only the abolition of slavery itself could restore the promise of just and humane laws to American democracy.

Slavery's defenders offered no justification for Mme. Lalaurie's conduct. Local notables may have shielded her from prosecution, but no one was willing to condone her behavior in print. The initial reports in New Orleans newspapers were forthright in their condemnation of her depravity, but within days of the 1834 fire, the city's papers fell silent on the topic. Proslavery advocates presumably recognized that it was far better to rebut the abolitionists' lengthening litany of atrocities with abstract statements of principle than to linger on the Lalaurie scandal. Although the Lalaurie outrages remained prominent in abolitionist lore for years, they quickly passed out of public discussion in the South. Even so, the shadow of Mme. Lalaurie's conduct, and that of other notoriously cruel masters, loomed over all discussions of the alleged benevolence of southern slavery, by posing two challenges to white southerners anxious to defend slavery.

First, any claims that her behavior was typical of, or inherent to, American slavery had to be refuted. Slave masters somehow had to distinguish between the physical coercion that they condoned as appropriate to slavery (and human society more generally) and the indefensible cruelty inflicted by some. In response, southern slaveholders strove to calibrate, both rhetorically and practically, their violence.

Second, defenders of slavery had to discredit claims that slavery coarsened the sensibilities of all those who came into contact with it. The sensibility and sympathy that informed northern attacks on slavery simultaneously influenced southern defenders of the institution. More generally, slavery's advocates argued that slave abuse like that uncovered in the Lalaurie home was rare because human nature mitigated against it. White southerners insisted that the innate human instinct for benevolence and charity dictated their actions no less than those of others. Indeed, they boasted that the institution of slavery facilitated the operation of this instinct by refining masters' sense of obligation and responsibility toward their dependents, especially their slaves. White southerners were adamant that they, more than their antislavery critics, possessed a refined faculty for sympathy.[61]

Slave masters rejected the accusation that slavery desensitized them to the suffering and pain of their human property. Theodore Dwight Weld voiced common antislavery sentiments when he lamented that where slavery prevailed, "cruelty has become a habit" and "the greatest cruelties" were inflicted "quite unconsciously."[62] Slave owners countered that it was the slaves themselves who were insensitive. In a widely consulted text on slave care first published in 1803, "A Professional Planter" admitted that there were no significant anatomical differences between slaves and their white masters, but he nevertheless insisted that slaves had "dulled sensitivities" that rendered them better "able to endure, with few expressions of pain, the accidents of nature."[63] Defenders of slavery recruited both medical and anthropological texts to substantiate their claims. An eighteenth-century medical text that remained in wide use even in the late nineteenth century declared, "What would be the cause of insupportable pain to a white man a Negro would almost disregard."[64] Common wisdom repeated in medical texts posited that black women, as compared to white women, experienced relatively little pain in childbirth.[65] This presumption regarding the slaves' "primitive" physiology not only mitigated the obligations borne by slave owners to provide for their slaves but also justified severe corporal punishments sufficient to compel obedience.

Defenders of slavery took pains to affirm that slaveholders harbored sympathetic natures that dictated their benevolence toward their dependents. In the decades preceding the Civil War, proslavery advocates aggressively defended slavery as a positive good that accorded with God's providential design for Africans in bondage and the advance of Christian civilization in the United States. Indeed, the Lalaurie outrages had provided an opportunity for whites in New Orleans to demonstrate their sympathetic sensibilities. New Orleans newspapers applauded the public fury directed against the Lalauries, thereby underscoring that the city's residents were in no way inured to the slaves' suffering. Likewise, the florid language of the news accounts established that the city's journalists were conversant in rhetorical techniques appropriate to elicit humane horror at the atrocities inflicted on the Lalauries' dependents. The courageous rescue of the imprisoned slaves and the sacking of the Lalaurie mansion confirmed that the city's residents could and would act on the basis of their sense of revulsion and sympathy. The mob's actions made clear—to the satisfaction of New Orleans editorialists and contrary to abolitionists' attacks—that slaveholders had the moral refinement and resolve to punish any inhumane master in their midst.

For southern defenders of slavery, the exaggerated attention devoted to cruelties against slaves revealed a dangerous attack on the bedrock of civilization itself: patriarchy. Slavery, as white southerners intoned tirelessly, was a time-honored, biblically sanctioned "domestic" institution that properly came under the dominion of the household patriarch. The *Charleston Courier* explained, "Slavery with us is a parental relation."[66] The institution, like the family sphere itself, was and should remain beyond the proper reach of the state. The authority that the slaveholding patriarch exercised was exactly analogous to that asserted by a husband over his wife, a father over his children, and a master craftsman over his apprentice. Courts everywhere in the nation granted men wide latitude to discipline their wives, children, servants, and other dependents. Indeed, many nineteenth-century Americans were reluctant to infringe on parents' God-given authority to discipline their children. Corporal punishment, moreover, was a well-established component of military discipline. As proslavery advocates repeatedly pointed out, slavery may have become an institution "peculiar" to the South by the 1830s, but the use of violent forms of discipline was commonplace across the nation.[67]

The slave master, like all patriarchs, bore obligations to and responsibilities for all of his dependents, whether they were immediate family, apprentices, or slaves. These responsibilities were not only sacred but also crucial to the well-being of society. Benjamin Rush, whose ideas about the seclusion of criminals had been influential with prison reformers at the turn of the nineteenth century, had also vouched for the merits of stern patriarchal power. In contrast to tyrants who exercised arbitrary power, the father, schoolmaster, or employer who used physical discipline to "cure vice," in Rush's estimation, should be commended. It was a small step for southern slave masters to extend this argument to their power over their slaves and to festoon it with the language of paternalism.[68]

Far from admitting that they exploited their dependents, slaveholding patriarchs applauded themselves for nurturing a happy, contented labor force that was protected against the vicissitudes of day-to-day survival. Duty-bound to foster obedience and to enforce discipline, the idealized slave master was benevolent, sagacious, and dispassionate toward all his dependents, exercising his authority through force of character and intelligence. Just as a husband's power was purportedly tempered by the sacred and indissoluble bond of marriage, so too the slave master's power was leavened by obligation and affection. Slavery's defenders vouched for slave masters' reluctance to inflict bodily punishments, and they specifically denied that passion (or, worse, pleasure) played any role in their application. Unlike Mme. Lalaurie, conscientious slave masters professed to strive for control over all things, including their own emotions. According to the lawyer George Tucker, whose *Valley of Shenandoah* was a template for many subsequent plantation novels, the slave on a "well regulated estate . . . hardly feels" his chains. "Whatever coercion there is on his will it is so moderate and reasonable in itself, and above all, he has been so habituated to it," Tucker contended, "that it appears to be all right, or rather he does not feel it to be wrong."[69] The southern writer William Gilmore Simms similarly protested that the slave was "under no despotic power." To the contrary, he wrote, "There are laws that protect him, *in his place,* as inflexible as those which his proprietor is required to obey, *in his place.*"[70] Slaves, who appreciated the "tender care and protection" they received, demonstrated through their "affectionate attachment" to their masters that they accepted their lot.[71] Similar reasoning led the Virginia politico Abel Parker Upshur to boast that "in no part of the world has the laboring class been more distinguished by contentment, cheerfulness, and even gaiety."[72]

The wise patriarch understood that calibrated pain was useful. In manuals on plantation management and advice to overseers, slave owners avowed their rationality when handling slaves, especially when meting out punishment. Masters sought "a well regulated plantation" on which the certainty of moderate punishment lessened "the necessity of inflicting punishments almost entirely."[73] When the application of the whip was necessary, masters claimed to temper it with moderation. Joseph Acklen, the owner of a large Louisiana plantation, explained, "My rule is to whip, or pull the ear, or twist the nose, or slap them for every offense. . . . But always on the strictest rules of mercy." With language strikingly similar to that of northern prison wardens, he vowed that his punishments were never "cruel or severe," but were "repeated at proper intervals, until the most entire submission is obtained."[74]

The discipline necessary to achieve this "most entire submission" was a duty that fell upon the reluctant master intent on enforcing "obedience" and establishing "good order."[75] White southerners insisted that the disciplining of slaves could only be understood within the context of patriarchal authority. They rejected any suggestion that the corporal punishment of slaves was inherently cruel or unjust. Instead, corporal punishment was an essential and ethical complement to all patriarchal authority. Inflicting pain by itself was not the measure of cruelty, but inflicting unnecessary pain to demonstrate power was the essence of cruelty. According to defenders of slavery, slaves themselves, like disobedient inmates in northern penitentiaries, brought on their own punishment by their periodic ingratitude and sloth. Because slaves allegedly lacked a developed sense of guilt and responsibility, slave owners, like penitentiary staffs tested by disobedient prisoners, had to instill it in their charges. Invoking the analogy of prudent parenting, slave masters compared the disciplining of their children and their slaves. One master advised, "Negroes who do not do their work, like boys who will not get their lessons, must sometimes be flogged; but a few stripes are all that is necessary."[76] By scrupulously apportioning discipline and by justifying it as an essential foundation for social order, slave masters demonstrated, to their satisfaction, both their solicitude for their slaves and their desire to distance the institution from what they insisted were rare and inexplicable acts of deviant cruelty.

White southerners' justifications for corporal punishment were most fully (and openly) expressed during the late 1840s and early 1850s when southern senators defended flogging in the navy in the face of a northern-led campaign to abolish it. While on the defensive about slavery and anxious to downplay the violence on which the institution rested, southern legislators displayed no hesitation in defending the flogging of sailors and corporal punishment more broadly. Their endorsement extended from the domestic sphere to the decks of American frigates, representing a robust defense of the use of coercion and pain not only within the institution of slavery but wherever patriarchal authority prevailed.

Southern legislators warned that the attack on corporal punishment was yet another expression of corrosive "hyperphilanthropy" and dangerous northern fanaticism. They denounced the "mistaken philanthropy," the "flummery and humbuggery," the "sickly sensibility," and "this impatience of all just subordination and restraint" that sought to "strike out all sorts of punishment because they hurt." Moreover, the campaign against flogging was hopelessly naive and inanely utopian. H. N. McTyeire, writing in *De Bow's Review*, dismissed "the mawkish sentimentalism that pronounces against all corporal punishment and deals in moral suasion" as suitable only for "the millennium." He cautioned, "It does not suit the world as it is now and human nature as it is."[77]

To forswear the whip and the rod was to weaken the organic hierarchy of society, which rested on obedience and submission. In the campaign against flogging, southern congressmen discerned among their opponents a dangerous emphasis on consent, rather than submission, as the basis for society. Senator David Yulee of Florida challenged a colleague opposed to flogging as to whether he "would propose that the commanding officer should be elected, and that the government on board the ship should be a republican government; that it should emanate from the will of a majority of those on board." Such a principle, if applied broadly, would subvert all hierarchical relations. Yulee scoffed, "There must be discipline; there must, be, arbitrary power."[78] A fellow southerner agreed, holding that "all government, that is, all wise and just government, acts by the simple influence of hope and fear. . . . The end to be accomplished is obedience and submission."[79] Representative Abraham Watkins Venable of North Carolina concurred, thundering that "I dread nothing so much as insubordination to acknowledged law, whether in civil life, the camp, or on the deck of our ships of war." "Somebody," he roared, "must rule."[80]

Extolling duties over rights, senators and (proslavery polemicists more generally) argued that distinctions of rank were a natural feature of human society and should not be tampered with. The wicked, lazy, and feckless would never consent to what was in their best interest without the discipline imposed by benevolent patriarchs. Masters should not shirk their "duty" to "resort to punishment as seldom as possible, and to administer it in such a manner as will best accomplish its purposes."[81] By implication, the punishments imposed by patriarchs, including southern masters, were not only wholly consonant with civilization, but actually essential for its continuation. There were worse evils than corporal punishment to be contemplated, including a pending collapse of civilization brought about by anarchy and licentiousness.

White southerners chortled that northerners had made their peace with the harsh discipline that prevailed in penitentiaries even while they hypocritically ignored the poverty of the working poor who huddled in the alleys of northern cities. As Pliny, a proslavery essayist in the *Charleston Mercury*, asked of northerners in 1833, "What? Is nothing to be done for the poor?"[82] He rued that the atrophied and pinched patriarchy in the North offered nothing for the miserable, oppressed, and vulnerable poor there even while Yankees scolded white southerners for performing their appropriate duties as stewards of the enslaved.

Almost four years to the day after the Lalaurie scandal, Theodore Clapp, a noted New Orleans minister, delivered a sermon in defense of slavery. He chided the abolitionists for their fixation on slavery's purported cruelty. He conceded that "masters sometimes treat their slaves badly." He even acknowledged "rare and detached instances of inhumanity" within the institution. But he rejected the contention that on the basis of such isolated examples "the institution itself is, of necessity, a pure and unmixed evil." By extension, he argued, the same charge could be brought against the family and schools, because "the most shocking cruelties" sometimes occurred within both. The solution was not the abolition of the family, matrimony, education, or slavery, but instead the rooting out of personal evil. He concluded, "We must endeavor to remove the evils of life without assailing those relations essential to the very existence of society."[83] Wrapped in the language of humanitarian sentiment, Clapp offered a vision of social order in which discipline, coercion, and submission were complementary, inevitable, and salutary.

In 1828 Zephaniah Kingsley, a prescient Florida slaveholder, anticipated the challenge that defenders of slavery increasingly confronted: "The idea of slavery, when associated with cruelty and injustice, is revolting to every philanthropic mind; but when that idea is associated with justice and benevolence, slavery, commonly so called, easily amalgamates with the ordinary conditions of life."[84] He recognized that slavery's apologists could not succeed if they were constantly forced to defend the indefensible. Instead, they needed to restore slavery to the "ordinary

conditions of life," or, in other words, to render it so prosaic, so benign, that it aroused neither curiosity nor outrage. The challenge for
slavery's opponents, conversely, was to ensure that slavery and its attendant evils never receded from the imaginations of Americans.
Kingsley understood that the contest over slavery extended far beyond
an argument over "cruelty and injustice," but as long as the horrors inflicted on slaves by the Lalauries and others kept the issue of violence,
torture, and arbitrary power firmly in the foreground, attempts to distance slavery from cruelty and barbarism would be futile.

For all of their zeal and courage, abolitionists understood how little
headway they had made by mid-century in persuading Americans to
turn against slavery. While their revelations of cruelty animated the
antislavery ranks, powerful countervailing images of slavery persisted
and, indeed, proliferated. The enduring popularity of minstrelsy
throughout the United States demonstrated the appeal of a dramatically different depiction of slavery. Minstrelsy, of course, was never exclusively about slavery. It was a highly malleable form of popular en-
tertainment that allowed white performers to explore and satirize class
relations, inequality, politics, and race in the young republic. But black
phantasms of the white imagination loomed largest in minstrelsy. The
white performers who acted in blackface rendered blacks as simpleminded buffoons who had modest needs and ample cause to be contented with their carefree idyll. Like a vexatious child, the slave of the
minstrel show needed both protection and discipline. The true hardships of slavery went unacknowledged, and to the extent that violence
surfaced in minstrelsy it was the slave's potential for seemingly spontaneous and irrational violence. While most whites who attended minstrel shows probably were unaware of the burgeoning "scientific"
scholarship that purportedly demonstrated the unique fitness of Africans for slavery, they received a similar message every time they saw
minstrel performers depict slavery as benign and blacks as innately
suited to it.

Proslavery advocates drew comfort from minstrelsy when they
framed the agitation against slavery as an attack on the traditional authority that undergirded the nation's social order and mores. By doing
so, defenders of slavery tapped into the anxieties of countless teachers,
husbands, parents, and clerics who worried about reckless "leveling"

and excessive democracy eating away at the foundations of the republic. As Rev. Clapp had done during his New Orleans sermon, proslavery advocates shifted the debate from the malicious violence of the Lalauries and other wayward slaveholders to the preservation of patriarchy, which in turn was essential for the maintenance of liberty. The steady hands of patriarchs, after all, were needed to discipline their dependents, be they slave or free, to be productive, dutiful, and law-abiding. By doing so, slavery's defenders yoked the preservation of slavery and the defense of patriarchal authority to the cause of liberty, public order, and civic virtue. Slavery's defenders (and subsequent commentators well into the twentieth century) pointed to the abolitionists' fetishism of cruelty and suffering as evidence of their prurient fanaticism.

Even within the ranks of the broader antislavery movement, there were many whose opposition to slavery did not propel them to endorse the expansive ideas of freedom and rights advocated by radical abolitionists. So-called Free Soilers, for instance, condemned slavery for undermining the dignity of free labor, inhibiting social mobility, and obstructing true democracy, but they often displayed only passing interest in the plight of black slaves. Garrison and other abolitionists derided their stance for elevating white authority, or what Garrison called "white manism," instead of concentrating on the intolerable injustice of the enslavement of nearly four million who were subject to virtually limitless malice and violence at the hands of their masters and their agents.[85]

Over the course of little more than a decade between 1857 and 1870, the nation careened between these two divergent ideals of autonomy. In the *Dred Scott* decision in 1857, a majority of the Supreme Court held that "a negro," whether enslaved or free, could not be an American citizen. Writing for the majority, Chief Justice Roger Taney justified the ruling by invoking the inferior status that African Americans had been assigned throughout American history; they had been "regarded as beings of an inferior order, and altogether unfit to associate with the white race, either in social or political relations; and so far inferior, that they had no rights which the white man was bound to respect." The decision, which was a towering affirmation of the claims made by proslavery advocates, imposed a uniquely vulnerable status on African Americans. In Taney's chilling formulation, they had neither rights nor inherent dignity that commanded the respect of whites. At the outbreak of the Civil War, nearly four million enslaved Americans were bound within an institution that afforded their owners virtually limitless power. Regardless of how many of these enslaved Americans were actually tortured, they were abjectly vulnerable to the whims of their owners and had little recourse when they were abused.[86]

Southern slave owners predictably hailed the decision as a vindication of their preferred interpretation of the Constitution. Jefferson Davis, then a U.S. senator from Mississippi, gloated that the decision was a commonsensical answer to the simple question of "whether Cuffee should be kept in his normal condition or not."[87] For opponents of slavery, the decision was anathema. They assailed it for subverting the nation's principles of liberty by assigning all African Americans to a state of perpetual inferiority and legal invisibility. Frederick Douglass denounced the decision as "an open, glaring, and scandalous tissue of lies" that was an unconstitutional subversion of the nation's founding vision.[88]

The Civil War provided the resolution to the future of the "peculiar institution" that Taney had hoped the Supreme Court had resolved with the *Dred Scott* decision. Self-emancipation by tens of thousands of the enslaved, continual agitation by abolitionists, and military necessity during the war so transformed attitudes in the North that by 1864 it was clear that a northern victory would signal the death of the institution of slavery. Republicans in Congress rendered the *Dred Scott* decision moot by writing protections for African Americans into the Constitution with the Thirteenth, Fourteenth, and Fifteenth Amendments.

The significance of this revolution in the status of African Americans by 1870 should not be underestimated. At the turn of the nineteenth century, few white Americans acknowledged that the torture of the enslaved was an issue in which the public had an interest. That some slaves were tortured or treated cruelly by owners was perhaps lamentable but of no particular civic significance. Three-quarters of a century later, the formerly enslaved shared the same legal protections against torture enjoyed by other Americans.

Admittedly, these protections were tragically constrained until the mid-twentieth century. Not until then would the Supreme Court extend the protections of the Bill of Rights against transgressions by state actors. Previously, at least in the eyes of the Supreme Court, the Bill of Rights offered no more protections against torture for the formerly enslaved than to any other Americans. Similarly, the Court narrowly interpreted the protections that the Fourteenth Amendment provided to African Americans even as white supremacy crested at the end of the nineteenth century. And the most expansive ambitions of the abolitionists were not fulfilled by the unfinished revolution of Reconstruction. Hopes that the abolition of slavery would accelerate the dismantling of patriarchy more broadly were punctured during the debates over the Reconstruction-era constitutional amendments. Some supporters of the Thirteenth Amendment batted away opponents' warnings that the measure would erode the primordial foundations of society, especially the hierarchical structure of the family, by reaffirming the permanence of patriarchal power within the American family. The subsequent willful exclusion of women from the guarantee of voting rights in the Fifteenth Amendment was another telling confirmation of patriarchal privilege.[89]

Yet despite all of these glaring caveats, the abolition of slavery meant that the boundaries that placed a large group of Americans outside the law and the national community shrank. No longer would the United States harbor a population of millions of "mere naked human beings" in "a condition of complete rightlessness," to borrow the philosopher Hannah Arendt's evocative phrase.[90] As long as African Americans had been in the thralldom of slavery, they had been excluded from rights and claims of empathy. Indeed, they were deprived of the qualities that compelled white Americans to treat them as fellow humans. The "right to have rights" meant that African Americans, who had been uniquely and peculiarly vulnerable to torture, could now be, in the eyes of other Americans, victims of torture like any other fellow American.

FOUR

Torture in the Brothers' War

CAPTAIN THEODORE MCGOWAN and his soldiers had the tedious but vital assignment of maintaining security in Washington, D.C., during the Civil War. They had to contend with the drunkards, bullies, and shady characters who plagued most nineteenth-century cities. They also enforced a nightly curfew that emptied the streets of civilians and soldiers. And they were saddled with rounding up Union deserters who straggled homeward from the front lines in Virginia. Confederate deserters were yet another headache. They were not to be treated as prisoners of war because their desertion was encouraged as a war aim. But Union sentries could not easily discern whether a Confederate deserter was in fact what he claimed to be. As a result, officers ordered large numbers of apparent enemy deserters to be incarcerated and interrogated. Union forces were on the lookout for possible Confederate subversives. With the northern border of the Confederacy less than two miles from the White House, there was ample ground to be suspicious of any unfamiliar person lurking in the capital's byways.[1]

Confronted routinely with uncooperative prisoners, McGowan and other Union officers began using a "shower bath" to extract information from the men who passed through their hands. Endorsed by senior officers up to the rank of general, the shower bath was in nearly daily use at the Central Guard House during the last two years of the war. There, the provost judge ordered various classes of prisoners to undergo the procedure. Some were drunks who needed sobering up. Others were prisoners whose unruly behavior apparently warranted punishment. But the prisoners most frequently sent to the shower cell were those suspected of having lied during preliminary interrogation. More often than not, they were men who had been arrested for desertion but who would not admit to the offense.[2]

Prisoners sent to the shower cell were stripped naked and locked behind the cell's grated door. Outside stood a hydrant with a large hose attached to it. A guard climbed onto a small platform placed in front of the cell and turned on the hose. Out shot a high-powered stream of frigid water, which the guard aimed through the grating at the prisoner, who had no place to hide in the five-by-eight-foot cell. The guard would batter the prisoner with the torrent of cold water for about thirty seconds, then turn off the water. During the brief respite, a prisoner who confessed to desertion or some other offense would be spared further torment and be returned to the regular cells for prosecution. But a captive who did not confess promptly was targeted with the hose repeatedly for days at a time until he either confessed or was freed due to lack of evidence.

The systematic application of the shower bath in Washington, D.C., aroused no public controversy and might have escaped notoriety had it not been for Jacob Rubel's misfortune to undergo it on January 24, 1865. He was rounded up on suspicion of deserting and, after a night in confinement in the Central Guard House, was interrogated about his residence, occupation, knowledge of the city, and even local transportation fares. The commanding officer insisted that Rubel "owe[d] service to the government of the United States & [was] asked his regiment." When Rubel countered that he was a citizen of Prussia, he was sent to the shower room, where, according to Rubel, he suffered the shower bath three times, the last while handcuffed. When he was not being drenched with cold water, he was forced to stand "in a perfectly nude state in a cold and damp room." After two days' detention, Rubel still had not confessed and so was discharged. Furious about his treatment, which he claimed had seriously impaired his health, he appealed to the Prussian consulate to protest his ordeal, a step that eventually resulted in the court-martial of McGowan.[3]

A year earlier, the Confederate Home Guard in Randolph County, North Carolina, had improvised their own harsh interrogation techniques out of frustration with the incidence of Confederate desertion in that area. Fired up by the strongly worded proclamations of North Carolina governor Zebulon Vance, who had urged the Home Guard to punish the disloyalty of Union sympathizers and Confederate deserters by "making them feel the scorn and contempt of an outraged people," Home Guard soldiers adopted increasingly draconian measures to locate deserters and intimidate Unionists. They burned the genitals of some Unionist men, briefly hanged others, and beat many more, while threatening to rape Unionist women. In April 1864 the Home Guard detained and questioned the wife of Bill Owens, a notorious Unionist, deserter, and guerrilla leader. Skeptical of her claims that her husband was dead and buried in the local cemetery, they demanded proof. When she refused to show them his grave, the commanding officer tied her hands behind her back and suspended her by her thumbs so that her feet barely touched the ground. Uncowed despite her anguish, she refused to disclose her husband's hiding place. The guards next tied her hands together, then smashed her thumbs between two fence rails. Still defiant, she continued to swear at her persecutors and deny any knowledge of her husband's whereabouts. Only later was her husband captured and subsequently hanged by vigilantes while awaiting trial.[4] Even amid the grim violence of a war in its latter stages, Mrs. Owens's persecution aroused dismay and outrage. For Unionists in the state, the use of torture on a woman could not be excused as a military necessity, and the memory of the Home Guard's conduct lingered.

The charges against Captain McGowan and the torturers of Mrs. Owens paled in comparison to those against Henry Wirz, the only Confederate executed for war crimes during the Civil War. Born in Switzerland, he was a refugee from the revolutions of 1848 who settled in Kentucky before moving to Louisiana. There he practiced medicine until the start of the Civil War, when he volunteered for service in the Louisiana militia. His combat duty ended in 1862 when he was wounded during the Battle of Seven Pines. After he recovered, he joined the staff of General John H. Winder, who was in charge of the Confederacy's prisoner-of-war camps. In April 1864, Wirz took command of Camp Sumter in southwestern Georgia, a prison camp better known as Andersonville. There he presided over a ramshackle, fetid prison pen that held as many as thirty-two thousand prisoners of war, making it the fifth largest city in the Confederacy. And there thirteen thousand prisoners, or nearly 30 percent of the total, died of malnutrition, dysentery, disease, neglect, and violence. As early as the summer of 1864, accounts began leaking out about the appalling conditions at Andersonville. The reports so inflamed northern public opinion that when Union troops captured Wirz in May 1865 there was a clamor for his prosecution and execution. A military commission charged him with unjustified acts of brutality and violence against Union prisoners, including specific accusations of torture. Indeed, the overarching charge against Wirz was that Andersonville had been a machine for the systematic torment, dehumanization, and murder of Union prisoners. Given the accusations against him and the anger they provoked, few observers were surprised when he was found guilty of most of the charges and was executed on November 10, 1865.[5]

From the jail cells of Washington, D.C., to the prison pens of the Confederacy, Americans gained unwelcome familiarity with the intensity and devastation of modern war. Since the Revolution, Americans had boasted that they were building a new and innately superior society that represented humanity's best hope for the future. Neither the citizens of the Union nor those of the Confederacy abandoned this aspiration. But the fury with which they waged war called into question the progressive destiny that American civilization had seemed ordained to achieve before the war. "Atrocities" in Andersonville, the war-torn hinterlands of North Carolina, and elsewhere revealed that Americans were capable of wantonly breaching not just conventional rules of war but even the fundamental principles of the civilization they professed to defend.

Accusations of unconscionable violence were rife from the earliest months of the war. That the Civil War was routinely referred to as a

brothers' war magnified the heinousness of the accusations of internecine cruelty. Each instance was an act of pitiless violence against one's
own brethren. Here was inescapable evidence that white American
men would commit atrocities against their own. And because torture
was perceived to be among the most heinous manifestations of barbarism, accusations of it undercut the legitimacy of any cause to which
they became attached and confirmed beyond question the diabolical
and barbarous character of its perpetrators.

As reports of atrocities and torture accumulated during the war,
Confederates and Yankees alike sought explanations for behavior that
they previously had attributed to savagery or Old World tyranny. Each
side traced their enemy's proclivity for cruelty to the debased civilization of their foes. As the war dragged on, each side increasingly compared their adversary to the most reviled and fiendish savages they
could conjure.

Had the Civil War been the short and glorious conflict that warmon-
gers in both the North and South predicted in April 1861, its conduct
might never have provoked uncomfortable questions about Americans'
capacity for torture. The firing on Fort Sumter barely ceased before
newspapers on both sides of the Mason-Dixon line competed to fore-
cast swift and decisive victory. Supremely confident of Union success,
the New York Tribune crowed that "the hanging of traitors is sure to
begin before the month is over." The New York Times was no less smug
about the prospects for the North's triumph and dismissed the rebellion as "an unborn tadpole" and a "local commotion." Confederate secretary of war LeRoy Pope Walker was equally sanguine about the
prospects for his upstart republic; he proclaimed that the Confederate
flag would be hoisted over "the dome of the old Capitol of Washington
before the first of May." Such braggadocio discouraged any acknowledgment of, let alone preparations against, the violence that a drawn-
out war would unleash.[6]

Other Americans, in contrast, dreaded a dangerously destructive
and bloody conflict. The New York Herald worried that the war would
"leave nothing in the future but barrenness and desolation." They and
other pessimists fretted that the bloodletting, once started, might spiral

out of control. They doubted that the divided nation would wage a gen-teel war along the lines of the romantic renderings of past wars. In-stead, the conflict was likely to degenerate into something resembling the anarchic bloodshed in Bloody Kansas during the 1850s, when pro- and antislavery militias ravaged the territory. The nation's small number of professional soldiers understood better than most of their contemporaries that the nation was prone to fight an especially cruel war with itself. Even while Ulysses S. Grant, then a harness maker in Illinois, was eager to improve his fortunes by securing a commission in the Union army, he predicted that the established rules of war would not survive the contest. William T. Sherman was even more resigned; he anticipated that the conflict, "like a thunderbolt," would follow its own laws and, inevitably, "this country will be drenched in blood."[7]

The grim outlook of Sherman, Grant, and many other trained mil-itary men reflected their long-standing skepticism about the military traditions that their compatriots often lauded as the bedrock of the nation's enlightened civilization. Having repudiated large standing armies as engines of Old World oppression, Americans idealized citizen-soldiers who rushed to arms filled with a spontaneous sense of civic obligation and national spirit. The U.S. military consequently was slow to professionalize and remained extremely small, especially by comparison to European armies. The improvised manner in which the Union and the Confederacy organized for war was the inevitable con-sequence of both the tradition of citizen-soldiers and the inherited dis-trust of centralized authority that had characterized the nation since its founding.[8]

Longtime professional soldiers recalled with embarrassment, rather than pride, the conduct of many volunteer citizen-soldiers during the Mexican-American War waged fifteen years earlier. Although the vol-unteer troops in that conflict had been subject to the authority of the federal government, they often chose to answer only to their state mi-litia units. They had rebelled when officers imposed discipline, prompting one officer to complain that volunteers were too "thinking" and "capricious" to be "a mere moving and musket-holding machine." Even more alarming, volunteers displayed a disturbing propensity to violate laws and common notions of decency. General Winfield Scott wrung his hands over the "abominations committed by our troops."

While the war against Mexico raged, he disclosed to Secretary of State William L. Marcy that "our militia & volunteers, if one tenth of what is said be true, have committed atrocities—horrors—in Mexico, sufficient to make Heaven weep, & every American, of Christian morals blush for his country. Murder, robbery, & rape on mothers & daughters, in the presence of tied up males of the families, have been common all along the Rio Grande. . . . Truly it would seem unchristian & cruel to let loose upon any people—even savages—such unbridled persons." So dire were the infractions that Scott initiated unprecedented military commissions to prosecute and punish some of the "unbridled" volunteers.[9]

During the Civil War, Scott and other professional soldiers worried that vast armies of gung-ho but undisciplined amateurs would again swamp the small professional army. While Walt Whitman enthused about the "primal energies" of the wartime Union, professional soldiers and some civilian observers fretted that the Union's volunteers were wholly unprepared for the struggle they faced. When patriotic frenzy gripped both the North and South after April 1861, self-appointed officers, who often lacked any meaningful military experience, called for volunteers to join their hastily organized military units, which had fanciful names and even more fanciful uniforms. Other volunteers mustered into local militias that were haphazardly trained by officers who were either elected by their troops or appointed on the basis of social and political connections. Charles Eliot Norton, a prominent man of letters in the North, warned against the naive exuberance of those who failed to recognize that "enthusiasm will not supply the place of discipline."[10]

Volunteers betrayed little anxiety about their ignorance of even the rudiments of military training. They seldom envisioned themselves as deferential subordinates. Colonel Thomas Wentworth Higginson, a commander of one of the first African American regiments in the Union army, acknowledged the constant tension between military discipline and personal dignity. "One half of military duty," he observed, "lies in obedience, the other half in self-respect." Some volunteers bridled at the expectation of obedience and refused to concede that military life required anything more than limited and temporary abridgments of their autonomy. In their eyes, their self-motivation and self-discipline made military discipline superfluous. As Carlton McCarthy, a Confederate artilleryman, saw it, true soldiers were "manly and independent." Even some officers among the volunteers, such as Confederate officer James Jones White, deferred to their soldiers' independence. White singled out a soldier in his regiment as the ideal citizen-soldier; he was an "independent fellow [who] takes care of himself & allows nobody to interfere with his rights, which is very well understood."[11]

For men in either army who held similar attitudes, military discipline chafed, especially when it infringed on their expansive notions of personal dignity and independence. A Wisconsin volunteer, for example, bristled at the constraints he experienced while in service. It was, he grumbled, "irksome to be so closely confined and to have to implicitly obey all orders." Such a sense of self-mastery worked against strict obedience to military protocols under the best circumstances. More often, volunteers only grudgingly followed rules and obeyed their officers, while at every turn probing the limits of military permissiveness.[12]

Early in the conflict, some generals concluded that it was essential to establish and enforce rules of military conduct, especially with regard to the protection of civilians and their property. General George McClellan, for instance, stressed to his troops that their objective was to suppress the southern rebellion, not wreak vengeance against civilians. General Robert E. Lee endorsed similar principles when he led his troops into Union territory during the Gettysburg campaign in 1863. He announced that "we make war only upon armed men" and repudiated any impulse for retaliation: "We cannot take vengeance for the wrongs our people have suffered without lowering ourselves in the eyes of all whose abhorrence has been excited by the atrocities of our enemies."[13] Few commanders, however, had appropriate training to coax headstrong troops to comply with McClellan's and Lee's orders. Officers may have possessed some familiarity with parade drills and rudimentary tactics, but almost none had any training in contemporary laws of war or military discipline. Even fewer of the hundreds of thousands of the rank and file had any previous exposure to the laws of war or would receive any training in them during the war.

Through the use of harsh methods of military discipline, Union and Confederate commanders secured a modicum of sullen obedience in the ranks. Officers in both armies had wide discretion to punish any offenses that did not rise to the level of warranting a court-martial. Many officers seized on this prerogative to demonstrate their power by imposing capricious punishments. One punished soldiers for drunkenness by making them drink whiskey tainted with a laxative, while others ordered soldiers to carry heavy weights until they collapsed from exhaustion. Punishments included wearing a ball and chain for days, sitting astride a narrow pole for hours at a time with hands bound behind the back, being gagged and "bucked" (tied up in a fetal position), and being tied to trees in a stress position. One Union officer punished a soldier by tying him "up by his thumbs & keeping him in a cell on bread and water with the mercury below freezing." These customary techniques of discipline and punishment provoked outrage in some soldiers who believed they were exercises in cruelty as much as in obedience. Even commanders sometimes acknowledged that such punishments had "the character of torture" and cautioned against their overuse. So offensive were some of these techniques, especially hanging by thumbs and flogging, which evoked intolerable associations with slave punishments, that volunteers periodically rose up against them and freed imprisoned soldiers who were undergoing them.[14]

While the threat of stern military justice may have discouraged some soldiers from the most egregious transgressions, few commanders had illusions about the control they possessed over their troops. Sherman certainly did not; he dubbed his soldiers "refractory individualists" and confessed to his wife several months after the First Battle at Bull Run that he doubted that "our Democratic form of Government" was capable of producing any army other than "a mob."[15] To the degree that soldiers refrained from egregious violations of the recognized laws of war, this was as often a consequence of self-restraint at least as much as general orders from commanders.

For soldiers and civilians alike, the conflict unfolded as a grim cycle of daily atrocities only sporadically interrupted by decisive battles. Within months of the start of the war, lurid reports of callous butchery by the enemy tested the self-restraint of soldiers and outraged the sensibilities of civilians in both the North and the South. The litany of purported atrocities by the enemy that filled newspapers and circulated among soldiers inhibited compassion for the enemy and instead encouraged northerners and southerners to perceive the conflict as a struggle between civilization and barbarism. While reflecting on the course of the war on New Year's Day, 1862, Ella Gertrude (Clanton) Thomas of Georgia found solace that "one great advantage which will be gained by the war is the distinction which is made between the northerner and southerner." For her and many others, the early months of the war had revealed stark truths about the enemy; they were cruel, duplicitous, vindictive, and undeserving of the respect and compassion accorded an honorable foe.[16]

Northern reports of Confederate atrocities borrowed from well-honed abolitionist depictions of white southerners as crude, ignorant, filled with false pride, and prone to cruelty because they had been tutored in it by the institution of slavery. Their indefensible behavior confirmed that slavery as an institution poisoned everything with which it came in contact, not least the character and morality of slaveholders. As the Union army penetrated deeper and deeper into the plantation South in 1862, northern newspapers dwelled on discoveries of horrific "instruments of slave torture." After describing the assortment of devices found on plantations near New Orleans in 1863, the *Huntington Herald* in Indiana vouched that slaveholders were "creative in the refinements of cruelty." "The instincts of the masses in the South," the newspaper declared, "are brutal."[17] The Unionist editors of the *Nashville Daily Union* concurred, blaming slavery for predisposing slaveholders to "physical and mental despotism." Torture, lynching, and cruelty were "the natural and necessary tendencies of slavery" that were "manifested in savage forms toward the weak and defenseless."[18] Almost any act of depraved barbarism could be anticipated from an enemy that gloried in the abuse of the weak and powerless.

Confederate commentators were equally certain that northerners surrendered to immoral fanaticism even while they attempted to shroud their barbarism behind sanctimonious appeals to lofty moral principles. They were acquisitive, crude, immoral mercenaries or, in the words of Georgia private H. C. Kendrick, "a low" and "degraded" people. Even physiognomy apparently revealed the corrupt character of northerners; a Richmond newspaper, for example, dwelled on the "rough, repulsive personal appearance" of the Union soldiers captured

SOUTHERN CHIVALRY.
DEDICATED TO JEFF. DAVIS.

during the Battle of Ball's Bluff in 1861, implying that such uncouth men deserved whatever treatment their captors meted out to them.[19]

Northerners found in the actions of Confederate guerrillas conclusive evidence that the enemy were bloodthirsty barbarians bereft of compassion. Especially in the border states of Missouri, Kentucky, and Arkansas, semi-organized guerrilla gangs waged campaigns of assassination, pillage, and terror. The Confederate raiders who terrorized pro-Union civilians and fought federal troops garnered a measure of official sanction from the Confederate command. The 1862 Partisan Ranger Act, passed by the Confederate Congress, authorized the formation of such units and gave them legitimacy, at least in the eyes of Confederate authorities. Commanders of these units enjoyed such broad latitude to define their military objectives and methods that even the Confederate leadership eventually attempted to curtail their irregular warfare, fearing that the lack of discipline among rival partisan groups would offend civilians sympathetic to the Confederacy. But even after the Confederate Congress repealed the act in 1864, rebel guerrillas continued to operate until the end of the war.[20]

While claiming to defend the homeland from invaders, many Confederate guerrillas eschewed uniforms, relied on stealth, hoarded spoils of war, and were as likely to ambush civilians as enemy troops. More brigands than soldiers, guerrillas displayed even less regard for military discipline than did regular troops. Northern newspapers recounted the guerrillas' penchant for violating all conventional rules of war by preying on law-abiding civilians. During 1863, for example, northern newspapers carried graphic reports of the systematic torture by Confederate guerrillas of "women of loyal men" to force them to disclose the hiding places of their Unionist husbands, brothers, and sons. Confederate partisans in east Tennessee allegedly whipped women, hoisted them up by their thumbs, stripped them, and repeatedly threatened them with rape.[21] A year later Confederate guerrillas

FIGURE 4.1. *Southern Chivalry: Dedicated to Jeff. Davis.* In this 1863 illustration, Thomas Nast depicted many of the allegations of Confederate atrocities, including the torture and slaughter of wounded prisoners, the scalping of Union soldiers by Confederate Indians, and other examples of Confederate savagery. Nast sought to capture vividly the image of Confederates as a dishonorable and barbarous enemy.

in the same area "committed a series of acts which the demons inhab-
iting the lowest hell could not surpass in cruelty," including brutalizing a Unionist family, torturing and threatening to rape a white
woman, and sexually assaulting two slave women.[22] Heartrending
eyewitness reports of campaigns of terror came from across the South:
Kentucky civilians tortured to divulge the location of their horses
and arms; a victim in central Missouri whose toenails were pulled
off; and an Alabama Unionist who was tortured and executed, and his
body mutilated.[23] The atrocities charged against Confederate guerrillas included horrific and gratuitous acts against defenseless Union
prisoners. In Arkansas in 1864, for instance, guerrillas in Franklin
County captured a small Union unit and perpetrated "the most cruel
tortures and inhuman barbarities ever practiced upon prisoners in
this or any age," including cutting off their ears and noses before
stripping and castrating them.[24]

For Union soldiers who had to fend off guerrillas, the challenge of
distinguishing between civilians and partisans took on life-and-death
importance. Occupying troops had to calibrate their responses to guerrilla violence so as to crush partisan bands and intimidate defiant
civilians into acquiescence without provoking continued resistance.
In some locales, soldiers found it almost impossible to carry out this
task. Guerrillas could not be identified by uniform, and after they carried out attacks they ordinarily dispersed to their homes or to those
of sympathizers.

The ill-concealed enmity that many white civilians in the South
exhibited toward Union soldiers was a constant irritant. In the early
months of the war, General Henry Halleck complained that the
Union army in Missouri "is almost as much in a hostile country as
when in Mexico." Sherman subsequently concluded that "the entire
South, man, woman, and child, is against us, armed and determined."
With no clear battle lines and with ample evidence of civilian complicity with guerrillas, frustrated occupying soldiers adopted increasingly harsh attitudes toward and measures against civilians.
Union soldiers found in civilian defiance further license for escalating
acts of punishment. By 1864 an expansive and casual warfare of terror
had led to a redefinition of the enemy; no longer would war be confined
to the combatants. Simultaneously, the Union army demonstrated a

waning ability or inclination to compel soldiers to comply with military discipline.[25]

From the outset of the conflict, many Confederates anticipated harsh methods from the Union invaders. As early as May 1861 Alexander Cheeves Haskell labeled the Union army "an impious, piratical, bloodthirsty invader." Henry Ewing of Tennessee similarly charged that the Union had raised a "horde of vandals" to despoil the Confederacy by appealing to "the lowest & vilest passions." With its ranks filled with "mean and debased Devils incarnate," the Union army was "a fanatical mob animated by the most diabolical hate and revenge." Within two months of the attack on Fort Sumter, Confederate General P. G. T. Beauregard was accusing the Union army in northern Virginia of committing "acts of violence and outrage too shocking and revolting to humanity to be enumerated."[26]

As the Union army pushed into the southern hinterland, the behavior of the Union occupiers confirmed Confederates' worst fears. In August 1863, for instance, the *Staunton Spectator* in Virginia reprinted an account of "Yankee barbarity" near Canton, Mississippi. There, Union soldiers, aided by slaves, had tortured and whipped a sixty-five-year-old white woman to coerce her to disclose her hidden wealth. But because she had no money "she could not satisfy the savages," and so "she died under the torture of the lash." This and similar accounts demonstrated that plundering Union soldiers ignored conventional protections extended to defenseless civilians, including women and children. In other instances, Confederates pointed to the unconscionable violence meted out by Union forces. Especially notorious was Tennessee Unionist Fielding Hurst and the Sixth Tennessee Cavalry (USA). In retaliation for the murder of one of Fielding's nephews and an attack on his sister in 1863, he and his troops captured two soldiers from Nathan Bedford Forrest's 19th Tennessee Cavalry. After cutting off the tongue of one prisoner, "punching out his eyes, splitting his mouth on each side of his ears, and inflicting other mutilations," they left him to die. The other prisoner, Lieutenant Willis Dodds, was put to death by "the most inhuman process of torture." His "face was skinned, the nose cut off, the under jaw disjointed, the privates cut off, and the body otherwise barbarously lacerated and most wantonly injured."[27]

Equally horrifying to Confederate sensibilities was the Union campaign to foment slave unrest. Confederate secretary of war James Seddon charged the Lincoln administration with promoting a "servile insurrection" that would unleash the "brutal appetites of a barbarous race" and conclude with the "abandonment of all rules, conventions, mitigating influences, and humanizing usages." According to the *Richmond Enquirer*, the practical effect of the Emancipation Proclamation and other Union policies regarding slavery was to transform the conflict into "a war of extermination." Yankee fanaticism condoned a massive slave revolt that could only culminate in indiscriminate murder, rapine, and devastation not witnessed since the Haitian Revolution at the dawn of the nineteenth century.[28]

Northern and southern commentators agreed that history offered few precedents for the cruelty of their foes. For a generation of Americans familiar with sensational accounts of the Spanish Inquisition, comparisons of the methods of the enemy with the techniques of Spanish inquisitors were at once powerfully evocative and damning. Outraged by the treatment of Union prisoners of war in 1862, the *Cleveland Daily Leader* charged Confederates with a horrifying propensity for "worse than inquisitorial tortures and murder."[29] The same newspaper avowed that neither Fox's Book of Martyrs, a lurid catalog of Catholic atrocities that circulated widely during the nineteenth century, nor "the history of the Spanish Inquisition in its palmiest days" furnished "scenes that can surpass in atrocity" the conduct of Confederate guerrillas in Tennessee.[30] An Indiana newspaper contended that the manacles and torture devices that Union troops collected on slave plantations demonstrated that "chivalric Southern planters" would have made "excellent torturers for the Spanish Inquisition." Not even hated tyrants of old Europe, the editorialist insisted, had "more effective instruments" in their dungeons.[31]

Both sides invoked the horrors of Indian savagery to besmirch the legitimacy of their foe. Northern editorials denounced the conduct of Confederate guerrillas as the deeds of "fiends," not men. The *Louisville Journal* contended that the rebel bushwhackers were "more bloodthirsty and fiendish than the debased savage" and concluded, "We do not think that any savage nation or tribe upon the American continent was ever known amid all their innumerable atrocities to practice such terrible warfare."[32] Northern newspapers expressed little surprise over reports that the Confederacy had mustered Cherokees and other Indians "with their barbarous weapons" to join the campaign to destroy the Union. While the recruitment of Indians demonstrated Confederate treachery, northern commentators doubted that the presence of "Indian savages" could "greatly intensify" the "numberless atrocities and excesses" daily committed by Confederates.[33]

The *Richmond Dispatch,* in a single furious blast of indignation, cataloged all of the evidence of northern barbarity in an editorial in April 1864. The newspaper roared that the Union army's conduct "has proved them the most vicious and barbarous of nations." The war raging on the American continent was not a conflict between equals because white southerners abided by the laws of civilization, whereas "the Yankee is but a barbarian dressed in broadcloths." Not only were their "ideas of civilization" false but also "in the true sense of the term they have never been civilized." None of the much touted manifestations of northern civilization had elevated "the Yankee population above the animal passion of brutes." Indeed, the newspaper compared Yankees unfavorably with Indians: "The naked savage of the wilderness . . . could not be more brutal in his instincts, nor more ferocious in his hatred." The *Dispatch* closed by contrasting the innate honor of Indians with the irredeemable degradation of Yankees. "Let us not do injustice to the savages of North America" because the inescapable truth was that "the civilization of Yankees is the grossest and most indecent of all barbarians."[34]

Almost certainly the death and destruction of the "great slaughterhouse," as Whitman aptly labeled the war, would have clouded the consciences of soldiers with desires for retaliation even in the absence of sensational news reports that dehumanized the enemy.[35] The sensibilities of soldiers inevitably were hardened by the death they witnessed and the suffering they endured. After the war, Francis Lieber, the nation's preeminent philosopher of the law of war, would acknowledge that "a contest so comprehensive and so probing" as the Civil War "makes people abandon many things."[36] Many northerners and southerners seemingly lost their capacity for compassion, becoming inured to behavior that might previously have troubled their consciences. By 1862 Oliver Wendell Holmes Jr., the future Supreme

Court justice, expressed puzzlement at "how indifferent one gets to the sight of death."[37] Two years later Confederate Frank Myers reveled in the grim sight of Union corpses. Reflecting a hard-bitten stoicism that tolerated anonymous butchery, he gloated, "It does me good to the toes of my boots any time to see a dead yank and you may imagine how much good it does to look at miles of them."[38] Moncure Conway, a Virginia-born abolitionist, watched with mounting regret as the war coarsened men in the ranks. "The moralization of the soldier," he lamented, "is the demoralization of the man." This outcome was inevitable because "war is the apotheosis of brutality." He cautioned, "Should we continue this war long enough we shall become the Vandals and Hessians the South says we are."[39]

The cumulative effects of steady reports of atrocities and of the grim experience of combat was to stoke fantasies of revenge and justify a policy of systematic retaliation. Within days of the First Battle of Bull Run, the first major battle of the war, reports of Confederate attacks on Union hospitals and the destruction of Union ambulances prompted furious calls for vengeance. Colonel Robert McAllister could find "no parallel in history" for the behavior of the Confederate victors. "What a blot on Southern history!" He predicted that the Confederate cruelty "will tell in our future battles" when Union troops had an opportunity to exact revenge.[40] Reports of Union atrocities had a similar effect on Julia Whiting of northern Virginia, who fumed that "all one's feelings of indignation, hatred and revenge are daily roused by tidings of some fresh atrocity perpetrated by the Yankees."[41] Alexander Haskell, a Confederate officer from South Carolina, took solace that accounts of Union atrocities "lighted a fire of vengeance and desperate hate" in his compatriots.[42] When Lee's army invaded Pennsylvania in June 1863, H. C. Kendrick, a Georgia infantryman who would die at Gettysburg, eagerly anticipated the opportunity to bring the war to northern civilians. "I feel like retaliating in the strictest sense," he admitted to his mother.[43] Much later in the war, in December 1864, Colonel McAllister summarized the logic of retaliation to his wife after he and his troops came upon the site of the summary execution of Union soldiers by Confederate guerrillas. He recounted that the men had apparently been captured, stripped of their clothes, forced to kneel in a circle, and then shot in the head. After describing the scene, he asked rhetorically, "Need I now tell you why our boys burnt buildings?"[44]

The logic of retaliation was simple. Union soldiers rationalized that white southerners were solely responsible for the terror that was visited upon them. "Rebels deserved all they got and more" as the natural consequence of the war they had started.[45] "All considerations of mercy and humanity must bow," a Union officer calculated, before the inexorable logic of retaliation that justified harsh measures against civilians.[46] Confederates simultaneously pointed to the Union's war against southern civilians, the excesses of Union occupiers wherever they were, and especially the scorched earth tactics adopted by David M. Hunter in Virginia and William T. Sherman in Georgia.

Retaliation, northerners and southerners contended, was the one response likely to temper the excesses of the enemy. As R. H. Simpson, a Virginia soldier, saw it, only by way of the fear of retaliation "can we teach our uncivilized opponents a just appreciation of our rights and of the rules of war."[47] James Edmondson, an enthusiastic member of the Stonewall Brigade, offered the same rationale for resorting to harsh measures "until the Yankees are willing to accept the Code of Civilized war—blaze for blaze is my motto."[48]

While both warring sides used the rhetoric of retaliation, they simultaneously appealed to the laws of war to justify its application. To the extent that Union and Confederate officials consulted extant commentary on the laws of war, they looked to the eighteenth-century Swiss jurist Emer de Vattel's *The Laws of Nations.* Building on the work of Hugo Grotius, a sixteenth-century Dutch jurist, Vattel had considered both the relationship of the laws of war to civil wars as well as the legality of retaliation. With regard to the combatants in a civil war, he concluded that the two sides in a sundered state were "in every respect" equivalent to two distinct nations engaged in a conventional war. The import of this conclusion for the American conflict was far-reaching; the subjects of each of the warring sides in the civil war were enemies. Confederates, in other words, were enemies in the same way that Mexicans had been during the Mexican-American War fifteen years earlier. But Vattel did impose prohibitions on armies; military commanders

RETRIBUTION WILL BE SURELY GIVEN *A. Lincoln.*

THE TRAITORS IN COUNCIL

GEN. FORREST SHOOTING A FREE MULATTO

BELLE ISLE RICE

PADUCAH FORT WAGNER FORT PILLOW MARSHEN'S BEND

REBEL ATROCITIES.—[SEE PAGE 294.]

should not adopt measures of "an odious kind, nor unjustifiable in themselves, and prohibited by the laws of nature." Similarly, he only condoned retaliation by warring nations if it was intended to curtail illegitimate actions by the enemy and as long as the punishment bore "some proportion to the evil for which we mean to inflict it."[49]

Vattel's version of the laws of war proved inadequate to address the myriad questions that Union commanders confronted as the American conflict ground on, including guerrilla warfare, destruction and confiscation of civilian property, treatment of prisoners of war, prosecution of spies, and violations of the laws of war, especially the enslavement and summary executions of captured black soldiers. All of these issues were made murkier by the Lincoln administration's anxiety to avoid taking any actions that might grant formal recognition of the Confederacy as a legitimate nation (rather than a rogue rebellion). In practice, the Union treated Confederates in some instances as combatants and in others as traitors, resulting inevitably in contradictory and confusing policies.[50]

In an effort to bring some clarity to these issues, Major General Henry W. Halleck, the general-in-chief of the Union army, requested that Francis Lieber draft a timely compilation of contemporary laws of war. Halleck, the preeminent military expert on the laws of war of his day, had more than an academic interest in the topic; he had confronted all of the knotty issues while serving as a commander in Missouri at the outbreak of the war. Lieber enthusiastically tackled the assignment in early 1863, producing a short tract that the War Department subsequently issued as General Order No. 100 but more often referred to as Lieber's Code.

Lieber, who disdained Vattel's moderation, placed unprecedented emphasis on military necessity and the presumption that it was compatible with legal principles that restricted the violence of war. Lieber pronounced legitimate any methods to suppress the rebellion that did not entail outrageous cruelty. Men at war, he underscored, "do not

FIGURE 4.2. *Retribution Will Be Surely Given.* Thomas Nast depicted Confederate atrocities again in 1864 at a time of mounting outrage about the treatment of Union prisoners and demands for retribution against Confederate prisoners. The image left ambiguous who would inflict retribution upon Confederates, but it made clear that retaliation was justified.

cease on this account to be moral beings, responsible to one another, and to God."[51] In keeping with this injunction, Lieber specifically prohibited torture because it was inherently cruel. By definition, torture was the infliction of "pain for the sake of pain." Even if the purpose was to obtain important information for military purposes, the aim of torture was to inflict pain rather than to incapacitate a combatant. Similarly, he prohibited systematic assassinations or the use of poisons against an enemy.

Lieber, to a greater degree than Vattel, believed that retaliation was compatible with enlightened laws of war. He rejected revenge as an "elementary" and dangerous "passion" unless it was reined in. But if an enemy violated the laws of war and military necessity warranted a response, retribution was compatible with the laws of war. He endorsed retaliation as "a means of protective retribution" against "a reckless enemy" who must be dissuaded from "the repetition of barbarous outrage." Lieber explained to Halleck in private that "if Indians slowly roast our men, we cannot and must not roast them in turn."[52] If an enemy tortured and scalped prisoners, federal soldiers should not resort to the same illegitimate methods but instead could put enemy prisoners to death. If Confederates enslaved African American prisoners of war, the Union army could execute but not enslave Confederate prisoners of war. Enslavement of prisoners was an offense against the laws of war, but retaliatory execution was not. Even reprisals, in short, had limits.[53]

Lieber advocated that the private "unarmed, inoffensive, harmless citizen" should be spared "as much as the exigencies of war will admit." But he loosened these strictures when a "savage" enemy violated the laws of nations. For example, guerrillas and civilians who resisted occupiers were liable to "suffer the calamities of war," including destruction of property, taking of hostages, and reprisals. Recalcitrant civilians in occupied territory, Lieber contended, were "violators of the laws of war and are not entitled to their protection." Although he otherwise left vague the definition of a noncombatant, he was clear that the protections of the laws of war extended only to completely cowed and obedient civilians in occupied territory.

Lieber's expansive definition of military necessity and limited conception of military restraint were not easily reconciled. As Confederate secretary of war James Seddon pointed out, Lieber's Code could be read as defining as lawful all measures that are "indispensable for securing the ends of the war." Seddon complained that Lieber's definition of military necessity provided "an apology and defense" for "acts of atrocity and violence" that had "shocked the moral sense of civilized nations."[54] Although the code specifically forbade intentional cruelty, torture, the use of poison, and a few other forms of violence, it qualified its restraints on other violence by acknowledging the primacy of military necessity and the legitimacy of retaliation. Indeed, in the eyes of critics, Lieber's dictum gave Union soldiers the ethical freedom to do just about anything they wanted to citizens of the Confederacy in the name of military necessity.

The practical efficacy of Lieber's Code on the conduct of the war is hard to measure. When it was issued, Confederate commentators immediately denounced it as a charade intended to legitimize Union atrocities. More recently, defenders of Lieber's opus have argued that his code clarified the rules of war, encouraged restraint, and in turn kept the war's violence from claiming the lives of even more Americans. The code also bolstered the resolve of the Union military to insist on the proper treatment of black soldiers captured by the Confederacy. As such, General Order No. 100 is a milestone in the evolution of the laws of war and human rights. Skeptics, in contrast, contend that the code failed to modify the Union army's behavior in the field for the simple reason that "Union generals showed scant interest in the code and soldiers none." Because the scale of the war was so vast, the power of the Confederate and federal governments so diffuse, and the limitations of communication so substantial, field commanders and their soldiers inevitably formulated their own ad hoc policies with regard to civilians and combatants. Moreover, Lieber's elastic definition of military necessity gave commanders license to take almost any action against civilians. Finally, Lieber's Code contributed to the breakdown of the prisoner exchanges, which drastically worsened the conditions endured by prisoners of war. The code, in sum, gave a patina of legitimacy to everything but the most extreme methods of war.

Nowhere did the dehumanization of the enemy proceed further and with graver consequences than in prisoner-of-war camps. And nowhere were the accusations of torture and atrocities more commonplace than in the prison camps. Indeed, the prisoner-of-war experience became the paramount example of the barbarism and cruelty that contemporaries regretted had been unleashed by the war. Some contemporary apologists (and later historians) insisted that the horrors of Civil War prisons were a predictable consequence of a lack of know-how, planning, and resources. After all, Americans had little experience with mass incarceration. In 1860 the entire prison population of the United States totaled less than twenty thousand. Americans had even less experience with prisoners of war. The small number of prisoners during the Revolution and the War of 1812 had been exchanged by the respective sides so that few captives were imprisoned for long stints. At the start of the Civil War, both sides assumed that a similar exchange system would be adopted by the belligerents. No one anticipated that one of the tragic innovations of the war would be prisoner-of-war camps of unprecedented size and grimness. By the end of the war, probably between 150,000 and 200,000 Union and Confederate soldiers had spent time in these "furnaces of affliction."[55]

During the first months of the war, neither the Union nor the Confederacy made meaningful preparations for prisoners of war. This lack of preparedness went hand in hand with disorganization in the Confederacy. The Richmond government relied on a cumbersome chain of command to oversee prisoners until November 1864 when it finally created a centralized bureaucracy under the authority of General John H. Winder. By then prison conditions were already horrific, and the war was nearly over. The Union prison bureaucracy, by comparison, was more efficient, but it too was hampered by confusion in the chain of command and inadequate resources. Neither side committed the resources or demonstrated the resolve necessary to adequately, let alone humanely, address the needs of prisoners of war.

The consequences of this lack of planning and resources became apparent once both sides contended with large and unpredictable influxes of prisoners. As early as September 1861, Richmond housed nearly two thousand Union prisoners. Nine months later the prison population there exceeded eight thousand. The escalation of fighting in 1862 dramatically swelled prisoner populations, as was evident in the rapid growth of Camp Douglass in Chicago. Within three days of its opening in February 1862, it held more than seven thousand Confederate prisoners. With prisons already bursting, each successive battle produced substantial numbers of new prisoners for both sides, while mass surrenders of troops, such as of the Confederates at Fort Donelson, challenged officials to find space for almost as many prisoners as the total prison population in the United States at the start of the war.[56]

Providing housing for so many prisoners of war challenged both sides. Confederate officials especially struggled because the South had only a few rudimentary prisons, none of which were adequate to house the swelling ranks of prisoners of war. Meanwhile, virtually all of the forts and military sites in the new nation were needed for its defense and so could not be sacrificed to serve as prison camps. One measure of Confederate desperation was the offer by Governor Joseph Brown of Georgia to house prisoners in a slave market in Macon.[57] Brown's offer was not accepted, but Confederate officials improvised by adapting all manner of facilities to serve as prisons, including a rough cotton shed in Montgomery and an unfinished warehouse in Cahaba, Alabama; a slave pen in Vicksburg, Mississippi; an abandoned cotton mill in Salisbury, North Carolina; and fairground stables in Lynchburg, Virginia. Even the large and substantial tobacco warehouses used as prisons in Richmond lacked essential amenities, including adequate sanitation facilities, for thousands of prisoners. Union authorities, meanwhile, relied on far-flung forts and military training grounds to serve as prisons. While these facilities, in some regards, were suitable for their new purpose, they seldom were designed to house the number of prisoners crammed into them. Camp Chase in Columbus, Ohio, for instance, was built to house four thousand prisoners, but late in the war it held as many as ten thousand.

The chronic lack of preparedness extended to the staffing of the prison camps. Prisons were presided over by guards who lacked appropriate training and were understandably anxious about maintaining control of the prisoners, who vastly outnumbered them. Union and Confederate commanders were loath to assign battle-hardened troops to prison duty, leaving the task to a motley assortment of underage, overage, convalescing, and otherwise marginal soldiers. At many camps, prisoners discovered, to their dismay, that their guards were "a lot of boys who had never seen the front" and "new conscripts."[58] In some instances, such as the Macon prison camp, the guards were actually local civilians who "knew nothing of military discipline."[59] Elsewhere, former prisoners of war who had returned to the ranks were assigned to prison duty. At Camp Douglass in Chicago, local authorities relied on local police to guard prisoners there until former Union prisoners of war could take their places. Union commanders seem not to have second-guessed the wisdom of placing former prisoners, who almost certainly harbored resentment for their own previous treatment at Confederate hands, in charge of enemy prisoners. At Point Lookout in Maryland, Confederate prisoners claimed to have been terrorized by black guards who, according to one South Carolinian imprisoned there, "never let an opportunity pass to show their animosity and hatred towards us."[60]

Prison officers were no better trained than the guards. A federal prison inspector lamented that the officers at Camp Chase, the prison camp in Columbus, Ohio, displayed "the most astonishing ignorance" of even rudimentary military protocol.[61] A survivor of the Macon prison camp described the commander there as "a cold, canting, cadaverous excrescence that subsisted on cruelty," while a former Confederate prisoner at Rock Island labeled the commandant there "an imp of Satan."[62] Over time prisoners in both Union and Confederate camps concluded that prison staffs were incompetent, indolent, mercurial, callous, and worse. Samuel Fiske described the guards who tormented him at Libby Prison in Richmond as "worse than Italian brigands, Greek pirates, and Bedouin Arabs." His portrait of his tormentors jibed with those of countless Union and Confederate prisoners.[63]

Had an efficient and permanent system of prisoner exchange been adopted early in the war, the subsequent plight of prisoners almost certainly would have been reduced. During the fall of 1861, a haphazard procedure for prisoner exchanges did emerge. On a case-by-case basis Union and Confederate commanders haggled over the terms for exchanges of prisoners captured during combat. These ad hoc negotiations reduced prison camp populations but were unpredictable, time-consuming, and nerve-racking for prisoners and their families. The Lincoln administration's reluctance to take any step that might imply official recognition of the rebel government delayed the initiation of any formal exchange agreement with the Confederacy. With that aim in mind (and hopes of subsequent European recognition of the southern nation), the Confederacy jockeyed for formal prisoner exchanges along the lines of terms adopted by belligerents in previous wars. Finally, in July 1862 the Lincoln administration relented, and the warring governments agreed to a general policy for prisoner exchanges. To the delight of prisoners and their families, the policy drained both Confederate and Union prisons, and for a time overcrowding abated and prison conditions improved.[64]

Despite the manifest benefits of exchange protocol, both Union and Confederate authorities grew dissatisfied and looked for opportunities to gain advantage through it. Desperate to bolster depleted ranks, Confederate officials stretched the terms of exchange and exploited every opportunity to return former prisoners to active duty in the Confederate army as quickly as possible. Union generals, in response, dug in their heels at the idea of facing Confederate forces replenished with recently exchanged prisoners of war. Once Ulysses S. Grant began to pursue a war of attrition, Union commanders concluded that each imprisoned Confederate represented an irreplaceable reduction in the manpower at the disposal of the rebel army. A Confederate prisoner astutely summarized Union reluctance to continue prisoner exchanges when he observed that "Grant would rather feed us [as prisoners] than fight us."[65]

The enlistment of black soldiers in the Union army dealt the final blow to the negotiated exchange of prisoners. When the Lincoln administration announced in January 1863 that both former slaves and free blacks would be recruited by the Union army, Confederate authorities reacted furiously. They denounced the policy for encouraging "a general assassination" of slave masters by "several millions of human beings of an inferior race." Jefferson Davis condemned it as "the most execrable measure recorded in the history of guilty man," and his administration pledged to deny black soldiers and their white officers the protections accorded legitimate belligerents. Instead Confederate policy stipulated that black soldiers captured in combat could be sold into slavery, put to death along with their white officers, or punished, according to state laws, for "exciting servile insurrection." Confederate authorities pointedly made no distinction between free-born and enslaved black soldiers and stipulated that all African Americans taken in uniform would be assumed to be runaway slaves. In response, Union officials in May 1863 announced that prisoner exchanges would not resume until Richmond revised its policy regarding black prisoners of war. When Confederate authorities refused to do so, exchanges, with few exceptions, ceased until the final weeks of the war.[66]

After the suspension of exchanges, prison populations mushroomed, overcrowding increased, conditions deteriorated, and death rates among prisoners worsened. The rapid expansion of Andersonville Prison and the dire conditions there were one conspicuous consequence. Within two months of the prison's opening in February 1864, it housed more than seven thousand prisoners. By August the prison's population peaked at over thirty-three thousand and the site, which had no sanitation facilities, had a population density many times greater than that of the worst slums in any twenty-first-century city. By then, prisoners were dying at the rate of roughly one thousand per month.[67]

While prisoners understood that their fate would be determined by the twists and turns of the prisoner exchange policy, they blamed their immediate suffering on cruel camp guards and their commanders, who through willful neglect and malicious conduct, made the prison camps "hells of torture and insanity."[68] From the earliest reports of inhumane treatment that began appearing in newspapers during the fall of 1861 through subsequent firsthand accounts by exchanged prisoners, charges of intentional and wanton cruelty in the prison camps were rampant. They were augmented in the summer of 1864 by graphic woodcuts in the pages of the illustrated press of maimed and skeletal men recently released from southern prisons. Almost simultaneously, official reports by both governments, which included extensive testimony from released prisoners, further inflamed public sentiment.[69]

Appalled by the broken-down prisoners who straggled home at the war's close, both northerners and southerners continued to hurl recriminations at their former enemies for their merciless and indefensible treatment of prisoners. Such was the interest in the experiences of former prisoners that prison chronicles grew into a robust publishing genre that included several hundred titles by the end of the nineteenth century. Many were printed by small local presses and reached only local audiences, but some sold tens of thousands of copies, and a few sold hundreds of thousands. From the war's end until the last of the former prisoners of war died in the early twentieth century, prison veterans exploited every opportunity, from reunions and commemorative ceremonies to regimental histories and pension applications, to draw attention to the singular hardships they had endured and the unimaginable cruelty they had witnessed.[70]

When former prisoners set about compiling their narratives, they acknowledged the soul-numbing monotony and quotidian traumas of prison camp while dwelling especially on the extraordinary courage and resolve displayed by their fellow prisoners. At a time when audiences were bombarded by heroic renderings of the war, especially of battlefield deeds, former prisoners had to overcome the perception that, as the Irish poet William Butler Yeats would observe when reflecting on World War I, "passive suffering" like that of prisoners of war was inherently less inspiring or captivating than battlefield valor.[71]

Intent on demonstrating both their courage and the depravity of the enemy, prison camp narrators insisted that they had passed through a crucible of suffering that defied simple description or easy comprehension. A recurring motif in the accounts is the lament that the authors lacked sufficient craft to render in prose the full horror of their prison experience. Prison narrators simultaneously invoked conventions of common decency as justification for expurgating especially lurid details from their accounts. Prison memoirs made it clear that neither civilians nor even veterans who had not experienced imprisonment could ever fully understand the iniquity of the camps. And because the prisoner-of-war experience was so far outside the ken of contemporary life, prison survivors anticipated an incredulous reception for their accounts. So to establish their veracity and to comply with contemporary conventions of autobiography, prison narrators pledged that their narratives were humble testimonials free of all artifice. This aim almost certainly explains why Robert Kellogg opened his account of Andersonville by invoking the New Testament verse "We speak that we do know, and testify that we have seen."[72]

For all the disclaimers by Kellogg and other prison chroniclers, their accounts of existence in the camps were intended to be vivid and haunting. The graphic descriptions of prison camp life were meant to wrench readers from familiar comforts of the contemporary age and plunge them into an abyss where prisoners endured unimaginable acts of cruelty, ceaselessly scratched at the lice-infested filthy rags that

clothed them, breathed the stench of thousands of unwashed and dis-
eased men, huddled in the rain and sweltered in the sun, scavenged in
the muck for grubs and undigested grains of corn to eat, waded through
quagmires of excrement, kneeled in putrid gullies to drink and bathe,
and gradually succumbed to dysentery, dropsy, and other diseases. Only
then could those who had not endured the camps grasp the hardships the
prisoners had endured and their lingering effects on camp survivors.

When reflecting on the torture and cruelty they had suffered or witnessed during their incarceration, prisoners concluded that the prison
camps were engines of torture intended to reduce them to a state of
abject subordination in the process of killing them. Prisoners predictably compared their suffering and oppression to that of slaves. In the
eyes of many Union prisoners, their ill treatment was an extension
of the debased morality of slaveholders. Samuel Boggs suggested that
slave drivers were selected as prison guards so that they could exercise
their "barbarous appetites on helpless captives" that had no property
value. Former Union prisoners interviewed by the U.S. Sanitary Commission in 1864 described overcrowded prisoners in Libby Prison
forced to huddle "like slaves in the middle passage." Not only were
they chained and disciplined like slaves, they also were chased down
when they attempted to escape by bloodhounds that otherwise were
used to track runaway slaves.[73]

Confederate prisoners were no less convinced that the goal of their
Union guards was to reduce them to a state below that of black slaves.
Lawrence Sangston, a Maryland legislator imprisoned for sedition, invoked the horrors of the Middle Passage when he compared the overcrowding at Fort Lafayette to "the between decks of a slave slip."[74] Joseph
Barbiere, a Confederate prisoner, observed that in the wake of triumphant
Union fanaticism the application of the lash and other punishments were
now considered appropriate for free white men.[75] And southern whites
fumed at the ignominy of being guarded by black soldiers, who apparently took every opportunity to delight in their power over slave drivers.

Although prison food was one of the most prosaic manifestations
of their systematic debasement, prisoners spoke and wrote at length
about it. In the best of circumstances, prison fare was sufficient to ward
off death. But too often, prisoners struggled to survive on tiny portions of
badly prepared food of little nutritional value. Even before Confederate

supply lines broke down, Union prisoners complained that fruits and vegetables were extreme rarities and meat rations were often rancid and maggot-infested. After 1863 prison fare became so irregular and inadequate that Union prisoners routinely lived on a diet of unrefined and undercooked corn meal that scoured their bowels. One prisoner recalled, with more humor than he probably had mustered when he was in the Andersonville stockade, that "the bacon had a habit of acting a little queer and lively at times, although we were repeatedly assured that it had been killed once."[76]

Confederate authorities acknowledged the deepening crisis but took no meaningful measures to address it. In response to the unaddressed conditions in Confederate prisons, Union officials retaliated by reducing rations for Confederate prisoners in Union camps. Although this policy was entirely consonant with the logic of retaliation, it tacitly demonstrated that the belligerents could and did calibrate the suffering of prisoners according to war aims. Henry M. Davidson, a Union soldier who had the misfortune to endure more than a year in several of the most notorious Confederate camps, attested that "there is no torture equal in intensity to the fierce longing for food."[77] A decade after the war, Charles Wright, a Confederate survivor of Rock Island prison camp, still vividly recalled the "continued gnawing anguish" of the hunger he had experienced while prisoner.[78] So desperate for food were the Confederate prisoners at Point Lookout that they sustained a robust market for "killed and dressed rats." "Quite a number of our boys," one prisoner recorded in his diary, "have gone into the rat business."[79] Another Confederate prisoner confessed that rats "smelt very good while frying" and that his compatriots "ate every rat they could find."[80] Meanwhile, at Belle Isle the scarcity of rations resulted in instances of Union prisoners "vomiting up their breakfast and this afterward was eaten by others."[81]

Prison recollections depicted a hellish world in which prisoners were denied the barest necessities that enabled humankind to elevate itself above beasts. Overcrowding created inhumane conditions at most camps. At Andersonville and Belle Isle, for instance, prisoners endured the winter cold without shelter other than the holes they scraped out of the earth and the tarps they fashioned out of rags and leaves. (Lumber that might have provided rudimentary shelter for prisoners at Andersonville instead was used for amenities for prison guards.) Three of the fifteen acres at Andersonville were swampland, which one prisoner described as "one animated mass of maggots one to two feet deep . . . moving and rolling like the waves of the sea."[82] Meanwhile, in some Union prisons Confederate prisoners lived a hand-to-mouth existence deprived of adequate protection against the bitter cold and even basic eating utensils. In most prison camps prisoners received cheap and poor-quality uniforms that chafed the skin even while rapidly disintegrating into rags. And because prisoners often lacked access to adequate sanitation and bathing facilities, they soon took on the appearance of primitive savages rather than civilian soldiers.

The ongoing, day-to-day degradation in the camps was punctuated by acts of excessive discipline and dehumanizing torture that seemingly had no apparent aim other than to cause pain and humiliation. Both Union and Confederate prisoners recalled being subjected to the excruciating torment of having their thumbs tied behind their backs and being lifted inches off the ground with all their weight pulling on their thumbs. A Confederate prisoner at Johnson's Island prison camp described witnessing prisoners suspended by their thumbs "who would grow so deathly sick that they would vomit all over themselves" and "the ends of their thumbs would burst open." A supervising surgeon would then take their pulse and "say he thought they could stand it a little longer."[83] Another prisoner recalled men who were hoisted by their thumbs screaming in pain and beseeching the guards "for God's sake, to shoot them." Elsewhere prison guards adopted thumb screws as a preferred method to torment prisoners.[84]

Another common "contrivance to punish and humiliate the manhood" of defenseless prisoners was the chain gang.[85] Prisoners were harnessed in chains and compelled to drag heavy metal balls wherever they went. At Andersonville, for instance, twelve men at a time were chained together to a single large ball while each prisoner simultaneously had to drag a small ball that was shackled to his other leg. In other instances, individual prisoners were shackled for "the amusement of the guards." For prisoners whose clothes were a swarming mass of lice and fleas, the torment of the chains was compounded by their inability to rid themselves of vermin.[86] In both Union and Confederate camps, prisoners who somehow crossed their guards were likely to be bucked and gagged. A survivor of Fort Delaware, for instance, recalled that prisoners were bucked and "rolled out onto a stone pavement and left for hours, though the thermometer was at zero."[87] A Union prisoner at Andersonville described a similar scene of a prisoner's gagged and bucked body twisted in "the manner of a calf going to the market."[88] So heartless was the practice that one Confederate vowed, "I would not punish a dog in that way."[89] Prison officers regularly sentenced prisoners to endure hours in stocks or other taxing positions. In his prison memoir, Samuel Boggs provided a gruesome portrait of a bleeding Union prisoner whose arms and legs were fastened into the stocks for twelve hours, during which "maggot flies deposit[ed] their eggs in his wounds" so that days later his unattended wounds were a "working mass of maggots." Typically situated in plain view of the prisoners, the stocks served as a graphic warning of the consequences of offending prison staff.[90]

Complementing these systematic techniques of degradation were acts of capricious cruelty by prison staff. Acts of petty humiliation sometimes were as painful as the harshest discipline. Henry Davidson bitterly assailed the decision by the Confederate commandant at the Danville, Virginia, prison camp to withhold mail sent to Union prisoners. When the policy was enforced, Davidson claimed that "poor fellows who had stood in the stocks for 'four and twenty hours, under a boiling sun and had endured exposure and famine for months without a murmur, wept like children.'"[91] Almost without exception, prison survivors claimed that guards shot prisoners in cold blood. Confederate prisoner John Dyer reported that every Union guard at Camp Chase "seemed to think he ought to kill a rebel."[92] At Point Lookout, African American guards allegedly shot at prisoners "as they would at game," and at the Cahaba camp in Alabama a guard allegedly went unpunished after he randomly shot four Union prisoners. "It was," a prisoner recalled years later, "the unprovoked deed of a demon." He, like many prisoners on both sides, believed rumors that guards were rewarded for their impulsive violence, including a three-month furlough for each prisoner they shot.[93] And then there were the acts of violence that seemingly had only one aim: the complete degradation of the victim. How else can we explain why Charles Loehr, who was a Confederate prisoner at Point Lookout, was "bound and dipped head first into a urine barrel"?[94]

The cumulative effect of these degradations was to reduce prisoners to an animal state that seemingly affirmed the distance that separated them, now reduced to mere bodies, from their captors. Their systematic humiliation exposed the logic of retaliation and its capacity to sanction conduct that seemed to contradict the laws of civilization. The "law" of retaliation not only provided the pretext for both sides' intransigent policies regarding prisoner exchange, but also fueled the day-to-day treatment of prisoners. No official or officer had to give explicit orders to prison staff to abuse prisoners of war as long as a rhetoric of vengeance permeated the reporting on the war or the discussion of prisoner-of-war policy in particular. Indeed, civilians forthrightly advocated even harsher practices than those that prevailed in many prisoner-of-war camps. Only six months after the start of the war, the *Charleston Mercury* reported that residents of Richmond complained that rations for the burgeoning population of Union prisoners were far too generous: "Some people think we ought to feed them on fodder or mixed horse feed," he wrote, "while others say the cheapest plan would be to destroy them outright."[95] With such severe measures, including summary execution, bandied about in public, officials and prison staffs were by comparison restrained in their treatment of the prisoners under their control.

While the logic of retaliation claimed its greatest toll in the prison camps, its consequences were felt across the war-torn nation. The "law" of retaliation created a context in which the threat of an endless cycle of escalating retaliation and atrocities loomed over the conduct of the war. Appeals to the logic of retaliation gave sanction to otherwise unjustifiable methods of war and treatment of civilians.

But the logic of retaliation also constrained the violence of the war. We cannot easily know how often combatants refrained from acts that they judged to be excessively provocative or that offended their consciences. But there were instances in which officials and soldiers reflected on the likely consequences of retaliation and elected to forego it. Governor Vance of North Carolina, for instance, grew increasingly troubled by reports of the conditions at the Confederate prison in Salisbury. "Accounts reach me of the most distressing character in regard to [the prisoners'] suffering and destitution," he wrote. More than just humanitarian sentiment aroused his concern. He cautioned that such conditions, if unaddressed, "would lay us open to a severe retaliation."[96] Similarly, the logic of retaliation did not provide comfort to the troubled consciences of some combatants. A twenty-three-year-old Wisconsin schoolteacher who had participated in Sherman's March to the Sea confessed in a letter: "The cruelties practiced on this campaign towards citizens have been enough to blast a more sacred cause than ours. We hardly deserve success."[97] Even some civilians caught in the maelstrom of guerrilla warfare recoiled from the cycle of atrocities that the logic of retaliation fueled. A Missouri letter writer in the *St. Joseph Morning Herald* warned his Unionist neighbors against succumbing to the allure of vengeance. "If we fight with cannibals, we don't eat our prisoners; if with Indians we don't burn and otherwise torture them to death. Why then because we are fighting these half-civilized pro-slavery rebels should we do as they do?"[98]

Despite the magnitude of the trauma they had endured, Americans after the Civil War did not reflexively shy away from pondering the scale and intensity of the war they had waged. Having experienced bloodshed on an unprecedented scale, they set about describing, quantifying, and justifying it. Making sense of the Civil War was one of the enduring cultural strivings of late nineteenth-century Americans. While reflecting on the recent war, they could not easily avoid weighing the import of wartime atrocities. Had the barbarous lapses been the inevitable by-product of the prewar culture of the Yankee North and slaveholding South? Were they worrisome divergences from the forward march of American civilization? Or could wartime atrocities be rationalized and excused in a manner that allowed Americans to avoid acknowledging their capacity to transgress the principles of civilization that justified their nation's very existence? As Herman Melville pleaded in his *Battle-Pieces* shortly after the end of the war, "Let us pray that the terrible historic tragedy of our time may not be enacted without instructing our whole beloved country through pity and terror."[99]

Wartime loyalties and the logic of retaliation, however, foreclosed consideration of the deepest, most universal implications of the conduct of the war for most of the war generation. Late nineteenth-century Americans forthrightly argued over the breaches of the norms of civilized war, but their conclusions as a rule conformed to a Manichaean view of the war that assigned base motives and inexcusable transgressions to the enemy while ascribing unassailable virtue to their own side.

Apologists for each side insisted that they and their compatriots had upheld the laws of civilized war despite countless provocations that would have justified harsh responses. The enemy, in contrast, had exposed the illegitimacy of their cause by committing torture and other indefensible atrocities. And in those rare instances when apologists conceded severe measures by their side, they invoked the logic of retaliation to justify their conduct and affirm the purity of their motivations.

Of all the war's participants, prisoners of war were some of the most tenacious opponents of any facile reconciliation with their former enemies. They were tireless in assigning blame and tallying war crimes; after all, they had witnessed unbridled evil and consequently had unique insight into the moral depravity of the enemy. And because many prisoners of war refused to disavow their charges against their former enemies, their memories of the war remained a jarring riposte to those who appealed for sectional reconciliation in the decades after the war.

Neither could the memory of the guerrilla war and the efforts to hound dissidents be easily reconciled with the goal of national unity. In North Carolina, a state that had been riven by opposition to the war and desertion from the Confederate army, Thomas Settle and his Republican supporters labored to keep alive the memory of the "barbarity and savageness" of the campaigns to suppress Unionism and desertion during the war. During state elections in 1872, Settle, who himself was a North Carolinian who had served (briefly) in the Confederate military, reminded audiences about the rounding up of Unionists in "bull pens," the torture of Unionist Bill Owen's wife, and the brutality of the Home Guard in general. He linked the violence that was condoned by Confederate authorities during the war to the postwar terrorism carried out by former Confederates who directed the Democratic Party in the state.

Four years later, while campaigning for the governorship against Zebulon Vance, the former Confederate general and wartime governor of the state, Settle sharpened his attacks, targeting Vance's role in the wartime atrocities in the state. Settle's effort to align the memory of wartime violence with the Republican Party was undeniably partisan, but it was also a compelling challenge to the emerging Confederate commemoration. Vance responded to Settle's charges by distancing himself from the wartime atrocities but simultaneously vigorously championing the Confederate cause. His supporters attacked Settle as a demagogue who continued to pick at "the scabs of old sores of the Confederate war" and who refused to leave behind "the smoke and ruin of dark, devastating war." Settle's campaign garnered almost 47 percent of the vote in 1876 and did especially well in areas where opposition to the war had been strongest. But his electoral defeat also demonstrated the limits of his message, including his account of the war. In subsequent years, Vance, his allies, and their counterparts across the South would assert a stronger and stronger grip over the public commemoration of the war.[100]

Champions of national reconciliation worked to marginalize the memory of wartime retaliation and the atrocities associated with it. Just as they downplayed the importance of slavery and emancipation as a cause and consequence of the war, so too advocates of reconciliation dismissed their contemporaries who continued to stir up wartime animosities as retrograde sectionalists, crass demagogues, special pleaders angling for pensions, hucksters given to chronic exaggeration, and aging veterans desperate for recognition. Proponents of reconciliation simultaneously urged Northerners to curb their self-righteousness and Southerners to temper their acute sensitivity. Even some former prisoners of war were apparently swept up by the growing enthusiasm for sectional rapprochement. T. H. Mann, who published an account of his experiences in Andersonville in *Century Magazine*, perhaps the foremost organ of reconciliation, confessed that he had toned down his account, "leaving out much of its bitterness and nearly all of the explosive adjectives."[101] Clearly, there was no place in the project of reconciliation for assigning blame or even lingering on the horrors of guerrilla warfare, prison camps, or abuse of civilians. Indeed, because the sectional memories of the brutality of the war were irreconcilable, they could not be easily incorporated into an emerging view of the war as a tragic yet heroic struggle fought by courageous and principled soldiers.

With the inevitable passing of veterans, particularly prisoners of war, and as the war receded further into the past, custody of the memory of the Civil War passed from veterans to historians. After the dawn of the twentieth century, historians played an oversized, arguably even crucial, role in revising the memory of the war, especially the war's atrocities. Their devotion to objectivity, insistence on the supremacy of certain forms of historical evidence, and deep suspicion of the trustworthiness of "witness" accounts justified, in their eyes, the dismissal of many of the darkest chapters of the war. Like the postwar proponents of reconciliation, historians were predisposed to dismiss the accounts of prisoners of war, veterans, and wartime civilians as biased, lurid, and unreliable. Claims that the horrors of the prison camps were the result of clear intent, for example, were dismissed out of hand, and instead the terrible conditions were explained as the tragic consequence of the naïveté of military officials and politicians.[102]

The apotheosis of the cleansing of the memory of the Civil War of its brutality, perversely, occurred at Andersonville. In 1970, Congress created Andersonville National Historic Site, which brought together the national cemetery where tens of thousands of dead Union prisoners were buried and a wholly inadequate museum of sorts maintained by the army. Averse to reviving sectional recrimination and committed to honoring the sacrifice and heroism of all American prisoners of war, the National Park Service used the new site to depict "life and death in military prisons throughout the ages of man."[103] During the 1980s the Park Service allied with former prisoners of war from World War II, the Korean War, and the Vietnam War to advocate for the construction of the National POW Museum at Andersonville. When the new museum opened in 1998, it further distracted attention from the atrocities of the Civil War era by situating them in the larger history of prison camps, gulags, and death marches. Andersonville and the Civil War dissolve into the background, overwhelmed by the prodigious record of "man's inhumanity to man" during the modern era.[104]

Apparently unable to reconcile the violence of the conflict with American innocence, Americans instead practiced selective amnesia and consigned wartime torture and atrocities to the silences of the past. Yes, torture, cruelty, and atrocities had occurred, as they did in most wars. But they could be explained away as exceptional and tangential to the main conduct of the struggle, which was waged in a manner that demonstrated the superiority of American civilization. In this telling, the conduct of the war was a testament to the high principles that Americans held in common. The cumulative effect of this pruning of the memory of the war was an affirmation that the Civil War had not defiled American innocence.

FIVE

Imperialist Excesses

CAPTAIN GEORGE W. BRANDLE of the 7th Ohio Volunteers grappled with the challenge that tormented many of his fellow officers serving in the Philippines in 1900. When American troops occupied the Spanish possession after the comically short war with Spain in 1898, they had responsibility not only for imposing order in a society turned topsy-turvy by revolution and war but also for suppressing an insurgency of Filipino nationalists intent on ending three centuries of colonial domination. Brandle and his troops simultaneously had to maintain the peace and wage war in a foreign land among people whose language and customs were alien. Conventional military procedures often seemed ill-suited to the circumstances that he and his men confronted.

In early May reports of the abduction of a Filipina woman in Marikina (or Mariquina) on the outskirts of Manila set off a sequence of events that foreshadowed both the severe tactics Americans would employ against the Filipino insurgency and their justifications for doing so. When word of the kidnapping reached Brandle, he ordered a small unit of soldiers to track down a Filipino witness who purportedly could locate the kidnappers. The man led the soldiers to a house from which someone opened fire, killing the commanding sergeant. The troops returned fire and killed two men in the house. There, the soldiers found the abducted woman. Convinced that the incident had been a planned ambush, the troops arrested their informant as well as an armed man in a neighboring house.[1]

During subsequent interrogations, the Filipino captives refused or were unable to name the culprits responsible for the ambush. Determined to punish someone for the death of his comrade, Brandle resorted to harsher methods of interrogation. Taking elaborate steps to increase the violence of the interrogation, he ordered the prisoners to be hanged by the neck until they talked. He assigned two lieutenants to oversee the procedure and appointed a sergeant to direct the enlisted men who would carry out the hangings. He recruited a hospital steward to ensure that the mock hangings did not pose undue risk to the captives. After the assigned staff had gathered and preparations were complete, the steward placed a rope around each prisoner's neck. Soldiers hoisted them off the ground, dangling each man for fifteen seconds or less, then lowered the gasping prisoners and questioned them. Although the procedure was repeated multiple times, it failed to extract any credible evidence.

Brandle's methodical interrogation, however, did provoke his trial for "willfully and cruelly" torturing the two prisoners. His court-martial in June 1900 occurred before the use of torture by American forces in the Philippines was widely known in the United States. Eighteen months later, reports of widespread cruelty in the new American possession would ignite an intense debate in the United States about the systematic use of torture as an instrument of American imperialism. In his own defense, Brandle anticipated many of the justifications offered by defenders of the severe methods used by some American occupiers to impose "benevolent assimilation" on the Philippines. Yet, that he was tried for his actions in Marikina and that his commanding officer displayed a pronounced interest in his case underscore the deep unease of some Americans, including soldiers, with their nation's plunge into overseas imperialism.

Brandle offered a forthright and unapologetic defense of his actions. He rejected the charge that he and his troops had engaged in torture. His method of interrogation, he insisted, had not risen to the level of torture. According to the hospital steward who had overseen the prisoners' ordeals and who had tied the nooses, neither man had been in danger of suffocation. After the interrogations, the steward testified, neither man had any evident injuries other than "very slight marks" on their necks. (One of the interrogated men, however, testified that his neck and throat had been sore for a week after his ordeal.)

Brandle reiterated that he had not engaged in torture because his intentions had been justified and legitimate, and so his methods were necessarily justified and legitimate. His motivation had not been to torment or maim the prisoners but to gain information. His goal, furthermore, had been consonant with military necessity and therefore had not violated the rules of war. In sum, because he did not intend to torture his prisoners, he insisted that his actions could not be defined as torture.

To bolster his claim that his methods were neither exceptional nor cruel, Brandle recruited a soldier who previously had been an officer in the Washington, D.C., police force to testify about routine interrogation methods used in the United States. The former policeman described methods, ranging from "sweating" prisoners in sweltering and confined spaces to hanging suspects by the neck, that he and his police colleagues had used to extort evidence and confessions from suspects. (Both at the time and for decades to come, the police in the nation's capital were notorious for the violence of their interrogations.) Brandle contended that if such methods were commonplace and tacitly condoned in the United States, then they surely were no less appropriate in the American-occupied Philippines.

Brandle's final line of defense was that the victims of his interrogation were not lawful combatants so he had no obligation to extend prisoner-of-war protections to them. Had the Filipinos been in military uniform and had they been captured during a conventional military operation, he conceded that he would have been legally bound to treat them as prisoners of war. But the captives were, Brandle claimed, bandits or insurgents who refused to accept American sovereignty or to comply with the codified rules of war. Because they were unlawful combatants, his treatment of them had not violated of the rules of war.

The prosecution dismissed Brandle's claims as groundless. His victims had not been unlawful combatants. Indeed, they had not even been charged with a crime when he interrogated them. His professed motives for the interrogation were irrelevant. Regardless of whether his intent had been to abuse or interrogate his prisoners, they had been treated in a manner that caused not only "bodily pain" but also the "mental torture" of a reasonable fear for their lives. Moreover, General Order No. 100, the code of military law drafted by Francis Lieber during the Civil War that remained the cornerstone of the American rules of war in 1900, explicitly forbade "torture to extort confessions." This prohibition applied to soldiers, unlawful combatants, and everyone else.

The prosecution's argument failed to impress the court. Whether persuaded by Brandle's defense or swayed by sympathy for a fellow officer, the court acquitted Brandle of all charges. But Major General Arthur MacArthur Jr., the departmental commander for the region that included Brandle's post, refused to let the court's decision stand. His motivation for intervening in the case is unclear. Despite his long military career and keen devotion to the army, he was not a hidebound martinet. While a teenage Union soldier, he had won a Medal of Honor for his heroism at the Battle of Missionary Ridge and then rose rapidly through the ranks. After the war he briefly returned to civilian life and studied law before receiving a commission in the army, in which he served for the remainder of his life. During the three decades when he held various commands in the American West, he advocated reforms to modernize the army and to make it more meritocratic and professional. Perhaps his upbringing as the son of a prominent jurist and his brief flirtation with a legal career instilled in him an uncommon interest in military law. Whatever the cause, he exercised his right to review the Brandle verdict, overturned the acquittal, and remanded the case back to the court.[2]

MacArthur provided a vigorous charge to the court. He skewered the claim that Brandle had not committed torture. Brandle had committed "a most serious offense" because "any corporal punishment, illegally imposed, that causes anguish of body or mind is torture." MacArthur likewise dismissed the argument that the victims of Brandle's violence were unlawful combatants. They had not been caught in any illegal act, and their guilt was not proved. Moreover, nothing in military law authorized officers to torture prisoners to find a pretext on which to prosecute them. And police practices in the United States had no bearing on the conduct of military officers serving on a military mission. The military operated according to its own, and by implication superior, code of conduct and law. MacArthur concluded by lamenting the dangerous implications of the court's acquittal of Brandle. It had been tantamount to "a deliberate declaration by the court that torture of prisoners in military custody is an authorized American practice—a declaration that would be alike repugnant to the civilization of the Republic."[3]

MacArthur's charge to the court compelled it to return a guilty verdict, but the court displayed its continuing sympathy for Brandle by tempering its verdict. It gave him a slap on the wrist by reducing his offense from torture to causing "mental anguish," deleting any reference to his willful or cruel intentions in the verdict, and sentencing him to a reprimand. Apparently stymied by the court's resistance, MacArthur accepted the new verdict but pointedly rejected its overly generous interpretation of Brandle's actions. In a final salvo, MacArthur again condemned Brandle's methods as criminal torture. He placed Brandle's violence in the larger context of the nation's new international standing and imperial ambitions. He warned that methods like those employed by Brandle risked inflicting "permanent injury upon the essential interests of the Nation." If the United States "is to introduce and plant republican institutions" in the Philippines, MacArthur stressed, the army was obligated to "maintain the highest standards of American civilization." It also had to conduct itself in a manner that would retain the "confidence and attachment of the American people." As if to make up for a sentence that he believed to be excessively lenient, MacArthur reminded Brandle that his "reckless defiance of the ethics of his profession" had "cast an unwarranted aspersion upon the reputation of the United States Army for sentiments of honor and humanity."[4]

The Brandle court-martial sparked no controversy and merited only passing mention in the popular press. Contrary to MacArthur's stated intent, his intervention did not inhibit other soldiers from employing torture and severe interrogation methods in the field during the American occupation of the Philippines. Nor did the trial apparently interfere with Brandle's military career. Six months after the court-martial, he accepted a commission as first lieutenant in the U.S. Army. His service in the Philippines, however, did shadow the remainder of his life. Eventually his actions in 1900 resurfaced amid the growing public controversy over the American occupation of the Philippines, and in 1903 he was called to testify in the court-martial of another army officer accused of cruelty toward Filipinos. He also suffered from recurring bouts of acute gastritis that he traced to his service in the Philippines. Two years after finishing his tour in the Philippines, on October 30, 1905, while gripped by acute "melancholia," Brandle laid down on his bed in his quarters at Fort Porter, New York, and shot himself in the head.[5]

The "pacification" methods employed by Brandle and other American soldiers in the Philippines might have passed without much public controversy had opponents of American imperialism not latched onto exposés of torture as the means to illustrate how the nation's global adventurism violated sacred American principles and inexorably eroded liberty. So-called anti-imperialists had been unable to stop the rush to war in 1898, to impede the American annexation of the Philippines, or to sway the Supreme Court to repudiate American expansion into the Pacific and Caribbean. But in 1901 they became convinced that if they could foment sufficient public outcry against the military tactics used in the Philippines, they could pressure President Theodore Roosevelt to curtail or even abandon the nation's new empire. Although short-lived, the controversy challenged long-held assumptions about how American democracy and civilization would exert their beneficent influence over the world and whether the United States was conducting itself according to higher principles than those of other nations.

The ensuing debate over the American occupation of the Philippines, like the Spanish-American War that preceded it, was waged in the name of civilization. The aims of the occupation and the methods employed during it were scrutinized to confirm or expose Americans' fealty to their professed principles. Given the long associations of torture with tyranny and barbarism, the acknowledgment that Americans in the Philippines employed torture compelled turn-of-the-century

Americans, if only briefly, to reflect on shibboleths of American civilization and progress.

General Arthur MacArthur was not alone in noting the irony that American soldiers charged with planting the flag of American democracy in the Pacific engaged in torture and acts of cruelty in a former Spanish colony. Spain and its colonial possessions for several centuries had been associated with tyranny and bloodthirstiness in the American imagination. Among Protestants, the Spanish Inquisition had been a byword for cruelty and ignorance since the Reformation. Many Anglo-American colonists had been quick to believe and amplify sensational accounts of Spanish barbarism against the indigenous peoples of Central and South America. During the early nineteenth century, American commentators regularly condemned the remaining husk of the Spanish Empire for its "horrid tyranny" and its "idleness, ignorance, and inquisition."[6]

Spain's lingering influence in the Caribbean continued to sustain this time-worn critique of Spanish imperialism. From the vantage point of many Americans, the ossified Spanish Empire stifled the potential of Spain's possessions, especially Cuba. Americans were heartened during the 1880s when Cuban insurgents began to loosen Spanish control of the island. As the struggle for Cuban independence intensified, it stirred the American imagination and prompted calls for American intervention there. Cuban nationalists in the United States and their American allies launched an adept campaign to garner support and with each new sensational report of Spanish atrocities against the Cuban population, sympathy for the insurgents mounted.[7]

As late as the winter of 1898, President William McKinley, his closest political allies, and influential capitalists remained wary of any actions that might prolong unrest in Cuba. Some business interests even urged McKinley to work with Spain to restore order there. But after the U.S.S. *Maine*, an American battleship, exploded and sank while anchored in the Havana harbor in February 1898, calls to avenge the ship's destruction overwhelmed McKinley and his closest political allies, and they too succumbed to war fever. On April 11, McKinley asked Congress for authority to send American troops to Cuba for the purpose of ending the civil war there. On April 19, Congress passed joint resolutions supporting Cuban independence and renouncing any plans to annex Cuba. By April 25, Spain and the United States were at war.[8]

When the United States declared war on Spain, it became an active if junior participant in global imperialism. Cuba was the idée fixe in the minds of many Americans who exhorted war, but the Spanish Empire with which the United States now fought stretched from Africa to the South China Sea. The outcome of the war would determine the disposition of many of Spain's most strategic possessions, including Puerto Rico, Cuba, Guam, and the Philippines, at a time when the European powers were consolidating their global empires.

Within a week of the start of the war with Spain, Americans had to contemplate their nation's responsibilities toward the Philippines, which most citizens probably had difficulty locating on a map. On May 1, 1898, an American fleet under the command of Commodore George Dewey swiftly and efficiently destroyed the antiquated Spanish naval force that huddled in the Manila harbor. (Anticipating the outcome of the battle, the Spanish commander had positioned his ships in shallow water with the hope that the crews from sinking ships would be better able to save themselves.) Beleaguered Spanish authorities in the Philippines, who entertained little hope of rescue by overstretched Spanish forces from elsewhere in the empire, were keen to surrender to the Americans rather than suffer defeat and possible retribution at the hands of Filipino nationalists. With the virtual collapse of Spanish authority everywhere in the islands except Manila, the Philippines appeared to be free for the picking. Even while Dewey's flotilla anchored in Manila's harbor, British, French, German, and Japanese warships began crowding the waters. With some cause, American officials assumed that each of these imperial powers intended to snatch the archipelago.[9]

Seemingly an afterthought in the rush to war, the Philippines became the principal laboratory for American imperialism. Yet American ignorance of the islands and their history had profound significance for the American occupation. During the three centuries of Spanish rule that preceded the American victory in Manila Bay, the Philippines had developed into a remarkably diverse but fragmented colony, marked by religious, linguistic, economic, and geographic differences. Within its major cities and towns, some of the Spanish-speaking Filipino elite and middle classes had embraced liberal ideas emanating from nineteenth-century Europe and had agitated for greater autonomy from Spain. Elite Filipinos also were keen to participate in the thriving trans-Pacific trade without the encumbrance of Spanish colonial bureaucracy. Almost contemporaneous with the resistance to Spanish rule in Cuba, Filipino nationalists launched their own revolt against their colonial status. Although Filipino revolutionaries had acceded to a truce and their leaders had gone into exile on the eve of the American war with Spain, Spanish authority in most of the colony was nominal in 1898.[10]

The American victory was so swift and so complete that Dewey and the troops that had accompanied his fleet were unprepared to occupy Manila, let alone its environs. They could do little more than besiege the Spanish forces and await the eventual arrival of reinforcements from California. Two months later, fourteen thousand American troops reached Manila. By then they confronted both exhausted Spanish troops eager to surrender and a revived nationalist insurrection. With Spanish forces hunkered down in Manila, Filipino nationalists under Emilio Aguinaldo's command took control of most of the islands and proclaimed the independence of the Philippines. Thus in August 1898, the United States was at war with an imperial power that had only the appearance of sovereignty over the islands even while American authorities scrupulously avoided recognizing the nationalist movement that actually exercised effective power.[11]

Wars are inherently chaotic, but the Spanish-American War was uncommonly so. The American army was, in most regards, completely unprepared to wage war simultaneously on two fronts on opposite sides of the globe. In 1897 its officer corps totaled roughly two thousand, and its enlisted ranks had twenty-six thousand, numbers wholly inadequate to wage war against the Spanish Empire. Once the war began, the McKinley administration issued a call for volunteers to fight, which prompted a flood of men flush with patriotic fervor who swelled the army by more than 200,000 and overwhelmed its archaic bureaucracy.

Exacerbating the military challenges was the lack of any overarching strategic planning by the McKinley administration. The United States pledged to free Cuba from Spanish tyranny, but otherwise its goals in waging war on Spain were undefined. With the arrival of American occupation forces in the Philippines in August 1898, the McKinley administration had to begin to clarify its plans for the Philippines. The newly arrived Americans had only one clear goal: the defeat of the remaining Spanish forces in the Philippines. Major General Wesley Merritt and the Spanish governor-general agreed that the Spanish surrender would take place after a mock battle, which would be staged to both demonstrate and assuage Spanish military honor. After the sham clash took place on August 13, 1898, Spanish authorities promptly surrendered the city to the Americans, and hostilities with the Spanish ended in the Philippines.

American commanders now had to translate the McKinley administration's murky strategy for the newly occupied former colony into tangible policies. American troops and Filipino nationalists, no less than others, struggled to discern McKinley's plans. American newspapers and magazines were filled with proposals for the disposition of the former Spanish colony, ranging from virtual incorporation into the United States to complete independence. President McKinley himself gave only the vaguest indications as to his plans for the islands. In the eyes of many contemporaries, the McKinley administration suffered from almost paralyzing cautiousness. The president seemingly had no clear plan beyond a general commitment to an assertive foreign policy that would augment the nation's influence in the Pacific. His certainty of the superiority of Americans, on the basis of both their race and their Christian civilization, imposed obligations on the nation that could not be ignored without calling into question the nation's character. He subsequently explained that at first he had opposed the retention of the Philippines but later concluded that there was no viable alternative. To return them to Spain would have been "cowardly and dishonorable," to leave them to "our commercial rivals" would have been "bad business," and to turn them over to Filipinos was unthinkable because they were "unfit for self-government."[12]

American commanders understood that their victory over the Spanish established American authority in name only. The choreographed surrender of Spanish forces had undercut the prospects for fruitful collaboration between Americans and the Filipino revolutionaries, who bitterly resented that American troops had prevented insurgents from entering Manila after the Spanish surrender. The American occupation of Manila and the American refusal to recognize the newly declared Republic of the Philippines was an affront to those Filipinos who hungered for national independence.

Finally, in December 1898, six months after Dewey's victory, the peace treaty between Spain and the United States revealed that the McKinley administration intended to retain the Philippines. In a proclamation to the Filipino people, McKinley pledged that "we come, not as invaders or conquerors, but as friends," while vowing that the intent of the occupying troops would be to win their "confidence, respect, and affection." Eschewing the crass motivations and heavy-handed techniques of other imperialists, Americans, he announced, would pursue a mission of "benevolent assimilation" that would substitute "the mild sway" of American justice and right for the "arbitrary rule" of the Spanish. Senator Knute Nelson of Minnesota concurred on the floor of the Senate, attesting that "we come as ministering angels, not despots." In the minds of McKinley and Nelson, the United States was occupying the Philippines for the good of Filipinos.[13]

If McKinley's proclamation clarified the disposition of the Philippines, it did little to lessen the ambiguity inherent in his pledge to pursue "benevolent assimilation" there. While the slogan "benevolent assimilation" may have eased the anxieties of those Americans who worried that the nation had exploited the war with Spain to become, in the words of Senator George Frisbie Hoar of Massachusetts, "a vulgar, commonplace empire," it offered little clarity as to the methods of the American occupation of the Philippines.[14] Left unaddressed was the boundary between civil and military authority in the archipelago or the role, if any, for Filipinos in the colony's affairs. Did the Constitution apply in the Philippines? If not, what rights did Filipinos have as residents of an American-occupied territory? By early 1899, perhaps the only issue that had been resolved was that the McKinley administration was intent on establishing American sovereignty over the Philippines.

Complicating the American military's vague mission were nonmilitary considerations. For instance, a severe international shortage of Manila hemp, which was essential for the manufacture of ropes, especially ship riggings, influenced American plans almost from the outset.

Intent on restoring hemp production that had been disrupted first by the war with Spain, Secretary of War Elihu Root in 1899 ordered a coordinated campaign by American forces to establish control over hemp-producing regions. This objective compelled overextended American forces to expand their influence into remote areas, such as the southern island of Samar, where tenacious insurgents provoked American troops into employing some of their harshest and most controversial tactics.[15]

As American intentions became clear to Filipino nationalists during spring 1899, they recognized that their quest for autonomy could not be reconciled with American sovereignty. In January 1899, with mounting impatience, Aguinaldo assumed the presidency of the newly christened Republic of the Philippines, even though the United States refused to recognize either the new nation or his office. By then relations between American troops who occupied Manila and nationalist soldiers who ringed the city were volatile. Yet even after fighting between the new republic's army and American soldiers erupted in February, Aguinaldo and the Filipino Revolutionary Congress continued to appeal to American authorities to restore peace by acceding to a modicum of local autonomy. Not until July 1899 did Aguinaldo acknowledge the futility of negotiations and declare war against the United States.

American military superiority was evident even before the formal start of war. Although the Filipino army substantially outnumbered the American forces, American troops had a clear advantage in weaponry, discipline, and organization. The republican army, which relied on captured rifles and munitions for much of its firepower, lacked adequate training in conventional warfare. Consequently, its forces suffered terrible losses whenever they faced American troops in battle. By November 1899 the Americans had routed the nationalist forces in central Luzon, captured the provisional capital of Aguinaldo's fledgling republic, and sent its leader fleeing helter-skelter into the hinterlands. Any lingering prospects for nationalist success evaporated with the arrival of American reinforcements, including battle-hardened veterans from Cuba as well as a thirty-five-thousand-man volunteer force raised specifically for service in the Philippines.

The deteriorating fortunes of the republican army posed an existential threat to the Filipino nationalist movement. In a society frag-

FIGURE 5.1. *How United States Soldiers Were Met by Conquered Natives.* This stereograph depicted grateful and jubilant Filipinos welcoming Americans after the defeat of the Spanish in 1898. Imperialists contended that only a small minority of Filipinos opposed the American occupation, which promised to bring civilization and democracy to the islands. Not until 1902 did anti-imperialists tarnish this romantic image of the United States as a benevolent imperialist.

mented by region, religion, language, and class, the republic's army, in many regards, was the institutional embodiment of Filipino nationalism. Its ranks came closer to mustering a cross section of Filipino society than any other institution in the islands. Equally important, nationalists pointed to the existence of a conventional army, armed, organized, and uniformed along familiar European and American lines, as a compelling demonstration of both their aspiration to self-government and their attainment of a level of civilization necessary to field a disciplined military. But with the republican army decimated by mounting casualties and sagging morale, nationalists had either to concede defeat or to adopt a new strategy to thwart American victory.

Out of necessity, Aguinaldo formally announced the adoption of guerrilla warfare in November 1899. He hoped that a war of attrition would exhaust American will and prompt weary Americans to pressure their leaders to end the occupation of the islands. He and other nationalist leaders recognized that adopting unconventional war tactics was risky. Filipino soldiers who were loath to fight in trenches or with conventional tactics were often more adept at guerrilla fighting, in which their local loyalties superseded broad principles and national goals. But while guerrillas could rally local support and harass American forces, they could also be dangerously independent and disorganized. Guerrilla leaders could, and sometimes did, become regional warlords who operated with little common purpose while adopting tactics that embarrassed the titular leaders of the nationalist movement. By adopting guerrilla tactics, moreover, the nationalists eroded their movement's international standing and provided American imperialists with grounds to denounce them for devolving into uncivilized banditry.[16]

Some practices of the guerrillas gave credence to the imperialists' insistence that only the United States could prevent the Philippines from succumbing to internecine butchery. Where possible, the nationalists infiltrated local institutions sanctioned by the American occupiers and undermined their control. Elsewhere the guerrillas formed secret corps that humiliated, abducted, tortured, and assassinated Filipinos who aided Americans. Lacking the conventional punishments of a formal state, guerrillas adopted stern and swift measures. American officials, who tallied the reports of Filipinos hacked, beaten, and tortured to death, were not mistaken when they concluded that the insurgents intended their ongoing bloodletting to terrorize any Filipinos who acceded to the American occupation. Each tortured or assassinated "amigo," as the collaborators were known, bolstered the American perception of Filipino nationalists as bloodthirsty marauders.[17]

Meanwhile guerrilla tactics inflicted a small, if troublesome, number of casualties on the American occupiers. With rifles and ammunition scarce, guerrillas relied on subterfuge. Frequently they staged ambushes during which they hacked at Americans with their bolos, a machete-like knife. Such attacks, as well as ingenious booby traps, produced horribly mutilated casualties that outraged American sensibilities. Guerrillas typically treated captured Americans humanely, but on occasion insurgents did commit atrocities; accounts of wounded soldiers who had their eyes gouged out and their limbs amputated or who were tortured for hours before being burned alive reinforced claims that Filipinos waged a lawless, immoral rebellion.

Further bolstering the idea that nationalist resistance was abjectly illegitimate was the widely parroted claim by President McKinley and his allies that the majority of Filipinos anticipated American control of the islands "with every hope of their hearts." Taking for granted that the majority of Filipinos welcomed American tutelage, advocates of American sovereignty assailed resistance to it as the handiwork of a small minority of fanatics whose commitment to nihilism and terror offered nothing but suffering to their countrymen. Early in 1900 Secretary of War Root avowed that there was no opposition to American occupation except from "fugitive bands, half guerrilla and half bandit." Only American troops, he warned, could protect the "patient" millions of Filipinos who "had never consented to the nationalist cause." For American imperialists like Root, the guerrilla insurgency was irrefutable confirmation of Filipinos' incapacity for self-rule and the urgent need for American dominion over the archipelago. These seemingly unshakable convictions not only shaped the grand strategy for defeating the nationalist insurgency but also encouraged Americans to adopt their own unconventional tactics to defeat their vexing and shadowy adversary.[18]

As late as fall 1899, General Elwell S. Otis, the second military governor in the Philippines, was optimistic that in short order American largesse would win over Filipinos to American rule. He and other military and civilian officials translated McKinley's "benevolent assimilation" into a program to modernize Filipino society by improving sanitation in cities and towns, building roads, opening schools, extending communications, initiating judicial reforms, and reorganizing civil government under American tutelage. In perhaps half of the Philippines, the tangible benefits of American rule contributed to a restoration of order and grudging acceptance of American hegemony. In these areas, the day-to-day struggles of American troops were with isolation, the tropical environment, and the monotony of military service rather than guerrillas.[19]

Elsewhere, especially in southwestern Luzon, Cebu, Negros, Samar, Leyte, and Panay, Americans battled insurgents who were unyielding despite American munificence. In these areas the obstacles that hindered

American military operations were conspicuous. The occupying force was too small to impose its will on a large and fractious population dispersed across mountainous and jungle covered islands. In 1900 American troops were spread among more than five hundred garrisons, many staffed with a single company of troops. Geography and climate rendered communications between these posts difficult even when insurgents refrained from cutting telegraph lines or attacking convoys. Consequently, field commanders, much like their guerrilla counterparts, often had to operate autonomously.[20]

Further confounding the task before the occupation force was wholesale ignorance of almost every facet of Filipino society and history. So desperate for background on the islands was General MacArthur that he ordered all available English-language books on the Philippines from booksellers in Hong Kong. That he relied on English-language sources underscored the difficulties that American officials had in gathering firsthand knowledge. The profusion of Filipino dialects that were unknown to Americans meant that most exchanges between Americans and Filipinos involved interpreters, with all of the attendant confusion and misunderstanding that translation introduces into any conversation. Struck by the mutual unintelligibility of Americans and Filipinos, a correspondent in Manila in 1902 worried that neither side knew enough of the other's language to exchange ideas "even under the most favorable circumstances." When language barriers were overcome, Americans complained that Filipinos were exceptionally reticent to divulge useful or truthful information. Dredging up stereotypes of inscrutable "Asiatics," American soldiers complained that Filipinos dissembled, telling Americans whatever they wanted to hear. Confronted by allegedly duplicitous Filipinos, American soldiers struggled to determine whether they covertly supported the nationalists or were merely terrorized into silence by them. In either case, American troops were acutely aware that they were, as one officer explained, "a blind giant" stumbling around swatting haphazardly at an invisible enemy.[21]

Desperate for translators and reliable local allies, Americans began exploiting ethnolinguistic divisions within the islands to recruit Filipinos to join the occupation force. Filipino auxiliaries such as the Macabebe Scouts and Philippines Rangers not only had firsthand famil-

iarity with the geography and cultures of the islands but also were
highly motivated by self-interest and long-nurtured grievances against
supporters of Filipino independence. American commanders looked to
these Filipino recruits to secure intelligence and ferret out insurgents
who were hiding among civilians. But while American officers applauded the effectiveness of Filipino auxiliaries, one correspondent
warned of the "awful possibilities for mischief" they presented. Sometimes their "mischief" included widespread looting, cruelty, rape, and
murder. American officials dismissed most of these charges as an unfounded smear while excusing other incidents as the inopportune excesses of a semi-savage people.[22]

The crux of the American dilemma in the Philippines was the impossibility of distinguishing insurgents from compliant and peaceable
civilians. The most adept guerrilla leaders infuriated their American
adversaries by safeguarding their weapons and ammunition while
melding into the local civilian population. As early as the second day
of the hostilities between Americans and Filipino nationalists in
February 1899, American troops groused that the enemy escaped certain
defeat by skulking back to their homes disguised as civilians. General J.
Franklin Bell, who was charged with suppressing an especially aggressive insurgency in Batangas, cautioned his soldiers to presume that all
Filipinos were foes. He asserted that it was virtually impossible to distinguish "the actively bad from the passively so." Neutrality, he pledged,
would not be tolerated. Every Filipino, he demanded, "should either be
an active friend or be classed as an enemy." These precautions were necessary because "with very few exceptions practically the entire population has been hostile to us at heart."[23] Brigadier General Jacob H. Smith
shared similar convictions. He ordered troops who participated in the
campaign against insurgents in Samar to apply a strict measure of
Filipino loyalty. Every "native," he commanded, was to be "regarded
and treated as an enemy until he is conclusively shown to be a friend."
Smith expected "natives" to demonstrate their loyalty by undertaking
"some positive act or acts that actually and positively commit him to
us." Summing up his view, Smith divided the population into two
clearly defined camps: "If not an open friend, he is an active enemy."[24]

When General Otis's program of public works failed to end resistance by 1899, the McKinley administration concluded that sterner

measures were needed. Growing anxiety that the United States might become bogged down in a conflict like the decade-long struggle that France had waged in Algeria prompted calls for a new strategy in the Philippines. Henceforth each newly elevated military commander felt the need to announce that he would fight the guerrillas with greater urgency and severity. General MacArthur, Otis's successor as military governor in late 1900, effectively contradicted the position he had taken during Captain Brandle's court-martial and adopted policies that seemed to condone reprisals against Filipinos who resisted American rule. When General Adna Chaffee succeeded MacArthur in 1901, he announced that he would impose "bayonet rule" in the Philippines and groused about the timid tactics that had been applied previously. He justified his approach on the grounds that "the whole Philippine people are now engaged in making war in a manner not in accordance with the recognized laws of war." Chaffee urged the necessity of a "wholesome fear of these people of the army." Vowing that he did not advocate "inhuman treatment" of any islanders, he nevertheless pledged to wield "stern" and "inflexible" military power. President Roosevelt, who assumed office in 1901 following McKinley's assassination, joined in the escalating rhetoric by ordering Chaffee to adopt "the most stern measures" to punish the island of Samar, where nearly fifty American soldiers had been killed in an especially well-orchestrated massacre. General Bell summarized the prevailing attitude of American officers when he recommended that similar methods be employed throughout the islands. "These people," he testified, "need a thrashing to teach them some good common sense."[25]

The demands for stern measures prompted some officials and military officers to recall previous military campaigns as models for the pacification of the Philippines. Fulfilling the adage that armies often prepare to fight the last war they fought, Brigadier General Samuel B. M. Young warned that the insurgency would persist until the army applied "the remedial measures that proved successful with the Apaches." Just months before Colonel Lyman W. V. Kennon became military governor of the province of Ilocos Norte, he contended that the Filipinos "must be subdued in much the same way" as American Indians had been. In 1901 Secretary of War Root concurred, announcing that the army would adopt the "methods which have proved successful in our Indian campaigns in the West."[26]

The invocations of Western frontier experience had a certain logic. Many army officers had spent the bulk of their careers devoted to the pacification of American Indians west of the Mississippi. They understandably sought to draw on those experiences when they faced off against the insurgents in the Philippines. But Root and like-minded strategists exaggerated the relevance of the military campaigns in the American West for the occupation of the Philippines. Officers who had been stationed in the American West did gain some experience with "unconventional" warfare, but by the late nineteenth century the army had considerable familiarity with the diverse Indian nations within the continental United States. Many soldiers in the West unquestionably harbored racist attitudes toward Indians and displayed marked ignorance of Indian culture, but others had much more than a cursory understanding of Indian societies. American officers nurtured important alliances with some Indians, who served as scouts and were essential to the army's campaigns in the West. Moreover, the various Indian nations were dispersed and vastly outnumbered by white Americans (if not by actual troops). In the Philippines, in contrast, Americans proposed to rule a population of more than eight million Filipinos, about whom they knew virtually nothing, with a small occupation force.[27]

The American Civil War, more than the Indian Wars, informed the methods adopted by American commanders in the Philippines. Indeed, the harsh collective punishments that American forces adopted in areas rife with insurgents were familiar to those officers who were Civil War veterans. The lesson many drew from the campaigns of Generals William T. Sherman and Philip H. Sheridan during the Civil War was the value of waging the harshest war compatible with American objectives. Brigadier General Jacob Smith, a Civil War veteran who bore a scar and carried a Minié ball in his hip from the Battle of Shiloh, parroted Francis Lieber when he invoked the conventional wisdom drawn from the Civil War: "Short severe wars are the most humane in the end." "No civilized war, however civilized," he declared, "can be carried out on a humanitarian basis."[28] Smith's commander, General Chaffee, agreed. He denounced the "false humanitarianism" that impeded the swift suppression of the Filipino insurgency. Such attitudes were echoed in American newspapers like the *Providence Journal*, which defended even the most severe and controversial tactics employed on behalf of American imperialism as "one of the necessities of war."[29] Adding to the impatience with allegedly naive humanitarian restraints on the conduct of war was the festering anger over the inability of American forces to distinguish disguised Filipino guerrillas from civilians. Commanders and rank-and-file soldiers concluded that the most prudent response was to avoid the folly of attempting to do so and instead impose the harshest sanctions swiftly, relentlessly, and widely. For these reasons, by fall 1899 American forces fixated on finding means to compel Filipinos to turn against the insurgents or suffer the full weight of American occupation.[30]

Intent on demonstrating their resolve to crush the insurgency and their willingness to use every means at their disposal, Americans resorted to collective punishments. They engaged in the wholesale destruction of property, including seizing and destroying crops and livestock. In areas that were purported to be insurgent sanctuaries, American forces often reduced everything in their path to ashes. While surveying conditions in the Philippines, General Nelson Miles described a ride through thirty-eight miles of desolate landscape denuded of inhabitants, livestock, or crops. Several regional commanders forcibly herded tens of thousands of Filipinos into fetid and primitive "reconcentration" camps. The depopulated regions were then razed so that they could provide neither protection nor sustenance for guerrillas. Anyone discovered in these wastelands was assumed to be an insurgent and was subject to arrest or worse. The irony that many Americans had denounced similar Spanish camps in Cuba during the 1890s and British camps in South Africa during the Boer War was not lost on opponents of American imperialism. American defenders of the policy countered that the forced migrations were carried out in strict accordance with military law, and they boasted that relocated Filipinos allegedly luxuriated in the amenities of the reconcentration camps.[31]

More sinister was the widespread adoption of a policy of not taking prisoners or of shooting down prisoners when they "attempted to escape." By the fall of 1899 many officers had a tacit understanding with their soldiers that they were not to take insurgent prisoners. Soldiers, in their letters home and to newspapers, displayed no reticence in bragging about the number of captured guerrillas they had executed. Sergeant Howard McFarland of the 43rd Infantry recounted in a hometown newspaper that his company had killed "seventy-five nigger bolomen and ten of the nigger gunners." He and his comrades did not concern themselves with wounded or captured guerrillas: "When we find one who is not dead, we have bayonets." Officers and soldiers alike viewed with suspicion anyone who deviated from this policy. A journalist for the *Boston Transcript* revealed that fellow officers sternly criticized Major Littleton Waller for taking prisoners during his initial command on the island of Samar in 1901. His peers noted with approval that he did not repeat his "mistake" once he became "better acquainted with the conditions in Samar."[32]

Any estimate of the number of Filipino prisoners who were executed is sheer conjecture. In many instances, officers gave explicit orders not to take prisoners, and field reports confirm that the orders were duly followed. More often the policy was unspoken but widely understood. In their boastfulness, some soldiers probably exaggerated the blood on their hands. Nevertheless, with good reason, critics of the American occupation concluded that summary executions, as opposed to battlefield casualties, accounted for a substantial portion of guerrilla casualties.[33]

Of all the "sterner measures" adopted in the war against Filipino insurgents after 1900, the most controversial was the commonplace use of coercive interrogation—torture—by American troops. Reports of the torture of Filipinos surfaced as early as spring 1899, and by 1900 they were sufficiently widespread to attract periodic comment in American newspapers. In some instances, as in the interrogation conducted by Captain Brandle, Filipinos were hanged to elicit information or as a reprisal for alleged guerrilla activities. Others received severe beatings or endured threats of murder by having loaded guns placed against their heads. Many were deprived of sleep, water, and food for extended periods of time. Some insurgent suspects were fed heavily salted foods while being deprived of water; one officer who employed this method crowed that "this diet had excellent results," prompting the men subjected to it to give "more or less information." Others were hanged by their thumbs or forced to stand in stress positions for hours on end. American troops in the Philippines seemingly employed much of the time-honored repertoire of bodily torments.[34]

The most notorious interrogation technique, which became synonymous with the conflict, was the so-called water cure. With origins in the deep recesses of human history, it was a less elaborate version of the mock drowning that had been applied at Eastern State Penitentiary in Philadelphia and in other American prisons during the nineteenth century. Apologists subsequently claimed that the water cure could be traced to the Spanish Inquisition and that American soldiers had learned the technique from Filipino irregulars, especially the Macabebes. But there is little reason to doubt that American ingenuity was sufficient to adapt the water cure familiar in the United States to circumstances in the Philippines.

When testifying before a Senate Committee, Grover Flint, who served in Cuba and then in the Philippines, provided a graphic description of the application of the water cure, which he had witnessed in May 1900:

> A man is thrown down on his back and three or four men sit or stand on his arms and legs and hold him down; and either a gun barrel or a rifle barrel or a carbine barrel or a stick . . . is simply thrust into his jaws and his jaws are thrust back, and, if possible, a wooden log or stone is put under his head or neck, so he can be held more firmly. In the case of very old men I have seen their teeth fall out,—I mean when it was done a little roughly. He is simply held down and then water is poured onto his face down his throat and nose from a jar; and that is kept up until the man gives some sign or becomes unconscious. And, when he becomes unconscious, he is simply rolled aside and he is allowed to come to. In almost every case the men have been a little roughly handled. They were rolled aside rudely, so that water was expelled. A man suffers tremendously, there is no doubt about it. His sufferings must be that of a man who is drowning, but cannot drown.[35]

A contemporary correspondent who witnessed a similar application of the torture recalled grimly that the victim's body was "an object frightful to contemplate."[36] Filipinos subjected to the "cure," one soldier explained, "swell up like toads."[37]

By the time Brandle conducted his interrogation in 1900, the water cure and other tortures were becoming routine among American forces in the Philippines. Military commanders unquestionably were aware

FIGURE 5.2. *Those Pious Yankees Can't Throw Stones at Us Any More.* The 1902 cover of *Life* depicts American soldiers in the Philippines subjecting a Filipino to the "water cure" as a chorus of European imperialists watches. The casual indifference of the supervising officer reflects American complacency about the violence required to export American civilization and democracy. The image mocked Americans for adopting methods of military imperialism that they had previously denounced.

of the widening use of torture and other extreme measures in the field. In June 1900 military governor General MacArthur issued an order explicitly banning torture. Two months later he again banned severe interrogation techniques. But with the sharp escalation of guerrilla attacks in the fall of 1900 and the mounting pressure from Washington, D.C., to put down the insurgency, the substance and tone of the orders from senior officers in Manila changed markedly. On December 20, 1900, MacArthur himself issued a lengthy proclamation that revealed that he and his high command were aligning formal policies so that they more closely conformed to military practices in the field. The principal innovation of MacArthur's edict was his declaration that insurgents and their supporters were guilty of violating the rules of war. Consequently, anyone who actively opposed American forces or supported the insurgency was a common criminal and was subject to "exemplary punishments," ranging from confiscation of property to summary execution. MacArthur made clear that General Order 100 would now be applied not only to the American occupation forces but also to Filipinos.[38]

For months prior to MacArthur's proclamation, soldiers and officers alike had improvised as they battled nationalist guerrillas. Reflecting the murkiness of the McKinley administration's policy toward the Philippines in general, military commanders had wrestled with balancing strenuous pacification of the insurgency with "benevolent assimilation." Some commanders, like Brigadier General James F. Smith on the island of Negros, stipulated that troops under their command were expected to abide by the terms of General Order 100. As interpreted by Smith and a few others, the rules of war imposed clear obligations and significant constraints on American troops. Similarly, MacArthur demonstrated that he expected American occupiers to operate within a strict reading of the general order when he denounced the verdict of Captain Brandle's court-martial.[39]

But just as had been true during the Civil War, the order was open to sharply divergent interpretations, and the longer the insurgency continued, the wider the divergence in its interpretations. As Brandle did during his court-martial, officers familiarized themselves with the order and seized on its ambiguities to give sanction to their actions as occupiers. And, as MacArthur's December 20 proclamation made clear, even a commander, like MacArthur, who was intent on demonstrating the sanctity of military law could invoke General Order 100 while shifting the emphasis from the constraints imposed on the occupiers to the responsibilities borne by the occupied.

Some of the difficulties of applying General Order 100 to the circumstances in the Philippines were spelled out by Major Charles Judson Crane in a plaintive commentary published in 1903. Crane had acquired considerable expertise in military law during a career that stretched from the Civil War through tours of duty in the American West and in Cuba before his three years in the Philippines. But this knowledge could not resolve crucial questions relating to General Order 100. He lamented that the order left unclear how much coercion was compatible with the rules of war. Lieber's Code, as MacArthur pointed out in his rebuke to Brandle, banned torture, but it sanctioned the coercion of "guides" to provide vital information necessary to pursue the enemy. Crane asked, "Where is given to us the definition or limit of the nature and amount of force allowable?" What was the line between coercion and torture? And what information could be elicited by coercion? He also wrung his hands over the question of how widely and aggressively exemplary punishments should be applied to partisans. Given that American forces were "fighting an Asiatic nation in arms and almost every man a soldier in disguise" (and hence a criminal unprotected by the rules of war), the number of Filipinos who were eligible for "exemplary" and "summary" punishment was vast. Commanding officers necessarily had to make choices about which unlawful combatants they would subject to the harshest penalties. But officers looked in vain for "positive instructions" on the subject in General Order 100. As though throwing his hands up in exasperation, Crane asked, "Who was to be the judge, jury, and executioner in such a summary process?" In each instance Crane highlighted the degree to which Lieber's Code provided broad discretion to officers in the application of its provisions.[40]

Some commanders, like General Frederick Funston, displayed no evident trepidation in serving as judge, jury, and even executioner. When Funston and his troops captured two apparent insurgents who were hacking away at Filipino auxiliaries, Funston informed the guerrillas that they would be executed under the authority of General Order

100, and "within ten minutes after the commission of their brutal crime the two had paid the only appropriate penalty." Because of the military exigencies in the Philippines, where far-flung commanders could not be expected to solicit specific guidance from Manila every time they captured an insurgent or needed to interrogate a local resident, Funston and other soldiers in the field wielded the widest possible discretion.[41]

This broad discretion was evident in the articles of General Order 100 devoted to sanctioned retaliation. Articles 27 and 28, with only the vaguest constraints, authorized retaliation and "protective retribution." Retaliation, according to the code, was never to be "a measure of mere revenge." Instead it was to be adopted only "cautiously and unavoidably" and as a means of protective retribution, or in other words, to discourage the enemy from subsequent outrages or violations of the rules of war. So vague were these articles that officers routinely invoked them to justify almost any action against the insurgents. After several soldiers in his district were murdered, Brigadier General Jacob H. Smith raged that "a few killings under General Order 100 will aid very much in making the enemy stop these assassinations."[42] In December 1901, General J. Franklin Bell cataloged all of the breaches of General Order 100 by Filipino insurgents and then stated, explicitly, that henceforth he intended to "severely punish, in the same or lesser degree," these violations of the rules of war. He extended the logic of "protective retribution" as far as to propose violating the same rules of war that he complained his Filipino enemy had transgressed. In this and other situations, officers and soldiers demonstrated that they looked on the order as a set of general principles rather than a coherent or strict code of conduct.[43]

More than practical necessity or ambiguity lay at the root of the loose interpretations of General Order 100 that often prevailed among American troops in the Philippines. The rationale for the American occupation rested on the long-established dichotomy between civilization and barbarism. As presented by imperialists, a moral chasm distinguished Americans, who were agents of the most advanced civilization in history, from Filipinos, who were well-nigh savages. By pitting American civilization against Filipino savagery, American imperialists cast the struggle as both part of the larger march of civilization and as another front in the racial struggle between the superior white race and its racial inferiors. The logic of the McKinley administration's "benevolent assimilation" rendered even peaceful Filipinos as inferior, backward, and incapable of self-government. When General Funston referred to Filipinos as "treacherous savages," he believed he was stating a fact, not spouting invective.[44] Another officer affirmed conventional wisdom among the American occupiers when he described Filipinos as "a cruel and vindictive lot of savages."[45] Testifying before Congress, General Robert Hughes vouched that "these people [Filipinos] are not civilized."[46]

Such attitudes permeated the highest levels of the McKinley and Roosevelt administrations. When General Otis completed his assignment in Manila, President McKinley congratulated him on his "victory over the forces of barbarism in the Philippines." Roosevelt's closest allies, such as Senators Henry Cabot Lodge and Albert Beveridge, harangued Americans about the debased character of the foe in the Philippines. They and other imperial enthusiasts acknowledged no doubts regarding the innate inferiority of Filipinos or their incapacity for self-government. After all, they lacked the centuries of civilizing progress that Americans and western Europeans could claim. As Beveridge explained, "We are dealing with Malays instructed in Spanish methods. They mistake kindness for weakness, forbearance for fear. It could not be otherwise unless you could erase hundreds of years of savagery, other hundreds of years of Orientalism, and still other hundreds of years of Spanish character and custom." Apparently only Americans could be trusted to redeem these benighted people and to impose civilization on them. Beveridge announced, "The Philippines are ours forever. . . . We will not renounce our part in the mission of our race, trustee, under God, of the civilization of the world."[47]

Americans, especially champions of Protestant missionary work in the islands, dismissed Filipino Christianity, which had been practiced since the founding of the British colonies in North America, as ignorant and superstitious idolatry. Even American Catholic prelates embraced the imperial mission with the hope that their influence would displace that of retrograde Spanish Catholic prelates. Simultaneously, the Muslim Filipinos of the southern islands inherited all of the pejorative traits that American Christians assigned to followers of Islam elsewhere in the world. The rhetoric of civilizing imperialism helped resolve the apparent contradiction between long-professed American democratic principles and the newly undertaken imperialist adventure. If the United States was the engine of civilization and progress in the Philippines, Americans need not succumb to undue anxiety that their rule there rested on coercion and was otherwise indistinguishable from Old World imperialism.[48]

The rhetoric of civilization and racial superiority that figured so prominently in the occupation of the Philippines also was wholly consonant with cresting white supremacy in the United States. With cavalier disregard for the complexity of Filipino society, Americans in the Philippines applied familiar American racial categories to the polyglot population of the islands, reducing it to the crude white/black racial binary that white Americans were then cementing firmly in American law and daily life. Within six months of the American occupation of the Philippines, American soldiers already routinely referred to Filipinos as "niggers." The significance of this label was not lost on contemporaries. White soldiers intentionally used the term to demean their foe, whom, according to one correspondent, they viewed as "little better than a dog." To dismiss the Filipino as a "nigger" was, according to one white correspondent in Manila, to assign him "to a class beneath our notice."[49] The use of the epithet to refer to Filipinos suggested that not only were Filipinos to be assigned the same place in the hierarchy of races as Africans and African Americans but also that the methods used to coerce African American subordination to the American racial hierarchy were appropriate for Filipinos. Many of the sizable contingent of African American soldiers who served in the Philippines took understandable offense at the routine use of the crude term to refer to both African American soldiers and Filipinos, including insurgents. An unidentified black soldier railed in a letter to an American newspaper against the insidious conflation of Filipinos and African Americans, complaining of having to listen to white soldiers talk "with impunity of niggers" without ever "thinking that they were talking to home 'niggers.'"[50]

The passions of war further enflamed the rhetoric of American civilization and Filipino barbarism. Advocates of "severe measures," whether in the ranks or on newspaper staffs, cataloged every instance of alleged Filipino cruelty and treachery to illustrate the nature of the enemy that American troops faced. The clear implication of these exercises was that no one could expect the rules of civilized warfare to prevail in a struggle against such a foe. Defenders of the campaign to pacify the islands repeatedly invoked the natural desire for vengeance and the strain of war to mitigate American tactics. Secretary of War Root dismissed any American excesses by insisting that the fact that "soldiers fighting against such an enemy with their own eyes witnessing such deeds [of savagery] should occasionally, regardless of their orders, retaliate by unjustifiable severities is not incredible."[51] Military Governor Chaffee offered a similar, if less florid explanation in a memorandum excusing alleged atrocities by American soldiers: "Sorely impossible to convey in words [the] correct idea [of the] difficulties [that have] been met with by officers in prosecution [of] this war." He conceded that "[their] blood [had] grown hot in their dealings with deceit and lying," and hence they had resorted to "severity [in] some few occasions."[52] According to Senator Henry Cabot Lodge, harsh measures that Americans would recoil from using against a civilized opponent were necessary in the Philippines. That Americans retaliated was the inevitable consequence "of the war that was waged by the Filipino themselves, a semicivilized people with all of the tendencies and characteristics of Asiatics, with the Asiatic indifference to life, with the Asiatic treachery and the Asiatic cruelty, all tinctured and increased by three hundred years of subjection to Spain."[53]

When viewed in the context of strident rhetoric regarding the urgency of pacifying the islands, of ambiguous interpretations of the existing rules of war, of pervasive racism, and of the inherent challenges of waging guerrilla warfare in a foreign environment, the torture and other atrocities carried out by Brandle and other American troops can be properly understood. Captain Brandle's application of "stern measures" when interrogating his Filipino captives in 1900 was the consequence of more than a personal character flaw or a single order. Rather, it was a consequence of a concatenation of attitudes, decisions, and circumstances. The excesses of the American occupiers like Brandle were the actions not of wayward troops but of soldiers who sometimes followed explicit orders and other times used their discretion to try to satisfy their understanding of an ill-defined mission.

Based on the rhetoric emanating from the highest levels of the American government, soldiers and citizens could be excused for assuming that almost any "severity" could be justified in the jungles of the Philippines. Certainly respect for the adversary provided few if any constraints on American behavior. President Roosevelt himself said, "I have taken care that the army should understand that I thoroughly believe in severe measures when necessary and am not in the least sensitive about killing any number of men if there is adequate reason." This and similar statements left the impression that all constraints on American violence were contingent. When reports of the summary execution of Filipino captives finally provoked a full-blown controversy in 1902, correspondent Jos Ohl, writing in the *Atlanta Constitution*, traced the line of complicity for the atrocities from the commanding officers through military governor General Chaffee to Secretary of War Root and finally to President Roosevelt. The controversial murder of the prisoners, he concluded, "can be legitimately attributed to the methods of campaigning which had the fullest and hardiest approval of the present administration."[54]

By the spring of 1902 Herbert Welsh of Philadelphia probably knew as much as any American about the use of torture by American soldiers in the Philippines. His research informed his single-minded campaign against the nation's imperialist project. He was not the most famous critic of the McKinley and Roosevelt administrations' policies, but he made the use of torture by American troops a focal point in the debate over the legitimacy of American imperialism. He gained his grim expertise by scouring newspapers and public records and by tracking down former soldiers who could provide firsthand accounts of atrocities. His abiding belief in Christian civilization and American democracy, while in some regards consonant with those of contemporary imperialists, defined and sustained his opposition to American policy in the Philippines. His jeremiads against American atrocities there are a reminder that paeans to civilization and American exceptionalism were marshaled to assail no less than to excuse torture in the name of empire.

Born in 1851 to a family of wealth and influence in Philadelphia, Welsh grew up in a milieu in which religiously inspired philanthropy and reform activism were so commonplace as to be taken for granted. His father and grandfather had been successful merchants, and his brother eventually became one of the richest men in the city. After graduating from an exclusive preparatory school, Welsh attended the University of Pennsylvania. Instead of following family tradition and entering business, he traveled in 1873 to Paris, where he studied painting. When he returned to his hometown a year later, he devoted himself to art and church affairs. Not until 1882 did Welsh discover the cause that consumed much of his energy for the next two decades: the plight of American Indians. During a trip to the Dakota Territory to visit Episcopal missions, he absorbed the prevailing white wisdom about the most humane measures to uplift Indians. Members of his family had previously taken an interest in American Indians, but Welsh embraced the cause fully, and six months after his return from the West he took the lead in organizing the Indian Rights Association. Within three years it employed a lobbyist in Washington, D.C., had a permanent office in Philadelphia, boasted a network of benefactors across the Northeast, and arguably was the most influential philanthropic organization devoted to Native Americans.[55]

The association's mission, at first glance, might have served as a blueprint for the McKinley administration's "benevolent assimilation" policies in the Philippines fifteen years later. Welsh advocated the complete assimilation of Indians into American society by means of Christian education, preferably at boarding schools, that would tutor Indians in modern civilization. Welsh's paternalism, however, was leavened by a sincere respect for Indians that was markedly different from the McKinley administration's attitude toward Filipinos. He was certain that Indians, as much as whites, possessed "the best and deepest instincts of human hearts" and that they deserved a place within American society. But until they were assimilated, they needed protection from rapacious and malevolent whites, and wise and principled federal oversight of Indian affairs was crucial. Whereas imperialists at the turn of the twentieth century looked to the conquest of western Indians for a precedent for the occupation of the Philippines, Welsh saw in that same history a tragic record of American cupidity and moral failure that he hoped would never be repeated. For him, whites were agents of violence and destruction as often as civilization.[56]

By 1898 Welsh's activism extended far beyond Indian affairs. Dismayed alike by venal Indian agents and corrupt officials in Pennsylvania, he became a prominent advocate of "clean government" during the late 1880s. Among his allies in this crusade was Theodore Roosevelt, then a high-spirited young reformer appointed to the Civil Service Commission by President Benjamin Harrison. In 1895 Welsh launched *City and State,* a Philadelphia weekly devoted to civic reform that later circulated his anti-imperialist exposés. He simultaneously took up international humanitarianism by championing the cause of Armenian victims of Turkish atrocities and the promotion of international arbitration. When the United States started the war with Spain, Welsh viewed the conflict as an unprecedented and tragic folly that impinged on many of the causes he had championed for years.

The anti-imperialist campaign to which Welsh devoted himself appeared to be, and sometimes was, disjointed. Anti-imperialists never nurtured a broad grassroots movement. Instead, while Welsh and some opponents of American expansion joined together in the American Anti-imperialist League, others remained unaffiliated and used their pens, lecterns, or pulpits to voice personal protests. For Welsh and anti-imperialists of his ilk who were active in overlapping reform communities, it was second nature to direct their appeals against the policies of the McKinley and Roosevelt administrations to elites and right-thinking shapers of opinion like themselves.[57]

Although the leadership of the anti-imperialist movement was drawn from a narrow stratum of American society, it nevertheless rallied men with widely disparate motivations. Some anti-imperialists, like Carl Schurz, had been active in the abolitionist movement a half century earlier; they viewed the campaigns against slavery and imperialism as essential and complementary struggles to defend and extend democracy. They were joined by a who's who of American letters, including Mark Twain and William Dean Howells. Disdainful of what they perceived as the crass braggadocio and avarice of American imperialists, the anti-imperialist intelligentsia saw in foreign adventurism a sordid travesty of American values. Altogether different concerns motivated the anti-imperialism of southern Democrats, such as Senators Benjamin Tillman of South Carolina and Augustus Bacon of Georgia, whose opposition to the annexation of unassimilable foreign peoples was consonant with their full-throated advocacy of white supremacy in the American South. A few Republicans who did not share the imperialist enthusiasm of their party, most notably Senator George Hoar of Massachusetts, protested that imperialism contravened cardinal principles of American democracy and would draw the republic into dishonorable foreign entanglements. Finally, the anti-imperialist cause recruited newspaper editors ranging from Democratic partisans intent on tarnishing the Republican Party to reform editors who saw in the Philippines glaring evidence of the accelerating erosion of American principles.[58]

This disparate collection of turn-of-the-century critics of American imperialism has not fared well in chronicles of the era. Their cause suffers the disdain often attached to seemingly failed movements in American history. Imperialists dismissed them as naive busybodies at best, and traitors at worst. Their innate elitism made some of them easy targets. Welsh himself was mocked as a "one of those fussy, self-opinionated men" and as an effete patrician who carried a silk umbrella and "lived off his dead father's hard earnings."[59] Subsequent historians described them as backward-looking ideologues, dysfunctional nonconformists, and racist hypocrites whose proclamations of principled anti-imperialism masked narrow partisan maneuvering. Yet some, like Welsh, were resolute and prescient critics of the nation's lurch into imperialism. To them should go the credit for exposing the extent of torture and atrocities in the Philippines and the facile predictions, unacknowledged half-truths, and muddled assumptions that informed American imperialism. The anti-imperialists saw themselves as the nation's conscience—in this instance, justifiably.

Anti-imperialists repeatedly had to change strategy as they tried to outflank the McKinley and Roosevelt administrations. As war fever mounted before the declaration of war, anti-imperialists' first goal was to ensure that the McKinley administration did not use the war to expand the nation's boundaries. Anti-imperialists succeeded in attaching a joint resolution, sponsored by Senator Henry Teller of Colorado, to congressional approval of McKinley's declaration of war. On the basis of this pledge, anti-imperialists were hopeful that the conflict would not be a pretext for "greedy ambition, conquest, and self-aggrandizement."[60] But the Teller amendment contained no provision to prevent the

annexation of other Spanish possessions, and the McKinley administration's murky policies toward the Philippines soon provoked concern.
Within three months of Dewey's triumph in Manila Bay, Welsh
warned that retaining the Philippines would violate "our fundamental
principles," require "a great naval and military establishment," and
transform the United States into "a national highwayman."[61]

After the McKinley administration rejected these appeals and
launched its campaign against Filipino nationalists, Welsh shifted to
warning of the unacknowledged challenges American occupiers would
face. In February 1899, Welsh accurately foretold the course of the war
when he asked, "How will it be when the rainy season, the impassable
jungle and the fever become their allies and when they adopt guerilla
tactics wholly?"[62] Anti-imperialists anticipated that mounting casualties in the Philippines eventually would spark opposition at home
and pressure the administration to change course. In the meantime
they sought to turn the presidential election of 1900 into a referendum
on American imperialism. Welsh declared early in the campaign,
"Imperialism is the greatest public question which has arisen in the
United States since the questions of slavery and secession were settled."[63] But Democratic presidential candidate William Jennings
Bryan proved to be neither a steadfast nor trenchant critic of the occupation of the Philippines. Instead of an elevated contest over imperialism, the election descended into crude caricature, and the rancor
over the status of the Philippines had only a small role in its outcome. The Republicans' resounding victory emboldened imperialists
while chastening anti-imperialists, who searched anew for a way to
slow imperialist momentum.

Welsh and the anti-imperialist ranks looked to the Supreme Court,
which they hoped would rule against the extension of American sovereignty over the Philippines and Puerto Rico. But in 1901 the Court sanctioned the nation's new colonial possessions where subject populations
were denied the rights guaranteed by the Constitution. Rebuffed by
both the McKinley administration and the Supreme Court, anti-
imperialists yet again pivoted. But with the assassination of McKinley
in September 1901, they now confronted President Roosevelt, who
was one of the most ardent and resourceful advocates of American
imperialism.[64]

Anti-imperialists recognized that they had to fire up public indignation to pressure the new president to change course. After December 1901 Welsh became single-minded about exposing the atrocities that he believed were inherent to American tactics in the Philippines. This focus was more than a desperate attempt to broadcast sensational falsehoods, as imperialists contended. Instead it was the culmination of criticisms and concerns that he had voiced for at least a year, and by 1901 he had sufficient evidence to weave it into a blistering critique of the occupation of the islands. As Welsh explained, "The tortures and cruelties which have been rife under our flag in the Philippines follow logically from the false policy we have pursued there."[65]

For Welsh the application of torture by American occupiers was the bellwether of American imperialism because torture was indelibly associated with tyranny. In an age when empires and militarism were ascendant across the globe, the United States had stood almost alone as a popular democracy. The sudden embrace of imperialism besmirched the nation's mission as the exemplar of liberty in a world of despots and empires. Welsh affirmed that the glory of American democracy was, as the Declaration of Independence had established, that it rested on the consent of the people. He reminded his contemporaries that Abraham Lincoln had distilled this transcendent principle into the pithy phrase "government of the people, for the people, and by the people." On occasion Welsh harrumphed about some of the nation's electorate who were feckless and ignorant, but he never equivocated about the right of every citizen to participate in the nation's public business. This conviction led him to advocate for women's suffrage, defend African American voting rights, and oppose the restrictions imposed on Asian immigrants. Especially offensive to Welsh was the explicit repudiation by imperialists of the universal truth of the nation's founding principles and their relevance for Filipinos and other subjects of the nation's new overseas empire.

Not only did American imperialists profane timeless principles, but they did so while professing patently false motives. Their hypocrisy, anti-imperialists fumed, was boundless. How, asked Welsh, was it that they intended to bring democracy to the Philippines at the point of a bayonet? How was it that American authorities suppressed polygamy in Utah even while they recognized it in the Philippines, or that the republic that had fought a bloody civil war to destroy slavery now recognized it, by treaty, on the island of Sulu in the Philippines?[66] Especially insincere were the efforts of imperialists to draw distinctions between the cruel methods of the Spanish and the "benevolent assimilation" employed by Americans. After all, Roosevelt himself had campaigned for the vice presidency in 1900 by boasting that the United States had liberated Spanish colonies that had been "writhing in hideous agony under a worse than medieval despotism." Such gall prompted Welsh to muse that "injustice and cruelty when practiced by us wear a different face from that which we see in them when used by another; they are no longer plain injustice and plain cruelty but only rather harsh means to a very necessary end."[67] Rather than allow Filipinos to develop their own democracy, American officials instead were intent on transforming Filipinos into an oppressed racial underclass deprived of their innate rights. Only by means of violence and intimidation could the United States stifle, if only incompletely and temporarily, the long-thwarted democratic aspirations of the Filipino people. Welsh foresaw the perpetual colonial status of Filipinos as comparable to the reprehensible dispossession and oppression of American Indians.[68]

Atrocities in the Philippines, Welsh proclaimed, were the most glaring manifestation of the crisis brought on by American imperialism. But the consequences of imperialism for American domestic institutions were also dire. Whichever direction Welsh looked after 1898 he saw unmistakable evidence of American democracy imperiled. He was certain that, unless Americans were vigilant, "the machinery of war will grind on pitilessly."[69] As early as November 1898 he pointed to the imperialists' pining for an enlarged army and military budget as a dangerous reversal of the nation's traditional hostility to a large standing army.[70] He was unswayed by imperialists who pointed to the disorganization and inefficiency of the volunteer army that fought in Cuba as evidence of the need for an expanded and professional army. Nor was Welsh persuaded by the imperialists' insistence that military expansion was needed to protect the nation's interests in Asia and the Caribbean. Had the nation not undertaken imperial adventures, he countered, it would be at peace and would not need an enlarged army, with its extravagant costs, to terrorize Filipinos into sullen resignation.

With the advent of an expanded military, Welsh warned that military leaders and politicians would pursue their respective narrow interests while ignoring the nation's needs. Although Welsh respected some officers he had met in the American West, he also had intimate knowledge of the networks of corruption forged by military officers, Indian agents, and local politicians in the region. After denouncing the corruption that racked the nation's policies towards Indians, Welsh in September 1898 predicted, "Now we shall transport the system to the tropics."[71] The rapid elevation through the ranks of military officers who were favorites of Roosevelt and other influential imperialists appalled Welsh, who viewed it as confirmation of invidious favoritism within the military ranks comparable to the venal patronage that cursed his home state of Pennsylvania and the nation in general. "Clean government," he rued, was a lofty and still unfulfilled goal in the United States even where public affairs were subject to the scrutiny of a free press. In the nation's new far-flung colonial possessions, where the military operated with only minimal public scrutiny and without local consent, widespread graft and corruption were certain to flourish. By 1900 he could point to revelations of corruption in the provisioning of troops in both Cuba and the Philippines as confirmation of his warnings. Equally alarming was the widespread and seldom punished looting of Filipino property by American troops, whose penchant for pillage, which was apparent as early as April 1899, contradicted the McKinley administration's promise of the humanitarian intentions of the American occupiers.[72]

An especially menacing erosion of democracy was the heavy-handed censorship imposed by both military and civil authorities on news about the Philippines. To Welsh, a commitment to free press and free speech was a prerequisite for an informed and engaged citizenry. He upheld both principles in his own newspaper, in which he published verbatim all letters to the editor, including scathing denunciations of his positions. In the Philippines, military authorities aggressively censored any news that contradicted the appearance of imminent American success, while government leaders in Washington, D.C., were equally intent on presenting the occupation as a crowning example of

American generosity. Military and administration officials, Welsh protested, colluded to "stretch the mantle of secrecy over our acts."[73] After American correspondents unsuccessfully protested against this censorship, Welsh repeatedly compared it with the much reviled suppression of information in czarist Russia.[74] Invoking the notoriously autocratic Ottoman Turks, Welsh took to referring to the Philippines as "Turkish America, where free speech does not exist but where slavery and torture do."[75] Welsh's disgust mounted when American officials responsible for establishing American civil authority in the Philippines, led by future president William Howard Taft, imposed a sweeping definition of treason and sedition that rendered almost any criticism of American authority as grounds for prosecution. "Resistance to arbitrary rule imposed on a people from without," Welsh railed, was "not a crime."[76]

The challenge that confronted Welsh and other anti-imperialists was "how to bring the facts" before a public that had been misled by "suppressed truth, distorted truth, and by the natural unwillingness of honorable minds" to believe ill of elected leaders.[77] Gradually anecdotal accounts of executions of unarmed prisoners, the use of the water cure, and the indiscriminate destruction of villages surfaced in letters from soldiers to their families and hometown newspapers. Within three months of the outbreak of the "insurrection" in 1899, Welsh used the columns of *City and State* to appeal to the War Department to investigate rumors of the summary execution of prisoners.[78] By 1900 a few commentators with firsthand knowledge of the Philippines, such as the explorer and journalist George Kennan, confirmed the "implacable resentment" that American methods had aroused among Filipinos. Kennan in particular contrasted the occupiers' "many verbal assurances of benevolent intentions" with the execution of "unresisting wounded," the use of "Spanish inquisitorial methods" such as the water cure, and the indiscriminate mass incarcerations of Filipinos.[79] As the rhetoric of American officers in the Philippines grew strident and news reports on American tactics became less circumspect during late 1900, Welsh's fears seemed confirmed. A Manila correspondent for the *Philadelphia Ledger* gave American readers a revealing glimpse of the war that Americans were waging in the Philippines. "The present war is no bloodless, fake, opéra bouffe engagement," he observed. American soldiers "have killed to exterminate men, women and

children"; they "have pumped saltwater into men 'to make them talk'";
and they have taken prisoners, "without an atom of evidence" that they
were insurgents, and "shot them down one by one."[80] Alarmed by this
report and hearsay of widespread use of the water cure, Welsh repeatedly urged the McKinley administration to stop prevaricating and investigate the accusations.

By December 1901 Welsh and other leading anti-imperialists concluded that the only way to circumvent the censorship and arouse
opposition to the conduct of the war was to petition the Senate to conduct an investigation. In a personal letter to his erstwhile friend
President Roosevelt, Welsh laid out the evidence of torture in the Philippines and urged him to probe the allegations. Anti-imperialists anticipated that an investigation, whether conducted at the behest of the
president or the Senate, would shift the debate from the general
principle of imperialism to the practice of imperialism in the Philippines. Imperialists heretofore had managed to portray the occupation
as a humanitarian undertaking consonant with American values. A
public investigation would compel imperialists to justify the use of reconcentration camps like those that had been denounced in Cuba, torture that evoked the Spanish Inquisition, and the extraordinary disparity between American and Philippine casualties (which suggested
to anti-imperialists an unacknowledged policy of executing wounded
insurgents). A Senate investigation, moreover, would restore a measure
of public oversight to military and administration policies that hitherto had been shielded from scrutiny.

In January 1902 Senator George Hoar introduced a resolution to establish a special congressional investigating committee. He had long
rankled his imperialist colleagues by scolding them, but otherwise had
remained a loyal Republican partisan. His support for an investigation
now risked exposing the Roosevelt administration to partisan attacks
in Congress and withering editorials in the press. Fellow Massachusetts senator and zealous imperialist Henry Cabot Lodge blocked the
resolution until Hoar agreed that any investigation would be conducted
by the standing Philippines Committee, which Lodge chaired. Hoar ac-
quiesced, naively assuming that the bipartisan membership of Lodge's
committee would ensure a full vetting of the evidence.[81]

Welsh, however, fretted that the investigation was a Pyrrhic victory
because Lodge was certain to use his powers as chairman to subvert

the inquiry. Most Republican members of Lodge's committee, Welsh anticipated, would not risk crossing the chairman. Besides, as Senator Charles Dietrich of Nebraska brazenly admitted to a correspondent, "Things might get out if the doors [on abuses in the Philippines] were thrown open that we don't want to reach the public."[82] Lodge was, Welsh regretted, a master of tactics of "obstruction" and "suppression." The senator, for example, limited the number of reporters who could attend his committee's hearings to representatives of the three major wire services. He claimed that the presence of additional journalists was redundant, but anti-imperialists pointed out that the wire services were openly sympathetic to the administration and were likely to downplay any damaging testimony. Lodge also limited witnesses who could testify, refused to hold hearings in the Philippines where many important potential witnesses were located, and discouraged testimony from Filipinos. During committee sessions, he allowed witnesses favorable to government policies to talk at length without interruption whereas those whose testimony bolstered anti-imperialist claims had to parry frequent interruptions from Lodge and other Republican loyalists.

Anticipating Lodge's obstructionism, Welsh worked tirelessly throughout 1902 and 1903 to bring evidence of torture and cruelty in the Philippines before Lodge's committee. Although allegations of atrocities had circulated since 1900, they seldom included details essential to establish culpability. Imperialists summarily dismissed such accusations as sensational exaggerations from disgruntled publicity seekers. Aided by his business partner, a Philippine army veteran, and another anti-imperialist activist, Welsh sought out veterans of good reputation who had firsthand knowledge of atrocities. Then he and his team interviewed them and shared their sworn affidavits with the Senate committee. Welsh simultaneously filled the columns of his newspaper with the accumulating evidence.[83] Welsh's prodigious research provided the bulk of *Secretary Root's Record: "Marked Severities" in Philippine Warfare*, a compilation of harrowing first-person accounts of atrocities by American soldiers that the Anti-imperialist League published to compel the Lodge Committee and the Roosevelt administration to investigate the conduct of the American occupation.

Just as abolitionists had used accounts of the torture of slaves to revise popular ideas about African American humanity, so too Welsh sought to change the popular perception of Filipinos. Beyond compiling details of specific atrocities, he depicted Filipinos as victims with whom Americans could sympathize. In a manner similar to Ida Wells-Barnett's contemporaneous rebuttal of the justifications that whites offered for lynching in the American South, Welsh inverted the conventional American understandings of the civilized and the savage. Whereas imperialists presented the struggle as pitting philanthropic American agents of modern civilization against treacherous savages, Welsh recounted a war in which vengeful Americans preyed on innocent peasants, vulnerable women, and defenseless priests. He simultaneously portrayed Filipinos as modern-day counterparts to America's founders, possessed of an innate desire for self-government and a praiseworthy contempt for foreign occupation of their lands.

Had Lodge been able to control the testimony of witnesses before his committee as completely as he intended, the anti-imperialists would have been stymied. But even administration witnesses like Governor-General William Howard Taft stumbled in their efforts to dismiss the anti-imperialists' charges. While trying to brush aside allegations regarding the water cure, for instance, Taft conceded that the practice was used in the Philippines and that he was aware of its use. Recognizing the damage done by his admission, Taft downplayed the severity of the procedure. But his testimony, as the highest American civil authority in the archipelago, flatly contradicted imperialists' repeated assertions that allegations of torture were a malicious lie.[84]

Even more damaging was the testimony of several former soldiers, especially Sergeant Charles S. Riley, a veteran Welsh had brought to the attention of the Democrats on Lodge's committee. Riley had served as first sergeant in the 26th U.S. Volunteer Infantry in the Philippines from 1899 to 1901. While stationed in the town of Igbaras on Panay, he had witnessed the techniques applied to coax information from suspected insurgents. In November 1900, Major Edwin F. Glenn, who conducted intelligence operations in the district, and a contingent of scouts on "water detail" had subjected the town's mayor to the water cure twice, once on a public street. Subsequently, Glenn had ordered the town, with its hundreds of dwellings, razed. Troubled by what he had witnessed, Riley wrote home a detailed letter, which was later published in a local newspaper. Welsh and other anti-imperialists had seized on the letter as confirmation of their accusations, but Secretary of War Root, after a purportedly thorough investigation, had dismissed Riley's charges as grossly exaggerated. Riley, however, proved to be an unimpeachable witness when he testified. Despite Lodge's and Beveridge's efforts to impugn his testimony, he remained unperturbed and provided evidence that could not be dismissed as the fabrication of an opportunistic partisan or an anti-imperialist stooge.[85]

Riley's testimony, in conjunction with news accounts of the devastation wrought by American tactics in Samar, threatened to undermine support for the administration's policies in the Philippines in April 1902. Intent on tamping down the anti-imperialist surge, President Roosevelt and Secretary of War Root responded with a vigorous public relations campaign. They promised to investigate and punish any violations of the laws of war by American soldiers while they also denounced critics of the military as disloyal and craven partisans. Anti-imperialists were branded "Copperheads," the epithet applied to traitorous northerners who had supported the Confederacy during the Civil War, and outspoken military officers, especially General Frederick Funston, advocated their summary execution as traitors. In Congress Beveridge and Lodge joined the campaign, conceding that American soldiers might have applied "severe measures" but arguing that their actions had been mild in comparison to the outrages regularly perpetrated by insurgents. Republican loyalists answered any mention of atrocities by recounting a litany of horrific cruelties that Filipinos had inflicted on American soldiers.[86]

To give credibility to the pledge to investigate plausible allegations and thereby blunt the attacks from anti-imperialists, Root ordered Major Glenn, Riley's commanding officer and the officer responsible for the events in Igbaras, to be court-martialed. Root may have hoped that Glenn would serve as a scapegoat, but his court-martial risked exposing the extent to which his superiors had condoned his methods. Wherever Glenn had been stationed he had forthrightly used the water cure in his pursuit of alleged insurrectionists. The interrogations that Riley had witnessed were only two among scores that Glenn had carried out.[87]

Glenn's trial, unlike Captain Brandle's court-martial two years earlier, attracted national attention. Glenn was a West Point graduate who had a long record of service as well as a reputation as a published authority on international law. Rather than deny the charges against him, Glenn made a vigorous defense of his use of the water cure. He offered the same justifications that Brandle had used during his court-martial. Glenn avowed that "force is absolutely needed to obtain information from natives," who were primitive peoples motivated more by fear than reason. At the same time, he shrugged off the water cure as a mild punishment that was "not unusual in the United States." He and defense witnesses assured the court that the water cure had no lingering effects; it was equivalent to the dunkings that playful children inflicted on each other at swimming holes. Despite its mildness, the procedure had been effective. Glenn explained with florid imagery, "Water was administered only until it touched the fountain of information, and truth gushed out."

Given that Root had ordered Glenn's court-martial and that Glenn shamelessly justified his routine use of the water cure, the outcome of his court-martial was a foregone conclusion. The court found him guilty. It scolded him for his use of the water cure, which the court regretted was prone to abuse. Otherwise the court imposed a punishment that was hardly more severe than that imposed on Brandle two years earlier. Glenn was suspended for one month and fined $50. The members of the court-martial even petitioned for leniency for him on the grounds of his distinguished service, especially on Panay, even though it was there that his use of the water cure had precipitated his court-martial.[88]

Although Glenn received a trivial penalty, Root and administration loyalists pointed to his and subsequent trials as evidence that violators of the rules of war would not escape punishment. Among the court-martials that followed on the heels of Glenn's trial was that of First Lieutenant Julien E. Gaujot, who, like Glenn, boasted of employing the water cure. He defended its use by claiming that he had confronted inhabitants who were "crafty, lying, and treacherous" and had no respect for any law. In the absence of coercion, he found it impossible to obtain intelligence about insurgents. His methods, he insisted, had been in compliance with General Order 100 because he had not tortured his victims "for my own gratification, but for the purpose of obtaining information that would enable us to strike a blow at the insurrection." In short, military necessity justified his use of the water cure. Gaujot apparently made a slightly less favorable impression on the court than had Glenn; it sentenced him to a three-month suspension and a $150 fine.[89]

A month after Gaujot's trial, Captain James A. Ryan stood before the court, represented by Major Glenn. That Glenn, a convicted violator of the laws of war, could serve as defense counsel in a court-martial is indicative of the informality of courts-martial of the era. Ryan, like Glenn and Gaujot, was accused of subjecting Filipino functionaries to the water cure. But unlike his two predecessors, Ryan pleaded not guilty. He conceded that he had ordered a local mayor to undergo the water cure repeatedly but testified that the procedures had been so brief as to have been trivial. In apparent agreement, one defense witness admitted that he had found them "rather amusing." When the prosecution introduced testimony from an American prosecutor in Manila that Ryan had been needlessly harsh in his treatment of Filipinos, counselor Glenn lashed out at the witness by badgering him about his lack of military service. Glenn's intent seemingly was to suggest that only someone with military service could properly pass judgment on a soldier's conduct. The court apparently agreed with Glenn and acquitted Ryan.[90]

The Roosevelt administration finally found a scapegoat in Brigadier General Jacob H. Smith, who had commanded the expedition that crushed the insurgency on Samar in 1901. Smith was in many regards a convenient target. Despite his service during the Civil War and nearly four decades in uniform, he had a long and shady record of insubordination, dishonesty, and corruption. His promotion to the rank of brigadier general had been on the basis of seniority and on the assumption that he would promptly retire. Instead he hung on and received command of the Samar expedition. The brutality of that campaign was reported in broad terms in the press, but not until the court-martial of one of Smith's subordinates for the summary execution of eleven Filipinos did the American public learn that Smith had issued orders to kill all Filipinos over the age of ten and to transform Samar into "a howling wilderness." Smith's orders were so embarrassing to the administration that some rebuke was necessary. In May 1902, Smith faced court-martial not for violating the rules of war but for "conduct to the prejudice of good order and military discipline." Smith helped neither his case nor the imperialist cause with his blustering testimony. Few could have been surprised when the court found him guilty. President Roosevelt, at the recommendation of Secretary of War Root, ordered Smith's retirement from the army, but no additional punishment.[91]

Following this spate of courts-martial and the surrender of one of the last active insurgent generals and his forces, President Roosevelt seized the moment in June 1902 to declare an end to hostilities in the Philippines. Henceforth military campaigns would be described as police actions against bandits and lawless elements. In the meantime, the military ceded authority to American civil administrators, thereby affirming that the insurrection had been quashed.[92]

In fact, Roosevelt's announcement was more symbolic than factual. American forces had yet to compel deference from the Muslim inhabitants of the southern islands who had previously been ignored while Americans concentrated on suppressing insurgents in the northern islands. Subsequent campaigns in Sulu and Mindinao were marred by some of the excesses that had characterized earlier American actions. Arguably the worst atrocity of the war occurred in 1906, when Americans massacred hundreds of besieged Tausūg at Bud Dajo. Nevertheless, between mid-1902 and the bloodbath at Bud Dajo, the Roosevelt administration succeeded in promoting the notion that Filipinos now acknowledged and even embraced American control over their islands.[93]

The business of "benevolent assimilation," Americans were told, now proceeded unhindered, and the water cure and other "stern measures" that previously had been necessary to suppress the insurrection were passé. But while American troops refrained from torture, the Philippine constabulary, which was manned by Filipinos under American command, continued the practice as a complement to American benevolence. The constabulary became a laboratory for American advisers to develop and apply "innovative" police methods, including intrusive surveillance of dissidents, that would be repatriated to the United States in later decades. These modern techniques, however, apparently did not eliminate the need to routinely mistreat alleged "bandits" or kill countless prisoners "while escaping."[94] American imperialists dismissed this ongoing violence as a lamentable but necessary feature of imposing law and order on a chaotic and primitive society.[95]

Roosevelt's announcement of an end of hostilities did not assuage Welsh and other anti-imperialists. The defeat of the major insurgent forces in no way legitimated the American seizure of the archipelago. Nor, Welsh pointed out, did it provide justice to the victims of American atrocities or restore the integrity of American institutions that had been sullied since war with Spain. Welsh clamored for the ouster of Secretary of War Root for suppressing information about the conduct of the war and for failing to punish perpetrators of the water cure and atrocities. While Senator Lodge used every conceivable ruse to halt the hearings, Welsh tirelessly chided Lodge for thwarting public debate and continued to gather affidavits and press for investigations of atrocities committed by American troops.

In an attempt to embarrass Lodge and the administration, Welsh and his team organized an unofficial hearing in February 1903 before Democratic members of Lodge's Senate committee during which five witnesses gave vivid testimony about unprosecuted war crimes committed by American troops.[96] Among the atrocities described at the informal hearing was the murder of Father Augustine de la Pena, whose death was a mockery of McKinley's promised "benevolent assimilation." American troops seized the priest because he allegedly was an ally of the insurgents in Molos and knew where they had buried their gold. One of the priest's guards speculated in an affidavit that there had been a conspiracy to kill the priest because he had "lots of receipts for money." The cleric was transported on a naval vessel to Panay, where he was imprisoned and subjected repeatedly to the water cure. Despite warnings from at least one subordinate that further torture might kill Augustine, commanding officer Captain C. M. Brownell persisted until the priest perished. Members of the "water detail" responsible for the priest's death then secretly buried the corpse in an unmarked grave in a vacant lot where American soldiers played baseball.[97]

In this single wretched atrocity, Welsh discerned an encapsulation of the travesty of imperialism: a priest robbed, tortured to death, and secretly buried in unconsecrated ground, and his murderers unprosecuted. Worse yet, although Captain Brownell publicly acknowledged his role in the death of Father Augustine, military authorities claimed that no legal action could be taken against him because he had been mustered out of ranks and therefore was no longer subject to military justice. Indeed, defenders of the military shifted blame for this and other scattered atrocities to Brownell and volunteer soldiers who had been more zealous than professional in waging war against Filipino insurgents. Conveniently, by 1903 almost all of the volunteers had been mustered out of service and so could not be prosecuted. Welsh's pleas for a public accounting for the outrage of Augustine's murder and other alleged war crimes were to no avail.

By 1903 Welsh and his fellow anti-imperialists faced an uphill struggle to overturn the notion that the American possession of the Philippines was a fait accompli. The Roosevelt administration had no intention of recognizing Filipino independence and meanwhile had initiated a new imperialist scheme in the isthmus of Panama. Senator Lodge refused to conduct hearings into past atrocities, which he dismissed as old news. There had been, Lodge proclaimed, no new allegations since 1902. Moreover, he chastised the anti-imperialists for continuing to harass patriotic soldiers with accusations that were "often baseless, generally exaggerated," and motivated by the jealousy of subordinates toward their superiors. Wrapping his party in the American flag, Lodge promised that he and his colleagues would defend the army against "persecution," "injustice," and "wanton attacks."[98]

Anti-imperialists continued to press their case after 1904, but they were overmatched by Roosevelt and his imperialist allies. Further weakening the anti-imperialist cause was a pronounced thinning of its ranks. The deaths of Hoar and several other prominent anti-imperialists robbed the cause of men of irreplaceable stature. Welsh himself succumbed to exhaustion in 1904 and withdrew from most of the reform activities that had defined his public life. He shut down his paper, *City and State,* surrendered his leadership roles in the Indian Rights Association and the anti-imperialist cause, and took a restorative sabbatical in Europe. Anti-imperialists continued to rage against Roosevelt's global strutting but now were bereft of Welsh's dogged research and single-minded focus on torture.[99]

The incontrovertible evidence of torture as a routine practice applied by American soldiers could not easily be aligned with Americans' professed principles of democracy and liberty. The American military's response to the Filipino insurrection demonstrated how little regard America's leadership had for the democratic aspirations of the newly conquered colony. As long as white Americans had presumed that the expansion of American democracy would result in a republic populated by white Euro-Americans, they could persuade themselves that the torture was literally external to the modern and enlightened society they were fashioning. And when exposés of torture in antebellum prisons surfaced, they had been explained as either tragic or justifiable exceptions to American principles. The American occupation of the Philippines introduced a number of unprecedented challenges to these assumptions. Despite the insistence of Roosevelt, Lodge, and Beveridge to the contrary, American imperialism was neither clearly distinct from nor superior to Old World imperialism. There was never any likelihood that the United States would formally incorporate the Philippines into the nation. And once the Supreme Court ruled that the inhabitants of the nation's new imperial possessions did not possess all of the rights guaranteed under the Constitution, the United States ruled over more than eight million Filipinos whose formal rights were wholly contingent on American will. Simply put, the fundamental doctrine of American democracy that governmental power rests with the citizenry did not apply in the Philippines.

For all of the efforts of the anti-imperialists to stoke popular opposition to the occupation, the controversy over atrocities and torture in the Philippines demonstrated that partisan politics would contaminate any vetting of American imperial practices. To the dismay of the anti-imperialists, what they believed to be sacrosanct American principles of democracy were refracted by partisan allegiance. The anti-imperialists attempted to straddle partisan lines, but Republican intransigence forced them to forge an expedient alliance with some Democrats. The Democratic Party, however, was not well poised to thwart the imperialist impulse. After the elections of 1896, the Republican Party was ascendant, especially in Congress, where a sizable majority was in firm control. Consequently, any congressional investigation would inevitably deteriorate into a partisan scrum.

The occupation of the Philippines also demonstrated that the nascent movement to codify rules of war within the American military offered little protection to the population of America's Pacific colony.

Welsh's dogged investigation of American military atrocities exposed the limits of the military's willingness and capacity to prevent and punish violations of rules of war. The defenses offered by Brandle, Glenn, and the other court-martialed officers exposed the enduring ambiguities of Lieber's Code that had been apparent even during the Civil War. But unlike soldiers during the Civil War, who had only a superficial knowledge of General Order 100, officers in the Philippines had studied it closely. They referred to it in their orders and during interviews with the press. In Glenn's case, he had written a widely used text on international law that discussed Lieber's Code. Nevertheless, he and other soldiers continued to invoke the doctrine of military necessity to justify their coercive interrogations. They could do so because military authorities had effectively left the calibration of violence to the discretion of officers in the field. Equally important, military authorities had failed to clearly repudiate the widespread notion that General Order 100, as the defense counsel in General Smith's court-martial contended, "was never intended to apply to an inferior and savage race."[100]

Even when the nation's military and political leaders acknowledged that gross violations had occurred in the Philippines, the nation's military institutions were unwilling to punish abuses. The War Department never conducted a thorough investigation of the allegations of cruelty. Instead, individual officers, whether motivated by disgust, professionalism, or some ulterior motive, raised concerns about some incidents. In other cases, anti-imperialist agitation prompted action. The courts-martial themselves hardly instilled confidence in military justice. The officers who made up the courts were openly sympathetic to the defendants, and court-martial procedures allowed for wide latitude by the defense. Brandle, Glenn, Gaujot, and the other officers larded their defense with lengthy defamations of the culture of Filipinos and testimonials regarding the use of torture in the United States. And like the justifications of antebellum prison guards who defended their use of seemingly cruel punishments, officers facing courts-martial avowed that only someone who had faced similar challenges and dangers was qualified to pass judgment on their actions. This line of defense was sure to elicit sympathy from fellow officers while disqualifying any criticism from civilians.

Certainly, the war left few scars on the careers of the officers tried
for torture and cruelty. With the exception of Brandle, who came to a
tragic end at his own hands, and Gaujot, who never rose above the rank
of colonel, the rest of the court-martialed officers enjoyed celebrated
careers and retired with the rank of general. The War Department evidently attached no stigma to their deeds in the Philippines. Hence,
when the military identified the need for a modern handbook of the
rules of war to supersede Lieber's Code, they tapped Major Glenn, a
convicted violator of the rules of war, to compile it.[101]

American military and political leaders revealed the lesson they derived from the Philippine Insurrection during the American occupation of Haiti between 1915 and 1934. When confronted by a hostile population and stealthy insurgents on the Caribbean island, American
soldiers again resorted to torture and "severe measures" while offering
justifications that echoed those made by Brandle, Glenn, and others in
the Philippines. But officers in the field and in Washington, D.C., had
learned how important it was to avoid stoking controversy or opposition at home. In 1931, Marine Major Harold H. Utley distilled three decades of American military experience with "small wars" into a concise but revealing article for fellow Marines. Having recently completed
a tour of Nicaragua, where the Marines had been protecting American
interests since 1912, Utley drew on his firsthand experience there as
well as contemporary wisdom about European campaigns against guerrilla insurgents from Indochina and the Punjab frontier to sub-Saharan
Africa. For all of American imperialists' insistence that American imperialism would be distinct from and superior to the tawdry empire
building of European rivals, the military officers who had to translate
American global ambitions into day-to-day practice displayed few
qualms about aping their imperialist peers. Utley's article drew attention to the distinctive characteristics of "small wars" and the phases
of such conflicts before dwelling on the restraints on American commanders waging counterinsurgencies. The adversary that clearly vexed
Utley the most was "Public Opinion." He fumed that "there will always be so-called Americans who under one pretext or another will
assist in originating and spreading tales of alleged 'atrocities' said to
have been committed by our troops." He grumbled about the "countless 'Investigations'" that such allegations prompted and the benefit

that insurgents derived from them. So intent was Utley on making clear for his fellow soldiers the lesson of his analysis that he capitalized it: "MEASURES JUSTIFIABLE IN A REGULAR WAR, TACTICALLY SOUND, AND PROBABLY THE MOST EFFICIENT AVAILABLE, MUST BE FREQUENTLY ELIMINATED . . . AS NOT BEING IN ACCORD WITH PUBLIC POLICY." For Utley and others, there was a galling contrast between the most "efficient" and "sound" methods of using the American mailed fist and the pusillanimous measures that "public opinion" would allow. Had Brandle, Glenn, and the other veterans of the Philippine Insurrection been alive, they undoubtedly would have nodded in agreement with Utley's lament.[102]

Perhaps the most remarkable feature of the controversy surrounding cruelty and atrocities in the Philippines was how quickly it faded from American public discourse. For a decade after Roosevelt's proclamation of American victory over the insurrectionists, periodic exposés of atrocities in the Philippines would briefly revive debates about the failings of American imperialism. But these spasms of concern were quickly subsumed within the broader celebration of the nation's new-found status as a global power. By focusing on the liberation of Cuba from Spanish tyranny rather than the occupation of the Philippines, Americans could present themselves as reluctant imperialists who were kinder and gentler than their European and Asian peers. The Spanish American War provided an edifying focal point; the Philippine Insurrection, by contrast, was an awkward demonstration that American benevolence could not be accomplished without violence. Simultaneously, American authorities and Filipino elites who aligned themselves with the American occupiers found common ground in consigning the Philippine Insurrection and American atrocities to the shadows of history.[103] Little acknowledged in subsequent historical accounts of the nation, the imposition of American rule and the suppression of the insurrection are virtually absent from the monumental landscape that reminds the nation of the heroism of its soldiers.

SIX

Police Station Trespasses

O N SEPTEMBER 5, 1901, President William McKinley addressed a large audience of sweltering fairgoers at the Pan-American Exposition in Buffalo, New York. "Expositions are the timelines of progress," he proclaimed. "They record the world's advancement." After marveling at recent innovations in transportation and technology, he concluded with an optimistic flourish: "We hope that all who are represented here may be moved to higher and nobler efforts."[1] A day later, violence at odds with the advanced civilization celebrated by McKinley ruptured the fete honoring modernity and progress. After stalking the president for days, Leon Czolgosz, an anarchist, approached him while he was greeting well-wishers at the exposition. When McKinley reached out to shake his hand, his assassin fired two pistol rounds into his abdomen. While the gravely wounded president was hurried to a hospital operating room, police set upon his attacker and then hustled him to the Buffalo police headquarters. There, while mobs of would-be lynchers rushed the lines of police guarding the building, officials interrogated the badly bloodied and taciturn German American. When asked later whether Czolgosz had received "the third degree," a euphemism for strenuous grilling, a policeman boasted, "He got the thirty-third degree." Evening editions of newspapers revealed that he had been "given rigorous treatment" and predicted that "he will be tortured again."[2] Beyond gleaning the motive for the shooting, Czolgosz's interrogators were anxious to identify accomplices. On the basis of his confession, police in Chicago and elsewhere began rounding up anarchists.[3]

The specific interrogation methods that police used on Czolgosz were concealed by curious silences in the record of his incarceration. Because he had received a severe thrashing when he was first apprehended, it is virtually impossible to determine which of his extensive wounds could be traced to his arrest or to any subsequent beatings he may have undergone. Some observers speculated that he was not beaten but instead was forced to endure blinding light. Whatever the method, newspaper headlines proclaimed that he had undergone the third degree.[4]

The shooting of the president was as close as the nation had ever been to the mythical "ticking time bomb" scenario that present-day commentators often raise in their rhetorical jousting over the moral legitimacy of torture. Americans did not need to be reminded that, during the previous decade, anarchists had assassinated a French president, a Spanish prime minister, the king of Italy, and a Hapsburg empress and had attempted to murder many others. If the circumstances that precipitated the interrogation of Czolgosz were exceptional, there was nothing remarkable about the decision of law officers to employ violence during his interrogation. In theory, the practice of violent interrogation was illegal everywhere in the United States. Several state constitutions specifically prohibited torture, some states had laws banning coercive interrogations, and all states extended to citizens the right against self-incrimination. But only the willfully naive or transparently duplicitous could claim that agents of the state refrained from torture in the United States. Law officers in virtually every state used the third degree, and courts across the country routinely accepted confessions that had been violently wrenched out of prisoners. Notorious criminals and petty lawbreakers alike fell victim to it. Violent interrogations were so well known that the American soldiers prosecuted for war crimes during the Philippine Insurrection had repeatedly defended themselves by equating their actions with those of American police. Defending his use of the "water cure" against Filipino insurgents, one officer maintained that "it did not compare in cruelty with methods resorted to by American police officials to extort confessions." A newspaper editorial conceded that "there was more truth than poetry" in this defense.[5]

The proliferation of the third degree in the post–Civil War United States may be traced to the emergence of modern police forces and the shift toward state-initiated prosecution of crime. Until the mid-nineteenth century, most American communities relied on a time-honored system of night watches, often staffed by volunteers, to discourage lawless behavior and to alert residents when it did occur. Supplementing these watches were constables, who were law enforcement officers as well as jacks-of-all-trades who earned fees for performing a wide variety of functions, many of which had little to do with the prevention of crime. Simultaneously, the prosecutions of many forms of crime, ranging from private battery to illegal liquor sales, were initiated by private citizens or grand juries. But urban elites perceived both private prosecutions and constables as singularly ineffective at restraining working-class disorder and suppressing chronic illegal activity. Intent on diminishing the role of private citizens, reformers began during the 1840s to demand that agents of the state assume the lead in the initiation and prosecution of criminal cases. This campaign led directly to expanded duties for both police and district attorneys. Within a ten-year span after 1845, New York City, Boston, and Philadelphia established the nation's first professional police forces. By the end of the 1870s, virtually every major American city boasted a police force, as did many towns and smaller cities.[6]

These new police forces represented a significant innovation because policemen, unlike their predecessors, were full-time employees whose specific charge was to prevent crime, apprehend suspects, and complement the efforts of local authorities to prosecute criminals. For all of Americans' deep distrust of centralized power and standing armies, they tolerated police forces that enjoyed surprising autonomy. The newly established police departments developed an awkward relationship to preexisting local and state governments. Although typically enmeshed in local politics, the departments were subject to only limited legal and institutional restraints. Many police forces quickly developed powerful and insular cultures, in which unquestioning obedience, military-like discipline, and fierce loyalty to their precinct-level peers was expected. This professionalization and specialization sparked periodic controversy, especially because of the propensity of some policemen to be quick and heavy-handed with their batons while on the beat. But not until the 1880s did reports become commonplace that police employed torture to extract confessions and humiliate suspects in custody.[7]

These accusations of police torture were a testament to the evolving response of police to the headlong transformations in American society after the Civil War. The speed and breadth of change, especially in the nation's cities, fostered heightened anxiety about disorder and crime. Urban dailies gave readers the impression that neither life nor property was safe. At the end of the Civil War, only two of the nation's cities counted a half million inhabitants; by the dawn of the next century, six cities did, and three of these had more than a million. The arrival of nearly twenty-five million immigrants in the half century after Appomattox, with nearly a million arriving during some years, sustained this dizzying growth. Adding to the anxiety about the nation's stability was the pitched and violent struggle between "capital" and the developing labor movement. Defenders of capital responded with demands for a ruthless restoration of law and order. So acute was the anxiety about crime and labor unrest that many large businesses turned to private security services, most famously the Pinkerton Agency, to augment the stretched police forces of the era.[8]

Against this backdrop of perceived disorder and lawlessness, metropolitan police forces acquired new responsibilities and claimed unprecedented powers. Police continued to employ customary violence to impose their will even as they made increasing use of a new power—custodial interrogation—to expand their influence. Traditionally, interrogations of alleged criminals had been conducted by constables or officers of the court in the context of trials. Such interrogations often had been haphazard affairs, unfolding in public and with the participation of local notables and random witnesses.[9] Now police and district attorneys assumed as part of their official duties the responsibility of grilling accused wrongdoers while in custody.[10]

The innovation of custodial interrogation was a manifestation not only of increasing specialization but also of the nation's distinctive system of adversarial justice. A marked difference between the adversarial system that prevails in the United States and the inquisitorial systems that are common in Europe occurs when a criminal defendant admits to committing a crime. In American justice, the admission is likely to conclude a prosecutorial investigation, and the case may proceed to sentencing. In other systems of justice, a confession by a defendant is merely one more fact that is entered into evidence, and it does not free the prosecution of the obligation to present a full case. The exceptional weight assigned to the confession in American justice in turn encourages plea bargaining, which in other systems may be difficult, even impossible. The connection between coerced confessions and plea bargains is often direct. Once a criminal has incriminated himself through a coerced confession, he has compelling grounds to want to avoid trial and the likelihood of a severe sentence. Prosecutors also have ample cause to pursue plea bargains, which lightened crushing workloads, averted unpredictable decisions by wayward juries, and had the effect of shielding interrogation procedures and the integrity of the criminal's confession from the scrutiny of the court.[11]

The shift toward state-initiated prosecution during the mid-nineteenth century granted to district attorneys the discretion to dispense justice without resort to a trial. Consequently, for more than a century a large proportion of felony cases in the United States have been resolved through plea bargains and without trial. Studies of recent plea bargaining have estimated that at least half of all criminal cases conclude with confessions, and one study determined that the overwhelming majority of criminal investigations were solved through coerced confessions. How often suspects confessed and agreed to plea bargains during the late nineteenth and early twentieth centuries is unclear, but extant evidence suggests they did so as frequently, or more so, than suspects in recent decades.[12]

The police who began to gather evidence for criminal prosecutions, with rare exceptions, did so without any relevant training. Typically, they were recruited on the basis of political affiliation, patronage, and brawn. Virtually no police had any training in forensics. Indeed, the science of gathering forensic evidence barely existed in the United

States. Impressive feats of forensic analysis stirred the imaginations of journalists and readers of popular fiction, but not until the turn of the twentieth century did European scientists and jurists demonstrate the usefulness of ballistics, anthropometry, and crime-scene analysis. None of these advances displaced the haphazard methods that prevailed across most of the United States until the second decade of the twentieth century. Other crucial innovations, such as forensic serology, would not become a prominent crime-fighting tool until the 1930s.[13]

Given the new responsibility to secure evidence for the prosecution, the almost complete absence of effective investigative procedures and tools, and the weight accorded to confessions, it was altogether predictable that American police resorted to coercion to wrest confessions from perceived wrongdoers. In 1907 a thoughtful letter writer to the *New York Times*, identified as "A Jurist," conceded that the morality of the third degree might be questionable but declared its results "gratifying."[14] In the absence of confessions, police typically had only circumstantial evidence to substantiate charges against alleged criminals. Such evidence, to the great chagrin of law officers, could not be relied on to persuade juries to convict. As one early twentieth-century opponent of police brutality explained, when policemen "can pound a confession out of a man, it saves endless trouble in bringing about a conviction." Another observer noted curtly, "Applying the third degree is the easiest way."[15]

By the 1880s the practice of harsh interrogation had become sufficiently common and varied to generate a new lexicon. In his 1887 memoir, George Washington Walling, police superintendent of New York, introduced readers to the police slang of "sweating" and "getting the third degree" as euphemisms for violent questioning.[16] Gradually, after the turn of the twentieth century, "sweating" fell out of favor and the practice was most commonly referred to as "the third degree," perhaps with reference to the arduous initiation procedures endured to advance to the third degree of Freemasonry or to one of the levels of torture used to extract confessions during the Spanish Inquisition.[17]

Court appeals, civil suits brought against police departments, and news reports at the turn of the twentieth century revealed the reality behind the euphemism. The third degree typically occurred while the suspect was in custody of the police, before charges were brought, and in the absence of counsel. Instances might include physical abuse, deprivation, or psychological pressure; sometimes victims experienced all three. The varieties of physical abuse were limited only by the ingenuity of the interrogators. Common methods included cloistering suspects for extended spells in small, poorly ventilated spaces that were stifling hot or freezing cold. Police beat victims with fists, rubber hoses, ropes, belts, and clubs or subjected them to simulated drowning. By 1910 police were using electricity and modern technology to terrorize suspects. In one instance interrogators used a dental drill to coerce a confession from a suspect, and in another they drenched a fifteen-year-old with gasoline and held a lit match close to his dripping clothes until he confessed. Officers compelled suspects to stand in exhausting positions or hanged them by their wrists or necks for hours on end. Two prisoners in Gary, Indiana, for instance, were given a so-called head and ear massage, during which they were hung by the neck from a beam in the basement of the jail and beaten.[18] Other commonplace forms of the third degree included isolating suspects from counsel and family while depriving them of sleep, food, and water for days. And police routinely subjected suspects to grueling interrogations during which they were threatened with lynching, electrocution, or death. In one astonishing instance police held a criminal by his feet and dangled him out of a window high above a street.[19]

The methods of psychological pressure were equally varied. Suspects were routinely subjected to hours, even days, of continuous examination. Interrogators devised macabre techniques to exploit widely held beliefs about uncontrollable physical manifestations of guilt. In San Francisco, for instance, police coerced a Sicilian immigrant to implicate her husband in a murder by a series of escalating traumas. First, they took her infant child from her, grilled her for hours, and then showed her the mangled remains of the murder victim in the autopsy room and forced her to handle the blood-encrusted cleaver used in the murder and the blood-drenched blanket in which the victim had been concealed. They presumed that proximity to the corpse and the murder weapon would overwhelm her reluctance to divulge the truth and would implicate her husband. Instead, the ordeal induced an extended fit of hysteria that necessitated her hospitalization.[20] In New Jersey five years later, police forced a suspect to wear the blood-soaked vest of a murdered man and to hold on his left arm the blood-stained dress of a murdered woman, while placing his right hand on the Bible. He was ordered to maintain this ghoulish stance for twenty minutes.[21]

In contemporary news accounts, interrogations acquired a mystique as titillating features of the turbulent and hidden city life in which colorful but treacherous criminals faced off against crafty policemen. Major news dailies periodically published lengthy illustrated histories of the practice and its practitioners.[22] Such accounts often dubbed New York Police Inspector Thomas Byrnes the inventor of the third degree, but he almost certainly garnered his nickname only because he employed the technique more vigorously, systematically, and flamboyantly than his peers. Aside from his notoriety, Byrnes was otherwise typical of the early recruits to American police forces. After emigrating from Ireland to New York as a child, he first worked as a gas fitter before serving for two years in the Union army. Having completed his enlistment, he joined a firefighting company in New York until he was appointed a police officer in 1863. By 1880 he had risen through the ranks and headed the department's detective bureau, a position he held until 1895, when he was forced out for corruption. During his thirty-two years on the force, the number of detectives more than doubled, and the powers granted to his bureau expanded markedly. He adroitly used newspapers to publicize his mastery of "dramatic ordeals" and "mysterious arts" that he applied "without mercy" and, allegedly, with unfailing success. His methods for "breaking" criminals were presented as both a battle of wits as well as the extraction of information through pain and fear.[23]

As Byrnes's fame waxed, crime reporters from coast to coast identified his counterparts elsewhere who excelled at "sweating" alleged criminals and applying the third degree. In Chicago, for instance, Inspector John D. Shea of the Maxwell Street station garnered similar renown for "his ability to force confessions from the lips of even the most unwilling."[24] The *Chicago Tribune* alleged that "every police department in this country has its 'sweaters' or inquisitors, and long practice has made them adepts at the art."[25] News reports after the arrest of a suspect brought before Byrnes, Shea, and their ilk routinely predicted that they would apply the third degree. Subsequent reports would tally how long, strenuous, and productive had been the bouts of interrogation, with reporters weighing in on the strength of character displayed by the accused while under duress.[26]

No region of the country was free of the practice of coerced confessions. As one outraged contributor to *Lawyer and Banker* magazine complained in 1911, "From Seattle to Boston the action of the police has become a scandal."[27] A year later the same journal repeated its claim that the third degree was "generally established among police throughout the United States."[28] Reflecting the perception of the nation's cities as lawless and chaotic, metropolitan police had reputations as especially frequent practitioners of the third degree. But news accounts and judicial appeals demonstrated that small-town and rural law officers were also adept at it.

Despite the press attention devoted to the third degree, no comprehensive portrait of its victims at the turn of the twentieth century is possible. Contemporary news accounts, occasional court appeals, and suits lodged against police departments suggest that suspects accused of capital offenses, such as murder and rape, were most likely to experience it. A 1916 study of prisoners in the Western Penitentiary in Pennsylvania concluded that criminals accused of "predatory crimes," especially robbery, were the most likely to be given the third degree.[29] But blackmailers, forgers, burglars, safecrackers, and petty lawbreakers also endured it. Immigrants and African Americans may have disproportionately undergone it, but so too did white working-class Americans and those who had frequent brushes with the law.[30] Virtually anyone might be subjected to it. Newspapers periodically publicized instances of police applying it to lawyers, doctors, and businessmen.[31] The typical victim was a man, but women and youths underwent it on many occasions. Family members of suspects and witnesses, as in the case of the Sicilian wife in San Francisco, also experienced it. In Chicago, for instance, interrogators applied the third degree to a twelve-year-old boy in 1895, the nine-year-old daughter of an accused blackmailer in 1913, and a fortune-teller accused of murdering her husband in 1919.[32]

As the third degree became commonplace and received increasing scrutiny, police sought both to justify it and to shield it from public gaze.[33] Police commissioners grumbled that yellow journalists, misinformed do-gooders, and shyster lawyers in the pay of career criminals grossly exaggerated its frequency and intensity. The commissioner of police in Rochester, New York, scoffed at the third degree as a "vague newspaper term," while an officer in Baltimore claimed that he had "not yet heard anyone explain the exact meaning of the third degree."[34] Likewise, William Baker, the commissioner of police in New York City, mocked "sweating" as an "imaginary something" before claiming that it entailed a battle of wills and a test of intelligence rather than of stamina or tolerance of pain. He protested that "volunteer confessions" and "diligent inquiry of a prisoner for explanation of facts and circumstances" were the sum total of "the so-called 'third degree.'"[35] Richard Sylvester, the superintendent of police in the nation's capital and president of the International Association of Police Chiefs, dismissed "sweating" as "an effervescent term" in the "criminal vernacular."[36] Like other apologists then and later, Sylvester acknowledged that "some years ago a rough usage was resorted to in some cities in order to secure confessions," but he assured the public that "such procedure does not obtain at large nowadays."[37]

For decades to come, police spokesmen would parrot the bromide that the third degree was an archaic practice that had been superseded by modern scientific methods. In an editorial dripping with sarcasm, the *Chicago Tribune* in 1910 predicted that the Washington police chief would deny that the third degree was administered in his city, but that "it may be in some large cities." If the chief of police in Philadelphia was interviewed, he would say that "there was nothing of the kind there, but that there might be in New York." Police officials there would proclaim their innocence while referring the interviewer to Chicago, and on and on.[38] If the pronouncements of police were to be believed, the third degree was always practiced elsewhere by someone else.

Even newspapers that periodically published exposés of the third degree routinely dissembled about and excused police methods. For example, in a lengthy article the *Chicago Tribune* wrung its hands over the police's penchant for holding suspects incommunicado for days and employing rough methods of interrogation, before dismissing "the wild stories" told about "the brutal manner in which prisoners are bulldozed."[39] A decade later, the same newspaper groused that despite the

FIGURE 6.1. "Well, Captain, the Prisoner Has Confessed to Murder!" "O.K. Hold Him till There Is a Murder!" G. Burr Inwood's cartoon, published in *Judge* on July 19, 1930, depicts a group of exhausted policemen brandishing clubs and presenting a confession, apparently beaten out of a prisoner, to their captain. Jaded, the captain congratulates them. The cartoon captured the widespread cynicism about the trustworthiness of confessions extracted by police using the third degree.

effectiveness of the strenuous methods used by police, the public "did not take kindly to the idea of confessions extorted by the thumbscrew, the rack, the knout [whip], or their equivalents."[40]

Yet while apologists discounted as exaggerated most reports about the severity of police interrogations, they justified the occasional use of "stern measures," much like their predecessors who had defended retaliation during the Civil War or their contemporaries who excused "the water cure" in the Philippines. They insisted that only those engaged in the battle against the crime that racked the nation could fully understand the provocations that drove police to apply the third degree. Commissioner Baker of New York extolled police as "the guardians of civilization and progress."[41] Marshaling the language of a stern prophet, Superintendent Sylvester of Washington, D.C., justified police methods that protected "the public against the outrages and depredations of miscreants who are the declared enemies of the state." He concluded with a firm injunction: "If society is to be protected . . . force must be used against the very real and active simple wickedness of this selfish world."[42] Given the criminals the police battled, another commentator cautioned, "Policemen cannot have the manners of dancing masters," especially because "ten thousand men are trying to do a thirty-thousand-man job."[43]

Critics of police methods were dismissed as naive or worse. In Chicago, State's Attorney Maclay Hoyne acknowledged that "my police may have been rough with murderers, gunmen, highway robbers, drug crazed fiends" and may have been insensitive to their constitutional rights, but why, he asked, should the "liberty of criminals" be given precedence over "the life and safety of citizens"?[44] After a judge in Muncie, Indiana, harangued a prosecutor for submitting the coerced confession of an alleged thief, the prosecutor fumed that "it is no part the duty of a trial judge to make stump speeches from the bench in order to defeat the ends of justice."[45]

Few apologies for the third degree neglected to dwell on the alleged failings of American criminal justice. When newspaper editors, lawyers, jurists, and prosecutors lashed out at the nation's laws and legal profession, they tapped a deep reservoir of disenchantment with the legal system that reached a crescendo in the early twentieth century. Beset by serious problems during the late nineteenth century, the American legal profession faced attacks from both within and without its ranks. While state law associations began the difficult process of setting professional standards and of weeding out "preprofessional," old-time lawyers, the profession was the target of harsh criticism from the general public, which worried that due process of law was actually hampering the suppression of crime and the punishment of criminals. Discontent focused on the complexities of the law of evidence and of trial procedure—"the whole silly mass of trivial technicalities"—that contributed to a staggering number of technical errors in criminal cases.[46] State supreme courts had little choice but to routinely reverse large numbers of lower court decisions because of errors. The combination of "loopholes" and lenient (or incompetent) judges impeded the hard work of police and prosecutors. Penalties for crimes allegedly were so lax as to be farcical. Furthermore, "shyster lawyers" took advantage of every feasible legal maneuver to thwart justice.[47]

While incompetent judges, dishonest lawyers, and archaic laws impeded the work of the police, the purported stoicism of hardened criminals also drove police to adopt desperate measures to wrest information and confessions from them. Recurring references to a "criminal class" testified to the ascendant notions of innate racial, ethnic, and behavioral traits that leading practitioners of the new discipline of criminology promulgated at the turn of the twentieth century. The influence of Cesare Lombroso, a famed Italian criminologist, was especially pronounced. His widely publicized methods promised to differentiate criminals from the law-abiding, thereby providing "scientific" means to protect society against innate criminals whom he condemned as "ferocious beasts." So dire was the threat posed by the "criminal class" that some American criminologists championed the forced sterilization of criminals and even their systematic elimination by the state. Members of the "criminal class" were assigned traits that were often associated with the primitive and uncivilized; they were habitually lazy, dishonest, cruel, and violent. As defenders of police conduct were quick to claim, the nation's "criminal class" was inured to moral suasion and responded to only one stimulus: pain.[48]

If the innate attributes of many criminals justified the resort to violent coercion by the police, so too did the refined duplicity of white-collar lawbreakers, apparently. Newspapers and popular fiction at the end of the nineteenth century were awash with accounts of opportunistic crimes ranging from blackmail and embezzlement to fraud. Americans were fascinated by the paradox of apparently law-abiding individuals who harbored and acted on secret criminal designs. The apparent prevalence of such crimes posed serious challenges to law officers who struggled to wring evidence and confessions from culprits who were manifestly devious and subtle.[49]

Whether police used the third degree on a member of the criminal class or a suave grifter, an underlying logic, informed by long-held beliefs, bound together interrogation, the pursuit of truth, the body, and pain. If the police interrogated a suspect without resorting to violence, how could they be certain that the alleged criminal would not dissemble? The searing pain of a blow to the ribs or of wrists bound above the head enabled police to peer through the veil of inscrutability behind which the suspect sought shelter. By tormenting the body of the suspect, the police elicited information that corroborated the knowledge they already possessed. In the swirling and murky underworld of the late nineteenth-century and early twentieth-century United States, confessional speech provided a glimpse of authenticity, of transparency, of "truth."

When placed in a larger historical context, the third degree is consonant with the long-established if no longer state-sanctioned belief that coercion, and especially physical pain, can render truth visible and audible. Ancient Greeks bequeathed to Western tradition the belief that truth is not the outcome of public negotiation and the tedious accumulation of evidence but rather is an often hidden secret that exists independent of reason. Truth is a mystical and unitary artifact that can be recovered whole. It is telling that the Greek word for "touchstone" evolved into the word for a test for purity and eventually became the name for physical torture. For ancient Greeks, torture was a physical testing that exposed authentic truth just as a chemist's test revealed an ore's purity. This notion of truth resolved the challenge of locating truth in a society where human chattel was common. Because slaves purportedly lacked the capacity to reason, they could not give evidence—speak truth—in the same manner as a citizen, who by definition possessed rationality. Through the application of torture, the slave body could be compelled to offer up truth that would otherwise be inaccessible. Indeed, the ancient Greeks were more confident in the authenticity of the truth extracted from slave bodies than from the testimony of citizen slave masters. Truth extorted by torture was free of the distortions produced by guile and artifice. Consequently, Greeks looked to the truth extracted from the bodies of slaves to corroborate or discredit the evidence of free men.[50]

This classical concept of truth proved remarkably durable and influential. It subsequently informed Roman law and, after the thirteenth century, Western thought more broadly. The classical understanding of torture and truth exerted renewed influence beginning during the thirteenth century, when first religious and then secular authorities shifted from relying on God's intervention to discern guilt (whether of heresy or criminality) to accumulating evidence and applying reason to determine culpability. To divulge responsibility, whether in a church confessional or before a court of law, was to create truth. This elevation of confession to the highest level of religious and secular proof was, to a degree, a practical necessity. If culpability could no longer be ascertained by God's overt intervention, how could reason be applied and guilt determined in those instances when physical evidence or witnesses were absent? In the centuries after the thirteenth century reforms but before the advent of forensic science, what evidence other than confessions was accessible to civil authorities? Furthermore, at a time when the capacity of European states to coerce the compliance of their subjects was limited, the practice of confession enlisted individuals to assent to and thereby assume responsibility for their own subjugation. Predictably, perhaps even inevitably, confessions became the "queen of evidence" in the Western legal tradition.[51]

Practical considerations alone, however, are inadequate to explain the cultural importance attached to confessions from the thirteenth century on. With ample justification, the historian Jean Delumeau has observed that "the history of modern western reason passes by way of the confession." Perhaps best epitomized by Jean-Jacques Rousseau's *Confessions*, the self-exegesis of confession became the preeminent mode of self-knowledge and was understood to be the most authentic expression of selfhood possible.[52]

Because of the extraordinary cultural and judicial weight assigned to confessions in both ecclesiastical and lay justice, it may seem altogether inevitable that authorities would apply physical coercion to elicit confessions. Yet the rationale for physical coercion, including torture, in the early modern West had less to do with expediency than with ideas about the will, the body, and truth. The Christian theology of original sin encouraged the belief that the human will is inherently corrupt and that all willed acts are polluted by that corruption. As the historian Lisa Silverman has observed, "In this context, to tell the truth voluntarily is a near impossibility, precisely because human will is suspect." Given the likelihood of deceit in any act of will, such as the testimony of a suspect, medieval jurists employed torture as the preferred method to secure testimony that was uncorrupted by human guile. Through inflicting pain on an accused, the torturer destroyed the willful obfuscation that otherwise diminished or confused testimony. The expression of truth was a spontaneous ejaculation rather than a deliberate recital. Truth could be gleaned from the human body no less than from the verbal testimony of a suspect. Torture, in short, was the means by which the body revealed authentic truth.[53]

This ideal of corporeal truth came under attack from Enlightenment-era critics who contested inherited ideas about human suffering and whether violence to the body could produce truth independent of the mind. Voltaire, Montesquieu, Beccaria, and other eighteenth-century philosophes dismissed many of the justifications that had sustained and legitimated judicial torture. At the heart of their reevaluation was the conviction that pain corrupted and prevented the full exercise of free will. Whereas medieval jurists presumed that pain was needed to overcome the will and reveal truth, Enlightenment critics, including the founders of the American republic, identified pain as destructive of the self, corrosive of human identity, and stifling to truth.[54]

Nevertheless, as became apparent during the late nineteenth century, when methods of interrogation that contemporaries compared to those of medieval inquisitors proliferated, the Enlightenment ideals that condemned judicial torture as inhumane and barbaric did not sweep aside the countervailing conviction that the cumulative application of pain could overwhelm otherwise intractable human will and elicit truth.

In 1915 Coleman Blease had just ended his term as governor of South Carolina when he riled up an annual meeting of governors in Boston by contrasting lynching and the third degree. Three years earlier he had addressed the same group and had garnered international notoriety by offering an incendiary paean to the lynch mob. Now, he proclaimed that lynching "is a protection of our civilization," whereas the third degree was "a blow to the whole spirit of our institutions." "The third degree," he continued, was "barbarity in a sneaking form under the sanction of the law." Always looking for an opportunity to fan sectional prejudices, Blease claimed with smug pride that the third degree was practiced in the North, East, and West but "less frequently, I am glad to say, in the South." If he had expected his comments to produce a firestorm of controversy, he must have been disappointed. While some of the gathered governors took exception, several newspaper editors subsequently concurred with him.[55]

Although ham-fisted, Blease's address prodded his contemporaries to reflect on the relationship of two of the age's most conspicuous forms of extralegal violence—the third degree and lynching. At first glance, as Blease underscored, the differences between the two practices were most striking. Lynch mobs intended to execute their victims; police typically did not inflict the third degree with the intent to kill suspects. "The deed" of lynching, as Blease put it, was "open" whereas the "hypocritical, sanctimonious violation of fundamental rights" that was the third degree was carried out "under the cloak of law." And the geography of lynching was the obverse of that assigned by Blease to the third degree. While lynch mobs carried out their grim work in virtually every region of the country, and their victims included whites, Native Americans, Asians, Mexicans, and Mexican Americans, by the late nineteenth century mobs were most active in the South, and their victims were most often African Americans. Nevertheless, it was not coincidental that the heydays of lynching and the third degree overlapped so closely. The frequency of lynching rose sharply during the 1880s, crested during the last decade of the nineteenth century, then subsided slightly before finally declining during the 1920s. Neither Blease nor opponents of lynching were disposed to acknowledge how many attributes it shared with contemporary American justice.

Lynching, like the third degree, was a supplement to, rather than the antithesis of, the contemporary legal system. Intent on defending the sanctity of the law, opponents of lynching exaggerated the distinctions between the lurid excesses of lynch mobs and the orderliness and rectitude of law officers. The complicity of the law officers and legal authorities in the practice of lynching underscored the thin line that separated the formal legal system and the rough justice of mobs. Lynchers seized approximately two of every three of their victims from the custody of law officers. Sometimes, under the guise of transporting prisoners to safe and undisclosed locations, law officers orchestrated the surrender of their charges to mobs on isolated byways. Periodically, a bailiff, sheriff, or policeman faced down a mob. Less often police or local militia arrested or fired on would-be lynchers. Far more often, after the charade of token resistance, a sheriff, judge, or district attorney ineffectively grumbled while mobs cajoled law officers into surrendering their prisoners or broke into jails to secure them. Then too there were lynchings during which law officers themselves, along with elected officials and judges, took an active role. On these occasions, the boundaries that separated legally constituted authority and extralegal violence virtually disappeared.[56]

The parallels between lynching and the third degree extended well beyond the complicity of law officers in both extralegal practices. In those areas of the country where lynching was commonplace, especially the South, police routinely incorporated threats of lynching into their interrogations. In these locales, a recalcitrant prisoner could not cavalierly ignore the likelihood that police might act on a threat to turn him over to a mob. Such threats often quickly elicited confessions which in turn were used to justify hasty trials that critics began labeling "legal lynchings." These show trials inevitably ended with guilty verdicts, which advocates of law and order then applauded as evidence that the criminal justice system, when not obstructed by lynch mobs, could be trusted to render swift justice. In such cases, the third degree, the criminal justice system, and lynching worked together.[57]

The justifications offered by defenders of lynching and apologists for the third degree overlapped seamlessly. In the wake of a lynching, local newspaper editors typically exonerated the mob by deploring the threat that rampant criminality posed to modern civilization. Encumbered by an inefficient and corrupt judicial system and beset by savage criminals, otherwise law-abiding citizens were excused for taking the law into their own hands. Lynchers, the argument went, were lawless only in a technical sense; their actions bolstered the rule of law by demonstrating the lengths to which the citizenry would go to punish miscreants. Those who criticized lynching were denounced for wasting sympathy on criminals rather than their victims. Apologists seldom missed an opportunity to claim that those who lacked firsthand experience with the criminality punished by mobs could not understand the vengeance that animated lynchers. Virtually the same rationales were offered as justifications for the third degree.

Apologists for both lynching and the third degree insisted that the confessions wrested by the mob and the police legitimized both practices. The rituals of lynching aped those of traditional public executions at which the condemned were given an opportunity to confess their sins and beg for forgiveness. On those occasions when lynching victims were charged with attempted murder or murder, mobs sought confessions in hopes of identifying any alleged accomplices. That the confessions were made under extreme duress mattered little to mobs; the same logic that sustained the notion that pain and fear could elicit the truth during a police interrogation applied to the confessions drawn out of lynching victims. In both circumstances, at least in the eyes of the interrogators and lynchers, confessions provided prima facie justification for both their actions and the punishment that their prisoners received. Moreover, the act of confession made the suspects complicit in their own punishment. Thus both mob members and news accounts of lynchings placed particular emphasis on the confessions of the mobs' victims. The mob that lynched Tom Ruffin in Trenton, Georgia, in 1888, for example, was so intent on publicizing its victim's confession that it sent a white-robed member to the office of the county treasurer after the lynching to let it be known that the black man had admitted to having attempted to rape a white woman. News accounts in 1903 of the burning alive of George White, a black man accused of raping and murdering a white woman in Wilmington, Delaware, dwelled on the confession extracted from White while he was being led by the mob to his execution site. His earlier confession to law officers had not been made public out of fear that it would arouse public passions, and so his public confession allegedly spurred on the mob's lust for vengeance.[58]

Torture and confession were intricately linked in both lynchings and police interrogations. The methods and severity of torture typically differed between these two forms of extralegal violence. Lynch mobs inflicted torture as a precursor to death; police interrogators applied torture as a precursor to state-inflicted punishment. Nevertheless, both lynching victims and suspects undergoing the third degree experienced excruciating psychological terror and physical pain. For lynching victims, the terror often began with their arrest and escalated as they listened to the mob negotiate with law officers or watched as it assaulted their jail cell. Like the horror of a police prisoner who witnessed or heard another suspect undergoing the third degree, the imaginations of the victims targeted by mobs must have been consumed by the anticipated torments they would soon suffer. Once in the hands of the mob, they could expect their psychic torment to be magnified by physical suffering. Whereas suspects tortured by police could hope to survive their ordeal, those in the hands of a mob had no grounds for optimism. In the overwhelming majority of instances, mobs simply hanged their victims. But even in these cases, the victims often succumbed only after slowly choking to death or being riddled by bullets. In perhaps one in ten lynchings, especially following the most sensational alleged crimes, lynchers engaged in spectacles of systematic physical torture. The anonymity offered by the vast crowds who gathered at these lynchings incited participants to acts of almost unlimited sadism. James Irwin, who was tortured and burned for the murder of a white girl in Ocilla, Georgia, on January 31, 1930, suffered only some of the sadistic indignities devised by lynchers before he expired. Members of the mob cut off his fingers and toes, pulled out his teeth with pliers, and repeatedly jabbed him in the mouth with a pointed pole. After castrating the black man and collecting yet more souvenirs, the mob burned him alive.[59]

Such brutal fetes captured the attention of the nation. The graphic news accounts of lynchings and the consumer ephemera that many lynchings generated, including gruesome photographs of the executions, circulated the violence of the lynch mob far beyond the number who witnessed or participated in it. The columns of the nation's newspapers were given over to lurid stories of crimes and subsequent accounts of confessions violently extracted by harrowing acts of violence against lynching victims. Each lynching was further confirmation of the tolerance of law officers for extralegal violence, if not their outright complicity in it. Only a trivial number of mob members were ever prosecuted for their deeds. At the same time, each lynching demonstrated that a portion of the nation's citizenry was inured to torture and was even complicit in inflicting it. In light of these periodic orgies of violence, the violence of the third degree appeared comparatively restrained. Equally important, the nation's tolerance of violence in the name of law and order protected police interrogators no less than lynchers against any risk of prosecution. What was the likelihood that police who "sweated" an alleged arsonist would be disciplined if the lynchers who dismembered and immolated James Irwin in public went unpunished?

For some horrified Americans, the spectacle of police and lynch mobs using torture in the name of law and order was a scathing indictment of modern American civilization. Rejecting the justifications offered for the third degree (and lynching), opponents marshaled arguments against the practices that expanded on earlier critiques of torture. But whereas earlier campaigns against American torture had been directed against its use on specific classes of victims (for example, prisoners and slaves) or during exceptional circumstances (such as war), the contemporary threat—police torture—was banal and pervasive. Indeed, because of the ubiquity of the third degree, opponents of the practice worried that Americans blithely ignored the pressing menace that police violence posed to American democracy and justice.

The third degree, at a fundamental level, contravened the most sacred of Anglo-American legal traditions: the right against self-incrimination. Whereas police interrogations were still a comparatively recent innovation, the right against self-incrimination was centuries old and had been codified in the Fifth Amendment of the Constitution. Liberty, opponents of the third degree warned, was an empty slogan if agents of the state could coerce citizens to incriminate themselves. New York Supreme Court justice Henry A. Childs, speaking in 1902, summed up the principles that inspired him and other judicial critics of the third degree: "Liberty is the inalienable right of every citizen." The sacred right of habeas corpus was fundamental to American law, he and others cautioned, and Americans should not be complacent in its erosion.[60]

The third degree violated not only long proclaimed ideals but also the tenets of modern civilization. Opponents of it denounced police torture as characteristic of autocracies and retrograde societies rather than befitting a nation pledged to ushering in a new order in human affairs. At a time of rampant anti-Semitic violence in Russia, the *Jewish Exponent* in New York City leveled a stringing rebuke to American police by denouncing "the Russianization of police methods in many of the American cities." As if comparison to the reviled Russian autocracy was insufficient, the paper invoked the preeminent symbol of Old World cruelty: "The third degree process ... savors of the torture chamber and the Inquisition and should have no place on American soil."[61] After the shooting of President McKinley, the *Oshkosh Northwestern* implored that his assassin not be tortured. The paper dismissed the argument that the end justifies the means: "The same plea might be made with equal force by the members of the mob that strings up a colored wretch for committing some atrocious and aggravating crime."[62] A year later, Margaret Irving Hamilton, a law student at the University of Iowa, wrote to the *Chicago Tribune*, pleading, "As you would abolish lynch law and all other relics of barbarism from our system of jurisprudence, I beg you to abolish also the unlawful, inhuman physical tortures administered by means of 'the sweatbox' or 'third degree.'"[63] In Washington, D.C., where police violence was a recurring blight, the *Washington Post* denounced the third degree as an offense against principle and sentiment: "At its worst it is indescribable. At its best it is repugnant to the principles of good government, as well as to every natural instinct of decency and right treatment."[64]

Opponents, moreover, rejected the presumption that calibrated pain and suffering were certain to elicit truth. To the contrary, critics reasserted arguments against torture that would have sounded familiar to their Enlightenment-era predecessors. If Americans were unmoved by the other criticisms of torture, they presumably should have been impressed by abundant evidence of the unreliability of coerced confessions. With this goal in mind, opponents of the third degree lavished attention on the all too common occurrences of innocent citizens who were terrorized into giving false confessions. While cataloging the perils that suspects could expect during police interrogations, the *Chicago Tribune* acknowledged that "blunders are occasionally made and innocent men and women are subjected to repulsive and objectionable treatment." Once suspicion attached to a suspect, "the chance of escape" from the rigors of interrogation "is small."[65] Newspapers regularly reported cases of blameless citizens who were badgered into making spurious confessions. Some instances were so ludicrous as to call into question the basic competence of the police. In Baltimore in 1907, for example, police subjected George Washington Lamberger, an

African American, to the third degree until he confessed to the murder of a white man. But his confession crumbled because the alleged murderer was named "Al Carter" and Lamberger had been forced to sign a confession with that name. When he was eventually released, the shaken man explained, "I told them they had the wrong man but they kept telling me I was Carter so I told them I was."[66]

As concern over the risk of innocents confessing under duress gained currency, writers, especially those intent on rendering the milieu of the nation's tumultuous cities, seized on the dramatic possibilities of the third degree. Charles Klein, an English-born playwright and actor who immigrated to America in 1883, made the practice the dramatic center of *The Third Degree*, published in 1908. Now forgotten, Klein enjoyed great success writing stage melodramas until his death on the *Lusitania* in 1915. The inspiration for his 1908 play was the case of Richard Ivens, a simpleminded youth tried and convicted for the rape and murder of a Chicago woman in 1906. Despite the absence of any physical evidence linking Ivens to the crime and considerable testimony that provided him with an alibi, he was prosecuted on the basis of a confession that police had wrung out of him. The criminologist J. Sanderson Christison, in a pamphlet intended to exonerate Ivens, joined Ivens's defense lawyers in objecting that the police had effectively hypnotized the highly suggestible youth to extract his confession. After the youth's execution, Hugo Munsterberg, a psychologist at Harvard University, concurred, censuring the state for killing an innocent person on the basis of a coerced confession. While taking license with the specifics of the Ivens case, Klein's play centers on the plight of a weak man who succumbs during his interrogation and admits to a murder he did not commit. The play encouraged audiences who might otherwise uncritically endorse police methods to ponder the ambiguity of confessions and to sympathize with suspects broken by the third degree. Because of Klein's mastery of the melodramatic conventions of the day and the timeliness of its subject, the play was performed widely during the next two decades. It was also turned into a novel and provided the screenplay for three films between 1913 and 1926; the last was an acclaimed adaptation directed by Michael Curtiz of future *Casablanca* fame.[67]

While Klein explored the psychological dimensions of the third degree, he shed little light on the routine practice of prosecutors and courts accepting coerced confessions as legitimate and credible. Opponents of the third degree tirelessly proclaimed that the practice endured only because of the complicity of lawyers and judges who failed to abide by existing laws banning coerced confessions. While police bullied confessions and testimony, they were not responsible for using them to convict and sentence alleged criminals. On occasion a crusading lawyer during the first two decades of the twentieth century not only warned of the menace that the third degree represented but also skillfully defended clients against its consequences. In 1902 in Jackson, Mississippi, for instance, Dabney Marshall defended Edward Ammons, a black man who confessed while in police custody to stealing a pistol. Marshall's only viable defense strategy was to get his client's confession thrown out. During an adroit examination of the chief of police, the lawyer elicited an admission that his client had been sequestered for days in a five-by-six sweatbox that had been swaddled in blankets and that neither light nor fresh air penetrated. Testimony also revealed that Ammons had been isolated from visitors, had never been informed that he did not have to answer questions, and had been warned that "white people would come in here and hang him." The concession that Ammons had literally been "sweated" before he confessed neither troubled the presiding judge nor prevented the jury from convicting the black man. But Marshall was tenacious and appealed the conviction to the Mississippi Supreme Court, where he persuaded the justices to overturn it. Even in a state where the notion of white supremacy profoundly distorted criminal justice, the justices recoiled at the contention that Ammons's confession had been "free and voluntary." The court denounced the police's use of torture to elicit a confession, which violated "every principle of law, reason, humanity, and personal right" and threatened to "restore the barbarity of ancient and medieval methods."[68] Marshall's victory in Mississippi heartened lawyers opposed to the third degree elsewhere, leading a New York attorney to predict, incorrectly, that it would "establish a precedent that will practically overthrow the pernicious system" of the third degree.[69]

The legal profession as a whole, however, was largely apathetic, preferring to ignore the third degree or dismissing it as an unfortunate but infrequent affliction. Periodically, conversations within the legal ranks about the third degree arose after instances of police interrogation that were perceived as egregiously excessive. The Erie County Bar Association in New York in 1908, for example, conducted an investigation into the interrogation of the young daughter of Anna Sutherland, a middle-aged wife and boarding house operator who shot her husband during a struggle. The Buffalo police already had a bad reputation stemming from five years prior when they had subjected two innocent women to the third degree following a murder. Nevertheless, the police and district attorney held the young girl incommunicado for days while badgering her with questions about her mother and her mother's alleged romance with one of the boarders. Although held without charges, the daughter was prevented from attending her father's funeral, which she only learned about days afterward. At an informal public hearing organized by the bar association, the daughter testified that her interrogators were "very sharp" with her. The investigation also confirmed her unlawful detention and denial of legal counsel. But the local press was satisfied that no unjustified acts of official brutality occurred, and neither the police nor the district attorney responsible for her interrogation suffered any consequences.[70] Elsewhere, bar associations in New York, Colorado, and Maryland discussed the third degree, but they too took no systematic steps to oppose it.[71] For every activist lawyer like Marshall who combated the practice, there was another attorney who perhaps concurred with the American Bar Association member who summarily dismissed the third degree as a delusion, sneering, "There ain't no such animal."[72]

Judges, like the justices of the Mississippi Supreme Court, periodically ruled against the introduction of coerced confessions into court proceedings and even publicly denounced the third degree. Gutsy judges did so even in cases involving serious felonies, such as arson, murder, and burglary.[73] Some publicly urged grand juries to investigate the interrogation methods used by local police.[74] But judicial activism against the third degree was hampered by the practical benefits of plea bargaining (and coerced confessions). Like prosecutors, judges during the late nineteenth and early twentieth century were overwhelmed by their caseloads. Moreover, cases that went to trial typically took longer with each passing decade. Amenable to any reasonable measure that would lighten their criminal caseloads, judges sanctioned plea bargaining while ignoring the coerced confessions that often undergirded it.[75]

Equally important, the ambiguity of legal definitions of voluntary confessions gave judges plenty of latitude to admit even seemingly dubious confessions. For most of the nineteenth century, the Supreme Court adopted a generous interpretation of the admissibility of confessions. The Court privileged "voluntary confessions," which were, in Justice John Marshall Harlan's words, "among the most effectual proofs in law." But the Court did not display particular concern about confessions obtained in the absence of counsel or without any warning of the confessor's rights. Only haltingly between 1890 and 1930 did the Court begin to consider confessions to be of constitutional significance. Beginning with the *Bram v. United States* decision in 1897, the Court affirmed that the only valid confession was one "made freely, voluntarily, and without compulsion or inducement of any sort." Despite this strong wording, the Court left unspecified what forms of persuasion were violations. For example, not until 1924 did the Court rule that harsh detention and interrogation methods could render a confession inadmissible. And even then, neither this nor previous Court decisions impinged on questionable confessions that were entered in state cases.[76]

State legislatures in Colorado and Kentucky attempted to clarify the uncertainty regarding coerced confessions by passing laws that specifically banned them. In Colorado, Harry Eugene Kelly, a reform-minded attorney, proposed a state law against "the diabolical third degree monstrosity" in 1907, and two years later the state legislature adopted it. The new law provided a lengthy description of prohibited methods of coercion, ranging from "exhibitions of wrath" to torture, and imposed a one- to two-year prison sentence on any law officer who violated it. The Kentucky state legislature in 1912 passed an "anti-sweating" law that imposed similar penalties on police who "sweated" prisoners, although this law left ambiguous which interrogation methods were deemed illegal. Neither law seems to have prompted other state legislatures to adopt comparable measures, perhaps because the effectiveness of the laws was open to question. Although appeals courts in Kentucky repeatedly affirmed the legality of the state's anti-sweating law, both judges and newspaper editors soon dismissed it as a dead letter. Police subverted the law without fear of prosecution, while states' attorneys neglected to enforce it.[77]

Federal officials displayed little sustained interest in the third degree prior to the 1920s. Their apathy in part reflected the modest scope of federal police powers, which included little more than preventing counterfeiting, protecting the president, and corralling bootleggers. Nevertheless, when several notorious instances of the third degree sparked national debate in 1910, the U.S. Senate established a select committee to investigate possible abuses by federal law officers. Although the committee's jurisdiction was strictly limited to investigating federal law officers, it did have standing to scrutinize the Washington, D.C., police force, which operated under federal authority. Despite a well-earned reputation for violence, the D.C. police were unscathed by the investigation. Richard Sylvester, the force's superintendent, skillfully marshaled his reputation as a police reformer to persuade the senators that the third degree was uncommon everywhere and inconceivable in his city. The committee heard from Attorney General George W. Wickersham, who affirmed that he had never heard of a federal law officer resorting to the third degree. The committee's claim to have made a "diligent" but unsuccessful search for any credible evidence of the third degree should have aroused skepticism, especially after the committee conceded that it had no "clear definition of what constitutes the so-called 'third-degree' ordeal."[78]

The select committee's investigation highlighted the challenges that stymied opponents of the third degree. There was no simple or direct way to attack it. The autonomy of the nation's myriad police forces, the vigorous championing of severe police methods by district attorneys and states' attorneys, the indifference of many judges to coerced confessions, and "the indifference of the community," posed daunting challenges to reformers intent on suppressing the practice.[79] By the early twentieth century, the practice had become so deeply ingrained in the nation's fragmented system of justice that sporadic and local campaigns to curtail it were inherently ineffective.

Few contemporaries anticipated that the constitutional ban on the production, importation, transportation, and sale of alcoholic beverages, which began in January 1920, would eventually elevate the third degree to a national scandal. Former president William Howard Taft, then chief justice of the Supreme Court, correctly predicted the sweeping impact of Prohibition on nameless citizens: "The reaching out of the great central power to brush the doorsteps of local communities . . . will be a strain upon the bond of the national union."[80] As Taft recognized, Prohibition demanded an unprecedented level of collaboration between state, local, and federal authorities to curb the personal habits of millions of Americans. By the end of the decade, when the challenges inherent in enforcing the Eighteenth Amendment threatened to overwhelm the capacities of local and state governments, President Herbert Hoover seized the opportunity to launch the first comprehensive investigation of the nation's system of criminal justice. Hoover's priority was the efficiency and integrity of American criminal justice; police torture was at most a passing consideration. But any comprehensive investigation of the nation's law enforcement was bound to touch on the third degree, and for some of the jurists and scholars whom the president recruited to conduct the study, the third degree was a glaring example of the threat that official misconduct posed to civil liberties.

The enforcement of Prohibition quickly evolved into a matter of law and order. The vast clandestine world of illegal sales and consumption of bootleg spirits posed enormous challenges to the traditions of extreme localism in American criminal justice. Moral suasion alone was insufficient to eradicate either the nation's taste for alcohol or the capacity to manufacture it. Vigorous demand for spirits speeded the rise of organized crime, which previously had established beachheads in prostitution and gambling but now quickly expanded into the underground liquor traffic. In 1919, even before Prohibition, the Chicago Crime Commission had concluded that "the business of crime is being more expertly conducted. . . . Modern crime, like business, is tending toward centralization, organization, and commercialization."[81]

Intended to cleanse society, the Eighteenth Amendment instead produced, as one cynic put it, "the bootlegger, the speakeasy, and a spirit of deliberate revolt."[82] Prohibition effectively criminalized a huge number of the nation's previously law-abiding citizens who now refused to conform to it. In the American imagination, crime moved from remote immigrant enclaves to downtown business districts and leafy suburbs. Fierce competition by rival gangs to dominate local vice markets led to chronic violence, and bystanders were frequent victims.

Meanwhile, the exploits of gangs of kidnappers and bank robbers called into question whether there were any havens from crime in the United States. The public could take little comfort in the integrity of public officials; the influence of bootleggers and organized crime reached into judges' chambers, mayors' offices, and police headquarters.

The prosecution of Prohibition-related crimes overwhelmed the nation's law enforcement agencies and criminal justice system. The number of long-term jail commitments doubled or tripled in many locales while prison populations exploded, resulting in chronic overcrowding at many of the nation's prisons. Agencies ramped up their efforts to combat the now-criminalized practice of drinking, but without evident effect. In Washington, D.C., for instance, arrests for public drunkenness actually tripled in the four years after the adoption of the Eighteenth Amendment, indicating not only the persistence of alcohol consumption but also the defiant attitude of speakeasy patrons who showed little concern about the threat of arrest.[83] The resolution of cases through plea bargaining became a necessity because many courts otherwise could not prosecute their swelling caseloads. By one estimate, less than 2 percent of the felony prosecutions initiated in Chicago during 1926 went to a jury.[84] These conditions magnified the pressure on police to obtain confessions sufficient to secure a plea bargain.

Thwarted by the creativity of bootleggers and the dissipation of their customers, impatient advocates of Prohibition responded with furious demands for ever more vigorous enforcement. Whether police resorted to the third degree more frequently during the 1920s is difficult to determine. They were no more likely to openly acknowledge using the third degree than they had been previously, but more than ever their public rhetoric conveyed a sense of dire emergency that discouraged any second-guessing of police methods. Pointing to the prevailing climate of lawlessness, the expanding influence of organized crime, and worsening violence in general, police superintendents and district attorneys pledged to adopt no-holds-barred tactics. New local and state laws bestowed substantial financial rewards on law officers who located stills and nabbed bootleggers. The allure of these bounties discouraged scrupulous attention to legal protocols. Simultaneously, many police forces were bolstered by deputized citizens whose methods of enforcing Prohibition and restoring law and order resembled vigilantism, complete with excessive violence and willful violations of civil liberties.[85]

The third degree, which previously had seemed far removed from the concerns of most law-abiding citizens, came to be seen widely as one especially glaring example of widespread police lawlessness. The coercive powers of the state now were manifest in roadblocks, luggage searches, raids on private parties, and police wiretaps of private phone lines. Enforcement bore down especially on working-class and black neighborhoods, but huge numbers of Americans from all walks of life now experienced police custody. With the privacy of innumerable citizens violated by law officers charged with enforcing Prohibition, and at a time when state-imposed coercion was broader than ever before and extended from censorship of literature and films to laws against the teaching of evolution, the liberties promised in the Bill of Rights acquired new significance. Reflecting on the recent experience of Prohibition in 1929, Clarence Darrow, a vigilant defender of civil liberties, raged against "nine years of agitation, of outrage, of gross violations of individual rights and open warfare against citizens."[86]

Contributing to the anxiety about civil liberties was the repression of free speech, which began during World War I and continued in the postwar campaign against radicalism. Civil liberty advocates, who had long struggled to help labor activists escape the oppressive weight of injunctions on public meetings and strikes, now took up the cause of radicals and antiwar dissidents who were arrested and deported without the right to counsel or habeas corpus. In 1917 Congress had passed the Espionage Act with the aim of providing federal authorities with new powers "to regulate the conduct of the individual during war time." This expansive law provided a pretext to prosecute not only avowed opponents of the war but also, for example, skeptics who mocked war bonds as worthless and cranks who hampered Red Cross fund-raising. Taken together, first the Espionage Act and then Prohibition granted exceptional police powers to local, state, and federal authorities under the faulty presumption that they could be trusted to apply them efficiently and prudently.[87]

By 1928 even champions of Prohibition acknowledged that the exercise of these new powers was so marred by ineptitude, corruption, and brutality that it eroded support for the Eighteenth Amendment. If the "noble experiment" was to endure, its enforcement needed to be reconsidered. During his presidential campaign Herbert Hoover adroitly appeased "drys," who sought a renewed and robust commitment to Prohibition, without alienating the "wets" within the Republican ranks who advocated for profound changes in Prohibition policies. Once elected, Hoover promptly appointed a commission of "impartial, judicial minded experts" to evaluate the enforcement of Prohibition.[88] Reflecting his almost boundless faith in the power of such bodies to resolve knotty public questions, Hoover appointed within a year of assuming the office nearly fifty commissions to investigate issues ranging from child welfare to the economic depression. Few were as consequential as the National Commission on Law Observance and Enforcement.

When Hoover established the commission in May 1929, he intended it to accomplish ambitious, even unrealistic goals. Although Prohibition provided the catalyst for the commission, his charge to its members extended well beyond it and was an unprecedented expansion of federal involvement in crime. His vision for the commission extended to "cover the entire question of law enforcement and organization of justice."[89] The president was keen to modernize the nation's ramshackle criminal justice system in order to overcome the fragmented administrative responsibilities and traditional localism that hindered federal and state collaboration. With the capacities of local communities and states swamped, the resources of the federal government were essential to curtail lawlessness. Beyond the challenges that the poor coordination of police forces and the inadequate training of law officers posed, Hoover acknowledged that police behavior was itself often lawless. At the commission's first meeting, he emphasized the need to investigate "the abuses in law enforcement" as well as "the alarming disobedience of law" and "the growth of organized crime."[90] During his presidential campaign he had conceded, "Common sense compels us to realize that grave abuses have occurred—abuses that must be remedied."[91]

Hoover's expansive charge to the commission gave its members virtually a free hand to investigate all facets of American criminal justice. Composed of an incongruous collection of well-heeled corporate

FIGURE 6.2. *President Herbert Hoover Meeting with the Wickersham Commission, May 1929.* In 1929 President Hoover appointed former attorney general George W. Wickersham to lead a commission to study Prohibition and law enforcement in the United States. Under the influence of Roscoe Pound (*front, left end*) and others, the commission compiled extensive evidence of use of the third degree and contributed to widespread condemnation of police impunity.

lawyers, conservative jurists, leftist legal activists, and social scientists, the commission held divergent positions on Prohibition and the commission's scope. George Wickersham, a prominent corporate lawyer and the attorney general during President Taft's administration, accepted the duties as the commission's chair (and as a consequence the commission was commonly called the Wickersham Commission). Especially important was Roscoe Pound, the dean of Harvard Law School, who took a leading role in writing significant portions of the commission's reports and who recruited a cadre of like-minded scholars and legal experts to serve as research assistants. The other members included federal judges, a former secretary of war, and the

president of Radcliffe College. Despite vigorous lobbying by prominent African Americans to include a black member, Hoover elected
not to do so on the grounds that he did not want to give any group
"special representation."[92]

At the outset, a majority of commission members agreed with
chairman Wickersham that their work must begin with fact-finding.
Because of the localism that pervaded American criminal justice, almost no statistics about national crime rates existed, and no federal
agency had a responsibility to collect them. Wickersham maintained
that "a proper system of judicial statistics is a rudimentary requirement for any civilized system of judicial administration, and it is a
tragedy that we have nothing of the kind, either Federal or state."[93]
Three of the members of the commission had participated in nongovernmental crime commissions that had begun to collect data on crime.
Pound especially was conversant on the topic, having served on a pioneering commission in Cleveland and having published lectures that
drew on contemporary social science and legal theory to explore the
impact of crime on contemporary America. The task of collecting national data fell to Sam Bass Warner, who had already earned a national
reputation for his statistical work on crime and prisons.

Reflecting the scale of its undertaking, the commission divided its
inquiry into eleven topics, ranging from the causes of crime and juve-
nile delinquency to the cost of crime and "lawlessness by governmental
law enforcing officers." Oversight for the compilation of data and the
writing of the report on police lawlessness was assigned to Pound,
who in turn recruited several assistants, all of whom were nationally
prominent as advocates for strengthened protections of civil liberties.
Carl S. Stern was a Georgia-born lawyer who worked in New York City.
William Pollak was a Harvard-educated lawyer who was a tenacious
defender of freedom of speech. Together they collaborated on an extensive report for the commission on the conviction of Tom Mooney and
Warren K. Billings for complicity in the bombings that had occurred
during the 1916 Preparedness Day parade in San Francisco. The trial,
which had taken place more than a decade earlier, had virtually nothing
to do with Prohibition. But civil libertarians pointed to it as a glaring
example of the gross violations of civil rights routinely carried out by
prosecutors and police. Stern and Pollak would eventually conclude

that the prosecution had deliberately inflamed public opinion against Mooney and Billings while the police had deprived them of access to counsel and subjected them to the third degree. The third researcher appointed to the team responsible for the report on police abuses was Zechariah Chafee Jr. Like Pollak, Chafee had been educated at Harvard, where he was powerfully influenced by Pound's advocacy of "sociological jurisprudence" to replace the arcane legal formalism that had shackled American law to inherited shibboleths. While Chafee initially made his name as an expert in equity law, he gained notoriety for his outspoken opposition to the legal repression of radical speech after World War I. In *Free Speech*, published in 1920, Chafee argued for an expansive interpretation of the First Amendment and the protections of free speech. Although highly controversial when published, Chafee's arguments became foundational to subsequent defenses of free speech and gradually transformed even the Supreme Court's position on the First Amendment.[94]

Just as Theodore Dwight Weld had used published accounts of slave torture to make the case against slavery and Herbert Welsh had used affidavits from soldiers to confirm instances of brutality in the Philippines, commission researchers used unimpeachable sources to demonstrate the prevalence and effects of the third degree. They surveyed appellate court decisions between 1920 and 1930 and identified more than a hundred cases in which defendants had suffered the third degree. Researchers conducted interviews in fifteen major cities with law officers and prosecutors; equally important, they also interviewed public defenders, community officials, reporters, convicts, ex-prisoners, and correction workers. The interviews vividly confirmed the sense of invulnerability enjoyed by many police. In Newark, New Jersey, for instance, police boasted that they used whatever measures were necessary, including violating the Constitution, to coerce confessions. But elsewhere, such as Boston, researchers learned that police only infrequently employed torture or other severe methods of interrogation. The research team compiled information on state statutes and local guidelines intended to regulate police behavior, including interrogation procedures and the treatment of suspects. Confirming the conventional wisdom that laws like those in Kentucky and Colorado were a dead letter, the commission discovered that even comparatively robust

regulations, such as those in Denver, failed to deter police from flagrantly abusing suspects. Finally, the researchers compiled the first
comprehensive survey of reputable studies of police abuse at the local
level, further confirming the breadth and variety of evidence of the
widespread use of the third degree.[95]

The commission began issuing its conclusions in January 1931. The
first findings addressed the enforcement of Prohibition laws, and after
cataloging the failings to date, it concluded with a call for vigorous federal leadership. Neither "drys," who found the findings too tepid in
defense of the Eighteenth Amendment, nor the "wets," who regretted
that the commission endorsed the continuation of Prohibition, were
appeased.[96] But the commission's subsequent reports touched on almost every conceivable dimension of the nation's criminal justice
system, including prison administration, the treatment of foreign nationals by law officers, the causes of criminality, and police excesses.
The reports offered scathing denunciations of received wisdom: stiff
punishments did not necessarily discourage crime; ethnic and racial
identity did not predispose individuals to crime; and law officers were
not blameless guardians of civilization. Taken together, the findings
were the first systematic and thorough survey of American criminal
justice.[97]

Arguably, the commission's most significant report was *The Third
Degree,* which was published in the late summer of 1931. Dense with
data and footnotes, the volume summarized all of the evidence collected by the commission. It demolished the claims that police seldom
employed the third degree and underscored the national scope of the
problem. It hammered away at the consequences of the practice, from
convictions based on false confessions and sloppy police work to courts
cluttered with appeals from victims of police abuse and the widespread
erosion of esteem for all involved in the administration of justice. The
report warned that "the third degree, in its nature brutal, must brutalize
those who practice it."[98]

Chafee himself later recalled with disappointment the commission's impact. But it was folly to believe that a presidential commission would abolish a practice that had been routine in American criminal justice for more than a half century. Yet the commission did have
some immediate effects. Its findings gave new urgency to a Department

of Justice investigation of the third degree and the Washington, D.C., police department. The investigation, which revealed widespread corruption and commonplace brutality within the police department, culminated in the trial of five policemen and the conviction of two of them in late 1931.[99] Contemporaries recognized the symbolism of both the revelations of the third degree in the nation's capital and the campaign to root it out. But Chafee had cause to be disappointed by the response of some police and public officials to the commission's findings. Senator Smith W. Brookhart of Iowa made a familiar complaint when he grumbled that the attention paid to the third degree and the investigation of the police in the capital had emboldened criminals and debilitated the police there.[100] Across the country, police chiefs dismissed the findings as exaggerated and lamented the mollycoddling of criminals.[101] The commission's report failed to nudge state and local officials to take the steps that Chafee outlined as necessary to combat the third degree.[102] And in those few instances when legislatures did act, prominent politicians often denounced the initiatives. For instance, in 1937 after the New York State Assembly passed a bill to prohibit the third degree, Mayor Fiorello La Guardia of New York City blasted it as the "Magna Carta" for "punks, pimps, crooks, gangsters, racketeers and the shyster lawyers." He claimed that the third degree was essential to rid the city of organized crime.[103]

Without question, the report dramatically increased public awareness of the third degree. Major newspapers publicized the findings and decried the practice. Popular books and mass-circulation magazine articles disseminated the commission's findings even further.[104] References to the third degree peppered contemporary radio dramas and Hollywood films; several movies depicted it, sometimes vividly.[105] The attention lavished on the murder of Hyman Stark by police in Mineola, New York, in July 1932 illustrates the new sensitivity to and interest in police procedures. Stark, along with three associates, had allegedly robbed and assaulted the elderly mother of a Mineola policeman. After arresting Stark, police subjected him to such a severe interrogation that he died while undergoing it. Subsequently, neither police officials nor the district attorney denied that police beat Stark to death. But apologists for the police contended that Stark had been a career criminal, had engaged in organized crime, and had preyed on vulnerable citizens. Opponents of the third degree pointed out that Stark was a petty criminal, had accomplices but was hardly a gangster, and would not have been beaten to death if he had not victimized the mother of one of the Mineola policemen. Prior to the Wickersham Commission, Stark's death almost certainly would have elicited only passing mention in the local press. Now the naked display of police brutality in Mineola unleashed a torrent of public outrage across the nation and became a symbol of lawless police so emboldened that they deliberately killed suspects.[106]

Such notorious examples of police excess along with the Wickersham Commission's call for better police training and methods bolstered the ongoing efforts of reformers intent on raising the professional standards in American criminal justice. Led by J. Edgar Hoover, director of the Federal Bureau of Investigation, and August Vollmer, the pioneering police superintendent in Berkeley, California, reformers made the case that forensics, new technologies, such as the lie detector, and well-trained investigators provided effective alternatives to coerced confessions. They insisted that the abolition of the third degree need not hamstring police. Rather, the combination of expertise and modern science would simultaneously restore the integrity of law enforcement and convict the nation's lawbreakers. Equally important, the campaign for the professionalization of police provided compelling justifications for new resources and expanded staffs, which even retrograde police departments welcomed. Downplaying their long-vaunted brawn and playing up their new professionalism, police officials claimed with new vigor that the third degree persisted only in the nation's hinterlands. In some communities this new public stance on police behavior by law officers was mere window dressing, but it still marked a significant shift in public tolerance of the third degree. Within a decade of the publication of the Wickersham Commission reports, law officers and public officials would, at most, excuse the third degree, but virtually none would publicly defend it.[107]

The most important effect of the Wickersham Commission's report on the third degree, arguably, was on the Supreme Court's evolving stance on civil liberties. The impact was indirect but nevertheless significant. It was not coincidental that the commission consultants responsible for the report on the third degree strenuously urged the

Supreme Court during the 1920s and 1930s to revise its interpretation of the scope of the Bill of Rights. Chafee's interpretation of the First Amendment protections on free speech, which he spelled out at the close of World War I, first won over a dissenting minority on the Court during the 1920s and by the 1930s enjoyed the support of a majority of the justices. In 1925 William Pollak advanced the argument that the First Amendment's guarantees of freedom of speech applied to the states because the Due Process Clause of the Fourteenth Amendment protects "liberty" from abridgment by the states. Working on behalf of the American Civil Liberties Union (ACLU), Pollak represented Benjamin Gitlow, a New York radical convicted of publishing a pamphlet that violated New York's law against "criminal anarchy." Although Pollak failed to persuade the Court to declare New York's criminal anarchy law unconstitutional, he did persuade it to articulate for the first time an expansive interpretation of the Fourteenth Amendment that extended due process guarantees to state actions. Heretofore, the Supreme Court, with few exceptions, had held that the guarantees of personal liberties in the Bill of Rights restricted the powers of the national government but not state governments. Even after the adoption of the Fourteenth Amendment in 1868, which placed restrictions on state power, the Court had balked at interpreting the amendment to protect either substantive rights, such as free speech, or criminal procedure protections, such as coerced confessions, against state actions. The Court's openness to Pollak's argument in the *Gitlow* case set the stage for expanded oversight of criminal procedures.[108]

In 1932, a year after the completion of the Wickersham Commission's report on the third degree, Pollak again stood before the Supreme Court. He represented the "Scottsboro boys," nine young black men convicted of raping two white women on a freight train near Scottsboro, Alabama. In this instance he prevailed, and the court ruled that because the men had been denied competent counsel they had not received a fair trial. In so ruling the court took a major step toward interpreting the Due Process Clause of the Fourteenth Amendment as requiring states to provide defendants with fair trials in fact, no less than in superficial form.[109]

Carl Stern, the third of the consultants responsible for the Wickersham Commission's report on the third degree, participated in the appeal of the conviction of Tom Mooney, a one-time labor activist and one of the alleged masterminds of a 1916 San Francisco bombing. Mooney's prosecution and conviction had been marred by myriad irregularities, which Stern and Pollak had investigated at great length while serving on the Wickersham Commission. In 1935 Stern argued before the Supreme Court that the deliberate use of perjured testimony against Mooney by the prosecuting attorney had constituted a clear denial of due process of law. Although the Court ruled against the appeal on narrow procedural grounds, its decision expressed clear sympathy for Stern's argument.

Despite the drift of the Supreme Court's emerging understanding of the Fourteenth Amendment, it had still not addressed the question of whether coerced confessions should be condemned under the Constitution.[110] In February 1936, in *Brown v. Mississippi*, the court established that the third degree was a constitutional violation. The crime that precipitated the decision had occurred in March 1934, three years after the publication of the Wickersham Commission's findings, when Raymond Stuart, a white planter in Kemper County, Mississippi, was murdered. Within days, Arthur Ellington, Ed Brown, and Henry Shields, three black tenant farmers, were arrested for the crime. At their trial, the prosecution's only substantial evidence was their confessions, which were extracted while they were in police custody. Prosecution witnesses freely admitted that the defendants confessed only after being brutally whipped by police and, in one instance, being strung up by the neck from a tree. Nevertheless, the presiding judge admitted the confessions into evidence, and they were the basis for the defendants' convictions and death sentences. (The prosecutor at the trial level, John Stennis, went on to represent Mississippi in the U.S. Senate for forty-two years.) The men appealed, and the state supreme court agreed with state prosecutors that Mississippi had fulfilled its obligation to provide a fair trial and that the defense had failed to object to the admission of the coerced confessions at the appropriate moment in the original trial.[111]

Eventually the men's appeal reached the U.S. Supreme Court, which in a unanimous decision reversed their convictions. Speaking for the Court, Chief Justice Charles E. Hughes began the decision by asking "whether convictions, which rest solely upon confessions shown to have been extorted by officers of the State by brutality and violence are consistent with the due process of law." After a thorough summary of the original trial and appeal, Hughes made it clear that the Court was no longer hesitant to intervene when "the process of justice" was subverted by states. "The State," he conceded, "is free to regulate the procedure of its courts in accordance with its own conceptions of policy, unless in doing so it "offends some principle of justice so rooted in traditions and conscience of our people as to be ranked as fundamental." This privilege, however, was contingent on "the requirement of due process of law." Following these broad assertions of principles, the Court hammered its conclusion home: "The rack and torture chamber may not be substituted for the witness stand."[112]

Among the legal innovations of the twentieth century, the federal regulation of criminal procedures ranks among the most transformative. In *Brown v. Mississippi* and subsequent decisions over the next three decades, the Court incrementally made the protections of the Bill of Rights binding on the states and established judicial restrictions on coercive interrogation in the United States. Justice Felix Frankfurter in 1952 explained the Court's expanding understanding of its obligation to extend the scope of the Equal Protection Clause: "The requirements of due process impose upon this Court an exercise of judgment upon the proceedings resulting in a conviction to ascertain whether they offend those canons of decency and fairness which express the notions of justice of English-speaking peoples." Whereas his predecessors on the Supreme Court prior to the 1920s had been timid about interfering in criminal trials or law enforcement, Frankfurter now contended that the Court was compelled to act because due process of law is "so rooted in the traditions and conscience of our people as to be fundamental, or implicit in the concept of ordered liberty."[113]

Emboldened by such convictions, the Court waded deeper and deeper into criminal procedures after the *Brown v. Mississippi* decision. In 1940, in *Chambers v. State of Florida*, the Court agreed with Thurgood Marshall of the NAACP that confessions coerced through protracted intimidation and questioning were a violation of the Due Process Clause. In the same year in *White v. State of Texas*, the Court reversed the conviction of a black man suspected of rape, who was held incommunicado for a week during which Texas Rangers beat him each

night until he confessed. In 1942 the Court ruled for the plaintiff in
Ward v. State of Texas, who had been arrested without a warrant, held
incommunicado, beaten, whipped, burned, and repeatedly threatened
with lynching by police. In reversing the defendant's conviction, the
Court spelled out police behavior that was unconstitutional, including
threats of mob violence, protracted questioning, holding prisoners incommunicado, and terrorizing them in isolated environs at night. Then
in 1944 the Court determined that some interrogation situations were
so inherently coercive that any confessions thereby gained were inherently involuntary and therefore were not admissible in a court. In this
case, the defendant, who allegedly hired a man to murder his wife, had
been deprived of counsel, sleep, and any opportunity to leave the interrogation room for two days. Throughout his ordeal he had been subjected to continuous questioning while exposed to blinding light by a
team of interrogators. A year later, in *Malinski v. People of the State
of New York,* the Court ruled that a confession extorted by stripping a
suspect of his clothes and then withholding them until he confessed
was not voluntary and therefore should not be allowed as evidence. The
culmination of the Supreme Court's decades-long campaign to safeguard criminal suspects was the *Miranda v. Arizona* decision in 1966,
in which the court established precise guidelines for police interrogation procedures. Writing for the majority, Chief Justice Earl Warren defended the Court's long-standing efforts to protect individuals from
"overzealous police practices." Each citizen's privacy, which itself was
"the hallmark of our democracy," rested on the constitutional foundation that government will respect the "inviolability of the human
personality."[114]

These expanding constitutional protections of criminal procedures
provided a crucial opening for attorneys and activists to combat the
third degree. Now any defendant who had endured the third degree and
who had the good fortune of competent counsel and access to funding
to sustain the appeal process might prevail and have his conviction
overturned. And whereas previously a significant juridical restriction
on coerced confessions in one state was unlikely to have any effect in
the rest of the nation, the Supreme Court established legal precedents
that applied everywhere. Energized by these rulings, local citizens'
groups rallied to publicize police excesses, and national organizations

committed to civil rights, especially the National Association for the Advancement of Colored People (NAACP) and the American Civil Liberties Union, launched campaigns to systematically litigate cases of police brutality.[115]

For the NAACP, the campaign against the third degree was integral to its ongoing campaign to suppress lynching, end "legal lynchings," and root out racism in the criminal justice system. For this reason, the NAACP played a central role in *Brown v. Mississippi* and many of the subsequent cases regarding coerced confessions. That these cases involved southern law officers contributed to a perception that the third degree was, like lynching, a phenomenon now peculiar to the South. Nothing could have been further from the truth. But the customary treatment of black suspects by white southern law officers was often so egregious and so openly acknowledged that the NAACP focused its limited resources there. The organization also recognized that the Court displayed waning tolerance for the distortions that white racism imposed on criminal procedures in the South. Moreover, any Supreme Court ruling that curtailed the third degree below the Mason-Dixon line would do so beyond the boundaries of the South as well.[116]

The cumulative effects of the Wickersham Commission's exposé of the extent and brutality of the third degree, the advocacy of new "scientific" policing by police reformers, the Supreme Court's newfound interest in criminal procedures, and the adroit legal activism of the NAACP and other groups effectively drove the third degree underground. Henceforth instances of torture by police were unambiguous violations of the Constitution. The Enlightenment-era promise to constrain the power of the state to torture its citizens, which had been expressed in the constitutional convention in 1789, was at long last the established law of the land.

Yet as Chafee recognized, police continued to practice the third degree. Although convictions based on coerced confessions could now be overturned, it remained extremely difficult to convict police who engaged in torture. Except in extreme cases, district and state's attorneys were loath to prosecute policemen who otherwise were their essential allies and on whom they relied to carry out their jobs. Police and prosecutors alike had an interest in weakening the Supreme Court's restrictions on the third degree. Police consequently devised methods of coercion, especially forms of psychological intimidation, that did not produce conspicuous or lasting physical wounds. By doing so they sought to avoid inadmissible confessions and to escape even the minimal risk of prosecution. These new modes of coercion in turn drove the Supreme Court to develop ever more specific and comprehensive restrictions on interrogation practices, which would continue through the 1960s.[117] But as long as police were unlikely to face prosecution for torture, they had the same incentives to resort to torture as their predecessors who determined that pounding a confession out of a suspect could speed up a conviction.

The ordeal endured by Roosevelt Scott, a black man arrested for murder in Chicago in 1959, is a vivid reminder of the tenacity of the culture of the third degree in some locales and the evident confidence of police despite the previous three decades of Supreme Court decisions. During his twenty-four-hour-long interrogation, Scott was hit with a baseball bat, a blackjack, and a city phone directory and then was forced to strip and lie naked on the floor while police struck his testicles with a belt.[118] Despite Scott's harrowing experience and that of other residents, Chicago police spokesmen insisted that the third degree had long fallen out of favor there. Yet when the Chicago Police Department publicly banned the third degree in 1963, some officers grumbled that the prohibition would embolden criminals and impede police from doing their jobs.[119]

SEVEN

Cold War Brutality

ROBERT VOGELER'S FIRST WORDS to the American officials who met him after his release by Hungarian police were "Those dirty bastards!" Seventeen months earlier, in November 1949, he had been dragged from a car in Budapest and accused of being an American spy. American diplomats had been powerless to help the telecommunications executive while Hungarian authorities held him in a windowless cell adjoining a chamber where they tortured prisoners. Denied contact with a lawyer or his wife, he was deprived of sleep, exposed to blinding light, subjected to relentless interrogations, drugged, and beaten until he signed a ghostwritten confession. During his subsequent show trial, he briefly appeared in public, admitted to being a foreign agent, and received a fifteen-year sentence. Then he disappeared back into a Hungarian prison. After months of fitful negotiations, urged on by a publicity campaign led by his wife, American diplomats secured his freedom. But before his release, his Hungarian captors warned him, "Upon what you say will depend the treatment we give other Americans."[1]

In the weeks after his release, Vogeler gave halting interviews during which he appeared haggard, confused, and overwrought. Gradually he regained some of his former swagger and began publicly describing his ordeal. He presented himself as an ordinary American citizen who had been a victim of indefensible communist torture and manipulation. In an address to the National Press Club in 1951, he cautioned his fellow Americans: "It can happen to anyone, it can happen to you." Within a year he published *I Was Stalin's Prisoner*, a harrowing account of his captivity, and became a minor celebrity in the intensifying anticommunist crusade in the United States.[2]

Vogeler's prominence rested on his firsthand experience with communist terror at a time when torture loomed in the American imagination more persistently than at any time since the nation's founding. Torture, of course, had long been associated with despotic regimes, but Americans assumed that their institutions and their comparative geographic isolation offered ample protection against its malign effects. But recent history raised the very real prospect that torture, which had been condemned as an archaic form of barbarism that the march of progress would eliminate, was instead becoming the favored tool of regimes intent on crushing individual autonomy. The binary that contrasted civilization with barbarism and torture acquired renewed significance, with democratic civilization now pitted against totalitarian terror.

When listening to Robert Vogeler and other victims of communist torture recount the physical and psychological desolation that they experienced at the hands of interrogators, Americans had cause to worry that communists had pioneered alarmingly effective methods of coercion, including "brainwashing" and other forms of mind control. Torture now was much more than a vice of sadists, autocrats, and vengeful armies; it was a sophisticated weapon that could warp the individual human mind and squelch the collective soul of a nation. In the face of such a dire threat, the United States seemingly had only one course open. In a secret report to President Dwight Eisenhower, General James H. Doolittle admonished Americans, "Hitherto acceptable norms of human conduct do not apply. We must learn to subvert, sabotage, and destroy our enemies by more clear, more sophisticated, and more effective methods than those used against us. . . . It may be necessary that the American people be made acquainted with, understand, and support this fundamentally repugnant philosophy."[3]

The nation's military and newly established national security agencies scrambled to meet the menace of what Central Intelligence Agency Director Allen Dulles called "brain warfare." By recruiting the behavioral sciences to the challenge of communist torture and brainwashing, American Cold Warriors transformed the "science" of torture and incorporated it into the nation's arsenal. In practice, the application of this new science fell to American proxies in the developing world who battled insurgencies that threatened American interests and allies. As had been true throughout the nation's history, the torture that happened on the frontiers of the American empire could be ignored, dismissed, or excused as an unfortunate element of the struggle to extend democracy and defend civilization.

Most Americans were wholly unaware of the extent to which American national security agencies were deeply complicit in developing and disseminating the science of torture. During the three decades after World War II, many American observers voiced deep concern about the proliferation of torture and urged the United States to avoid adopting any practices that resembled torture. Their pleas were consonant with the long tradition of public assertions of the nation's innocence. But they also reflected the extent to which the militarization of torture was hidden from the nation. Not until the Vietnam War and investigations of secret CIA programs during the 1970s did most Americans come to understand the extent to which their nation had licensed torture around the world in the name of defending democracy.

The Manichaean binary that pitted democratic civilization against modern totalitarian barbarism emerged gradually. Some Americans recalled the Soviet "show trials" of the late 1930s when they contemplated the terror techniques that threatened American civilization after World War II. Between 1936 and 1938 Americans learned of the extraordinary public confessions made by prominent Soviets who admitted to being accomplices of disgraced former Bolshevik Leon Trotsky and the coordinated fascist and capitalist campaign to destroy the communist movement. Many Western commentators regarded the early trials as fair and believed the accused were clearly guilty. But as the purges expanded to include virtually every living Bolshevik other than Joseph Stalin, some sympathetic observers began to question the increasingly outlandish confessions of hitherto staunch Communists. Despite hints of the torture used to secure the confessions, enough ambiguity surrounded the trials to allow Americans to interpret them according to their prejudices. Not until 1956, when Soviet premier Nikita Khrushchev delivered a searing indictment of Stalin's reign, including the show trials, did diehard American communists concede the illegitimacy of the trials and the coerced confessions.[4]

Americans displayed more certainty about the perceived barbarism of the German and Japanese enemy during World War II. Even Americans who had overlooked the brutal treatment of Jews in Germany after Hitler's rise or the atrocities that accompanied the Japanese invasion of Nanjing in 1937 were appalled by German and Japanese behavior once the United States was drawn into the war. Reacting to reports ranging from Japanese making sport of torturing prisoners of war in Southeast Asia to German doctors and scientists conducting "scientific torture" on members of the Polish underground and civilians, Americans struggled to find adequate language to voice their horror before resorting to time-honored labels such as "fiends," "savages," "beasts," and "Spanish inquisitors" for German and Japanese torturers.[5]

Yet after the war, many Americans tempered their condemnation and offered surprisingly charitable views of the former enemy. Some were chastened by the indiscriminate devastation of Japan and Germany wrought by American aerial bombing. Accounts of summary executions by American troops in the Pacific, Sicily, and elsewhere also were disturbing at a time when the United States was prosecuting former enemies for similar atrocities. Without question, overt anti-Semitism informed the attitudes of some Americans. As the full scope of the Nazi campaign to exterminate Jews emerged, American skeptics dismissed the evidence as exaggerated by Jews intent on revenge. Yet other Americans, including the most strident anticommunists and white supremacists, had long viewed communism rather than fascism as the gravest threat to the United States. Now that Nazism had been eradicated, the thinking went, Germans would revive their civilized traditions and could be recruited to the global fight against communism.[6]

All of these attitudes surfaced in response to claims that American interrogators had tortured Waffen-SS soldiers charged with the massacre of hundreds of captured Americans near the village of Malmédy,

Belgium, in December 1944. Within days of the executions, firsthand accounts of them spread, prompting furious demands for retaliation. In the closing months of the war, American officials tracked down more than seventy German soldiers responsible for the atrocities and prepared to prosecute them for war crimes. When the German prisoners were brought before a tribunal in Dachau, Germany, during the summer of 1946, the prosecution seemingly had an overwhelming case based on eyewitness testimony and confessions of the alleged perpetrators themselves.[7]

Before the trial opened, however, several defendants leveled charges of cruelty and torture against their American interrogators, many of whom were prewar Jewish émigrés to the United States. Defense lawyers began tacking on ever more alarming allegations, including that the interrogators had kept the defendants in "dark, solitary confinement at near starvation rations up to six months; had applied various forms of torture, including the driving of burning matches under the prisoners' fingernails; had administered beatings which resulted in broken jaws and arms and permanently injured testicles." Unswayed by these accusations, the court imposed death sentences on forty defendants and prison terms on thirty more.[8]

In the eyes of critics, virtually every aspect of the trials smacked of victor's justice. Colonel Willis Everett, an American lawyer and the lead defense counsel for the German soldiers, relentlessly broadcast the accusations of his clients and recruited American politicians and jurists to press for an investigation. An official commission in 1948 confirmed that interrogators had held mock trials and used "irregular" interrogation methods. But it rejected the charges of pervasive torture. Unmollified, Everett persisted with his campaign and was abetted by Judge Edward L. Van Roden, a member of the commission, who began making inflammatory statements alleging that the German defendants "had been kicked in the testicles beyond repair," a method of abuse that was "standard operating procedure with our American investigators." These alarming charges elicited disappointment and anger from editorialists who regretted that American interrogators were lowering themselves to the level of their reviled Nazi prisoners.[9]

Goaded to action by the allegations and the controversy they aroused, a subcommittee of the U.S. Senate Committee on Armed

Services, chaired by Senator Raymond E. Baldwin, undertook a review of the trials in 1949. Senator Joseph McCarthy, then a junior legislator from Wisconsin who was desperate to garner national attention, routinely disrupted the subcommittee's hearings with extravagant claims and flamboyant behavior. Using many of the methods that would later distinguish his crusade against alleged communists in the federal government and U.S. Army, McCarthy seized every opportunity to magnify the accusations against the American interrogators. While badgering the secretary of the army, McCarthy grumbled, "We have been accusing the Russians of using force, physical violence, and have accused them of using mock trials in cells in the dark of the night, and now we have an Army report that comes out and says we have done all the things that the Russians were ever accused of doing." Impugning the interrogators because they were Jewish, he accused them of forming a "vengeance team" and persecuting the defendants out of their intense hatred for "the German people as a race."[10] Subsequent testimony from a lengthy list of witnesses punched huge holes in McCarthy's assertions and in Van Roden's credibility. When the subcommittee issued its final report, it dismissed the claims of torture and reaffirmed that the trials had been fair.[11]

The controversy surrounding the Malmédy war crimes trials revealed the complex crosscurrents that swirled around debates about torture during the Cold War. The allegations against the American interrogators aroused comment around the world, and no refutation by the Senate or any other government body was sufficient to discredit them. The controversy left the indelible impression that Americans were in no position to condemn Germans for transgressions that Americans had themselves committed. Although the victims of alleged torture were war criminals accused of summarily executing Americans with gunshots to the head, many Americans strenuously denounced the alleged use of torture against them. For the nation's political class, the outcry suggested that if Americans were unwilling to excuse the torture of Nazi war criminals, they were unlikely to condone the torture of any other.

In March 1950, six months after the Senate subcommittee issued its report on the Malmédy trials, *Time* reported that the State Department had answered "a question which has interested the West since the famous Moscow purge trials of 1936–38" and that had taken on new urgency since the show trial of Robert Vogeler: "How do Communist secret police extort 'confessions'?" A State Department report summarized the ordeal of a Bulgarian employee of the American embassy in Sofia who had been coerced to confess to being an American spy. He had been denied food and water, beaten, and forced to stand in painful stances for hours while fielding questions until he confessed to whatever charges his interrogators leveled against him. His description of his interrogation foreshadowed by a year Vogeler's account of his torture.[12] A striking feature of both the State Department report and the *Time* article was the suggestion that Communists had pioneered wholly original and uncommonly effective methods of coercion. Neither the report nor the article acknowledged the similarities between the third degree methods routinely employed by American police and the techniques used by Eastern European police. Instead the publicity stoked mounting anxiety that Communists were masters of psychological manipulation and that the United States was alarmingly vulnerable to their methods.

Three months later, the United States was at war against Communists in Korea. Almost immediately the United States reported that North Korean soldiers were torturing, beating, starving, marching to death, and summarily executing prisoners of war. (Four years later, Senator Charles E. Potter would claim that "approximately two-thirds of all American prisoners of war in Korea died due to war crimes.")[13] Within days of the start of the conflict, North Koreans began broadcasting radio messages by American prisoners denouncing the war. As the conflict dragged on, the statements issued by American prisoners became ever more provocative. In 1952 two captured Air Force officers professed their newfound contempt for capitalism while affirming that the United States was using biological weapons against North Korea. Within a year at least twenty-one other American airmen had made similar accusations in print, on camera, and during radio broadcasts.[14]

While scrutinizing these confessions American commentators discerned in the prisoners' "trance-like" mannerisms and speech unmistakable evidence of an "inhuman method for tampering with men's minds and souls."[15] Secretary of Defense Charles E. Wilson lashed out at the Chinese and North Koreans, accusing them of "a 'new' form of war crime, and a new refinement in atrocity techniques; namely, 'mind murder.'"[16] These fears were exacerbated in 1953 when the warring nations exchanged prisoners of war as part of a negotiated armistice. Twenty-one American prisoners refused to repatriate to the United States, to the dismay of their families and American officials. Instead, they enthused about the attractions of the communist way of life to journalists who had gathered to report on the prisoner exchange. Because most Americans found it inconceivable that any American prisoner of war would willingly remain in a totalitarian Communist society, the only plausible explanation for their behavior was sinister new forms of mind control.[17]

Sensational claims about communist torture, combined with anticommunist hysteria, impeded any accurate understanding of communist techniques. Purported experts insisted that communist torturers not only wore down their victims' resolve but actually rendered them brainwashed zombies bereft of individual will. Several psychiatrists claimed that Soviets and their Chinese allies had adapted techniques of negative and positive stimuli previously used to condition animal behavior. By alternately increasing and reducing a prisoner's suffering, whether through hunger, physical pain, or sleep deprivation, communist torturers allegedly altered their prisoners' thought processes and beliefs to imitate those of their captors. Even more alarming, the Soviets purportedly had devised a new form of lobotomy, and the Chinese advanced drugs to render tractable anyone who otherwise resisted the rigorous conformity demanded by Communism.[18] With even battle-hardened American soldiers being "broken" and transformed into slogan-spouting Communist loyalists, what hope was there that the average American, like Robert Vogeler, could withstand communist psychological warfare?

The Air Force, which was embarrassed by the number of captured airmen who leveled allegations of germ warfare against their own nation, concluded that its servicemen had not been adequately trained to withstand enemy torture and indoctrination. In response, the service expanded its World War II–era "evasion and escape" training and established a so-called brainwashing school at Stead Air Force Base in Nevada, where airmen underwent simulated captivity, including grueling interrogations, forced marches in bare feet, electric shocks, sleep

FIGURE 7.1. "The Evidence Is Piling Up." This cartoon, by Leo J. Roche, depicts a long line of "Returned UN prisoners" testifying before Uncle Sam about "Red Brutalities to PWs." The cartoon conveyed American outrage over American prisoners having been subjected to brainwashing, torture, and other cruelties, and over the apparent success of these methods in extorting false confessions.

deprivation, and confinement in a steel "sweatbox" and a hole filled with shoulder-deep water.[19] Its director, Colonel Burton McKenzie, explained tersely, "We have imported from Korea some of the gimmicks they [the communists] used in their interrogation."[20]

The U.S. Army and Marines established similar programs but were reluctant to excuse the traitorous behavior of American prisoners of war. The two services adopted a hard line toward their servicemen who had "collaborated." From the vantage point of the army and Marine Corps high command, the explanation for why prisoners during the Korean War, unlike their predecessors in other wars, had succumbed to the enemy's persuasion could be traced to alarming failings in contemporary American culture, not communist mind control. Experts who testified before a Senate probe of communist brainwashing leveled similar charges, including astonishing estimates that between 30 and 70 percent of Americans in captivity had succumbed to communist methods because of pervasive character flaws. So-called collaborators displayed a litany of defects, including too little patriotism, too little Christian piety, and too little understanding of the evils of Communism. Beyond the immediate task of punishing disloyal former prisoners of war, army and Marine Corps leaders advocated for an urgent national campaign to restore the national character.[21]

The behavioral sciences figured prominently in the nation's responses to communist psychological warfare during the Korean War. Reaffirming a fundamental lesson of World War II, American military planners stressed that war must be treated as a psychological contest as much as a military struggle. In a dangerous world buffeted by warped ideologies, military and political leaders looked to the behavioral sciences to provide the essential cultural and scientific understanding needed to defend the nation. As early as 1951, the Joint Chiefs of Staff had fantasized about "intangible" weapons that would transform warfare. To achieve this goal, the Joint Chiefs urged national action to "develop and rapidly implement a large-scale program of psychological warfare, including special operations, comparable in scope to the Manhattan District Project of World War II."[22]

Although no coordinated program akin to the atomic bomb program was established during the 1950s and 1960s, the U.S. military became, by far, the nation's most eager client for and generous bene-

factor of behavioral modification research. The services institutional-
ized psychological programs initiated during World War II while also
subsidizing a wide range of new academic projects, including behavioral sciences research units. Funded almost exclusively by the military and national security agencies, but nominally affiliated with and
located in universities, these new centers housed ambitious psychological and behavioral sciences programs whose principal clients in turn
were the Pentagon and national security agencies.[23]

Behavioral scientists embraced the opportunity to demonstrate the
unique relevance of their expertise for national security. They nodded
in agreement when President Dwight Eisenhower proclaimed in 1954
that "the world, is now split by hostile concepts of man's character and
nature."[24] While the behavioral sciences in the Soviet bloc had become instruments of totalitarianism, American scientists countered
that they had the expertise to analyze and mold human behavior to
forestall communist victory while preserving rational, modern democratic values in the United States and elsewhere. Although unquestionably opportunistic, behavioral scientists also were sincere in their
conviction that a multidisciplinary fusion of anthropology, psychology, medicine, sociology, and cybernetics held the key to the manipulation of the human motivation and behavior that were crucial to
any American response to the threat of communist science.

The nation's new national security agencies, especially the CIA,
were even more avid consumers of behavioral science research than the
military. In 1952 a CIA medical officer advised that communists "were
utilizing drugs, physical duress, electric shock and possibly hypnosis."
Given the alarming advances and the regrettable "laxity" of the American response to them, he exhorted the nation "to assume a more aggressive role in the development of these techniques."[25] A year later and
two months after assuming the directorship of the CIA, Allen Dulles
told an audience of Princeton alumni that too few Americans realized
"how sinister the battle for men's minds had become in Soviet hands."
The United States, Dulles warned, faced a foe who had mastered "brain
perversion techniques."[26]

To meet this urgent threat, the CIA pursued the development of sophisticated methods of individual and mass persuasion. By mastering
the techniques of ideological conversion and coercive interrogation, the

CIA pledged to be better prepared to defend citizens and soldiers against such methods. Simultaneously, proficiency in "brain warfare" would enable the American intelligence community to achieve, in the words of an internal CIA memorandum, the goal of "controlling an individual to the point where he will do our bidding against his will and even against such fundamental laws of nature as self-preservation."[27] With these aims in mind, the CIA poured several billion dollars into research related to mass persuasion, effective means of interrogation, and the effects of various forms of coercion. Organized through the Scientific Intelligence Division of the agency, the project, code-named MKUltra, began during the early 1950s and continued until 1973.

Among the earliest methods of furtive mind control investigated by the CIA were hypnotic suggestion and powerful psychoactive drugs. As early as 1949 a team began experimenting with using hypnosis during interrogations. But after hundreds of experiments, the agency concluded by 1953 that hypnosis had no practical applications in the world of espionage. Simultaneously, the CIA funded research to identify and develop drugs that would induce spontaneous confessions, promote illogical thinking, inhibit ambition and efficiency, enhance the capacity to withstand torture, produce amnesia, and boost susceptibility to suggestion. The program, which lacked meaningful oversight, quickly devolved into a tragicomic farce. Between 1953 and 1964, scientists administered LSD, mescaline, psilocybin, and other drugs to more than 6,700 unwitting subjects, including soldiers, mental patients, prisoners, drug addicts, and prostitutes. Although some drugs had dramatic, even catastrophic effects on subjects, they failed in most instances to produce either predictable or useful results. By the early 1960s the CIA grudgingly concluded that psychotropic and other drugs had only limited efficacy in "brain warfare."[28]

Sensory deprivation and disorientation proved far more promising tools in the CIA's quest to achieve mind control. Between 1951 and 1954, the CIA funded experiments that demonstrated the devastating psychological impact of sensory deprivation. More than a century before, Charles Dickens and other critics of the solitary confinement regime at Eastern State Penitentiary and elsewhere had described the crippling effects of primitive sensory deprivation on prisoners. Now Donald O. Hebb, a preeminent Canadian neuroscientist, brought to the assessment of sensory deprivation unprecedented scientific rigor and impeccable credentials. His broader ambition was to solve the riddle of the relationship between the biological functions of the brain as an organ and the higher functions of the mind. In pursuit of that goal, he readily accepted CIA funding to study how the presence and absence of stimuli affected consciousness. "The chief impetus" for his work, he later acknowledged, was "the problem of brainwashing." Dismayed by the "confessions" made at Communist show trials, he said, "We did not know what the Russian procedures were, but it seemed that they were producing some peculiar changes of attitude. How?"[29] Hebb's experiments demonstrated that humans deprived of light and other sensory stimuli for even comparatively brief periods often experienced hallucinations and severe disorientation. Thus debilitated, subjects could be rendered uncommonly suggestible and compliant during interrogation.[30]

The CIA found another willing research partner in Dr. Ewen Cameron, a renowned social psychologist affiliated with McGill University. With the aim of correcting schizophrenia by erasing memories and "reprogramming" psyches, Cameron subjected approximately one hundred patients, many of whom were involuntary subjects with only moderate psychiatric symptoms, to a three-stage "depatterning" process between 1957 and 1964. First they underwent a drug-induced coma for up to nearly three months. Next they endured extreme electroshock treatment three times daily for a month before wearing football helmets in which they listened to an endlessly looping tape recording of noise and terse statements. Labeled "psychic driving," the procedure attempted to wipe clean existing recollections while implanting new memories on a "clean slate."

Cameron described his "psychic driving" techniques at major professional meetings in the behavioral sciences and published his findings in prestigious medical journals. While some fellow scientists questioned the theories that undergirded his work, his research methods aroused few complaints and did nothing to damage his stature. Indeed, during the years of his work on "depatterning," Cameron served as president of four of the largest American, Canadian, and international psychiatric associations. His peers bestowed these honors on him even though his experiments produced no discernible benefits for his research subjects. Quite to the contrary, many of his patients suffered severe and lasting effects from the procedures, ranging from near-total amnesia and loss of speech to total incontinence.[31]

Cameron's research, nonetheless, was of considerable value to the CIA and the maturing science of "brain warfare." It confirmed and expanded knowledge about the profoundly destabilizing effects of extreme sensory deprivation and manipulation on individuals. Even in an era when the protocols for informed consent by research subjects were exceedingly lax, the CIA was unlikely to find contemporary scientists willing to carry out more invasive and extreme experiments on human subjects than those conducted by Cameron. He had found the threshold beyond which sensory deprivation and manipulation rendered humans so incapacitated that they were of no practical use as pliable tools in the superpower rivalry. The goal, after all, was to coerce enemy agents to talk, not babble. But with proper calibration, some of Cameron's techniques offered a promising method for controlling human thought and behavior.

Behavioral sciences research also clarified for the CIA how to achieve obedience from individuals in situations in which they might otherwise resist authority because of pangs of conscience. The research of Hebb, Cameron, and others provided the military and national security agencies with methods to coerce behavior in highly controlled circumstances, such as the research laboratory or an interrogation chamber. But short of recruiting and training sadists, the CIA and the other agencies needed to be able to find foot soldiers to wage "brain warfare" who would not recoil at the torment that they might be required to inflict on enemy subjects.

In 1961 Stanley Milgram, an assistant professor of social psychology at Yale, demonstrated, as he put it, that "human nature—or more specifically, the kind of character produced in American society—cannot be counted on to insulate its citizens from brutality and inhumane treatment at the direction of malevolent authority."[32] In what became one of the most notorious psychological experiments of the twentieth century, Milgram invited New Haven residents to a laboratory where they were told they were participating in a study of memory and learning. Assigned the role of teachers, the subjects began teaching word associations to fellow subjects (who actually were Milgram's assistants). Each time the learners made mistakes, the teachers administered incrementally more powerful electric shocks to them. Eventually, the alleged shock level reached a threshold at which the health of the "learners" purportedly was at risk and their cries of pain aroused concern among the teachers. Nevertheless, two-thirds of all of Milgram's subjects continued to administer shocks beyond levels that purportedly resulted in severe pain and possible death.

Milgram immediately recognized the implications of his experiment. He subsequently would explain that "the essence of obedience consists in the fact that a person comes to view himself as the instrument for carrying out another person's wishes, and he therefore no longer sees himself as responsible for his actions."[33] His experiment suggested that the likelihood of obedience could be increased by insulating subjects from the consequences of their actions. Subjects had been reticent to deliver the most powerful shocks to learners who were in close proximity and whose discomfort could not be ignored. Such restraint, however, evaporated if the learners were at a remove from the subjects. Milgram confided early in his experiments, "In a naïve moment some time ago, I once wondered whether in all of the United States a vicious government could find enough moral imbeciles to meet the personnel requirements of a national system of death camps, of the sort that were maintained in Germany. I am now beginning to think that the full complement could be recruited in New Haven."[34]

By the early 1960s the CIA had funded and compiled sufficient scientific research to refine and modernize methods of coercion that had been used for millennia. Through a mixture of physical deprivation and sensory disorientation, orchestrated by professional interrogators, the CIA had "brain perversion techniques" to rival those employed by the Communists in Korea and elsewhere. The cutting-edge science that informed these techniques provided a patina of moral legitimacy to them. Archaic thumbscrews and manacles gave way to antiseptic assaults on the mind and body that left no visible scars. Given that the same techniques had been applied to subjects in the laboratory and as part of psychiatric interventions, the new techniques of "brain warfare" were manifestly different from the brutish torture and coercion of yore. Indeed, when the techniques became the subject of controversy during the 1970s, CIA officials and their allies would insist that sleep deprivation, sensory disorientation, and the other methods did not meet the definition of torture.

The rudiments of this science of "brain warfare" could be discerned by anyone who waded through the dry-as-dust research findings produced by CIA-funded behavioral scientists. Cameron's research, for example, was widely publicized, although the source of his funding was not. Some researchers, like Hebb, knew they were conducting research with CIA funding, but others did not. Nor were the practical national security applications of the research publicized. From the outset, the CIA's program in psychological manipulation was covert, and its outlines became public only during the 1970s.

The secrecy of the CIA's investment in psychological warfare was in keeping with the intelligence community's innate predisposition for covert operations. The military and national security agencies were less motivated by concerns about the ethical scruples of scientists than by the ethos of secrecy that suffused the Cold War superpower rivalry. The fetish for concealment seemed prudent at a time when otherwise levelheaded government officials feared that communist agents had infiltrated all levels of the American state, including the national security agencies. Secrecy, moreover, was believed to be essential for the tactical effectiveness of the nation's covert operations.[35]

The absence of any tradition of democratic oversight of intelligence activities greatly facilitated the national security agencies' penchant for covert operations. Not until after World War II and enactment of the National Security Act of 1947 did Congress attempt to supervise intelligence activities. Even so, for all practical purposes the CIA operated with almost complete autonomy and had no statutory obligation to reveal its operations. Such oversight as did occur was the responsibility of two committees in the House of Representatives and the Senate. The budget for the agency was classified and, for security reasons, was hidden in nondescript line items of the defense budget. Only the chairmen and ranking minority members of the relevant subcommittees had even rudimentary knowledge of intelligence activities. Proposals periodically surfaced to create special committees with responsibility for intelligence oversight during the 1950s and 1960s, but Congress never adopted any of them. With good reason, critics of the CIA would later complain that it operated as a secret state within the state.

The nation's programs in "brain warfare" also were shielded from the public because the CIA had ample cause to believe they would be controversial if they were publicized. The public response to the accusations of torture during the Malmédy trials had been cautionary. Even more worrisome was the controversy that erupted following the publication of an article in *Newsweek* in 1955 that described the methods used at the Air Force's "brainwashing school." Commentators from across the nation questioned the ethical propriety of the school and worried about the likely impact of its methods on both the servicemen who attended it and the officers who conducted it. Methodist bishop John Wesley Lord proclaimed that the school was "revolting to any right-thinking American."[36] The editor of a small-town newspaper in Pennsylvania seethed, "Submitting American youngsters in the armed services to torture tests to 'teach them to take it' is the most repulsive idea we've heard yet. THAT isn't the answer to anything. It only puts the officers who permit it and carry it out in the same class as the Communists themselves."[37] An editor in Virginia concluded that the explanation for the Air Force's "torture academy" was that "sadists have gotten into the act."[38] The *Saturday Review* concurred, excoriating the "school for sadists" and warning that "brutality is like a bullet; you don't shoot a man to prepare him for war."[39]

The "brainwashing school" even elicited criticism from otherwise ardent Cold Warriors like Senator John Stennis, who expressed concern over the hardships that airmen might undergo there. Two decades earlier, when he was a Mississippi prosecutor, Stennis had shown no comparable concern about the ordeal of the three black murder suspects whose coerced confessions he used to secure their death sentences (and which prompted the Supreme Court to issue its landmark *Brown vs. Mississippi* decision). When even a former prosecutor well versed in the third degree was hesitant to condone the Air Force's training school, the military and national security agencies recognized the urgent need for discretion in all matters related to "brain warfare."[40]

In the face of rising protest, the Pentagon backpedaled swiftly. A week after *Newsweek*'s initial exposé, the Air Force announced that airmen would "undergo 'torture' techniques only if they volunteer," and three months later, the service disclosed that students would merely "watch instructors using Communist interrogation techniques on one another."[41] But by then the Air Force's brainwashing imbroglio already had stoked concerns about excessive secrecy within the Pentagon, prompting commentators to conclude that information about the "brainwashing school" had been "withheld deliberately in fear of nationwide criticism."[42]

The popular outcry about the Air Force program also reflected public expectations about the nation's commitment to individual rights that had been fostered by national leaders themselves. For more than a decade, human rights had been promoted first as a major Allied war aim and then as the foundation for postwar peace. President Franklin D. Roosevelt, in the Atlantic Charter and the declaration by the United Nations that he had helped craft, had declared that the Allies were fighting to guarantee self-government, freedom of speech, religious liberty, and economic security to peoples worldwide. But from the outset, human rights advocacy by Roosevelt and later by President Harry Truman was conservative in nature. Lofty general principles had to be squared with both respect for national sovereignty and inconvenient and enduring violations of human rights within the United States. The United Nations' charter, for instance, did not define or enumerate "human rights and fundamental freedoms," leaving the meaning of the two terms deliberately vague. Similarly, the United Nations' Universal Declaration of Human Rights, arguably the crowning expression of World War II–era human rights advocacy, was nonbinding on signatories and was barren of any meaningful enforcement schemes.[43]

President Dwight Eisenhower shared his predecessors' skepticism about any human rights advocacy that might open American race relations and capitalism to international scrutiny and censure. His reticence also reflected the power of isolationist anti-communists, led by Senator John Bricker of Ohio and the American Bar Association, who warned that human rights treaties undercut the Constitution, threatened racial segregation, promoted socialism, and were a calamity for American freedoms in general. Intent on halting creeping world government, Bricker and his allies advocated legislation to limit both the president's powers to negotiate treaties and the domestic impact of international treaties. Desperate to defend presidential autonomy in international affairs, Eisenhower retreated from pursuing treaties to expand and enforce human rights and instead launched a propaganda campaign against Communist-bloc oppression. He lashed out at the Soviet Union and communists for violations of human rights wherever they held sway. "Human rights," the historian Barbara Keys explains, "became one more tool in an anti-communist propaganda kit, used in the rarified world of the UN but with nearly undetectable resonance in the real world."[44]

Against this backdrop of the nation's leaders decrying Communist terror, especially "brain warfare," but offering only the sketchiest outlines of the American response to it, the American public eagerly lapped up fantasies about virtually every aspect of covert national security operations. By the early 1960s library shelves groaned under the weight of both espionage novels and nonfiction exposés of communist brutality that dwelled on the mysteries of brain control and torture. Simultaneously, moviegoers could see "brain warfare" enacted on the screen in slapdash B-movie science fiction thrillers and ambitious films such as John Frankenheimer's 1962 classic *The Manchurian Candidate.*

The popular culture of the era gave Americans titillating glimpses of the secret work of the state, but the reality of the deepening American investment in the science of torture took place with little public discussion and even less accountability. Perhaps some Americans took comfort that they did not know the disagreeable details of the nation's covert methods; like the subjects of Milgram's experiments, they preferred to be isolated from the consequences of the exercise of power. But many Americans presumably listened to the nation's leaders, who tirelessly affirmed their commitment to the defense of democracy, capitalism, and human rights while denouncing communist terror and torture, and assumed that any covert actions undertaken in the nation's name were compatible with long-professed American principles.

While Americans fretted about the threat that mind control posed to the nation's security, the battlegrounds where the science of "brain warfare" was applied were on the borders of the American empire. Like their predecessors in the Philippines a half century earlier, American officials looked to their foreign proxies to maintain internal order, serve American strategic interests, and suppress political movements hostile to the United States. Meanwhile, the United States assumed the responsibility to defend client states against aggression by an external power, especially the Soviet Union.

Instead of the rhetoric of the white man's burden to spread modern civilization that Theodore Roosevelt and like-minded imperialists had spouted during the conquest of the Philippines, Cold Warriors during the 1950s and 1960s embellished their pronouncements with jargon and ideas lifted from modernization theory and contemporary behavioral sciences. Nevertheless, the essential message was familiar. Americans continued to offer "homilies on the virtues of freedom and liberty" and to presume that the institutions and history of the United States uniquely qualified the nation to transplant democracy, free market capitalism, and the rule of law across the globe.[45] American planners expected developing nations to follow the path pioneered by the United States to modern levels of economic, political, and social development. American-led modernization, in turn, would render the developing world congenial to American national interest. In 1966 Charles Wolf, senior economist at the Rand Corporation, a global policy think tank, offered a succinct summary of American policy in Asia that applied equally to the rest of the developing world; the goal was "to help the Asian countries progress toward economic modernization, as relatively 'open' and stable societies, to which our access, as a country and as individual citizens, is free and comfortable."[46]

To make the developing world "comfortable," American strategists looked to a combination of economic largesse and robust military and security collaborations. Economic and social mobilization in developing nations would be sparked by American know-how that was "primarily *nonmaterial* in nature—political, social, economic, and psychological."[47] From the Andes to the Mekong Delta, behavioral scientists devised elaborate interdisciplinary programs that yoked modernization schemes to American strategic aims. The nitty-gritty work of sustaining modernization was assigned to the Alliance for Progress, the Peace Corps, the United States Agency for International Development, and a lengthening list of development agencies funded by the United States and its closest allies. But in many developing nations, American planners perceived the military and police to be the only institutions that had sufficient administrative capacity and institutional cohesion to serve as either enduring engines of modernization or reliable American proxies.

To cultivate alliances with police and military in client states, in 1948 the United States began distributing technology and training soldiers from Latin America and elsewhere in weaponry, technology, and military policing. After the Cuban Revolution in 1959 raised the specter of Communist insurgencies spreading across Latin America, American training emphasized counterinsurgency tactics. Simultaneously, roving American counterinsurgency specialists conducted overseas training, and by the end of the 1960s more than twenty-two thousand soldiers from client nations had received training. Simultaneously, hundreds of American police advisers fanned out across the globe to instruct more than a million police officers in forty-seven nations.[48] These programs enabled American specialists to share counterinsurgency tactics while simultaneously fostering networks of influence with military and police officers in client states.

Methods of covert intelligence gathering were integral to these training programs. Across the developing world, gathering intelligence from conventional sources, such as government and military functionaries, was wholly inadequate to disrupt and expose underground Communist insurgencies. The forces combating insurgencies needed timely and specific information about an enemy who was usually impossible to distinguish from civilians and whose location was seldom fixed. Only by infiltrating underground networks and systematically interrogating insurgents could insurgencies be dismantled. Thus the "science" of coercive interrogation was as relevant to the struggle against Communist insurgencies in the developing world as it was to espionage in the capitals of Cold War Europe.

Through a combination of American resourcefulness, the new science of "brain warfare," and refinements to the crude craft of interrogation, American military and intelligence agencies believed that they and the nation's proxies had the tools to snuff out insurgencies. In 1963 the CIA compiled a counterintelligence primer that was equal measures a summary of the latest behavioral science research (complete with a thirteen-page bibliography of scientific publications) and a how-to guide on interrogation methods. The *KUBARK Counterintelligence*

Interrogation manual incorporated the latest behavioral sciences research, stressing techniques that caused such severe disorientation that subjects typically became submissive and dependent, such as arresting subjects early in the morning, blindfolding them, stripping them naked, disrupting their sleep and other routines, and holding them incommunicado in windowless, soundproof, and dark rooms. Drawing on recent research on the capacity of subjects to withstand pain, the manual cautioned that crude torture techniques often backfired by goading subjects into renewed resistance. A subject's "resistance," the manual explained, "is likelier to be sapped by pain which he seems to inflict upon himself" than by suffering inflicted by interrogators. Far better to use noninvasive methods of coercion that left no physical scars, such as compelling subjects to endure painful stances for long periods of time, prolonged constraint, extremes of heat, cold, or moisture, deprivation of food and sleep, and solitary confinement. Better yet, the manual recommended confining detainees in "an environment still more subject to control, such as water-tank or iron lung." Application of these methods was sufficient to break even the most recalcitrant subjects.[49]

The KUBARK manual elided the definition of torture while describing methods of interrogation that could be intensified to exceed even the strictest definition of the term. Scattered passages advocated restraint and discouraged techniques that produced physical scarring. But the manual was conspicuously silent about what distinguished the methods of extreme psychological distress described in the manual from torture. With regards to torture, then, the manual was proscriptive rather than prescriptive; it coached interrogators in techniques that even in the most restrained application flirted with definitions of torture that the United States professed to recognize. Unless applied with restraint, most of the techniques described in the manual could quickly devolve into torture. By presenting interrogation as an antiseptic exercise in applied behavioral sciences, the manual obscured the pain and suffering of the detainees in a cloud of clinical language. The manual provided a patina of legitimacy to American and allied interrogators to use methods that would have been denounced if they had been employed by American enemies. Moreover, it fulfilled the charge laid out in the secret Doolittle report eight years earlier: to develop the means to subvert and destroy the nation's enemies even if the methods themselves were distasteful.[50]

The KUBARK manual may have been one of the worst-kept secrets of the Cold War. Although classified as top secret, it circulated widely within the military and security forces of American allies and served as a basis for collaboration between American security officers and their foreign counterparts for several decades. In the near term, Southeast Asia provided the field trial for the methods outlined in the manual. There, American strategists brought to bear all of the elements of counterinsurgency strategy that they had been developing during the previous decade. Millions of dollars were poured into rural reconstruction programs across South Vietnam; teams of behavioral scientists developed elaborate modernization schemes to transform Vietnam's peasantry into capitalist and democratic citizens; and more than eighty-five thousand South Vietnamese police received training from American specialists. And there the United States and its client state of South Vietnam confronted the kind of sophisticated revolutionary insurgency that American counterinsurgency strategy was intended to thwart.

The United States yet again faced the challenge of waging war without front lines and against an enemy that could not be distinguished easily from the civilian population. During the American Civil War, Union occupiers had struggled to identify Confederate partisans and guerrillas who harried them as they moved deeper and deeper into the Confederacy. During the occupation of the Philippines, American soldiers had found identifying insurgents so vexing that they concluded that the most prudent course was to assume that all Filipinos were hostile. Now in Vietnam the challenges were even greater. Although American leaders cast the conflict there in stark Cold War terms, it was never simply a straightforward clash between the Soviet Bloc and the United States–led "Free World." Americans confronted not only a war-hardened North Vietnamese army but also a large South Vietnamese insurgency in a rugged, geographically diverse, and densely populated nation. The lines of battle, moreover, were not just between Viet Cong insurgents and the North Vietnamese People's Army of Vietnam on one side and the South Vietnamese Republic of Vietnam and American forces on the other, but also between warring Vietnamese factions divided by ethnicity, religion, and political ideology.[51] Further complicating the human geography of the conflict were massive dislocations of the South Vietnamese population, including the forced relocation of hundreds of thousands of rural villagers into "strategic hamlets" reminiscent of the internment camps in the Philippines a half century earlier.

The American soldiers who began flooding into South Vietnam in 1965 as the war escalated were ill prepared to recognize these complexities. The basic training that American soldiers received included only rudimentary training in the rules of war or dealing with Vietnamese civilians. Recruits instead learned that the Vietnamese enemy were merciless terrorists who flouted rules of war and standards of human decency by resorting to assassinations, bombings, and booby traps. The most graphic images of torture and terror that Americans received were of the insurgents' campaigns to erode American and South Vietnamese morale by ambushing American soldiers and their South Vietnamese allies, torturing them, and leaving their mutilated bodies in prominent places. These grisly displays were chilling reminders to Americans and Vietnamese sympathetic to them that their superior weapons could not protect them.[52] American recruits also learned that Vietnamese insurgents exploited their ability to move among the civilian population with complete disregard for the consequences for civilians. If Americans struck back against insurgents lurking among civilians, any resulting civilian casualties undercut American claims to moral superiority over the insurgents. Predictably, soldiers often arrived in Vietnam wary of virtually all Vietnamese.[53]

The plight of American prisoners of war held by the North Vietnamese magnified perceptions of communist ruthlessness. President Lyndon B. Johnson's decision to forgo an official declaration of war out of fear that the Soviet Union and China would intervene in the conflict left unresolved the legal status of American prisoners of war. Following similar logic to that applied by Americans during the Philippine Insurrection, the North Vietnamese characterized American combatants as lawless "mercenaries" and "pirates" to whom they owed few formal protections as prisoners of war. From 1963 onward, the North Vietnamese and the Viet Cong insurgents in South Vietnam sought to exploit prisoners of war for propaganda purposes. In a repeat of communist techniques during the Korean War, American prisoners in Vietnam were pressured to confess to atrocities against the Vietnamese people, denounce the United States for intervening in Southeast Asia, and praise the benevolence of their captors. Then, beginning in 1965, the North Vietnamese began systematically torturing American prisoners to extract military information and propaganda statements. American commentators reacted to the spectacle of American soldiers "broken" by maltreatment and torture with dismay, anger, and disgust, much as Americans had to the ordeal of prisoners during the Korean War a decade earlier.[54]

For many American soldiers who presumed their innate superiority over the Vietnamese while dismissively referring to the enemy as "gooks" and "slant eyes," there were few incentives to draw distinctions between the civilians they were obliged to protect and the insurgents they were tasked with eliminating. Given the frustrations inherent in any counterinsurgency, many soldiers interpreted the incessant orders from military leaders for maximum "body counts" of slain enemies as a license to wage war indiscriminately. An army study in 1969 conceded, "The Vietnam war was characterized at all times by the lack of . . . precise distinctions between military and civilian personnel, between classical and guerrilla warfare, and between friendly and hostile territory." These conditions, the report concluded, promoted a rapidly escalating cycle of "reprisals and counter-reprisals."[55]

The ubiquity of danger from booby traps, the difficulty of identifying and locating the enemy, and the yearning for retribution for unavenged casualties complicated the job of counterinsurgency intelligence in Vietnam. Military intelligence officers, in particular, carried out interrogations in surroundings far removed from the near-laboratory settings described in the KUBARK manual. Expediency and frontline exigencies discouraged army interrogators from using elaborate methods of sensory disorientation and other techniques associated with the latest "brain warfare." Instead many army interrogators applied techniques commonly used by both South Vietnamese and Soviet interrogators. While training in the U.S. Army Special Forces, Master Sergeant Donald W. Duncan was taught torture methods borrowed from Soviet secret police, such as "the delicate operation of lowering a man's testicles into a jeweler's vise." When he asked his instructors whether he should use such methods, "the answer was, 'We can't tell you that. The Mothers of America wouldn't approve.'"[56] Other Vietnam veterans described similar experiences of being initiated in the "dual structure" of intelligence training: "a 'legal' education in the formal educational materials, and an illegal education taught orally by instructors."[57]

Without question, U.S. Army interrogators used the interrogation methods that had not been part of their "official" training. In the aftermath of the notorious My Lai Massacre in 1968, during which approximately five hundred civilians were murdered, army investigators compiled evidence of torture during the massacre that confirmed allegations that Duncan and others had been making since 1965. In the hours after the massacre, Captain Eugene Kotouc had repeatedly brought the dull edge of a knife down on the extended hand of an alleged Viet Cong suspect with the apparent intent of prompting the detainee to fear that his hand would be amputated unless he divulged information. Kotouc subsequently cut off the finger of another detainee during an interrogation. In the lead-up to the massacre, Captain Ernest Medina beat an alleged Viet Cong suspect during an interrogation before standing him in front a tree and then firing rifle rounds progressively closer and closer to his head in an effort to induce him to talk. Captain Earl Michles permitted suspects to be severely beaten and subjected to electrical shocks administered to their bodies.[58]

Subsequent army investigations confirmed other instances of American interrogators straying far from the guidelines laid out in the army's *Rules of Land Warfare*. Interrogators used field telephones to generate electrical shocks that were applied to sensitive parts of a prisoner's body, such as the chest and testicles. The technique, which could be intensified by wetting detainees and placing them in contact with metal objects, was so commonplace that army interrogators considered field telephones to be "tools of the trade."[59] Another common method was the so-called water rag treatment. An interrogator in the same division responsible for the My Lai Massacre explained, "I held the suspect down, placed a cloth over his face and then poured water over the cloth, thus forcing water into his mouth. The suspect, after becoming choked on the water, confessed that he was a VC [Viet Cong]."[60]

FIGURE 7.2. *Soldiers Torturing Viet Cong Suspect.* In this undated photograph, an American soldier, aided by South Vietnamese soldiers, interrogates a suspected Viet Cong insurgent. Images of South Vietnamese engaging in torture were much more common, which contributed to the belief that Southeast Asians were prone to cruelty and that Americans soldiers were reluctant participants in the war's atrocities.

As had been true in the Philippines, torture by army interrogators was not formal policy so much as customary practice. Prior to 1969, when mounting evidence of atrocities could no longer be ignored, the military high command displayed little interest in scrupulously enforcing the laws of war in Vietnam. Consequently, many soldiers in Vietnam displayed as cavalier an attitude toward the laws of war as had their predecessors in the Philippines. A survey of twenty thousand army officers and soldiers in 1969 revealed that a quarter of the officers and half of the soldiers believed they had legal immunity if they were following orders to torture or execute prisoners. Two-thirds of officers responded that they would order torture if they thought it would secure important information. Facing little risk of punishment, possessing a weak grasp of the laws of war, and confronting a tenacious insurgency, army interrogators concluded that "if we did not leave scars we could do exactly as we pleased."[61] "Nothing was sanctioned," an intelligence specialist later explained to journalists, "but nothing was off-limits short of seriously injuring a prisoner."[62]

While military intelligence concentrated on conventional combat and tactical intelligence gathering, the CIA and South Vietnamese intelligence undertook unconventional operations against the communist underground. The CIA conducted its covert campaign against the "Communist infrastructure" in South Vietnam without even the feeble constraints that curtailed the American military. Virtually until the end of the Vietnam conflict, the CIA operated behind the veil of secrecy with virtually no legislative oversight. In 1965 William Colby, the agency's senior field operative, launched an ambitious counterinsurgency program by recruiting teams "whose function was to use Viet Cong techniques of terror—assassination, abuses, kidnappings and intimidation—against the Viet Cong leadership." These Provincial Reconnaissance Units (PRUs) rounded up insurgents and civilians who were believed to have information and handed them to agents at interrogation centers in each of South Vietnam's forty-four provinces. There CIA operatives and contract employees extracted information that was then given to military commanders, who used it to plan subsequent capture and assassination missions by PRUs.[63]

Some CIA agents made a pretext of following the interrogation procedures outlined in the KUBARK manual. When CIA interrogators had the time and resources, they employed the full arsenal of "brain warfare," going as far as to import two CIA physicians and a civilian psychiatrist and equipment from the United States to apply massive electroshocks to alleged mental patients who suffered from schizophrenia, but in fact who were Communist insurgents, as part of interrogations. (The method was a failure; after three weeks of "treatment" all of the Viet Cong subjects had died.) But their South Vietnamese counterparts, who previously had been tutored in interrogation by French colonial administrators, employed less elaborate interrogation methods, including rape, electric shock to the genitals or other sensitive parts of the body, a "water treatment" reminiscent of the "water cure" commonly used in the Philippines fifty years prior, and the so-called airplane in which a prisoner's arms were tied behind the back and from which he or she was suspended above the floor.[64]

The incidence of torture in field interrogations and interrogation centers during the Vietnam War is virtually impossible to estimate with any precision. Anecdotal evidence from the accounts of veterans, military and security records, and contemporary news accounts suggests that it was commonplace. One student of interrogation programs during the war has concluded that "the large majority of South Vietnamese interrogators tortured some or all of the Communist prisoners in their care." So widespread were these methods that evaluators of the CIA operations in 1968 reported that "almost all advisers" witnessed instances of them. Claiming to have little leverage with their South Vietnamese counterparts, CIA interrogators "turned their backs" to what one CIA adviser described as "traditional Oriental interrogation brutality, aggravated by guerrilla war vengeance."[65] Some CIA agents resolved the contradiction between official CIA protocols and the methods that prevailed in the field by revising their definition of torture. One agent conceded that "prisoners were abused" but asked, "Were they tortured?" "It depends on what you call torture," he explained. "Electricity was used by the Vietnamese, water was used, occasionally some of the prisoners got beat up." But "were any of them put on the rack, eyes gouged out, bones broken? No, I never saw any evidence of that at all."[66]

Whereas Americans diligently tallied the body count of killed Viet Cong and North Vietnamese, they displayed no comparable zeal to quantify interrogation methods. The CIA would boast in 1972 that its counterinsurgency programs had neutralized more than eighty thousand communist operatives, informants, and supporters, of whom between twenty-six thousand and forty-one thousand had been killed. How accurate these numbers were and how many of these neutralized agents had been tortured is impossible to determine.

The use of torture by American troops and their allies in Vietnam might have remained mere hearsay had Americans continued to view the conflict as a stark Cold War confrontation between communist terror and democratic nation building. But the rapid growth of an international antiwar movement transformed the debate about the American conduct of the war. Like the campaign by anti-imperialists at the start of the twentieth century, the movement to end the Vietnam War came to focus on American atrocities and the moral bankruptcy of American global ambitions. In at least one important regard, however, the campaigns against the two wars differed markedly. Whereas Herbert Welsh and his fellow anti-imperialists failed to arouse a mass movement

against the American occupation of the Philippines, the opponents of
the Vietnam War mobilized soldiers, veterans, college students, house-
wives, unionists, clergy, and civil rights activists in one of the largest
social movements in American history.[67]

Disappointment and outrage at the perceived hypocrisy of American conduct of the conflict sustained opposition to the war. For all of
the claims that the United States was defending democracy in Southeast Asia, critics insisted that the logic of American imperialism placed
a priority on American interests rather than national self-determination.
They reminded Americans that American power was thwarting the aspirations of a people, as it had in the Philippines. As early as 1965,
Robert Scheer and other commentators began highlighting American
machinations to hinder any negotiated settlement that might strengthen
communist influence in South Vietnam while promoting antidemo-
cratic tendencies there. Oft-repeated claims that the overwhelming
majority of South Vietnamese opposed the Viet Cong and endured
their presence only because the "Viet Cong held the people in the grip
of terror by assassination and torture" were belied by the growth of
the insurgency and clear evidence that the South Vietnamese regime
lacked legitimacy in the eyes of its citizenry. Likewise, the claim
that the Viet Cong represented about "one-half of one percent of the
population of South Vietnam" was belied by American efforts to impose "an ironlike system of government political control over the population" because, as a high South Vietnamese official acknowledged,
"Frankly, we are not strong enough now to compete with the Communists on a purely political basis."[68]

While the war exposed the hollowness of the nation's commitment
to democracy overseas, it simultaneously eroded democracy at home
by intensifying the militarization of American institutions. The permanent mobilization of American society that anti-imperialists had
feared in 1899 had come to pass; democratic institutions had been hol-
lowed out while power was concentrated in an unaccountable elite who
practiced habitual public deception, secrecy, and hypocrisy. Reflecting
on his tour of duty in Vietnam, Master Sergeant Duncan regretted that
"we have allowed the creation of a military monster that will lie to
our elected officials" and then "both of them will lie to the American
people."[69] The clear intent of "the government's propaganda apparatus,"

another critic of the war lamented, was to render the citizenry ignorant of actual government policy and incapable of challenging it if they
did become aware of it.[70]

Above all, opponents of the war leveled a moral critique of the conflict. Not only were the war's aims illegitimate but the conduct of the
war was inhumane. When opponents of the war surveyed American
history, from the wars against Indians and the American occupation
of the Philippines to the conflict in Vietnam, they discerned a recurring pattern of callous disregard for the humanity of America's foes.
One commentator confessed to experiencing déjà vu when reading
about the Philippine Insurrection; it was "like sitting through a shabby
drama a second time."[71] Just as anti-imperialists had anticipated that
the American occupation in the Philippines would require "severe"
methods to impose American will, so too critics of the American intervention in Vietnam warned that atrocities were inevitable in a conflict in which the United States ignored popular will and unleashed
American technology without regard for the consequences. Within
months of the escalation of the war in 1965, scattered reports of torture and other atrocities began to surface in American newspapers and
magazines.[72] After two subsequent years of accumulating reports,
Noam Chomsky in 1967 pressed the readers of his trenchant critique
of the war to ask themselves "to what extent the American people bear
responsibility for the savage American assault on a largely helpless
rural population in Vietnam."[73]

The antiwar movement's emphasis on the brutality of the war
gained credibility when soldiers and veterans began to speak out against
it. Like their predecessors during the Philippine Insurrection, soldiers
spoke with the authority of witnesses to the war and its devastation.
Moreover, soldiers and veterans could not be easily dismissed as unpa-
triotic draft dodgers or wild-eyed leftists. Master Sergeant Duncan, for
example, had received the South Vietnamese Silver Star, the Combat
Infantry Badge, the Bronze Star, and the U.S. Army Air Medal and had
been nominated for the American Silver Star and the Legion of Merit,
before he declined promotion and returned to civilian life in the United
States. Deeply disillusioned by his experiences in Vietnam, he became
an early and outspoken critic of American counterinsurgency tactics.
In the February 1966 issue of *Ramparts*, a progressive Catholic journal

that had turned against the war in 1965, he published a poignant apology for his participation in the Vietnam conflict, entitled "The Whole Thing Was a Lie!" Tracing his evolution from an earnest Catholic anticommunist recruit into an opponent of the war, he dwelled on his disgust at the corruption and ineptitude of the government of South Vietnam and the brutal conduct of the conflict. By 1967 Duncan had expanded his critique of the war in one of the earliest veterans' accounts of the war in Vietnam and had established himself as one of the most widely respected veterans in the antiwar movement. Whether testifying in 1967 on behalf of an army doctor who refused to train Green Berets because American special forces were responsible for atrocities or at an unofficial "war crimes tribunal" in Denmark in the same year organized by the philosopher Bertrand Russell, Duncan offered specific, firsthand accounts of the use of torture during interrogations and of American complicity in the abuse and summary executions of prisoners by South Vietnamese proxies.[74]

As the ranks of veterans who had completed tours in Vietnam grew, so too did the number of testimonials that bolstered Duncan's allegations. Disenchanted veterans began gathering in Vietnam Veterans against the War (VVAW), an antiwar organization founded in 1967. Three years later, after its membership had swollen to twenty thousand, the organization began staging various forms of protest theater, including a three-day march in September 1970 from Morristown, New Jersey, to Valley Forge, Pennsylvania, during which hundreds of veterans reenacted "search and destroy" military operations and conducted mock interrogations in the communities along their path. Six months later, in Detroit, the VVAW held the Winter Soldier Investigation, where over one hundred veterans, including Duncan, testified about the war crimes they had witnessed or committed themselves. Soon thereafter Senator Mark Hatfield of Oregon summarized the veterans' testimony on the floor of the Senate, acknowledging the allegations of the torture and murder of suspects and prisoners of war by American and South Vietnamese forces, the wanton killing of unarmed civilians, and the rape of Vietnamese women. The cumulative testimony led the senator to conclude that the atrocities "were the consequence of reasonable and known policy adopted by our military commanders and that the knowledge of incidents resulting from these policies was widely shared."[75]

Within the military, the prevailing attitude seems to have been that most claims of war crimes were exaggerated or wholly unfounded. Military commanders and members of the Nixon administration assailed the credibility of soldiers who alleged to have witnessed torture and other atrocities. When Tom Glen, a private in the 11th Light Infantry Brigade of the American Division, wrote to General Creighton Abrams in 1968 with a lengthy denunciation of his division for its repeated brutality against civilians, the general forwarded the letter to Glen's commanding officer. Although Glen was assigned to the same division as the soldiers who had carried out the My Lai Massacre a few months earlier and rumors of their atrocities were ricocheting through the division, Glen's letter elicited derision rather than concern. Major Colin Powell, who decades later would serve as secretary of state during the Bush administration and its War on Terror, was tasked with investigating the allegations of torture and abuse. After interviewing a few officers but without requesting any additional information from Glen, Powell dismissed the accusations. Abuses were unthinkable, he contended, because the American troops had gone through an hour-long course on how to treat prisoners of war under the Geneva Conventions. "There may be isolated cases of mistreatment of civilians and POWs," Powell conceded, but in general "relations between American soldiers and the Vietnamese people are excellent." Glen's superior officer then closed the investigation with an indictment of his underling's character: "That he should write a letter in vague generalities," the officer complained, "makes his charges suspect and casts doubt on the moral courage he must possess."[76] The attitudes of Powell and the commanding officer were similar to that of another army officer who dismissed claims that there were extensive civilian casualties at My Lai because that was not "the American way."[77]

Had Glen ventilated his allegations in public, he might have faced an organized campaign of character assassination like that experienced ˙y Lieutenant Colonel Anthony Herbert. Despite having been one of the most decorated army soldiers during the Korean War and having had a distinguished career in the military before his tour of duty in

Vietnam, Herbert was denounced as a traitor and a media-hungry mal-content after he leveled allegations of war crimes against soldiers and officers in the 173rd Airborne Brigade. In April 1969, months before the disclosure of the massacre at My Lai, Herbert informed General John W. Barnes, commander of the 173rd Airborne Brigade, and his deputy, Colonel Joseph Ross Franklin, that two months earlier at Cu Loi he had observed an American adviser supervise South Vietnamese forces who serially executed detainees. Herbert also claimed to have witnessed American intelligence officers applying water torture during the interrogation of a prisoner. The day after Herbert made his allegations, General Barnes relieved him from his command and filed a harsh personnel evaluation accusing Herbert of being a perpetual liar. After a year of futile efforts to reverse the general's decision, Herbert filed formal charges against General Barnes and Colonel Franklin, accusing them of failing to investigate war crimes and of retaliating against him. By August 1971 the army had dismissed all of Herbert's accusations against both of his superiors. Simultaneously, they complained to the media that Herbert had not only failed to report atrocities but also was himself responsible for them. He was portrayed as a "keg of dynamite" who was "completely oriented to killing mercilessly." Moreover, he allegedly lacked credibility because the army claimed to have been unable to confirm the events he said he had witnessed. In fact, army investigators did confirm his accusations that military interrogators had used water, electric shock, and sticks to torture detainees in at least four instances. Investigators also identified twenty American and three South Vietnamese suspects, fifteen of whom admitted committing acts of torture. Yet this confirmation of some of Hebert's accusations remained undisclosed. While Herbert effectively was forced out of the army, only three of the confirmed torturers were punished (like Captain Brandt and the officers court-martialed during the Philippine Insurrection five decades earlier) with fines and reductions in rank.[78]

The revelation in November 1969 of the massacre of as many as five hundred civilians at My Lai the previous year transformed the deba᷈ from whether there were atrocities in Vietnam to how common they were. Army investigators discovered that some of the American soldiers who participated in the massacre had previously gained notoriety as serial rapists even before they committed at least twenty rapes during the massacre. Similarly, the platoon had a well-established reputation for abusing prisoners. Investigators also learned that American troops had been responsible for another massacre about a mile from My Lai during the same operation.[79]

American opinion divided sharply over the root causes of and culpability for the atrocities at My Lai and elsewhere in Vietnam. Some commentators and observers traced them to individual acts, dwelling on the responsibility of Lieutenant William Calley, one of the officers during the massacre, and individual soldiers for any atrocities committed in Vietnam. Americans were reassured that when a "few bad apples," as Vice President Spiro Agnew referred to the soldiers at My Lai, succumbed to the temptation to retaliate against communist cruelty, military justice would punish them appropriately. In words remarkably like those of Secretary of War Elihu Root in 1902, Secretary of the Army Stanley Resor reassured Congress in November 1969 that American troops in Vietnam had shown "decency, consideration and restraint towards the unfortunate civilians who find themselves in a zone of military operations."[80] At a time of declining support for the conflict in Vietnam, military officials were anxious to keep the focus on the conduct of individuals rather than on broader questions about the conduct of the war.

Others located the culpability for atrocities, now exemplified by My Lai, in the prevailing culture within the military in Vietnam, the policies of the military, and the nation's goals in the war. Veteran John Kerry in 1971 explained, "We cannot try a Calley for something which generals and Presidents and our way of life encouraged him to do."[81] Yet even while a substantial majority of Americans in 1971 apparently agreed with Kerry that senior military commanders bore blame for the massacre at My Lai, only 22 percent of respondents in a poll believed that senior commanders should be prosecuted for war crimes that they did not directly order.[82]

Another explanation, which was often voiced by supporters of the war, was that atrocities were inevitable in any war and that Americans were naive to assume that soldiers fighting in their name could sublimate the primal desire for retaliation in the face of communist provocations. Conceding pessimism about the capacity of soldiers to exercise

individual moral authority during war, 65 percent of Americans believed that atrocities and "incidents" like My Lai "are bound to
happen in a war."[83] Although the war was deeply unpopular among a
growing majority of Americans, there was an "overall sense," observed
the psychologist Robert Jay Lifton, that "this is a dirty war," and Americans continued to profess support for the soldiers in the field. A poll
of Americans in early December 1969 revealed that 67 percent of respondents did not believe that soldiers deserved punishment for killing
civilians while acting under orders. And in a January 1970 poll, only
23 percent confessed to feeling "moral repugnance" at the killing of
unarmed women and children in Vietnam. The war might be exceptionally brutal, but American soldiers were, on the whole, blameless.[84]

While peace activists denounced torture, murder, rape, and other
atrocities as routine facets of the war, pro-war Americans deplored the
excessive attention devoted to atrocities, which, Governor Ronald
Reagan of California proclaimed, gave "comfort and aid to our enemies." Instead of dwelling on the transgressions of American soldiers,
Americans instead should denounce the North Vietnamese who systematically tortured prisoners of war and the Communist insurgents
in South Vietnam who waged cold-blooded terror campaigns against
civilians and Americans alike. Whereas American atrocities were isolated deviations from our innately moral national culture, communist
outrages were vivid confirmation of the innate barbarism of the Vietnamese. While discussing the My Lai Massacre in November 1969,
ABC anchorman Howard K. Smith drew precisely this distinction:
"Nazi atrocities, like the daily ones of the Viet Cong, are acts of national policy. This [My Lai], if it happened, is a violation of national
policy."[85]

The response of Americans to the conviction of Lieutenant Calley
for his role in the My Lai Massacre revealed that a broad swath of the
public rejected the proposition that he bore singular guilt for the
atrocity. Despite the graphic evidence presented at his court-martial,
only 20 percent of respondents in a poll believed his actions had been
a crime. In poll after poll, large majorities of respondents located the
responsibility for My Lai elsewhere. Opponents of the war saw in Calley
a scapegoat offered up by military and political leaders intent on reclaiming legitimacy for an unpopular and inhumane war. Supporters

of the war also saw Calley as a scapegoat. His mistake had been to deviate from the timid and ineffectual strategy imposed by spineless American politicians by giving vent to his vindictive rage against a vicious but elusive enemy. More than 80 percent of respondents in a Gallup poll considered his conviction unfair, and more than two-thirds viewed Calley as a scapegoat for senior officers and government officials who were responsible for the way the war was waged. So strong was the disapproval of Calley's conviction that Indiana's governor asked all state flags to be flown at half-staff, and the legislatures in Arkansas, Kansas, New Jersey, South Carolina, and Texas requested clemency for him. Eager to somehow find a silver lining in the embarrassment of Calley's trial, President Richard Nixon calculated that he would garner popular approval by ordering Calley's transfer from military prison to house arrest in Georgia.[86]

The fact that, of the scores of American soldiers who had tortured, raped, and indiscriminately murdered civilians at My Lai, only Calley was convicted confirmed suspicions that the military was incapable of securing justice for atrocities committed by American soldiers in Vietnam. Of the fourteen officers accused of suppressing information about the My Lai Massacre, only one was tried, and he was acquitted. Captain Kotouc, who had been accused of torture and other atrocities, was court-martialed but found not guilty. Most of the men responsible for the acts of torture, rape, and murder at My Lai had already left military service and hence were beyond the reach of military justice by the time military authorities finally decided to punish them.

The lesson that many observers took from the official response to My Lai and other atrocities by American soldiers was that virtually everyone in the chain of command, from the "grunt" in the field to the "desk jockey" in Washington, D.C., abdicated individual responsibility. The soldiers at My Lai claimed that they had been ordered to "waste" the villagers, and so, like the subjects in Stanley Milgram's experiment, they had followed orders without apparent second thoughts. Calley himself claimed that his commanding officer had ordered him to "kill everything that moved," and he had followed those orders despite the strictures against the summary execution of civilians spelled out in the army's *Rules of Land Warfare*. Calley's commanding officers denied responsibility for tolerating a culture of casual violence, rape, and torture among their troops. However predictable it was that those involved in torture, rape, and murder would try to evade culpability, some observers were dismayed by the willingness of Americans to tolerate and even endorse their abdication of individual responsibility. One commentator complained, "Torture just happens, murder just happens, war crimes just happen. No one does it; no one is responsible." In addition to an unwillingness to assign responsibility, too many Americans in Vietnam were complicit in indulging those who did commit atrocities. A soldier or CIA agent in Vietnam might not torture prisoners and murder civilians, but "he merely makes murder and torture possible by refusing to prevent it." Whether confounded by the challenge of determining responsibility for war crimes in Vietnam or simply unwilling to acknowledge any obligation to do so, many Americans preferred to conclude that slaughter in war is habitual, beyond the control of human authority, and incapable of amends.[87]

Sordid revelations about how the war against Communism had been waged in Vietnam and elsewhere continued even after the signing of the Paris Peace Accords in January 1973 and the subsequent withdrawal of most American troops from South Vietnam by August of that year. The confirmation hearings of William Colby to be director of the CIA in 1973 provided an opportunity for Congress to probe the role of the CIA in Vietnam, which had been shielded from congressional oversight and was not widely understood by the American public. Colby had served as CIA station chief in Saigon during the early 1960s before returning to Washington. Then in 1968 he returned to Vietnam, where he oversaw the Phoenix Program, which targeted the political infrastructure of the Viet Cong by means of infiltration, capture, interrogation, and assassination. During the hearing, Colby maintained that abuses in the program were neither widespread nor officially sanctioned. Most Viet Cong, he insisted, had been killed during combat operations rather than while in South Vietnamese custody. But in the wake of My Lai and the widespread allegations of atrocities, critics were not persuaded that many of the eighty thousand Viet Cong allegedly "neutralized" by the program between 1968 and 1972, of whom more than twenty-six thousand had been killed, had not been tortured and summarily executed.[88]

Within weeks of Colby's bruising confirmation, damaging revelations about CIA skullduggery since the 1950s surfaced in major newspapers. Coming on the heels of the Watergate scandal, which had involved efforts to use the CIA and FBI for political purposes, these disclosures suggested to many members of Congress that intelligence activities, long ignored by the Congress, had strayed far beyond acceptable limits. Both houses of Congress established special committees to investigate illegal abuses, both foreign and domestic, committed by the CIA and American intelligence agencies. For the next year an almost daily stream of disclosures from these committees documented misconduct by the nation's intelligence agencies, including clandestine operations overseas, disclosures about the MKUltra program in "brain warfare," and questionable counterinsurgency methods in Vietnam and elsewhere. By the conclusion of the hearings in 1976, the veil that had shrouded the American intelligence agencies for two decades finally had been pulled back. And as General Doolittle had predicted two decades earlier, many Americans were disturbed by what they saw.[89]

In 1951 Robert Vogeler warned his countrymen that any one of them might be a victim of torture. Two decades later, Americans had cause to reflect that any one of them might become a torturer. By then psychologist Stanley Milgram's lament about the unexpected prevalence of "moral imbeciles" in the United States seemingly had been confirmed by exposés of the conduct of the war in Vietnam and of the Cold War in general. Any blanket presumption of American moral superiority and exceptionalism required either the willful denial of history or extreme naïveté. Taking stock of the blows to the nation's reputation in 1971, the theologian Reinhold Niebuhr proclaimed like a latter-day Jeremiah, "This is the moment of truth when we realize we are not a virtuous nation."[90]

Between 1945 and 1975, the American state to an unprecedented degree accommodated torture within the national arsenal. More than just a tolerated violation of formal policy, torture, as a weapon of democracy, was studied, refined, and applied. Whenever Americans caught a glimpse of the furtive methods used to fight the Cold War, defenders explained that the CIA had engaged in "brain warfare" in response to communist provocations and that the military had only become complicit in torture because of the terror tactics of the Communist insurgents. But such claims conceded that in the struggle to defend American democracy and capitalism, Americans had embraced forms of violence that other, less virtuous nations also employed. Some ardent supporters of American Cold War policies welcomed the perceived loss of innocence; henceforth, the United States could exercise its national power unrestrained by quaint obeisance to the maintenance of national virtue. Those Americans who recoiled from the gory spectacle of My Lai and chilling accounts of CIA interrogation methods viewed the puncturing of the myth of national innocence as overdue and the first step toward an acknowledgment of national culpability. The revelations of American covet activities and atrocities in Vietnam did not resolve the contradictions in American attitudes toward torture in subsequent decades. The United States would embrace human rights as a national obligation during the 1970s, and the American military would renew its commitment to rigorously observe the laws of war. But the imperatives of national security during the final years of the Cold War and then during the War on Terror would again expose and, indeed, intensify the contradictions at the center of the American tradition of torture.

EIGHT

The Enemy Within

E IGHT MONTHS AFTER THE invasion of Iraq in 2003, retired army colonel Stuart Herrington fretted that if the treatment of detainees in Iraq "becomes known, everybody who touched it will be in trouble." A month earlier he had assessed American intelligence operations in Iraq, an assignment for which he had impressive qualifications. His career in military intelligence began in the controversial Phoenix Program during the Vietnam War and continued during tours in Europe, Panama, and the Gulf War. After having witnessed the waterboarding of a nineteen-year-old female prisoner in Vietnam, he developed a strong aversion to torture. He instead practiced rapport-based interrogation techniques that took time but produced reliable intelligence. Even before he reached Iraq, he heard rumors that detainees there had been tortured and beaten by "[CIA] agency guys" and military interrogators. During his visit to Abu Ghraib prison in Baghdad, which held the largest number of alleged insurgents and former loyalists of Saddam Hussein, Herrington observed conditions so appalling that he worried the prison was "a pressure cooker" where "death, injury," and other "bad things" were destined to occur. Medical personnel told him that they routinely treated detainees who showed signs of abuse at the hands of their American captors. He also heard reports that Special Operations and CIA missions had been abusing detainees there using a secret interrogation facility to hide their activities. When he asked a commanding officer about the allegations of widespread abuse, he received a curt reply: "Everyone knows about it."[1]

Upon returning to the United States, Herrington shared his concerns with Deputy Chief of Staff Lieutenant General Keith Alexander. Herrington mistakenly assumed that his startling report would prompt a thorough investigation. Instead, in April 2004 he received a curt letter from the Office of the Staff Judge Advocate explaining that an investigator had been unable to confirm the conversations that Herrington had reported or "to pin down timelines and events in time." The cursory response closed with a finding that there was no evidence to substantiate his allegations of detainee abuse.[2]

The dismissal of Herrington's concerns was altogether predictable. For more than a year, credible allegations of prisoner abuse from Guantánamo and Afghanistan had been presented to the architects of the War on Terror in the Pentagon and the White House. But it was not until three weeks after the dismissal of Herrington's report, when *60 Minutes II* aired an exposé of the abuse of detainees at Abu Ghraib, that the Bush administration conceded that a few Americans might have committed human rights violations. Only a small number of the more than a thousand images and nearly one hundred video files of detainee abuse (as well as five hundred images of dead Iraqi detainees) at Abu Ghraib were aired, but even these few graphic photographs showing grinning military personnel taunting and abusing naked prisoners aroused global condemnation and elicited a furious defense of the War on Terror by the Bush administration.

Two decades earlier, in August 1983, Keith Griffiths, an investigator in the Chicago Police Department's Office of Professional Standards (OPS), was assigned the case file of Andrew Wilson, a convicted murderer who alleged that a year earlier police had tortured him to extract a confession. Included in the file was a letter from a medical doctor who described Wilson's troubling injuries when he had been admitted to the Cook County Jail following his arrest in 1982. Griffiths, complying with his supervisor's recommendation, assigned no urgency to investigating the allegations. During the following year, he completed his "investigation" by reading the sparse documentation in the file but without conducting any additional research or interviews. His perfunctory summary recommended a finding of "not sustained" for Wilson's allegations.[3]

There was nothing unusual about the laxness of Griffith's investigation. During the 1980s (and later as well), fewer than one in ten OPS investigations determined that Chicago police had used excessive violence. Even David Fogel, the director of the OPS during much of the decade, conceded that many of his investigators were "irremediably incompetent" and that his office "gives the formal appearance of justice but actually helps to institutionalize subterfuge and injustice."[4] Two decades of litigation would be required to rectify the summary dismissal of Andrew Wilson's allegations and to expose the extent of police torture in Chicago.

While the scale of police torture in Chicago was extraordinary, with hundreds claiming to have been tortured, reports of torture by law officials have surfaced across the country during the past four decades. There was Sheriff James C. Parker and his three deputies in San Jacinto, Texas, who during the early 1980s extorted confessions by draping towels over suspects' faces and pouring water over them until they gagged.[5] There was New York City Officer Justin Volpe who in 1997 arrested Abner Louima, a Haitian immigrant, following an altercation outside a Brooklyn nightclub. In addition to beating Louima, Volpe and Charles Schwarz, another policeman, took him into a restroom in the station house and plunged a broken broomstick handle into his rectum. The officers and two other colleagues then conspired to cover up the incident.[6] And there were the deputies in the sheriff's department in Los Angeles during the 2000s who formed a de facto gang, subjected inmates to racial insults, awarded one another points for breaking inmates' bones, and at least once made an inmate parade naked in front of other prisoners before sexually assaulting him.[7]

The torture carried out by Americans in Afghanistan, Iraq, Guantánamo, Chicago, Los Angeles, and elsewhere during the past four decades might be dismissed as regrettable but isolated lapses in a nation that otherwise had repudiated torture. But the contradiction between the United States' formal opposition to torture and the tolerance of

American officials for the actual practice of it has been repeatedly exposed during recent decades. At no previous point in American history has national opposition to torture been more vigorously professed. When President Ronald Reagan submitted the United Nations Convention on Torture to Congress in 1988, he vowed that it was a testament to "our desire to bring an end to the abhorrent practice of torture."[8] Subsequent presidents reaffirmed his pledge, including President George W. Bush, who proclaimed in 2005 that "any activity we conduct, is within the law. We do not torture."[9]

Yet even as the United States championed the international campaign against torture, the nation's national security agencies were deeply complicit in the use of torture by allies, from Honduras and Egypt to the Philippines. During the War on Terror, the nation's leaders urged the adoption of "enhanced interrogation" techniques that virtually all experts in human rights law, including many who served in the Bush administration, condemn as torture. And within the United States, some police departments, public officials, and courts, most notoriously Chicago's, tolerated and shielded the flagrant abuse of suspects that violated virtually every constraint on police power that the Supreme Court had imposed since the 1930s.

Equally important, at the turn of the twenty-first century the use of torture against enemy combatants and as part of the criminal justice system converged. This convergence was embodied in two Chicago police officers: Jon Burge, who learned interrogation techniques during the Vietnam War and later applied them on hundreds of African American suspects on the South Side of Chicago; and Richard Zuley, who transferred his use of prolonged shackling, threats against suspects' families, and coerced confessions from the interrogation rooms of Chicago to Guantánamo and then back again to the North Side of Chicago. Whether in the suites of the Executive Office Building or in a police station house in Chicago, agents of the state rationalized the use of torture as an expedient and effective method of interrogation. Their victims, they presumed, had forfeited any claims to protections that otherwise are accorded to citizens or members of the community of nations. Whether alleged terrorists sequestered by the CIA at a "black site" in a foreign country or career criminals in holding cells in Chicago, they were marooned in a virtual no-man's-land where they experienced the violence of American power but few protections of American or international law.

The public repudiation of torture during the 1970s was a direct legacy of the Vietnam War. Eager to put the tumult and national embarrassments of the previous decade behind them, Americans during the 1970s sought a restoration of national dignity. Americans hankered for transparent and "honest" government after the chicanery of the Johnson and Nixon administrations. Congress responded to these concerns by curbing executive powers that had been abused, including reining in the CIA by finally establishing a measure of oversight of it and banning or severely restricting its most controversial covert methods. Beyond restraining executive arrogance, some members of Congress justified their push by invoking the nascent global campaign for human rights. Offended by a perceived absence of ethical considerations in the nation's international relations during Henry Kissinger's tenure as secretary of state and appalled by revelations of American involvement in the 1973 Chilean coup, Congress began requiring the Department of State to compile reports on the human rights records of aid recipients. Congressional liberals warned Indonesia, Brazil, South Korea, the Philippines, and other repressive regimes that their violations of human rights threatened any future American aid.[10]

This new emphasis on egregious violations of human rights mirrored the attention devoted to state-sponsored torture by nongovernmental human rights groups during the 1970s. Previously, "human rights" were an ill-defined set of ideas and moral injunctions that infrequently surfaced in international negotiations as unenforceable aspirations rather than concrete policy. Amnesty International, which was founded in London in 1961, played an outsized role in elevating torture, above other abuses, to international prominence by pioneering grassroots, apolitical human rights advocacy. During the 1960s the organization barely gained a foothold in the United States, where its membership languished at a few thousand. Then, when the organization began focusing on state-sponsored torture, it expanded at a furious pace, claiming nearly a hundred thousand American members by the end of the 1970s.

Amnesty International's growth and influence demonstrated the continuing efficacy of the tradition of humanitarian reform, with its emphasis on empathy for the suffering of the weak and despised, that stretched from the late eighteenth century through the campaign against slavery. The organization focused on educating the public about credible abuses and advocated simple, direct actions by individuals on behalf of victims of persecution. Outside the corridors of conventional diplomacy, members of Amnesty International forged a direct and public connection with victims of repression while drowning offending governments in letters appealing for mercy. In 1972 the organization released a landmark global analysis of the problem, and in the following year activist Rose Styron published an influential article in the *New Republic* lamenting a renaissance of torture around the world. Many Americans who previously had thrown themselves into opposing the Vietnam War found a new focus by joining Amnesty International campaigns against continuing repression following a succession of right-wing military coups in Latin America. These campaigns complemented and urged on congressional inquiries into American involvement with right-wing dictatorships across the globe.[11]

The global influence of the human rights movement was bolstered by dissidents behind the Iron Curtain who had grown disillusioned by the failures of Communism during the 1960s. They coalesced into a small but highly articulate movement that protested the suppression of public debate, restrictions on free movement, and the prevalence of state torture in East Europe and the Soviet Union. Their denunciations of Communist oppression found a receptive audience among longtime anticommunists in the United States, many of whom viewed with suspicion and loathing the Nixon administration's warming relations with the Soviet Union and China.[12]

Human rights, especially the prohibition of torture, enjoyed support from an unlikely coalition both within Congress and among nongovernmental policy analysts and activists. With the Vietnam War finally over, the United States could resume its historical role as an exemplar of democracy and credibly reproach other nations about human rights. Depending on one's stance, the nation's newly assertive campaign for human rights, and specifically against torture, was a means either to embarrass the Soviet Union and other Communist states that practiced torture or to repair the reputation of the United States. Americans who had supported the Vietnam War and had tired of what they saw as excessive American self-criticism over the fiasco in Southeast Asia embraced the campaign for human rights. Moralizing against Soviet abuses directed attention away from American imperialism and complemented an aggressive assertion of American power to thwart international Communism. For those Americans who had opposed the war, aligning the United States with the cause of human rights offered the means to begin to erase the blot on the nation's honor.[13]

The potency of this campaign for human rights became evident during the Conference on Security and Cooperation in Europe (CSCE), which was concluded in Helsinki, Finland, in 1975. At the outset, few of the major participants anticipated that human rights would figure prominently in the conference. For the Soviet Union, the conference promised the formal recognition of its control of Eastern Europe. For Western Europeans, the conference was a means to institutionalize the détente between the West and the Soviet Union and its satellites. For Kissinger and others in the Nixon and Ford administrations, who viewed the conference with barely concealed contempt, it was a "meaningless" sop to western Europeans. The final agreement, which exceeded the participants' expectations, included a pledge by signatories to respect human rights and promote equal rights. Most participating nations assumed that these articles were virtually unenforceable. But they provided an opening for dissidents in Moscow and elsewhere to agitate for compliance with the agreement. By the end of the decade, most countries in Eastern Europe hosted robust grassroots human rights organizations that communist leaders could not suppress without flagrantly violating the Helsinki Accords.[14]

Against this backdrop of cresting international activism, Americans in 1976 elected Jimmy Carter, a presidential candidate distinguished mainly by his moral earnestness. Carter and his administration proposed a human rights strategy that was intended to distance the nation from the legacy of cynicism and suspicion fostered by the Vietnam War and American intervention elsewhere in the world. In his inaugural address in 1977, President Carter declared, "Our commitment to human rights must be absolute." He pledged that American policy would henceforth take into account the human rights record of other nations: "Our moral sense dictates a clear-cut preference for those societies which share with us an abiding respect for individual human rights." With these words, the rhetoric of American foreign policy was permanently altered, and the protection of individual human rights could no longer be cavalierly dismissed as Kissinger had only a few years prior. Carter's frequent invocation of human rights in 1977, along with the awarding of the Nobel Peace Prize to Amnesty International in the same year, augured a new era in the recognition of human rights. Now, regimes across the globe were on notification that their human rights records were subject to scrutiny by both aroused publics and the most powerful military and economic power on the planet.[15]

The Carter administration looked for opportunities to translate its human rights rhetoric into formal policy. The legal staffs of the Departments of State and Justice seized the opportunity to establish a far-reaching legal precedent expanding the reach of American courts to punish torturers in the case of *Filártiga v. Peña-Irala* before the U.S. Court of Appeals for the Second Circuit in 1979. At issue was whether the Alien Tort Claims Act, an obscure federal law that had been virtually dormant since it had been written two centuries earlier, conferred district court jurisdiction over a suit by two Paraguayan nationals against a Paraguayan official who had tortured their son to death in Paraguay. Positing an expansive interpretation of the law and its relevance to the prosecution of torturers, the administration insisted that the law established jurisdiction in the federal courts over a suit between two aliens, and that "the law of nations" was part of the federal common law. Because international law prohibited state-sanctioned torture, it followed that the right to be free from torture had become a principle of customary international law and by extension federal common law. The court agreed with the administration's interpretation and, in a landmark decision, ruled for the plaintiffs. The decision established that torture was such an egregious violation of international norms that torturers were now vulnerable to prosecution wherever they might dwell. Judge Irving Kaufman, in the court's opinion, admonished that "the torturer has become—like the pirate and slave trader before him—*hostis humani generis*, an enemy of all mankind."[16]

The clarity that marked the Carter administration's stance in *Filártiga v. Peña-Irala*, however, was too often absent from the administration's human rights policy. Conceived of as broad principles rather than a coherent program, it quickly became confused and confusing. Foreign leaders and policy experts alike were uncertain as to its crucial tenets. The administration seemed to shift its targets for reproach in an unpredictable manner: first Communist regimes, then African dictators, and later South American juntas. The administration, for instance, denounced torture in Guatemala but was virtually silent about Indonesia's rampant violations in East Timor. Likewise, American diplomats excoriated the junta in Chile even while President Carter showered compliments on the shah of Iran, whose secret police enjoyed an unenviable reputation for brutality that surpassed even that of the Chilean regime.[17]

The disarray of the Carter administration's foreign policy contributed mightily to Ronald Reagan's success casting himself as a decisive leader with a coherent vision to restore American credibility and prestige. An unwavering anticommunist, Reagan viewed human rights within a Cold War framework. His idée fixe was that international Communism posed the greatest threat to both human rights and American interests. While still a candidate, Reagan elevated Communist transgressions against human rights for severest censure. He acknowledged that various right-wing allies of the United States periodically violated human rights, but their transgressions were excused because they were provoked by communist insurgencies. When the assistant secretary of state for human rights in the Carter administration criticized the Argentine military for torturing and murdering thousands in 1979, Reagan fired back that she should "walk a mile in the moccasins" of the Argentine generals before criticizing them. Dismissing her charges as overblown, he conceded only "that in the process of bringing stability to a terrorized nation . . . a small number [of civilians] were caught in the crossfire, amongst them a few innocents."[18]

Once in office, Reagan and his administration adopted an aggressively interventionist international policy on a scale unseen since the 1960s. To beat back the menace of Soviet expansionism around the world, the United States now pledged to bolster any regime threatened by leftist insurgencies. Rather than single out human rights violations in allied nations as bleeding heart liberals and leftists had previously done, the Reagan administration aggressively defended the human rights records of allies. Jeane Kirkpatrick, who Reagan appointed as the nation's ambassador to the United Nations, codified the rationale for the policy in a highly influential article in which she abhorred the Carter administration's policy of "continuous self-abasement and apology vis-à-vis the Third World." Describing the shah of Iran and Anastasio Somoza, the longtime Nicaraguan despot, as "moderate autocrats friendly to American interests," she cautioned the United States to press for only gradual liberalization and democracy in the developing world, and only among those regimes that did not face violent overthrow. She granted that "traditional autocrats tolerate social inequities, brutality, and poverty." But far worse were "revolutionary autocracies" because they fomented and exploited brutality.[19]

Guatemala provided an important field test of the Reagan administration's policy of "constructive engagement" with friendly autocracies. The United States had long had an oversized influence on the Central American republic. During the Cold War, the CIA had orchestrated a 1954 coup against the democratically elected president, Jacobo Árbenz. Subsequently, both CIA and American military experts had trained and supplied the Guatemalan military during its campaign against leftist insurgents. By the 1970s, the brutality of the counterinsurgency in Guatemala attracted scrutiny from human rights activists, prompting the Carter administration to make gestures at withholding aid from the nation. When Reagan took office, he dismissed any hand-wringing over human rights violations there. He had no doubt that the unrest in Guatemala and throughout Central America was, at root, "a power play by Cuba and the Soviet Union, pure and simple." A state department white paper released in December 1981 concurred, blaming the violence on leftist "extremist groups" and their "terrorist methods" inspired and supported by Cuba. A year later the embassy in Guatemala protested that the government there was the victim of a communist-inspired "disinformation campaign" that traduced the nation's human rights record. While meeting with the commander of the military junta, Efraín Ríos Montt, in the White House, Reagan grumbled that his guest was getting a "bum rap" on human rights.[20]

More than just the tenor of American pronouncements on human rights changed during the Reagan administration. Covert operations by the CIA to influence the internal affairs of Guatemala and other countries were revived. William Casey, the director of the CIA from 1981 to 1987, had no patience for congressional oversight or the agency's recent compliance with the restrictions placed on it during the 1970s. Throughout his tenure the agency employed duplicity to shield its activities from congressional oversight and to skirt laws that impeded its plans. Its deceptions extended from substituting the innocuous-sounding phrase "human resources exploitation" for "interrogation," a word tainted by past controversies with embarrassing associations, to elaborate schemes to hide agency funding of illegal covert operations.[21]

Despite restrictions on American support for regimes that routinely violated human rights, the CIA was deeply involved in the brutal counterinsurgency campaigns in Central America and elsewhere during the 1980s. Operatives disseminated three decades of expertise in counterinsurgency and interrogation techniques to complement the training that Latin American military officers continued to receive at the U.S. Army School of the Americas, now relocated from Panama to Fort Benning, Georgia. In a revised version of the widely circulated 1963 KUBARK manual, American interrogation specialists advocated the effectiveness of psychological techniques developed decades earlier during the Cold War. As a Honduran interrogator recalled, his CIA training taught him "to study the fears and weaknesses of a prisoner" and to use simple but effective techniques to exploit them: "Make him stand up, don't let him sleep, keep him naked and isolated, put rats and cockroaches in his cell, give him bad food, serve him dead animals, throw cold water on him, change the temperature."[22] Such training encouraged the security services of allies to adopt American interrogation methods as well as to assume that their use would not attract unwelcome scrutiny from the international community.[23]

Recipients of CIA and American military training in Central America, however, displayed a penchant for physical torture as well as less invasive psychological methods, resulting in mounting allegations of sexual violence, maimings, and murders during the 1980s. The full extent of CIA involvement in the human rights violations in Central

America is impossible to determine at present. Certainly, tens of thousands in Guatemala, El Salvador, Honduras, and Nicaragua were tortured and killed by military units and "death squads" that received assistance, training, and intelligence from American agents. Periodically, American ambassadors in the region expressed dismay about human rights violations in private and even urged regional leaders to restrain their military and police forces. Nevertheless, the Reagan administration took no meaningful steps to rein in the CIA or to reprimand its proxies.

Jarring contradictions marked the Reagan administration's human rights policy no less than that of the Carter presidency. Even while the United States was deeply implicated in the carnage in Central America and sponsored governments that routinely committed torture, Reagan saw no inconsistency in urging an end to "the abhorrent practice of torture." For Reagan and his advisers, the eradication of torture was a noble dream that presumably would be fulfilled after the destruction of communism. Until then, the pressing challenge before the United States was to expose and denounce the torture carried out by communist regimes.

Reagan's opposition to torture, moreover, had clear limits that became evident in his reservations about the United Nations Convention against Torture. In 1975 members of the United Nations had issued a declaration denouncing torture as a violation of human rights but had not established any mechanisms to investigate, denounce, or punish torturers. The Convention against Torture, which was adopted in 1985, marked a significant step toward creating an effective international instrument on torture and capped a decade-long campaign against state torture waged by Amnesty International, the World Council of Churches, and other groups. When President Reagan submitted the Convention to the Senate for ratification, he explicitly rejected its broad definition of torture and instead substituted a narrower one that, whether by intent or not, did not prohibit most of the interrogation techniques endorsed by the CIA and used by its international proxies. Observers of the Reagan-era policies struggled to reconcile the apparent contradiction inherent in the nation's pledge to promote the abolition of torture even while American policies coddled friendly autocrats, national intelligence agencies flouted the law, and the administration advocated a definition of torture that deviated in crucial ways from international law.[24]

The end of the Cold War and the dissipation of the threat of international Communism during the early 1990s allowed American policy makers to sidestep these inconsistencies. Triumphant as the world's sole "superpower" and without any evident external threats, the United States was free of the strategic considerations that previously had tempered its commitment to prohibit torture. Policy makers no longer had to rationalize violations of human rights by allies or American agents during covert operations against leftist insurgencies. Congress took important steps to incorporate into federal law the protections against torture in the United Nations Convention against Torture. With the passage of the Torture Victim Protection Act in 1992, Congress granted both citizens and aliens the right to bring civil suits against individuals who, acting in an official capacity for any foreign nation, committed torture. Immediately after the passage of the law, Sister Dianna Ortiz, an American Roman Catholic nun, filed a civil action against former general and Defense Minister Héctor Gramajo of Guatemala, contending that he had been responsible for her abduction, rape, and torture in Guatemala in November 1989. Three years later, a federal court in Massachusetts ruled in her favor, awarding her $5 million in damages.[25]

The passage of the War Crimes Act in 1996 further bolstered federal law prohibiting torture. Congressman Walter B. Jones Jr., a conservative Republican, proposed the law after meeting a retired navy pilot who had been imprisoned and tortured by the North Vietnamese during the Vietnam War. With the goal of providing veterans with means to prosecute their abusers, the law criminalized breaches of the Geneva Conventions adopted after World War II, such as mutilation, cruel treatment, torture, and "outrages upon personal dignity, in particular humiliating and degrading treatment." The Department of Defense enthusiastically supported the law, even recommending that it include a longer list of war crimes. Because the United States followed the Conventions, the thinking went, American military personnel were unlikely to be prosecuted under the law but stood to benefit from its protections. While Jones intended the law to provide a remedy for future American troops who might be captured and abused while serving overseas, President Bill Clinton extolled the law within the context of expanding protections for human rights. Most of the bill's champions hoped that the law would seldom be invoked, and none could have anticipated that it would play a prominent role in shaping how the Bush administration would wage the War on Terror that it launched in 2001.[26]

"At 8:46 on the morning of September 11, 2001, the United States became a nation transformed."[27] Not since the attack on Pearl Harbor in 1941 had Americans suffered a comparable blow to their sense of collective security. The terrorist attacks that destroyed the World Trade Center in New York City and damaged the Pentagon in Washington, D.C., were the worst failure of the American intelligence services since their founding after World War II. So complete was the failure that President George W. Bush and his administration had no idea of the scale of the threat to the nation. A sense of acute vulnerability fed the belief that the nation faced an unprecedented crisis.

In the immediate aftermath of 9/11, the administration made several decisions that shaped fundamentally how it waged the subsequent so-called War on Terror. The administration cast the struggle in apocalyptic terms, imploring Americans to recognize that they were engaged in a cataclysmic confrontation with radical Islamic nihilism. Tapping into the notion that the "West" faced a "clash of civilizations" with Islamic societies, the administration sought to mobilize national and international support on the grounds that an attack on the United States was an attack on modern, democratic, capitalist civilization by an enemy that was savage, ruthless, fanatical, and unbound by any ethical code. They were, in the words of National Security Advisor Condoleezza Rice, "radical, freedom-hating terrorists [who] declared war on America and on the civilized world."[28] By proclaiming that the United States was the defender of civilization, the administration claimed for the American cause singular moral righteousness. Simultaneously, any suggestion of American responsibility for the disorder in the Middle East or the terrorism that it bred was deemed not only spurious but also traitorous. Champions of the War on Terror insisted that the United States had always conducted itself according to international norms and that to suggest otherwise was to aid and abet terrorism. In this battle between "civilization" and "barbarism," virtually any measures the Bush administration contemplated were justifiable against an enemy so despicable that they were banished from the human community.[29]

The administration interpreted the threat to the United States as tantamount to war and claimed the most expansive possible executive powers to wage its War on Terror. The horrifying images of the 9/11 attacks understandably fueled fantasies of retaliation. President Bush himself succumbed to them days after the attacks when he seethed, "We are going to kick some ass."[30] Even without the pretext of a national crisis, influential members of the administration were intent on buttressing executive power. Vice President Dick Cheney in particular had advocated broad executive privileges since his tenure in the Nixon administration, and he had deplored post-Watergate laws that restricted the capacities of the president. Now, in the wake of the 9/11 attacks, he and others in the administration saw an opportunity to reassert presidential authority on the grounds that the commander in chief's powers during national emergencies should be virtually unchecked. Assistant Attorney General John Yoo distilled this idea of presidential emergency powers in a succinct proposition: "In wartime it is for the president alone to decide what methods to use to best prevail against the enemy."[31]

This conception of executive power encouraged disdain for congressional oversight and a predisposition for secrecy. Cheney had displayed both while serving as secretary of defense in the George H. W. Bush administration. Alarmed that congressional investigations during 1992 risked exposing Project X, a long-running covert military program involving American participation in torture and assassinations, he ordered the collection and destruction of all extant records relating to it. A few innocuous documents survived the purge, but manuals and other records that documented possible human rights violations as part of the project were destroyed. Together, the predisposition to unilateral executive action and disregard for oversight undergirded the administration's conviction that the president was justified in adopting whatever interpretation of the law that he and his advisers believed the War on Terror warranted.[32]

As soon as the Bush administration began translating its assumptions about the enemy and executive power into war policy, momentum built to deviate from precedent in waging the War on Terror. The choice by the administration to define the enemy as illegal combatants was of inestimable significance in the chain of decisions that would culminate in the adoption of "enhanced interrogation" techniques. That the administration viewed members of Al Qaeda as stateless savages predisposed it to define them as "unlawful belligerents" and "illegal enemy combatants." But even after applying this label to the enemy, Bush and his advisers could have followed the Geneva Conventions and existing legal precedent regarding treatment of the enemy. Instead, the architects of the War on Terror seized on the murky legal status of unlawful belligerents to justify wide latitude in detaining, interrogating, and prosecuting them.[33]

The Bush administration took further steps to establish unprecedented procedures to deal with the terrorist enemy. Two months after the 9/11 attacks, the president signed a military order that established that captives in the War on Terror would be tried for "violations of the laws of war" by military tribunals and that "the principles of law and rules of evidence" that prevailed in American courts would not be applied to the military tribunals. In January 2002 Secretary of Defense Donald Rumsfeld proclaimed, "Unlawful combatants do not have any rights under the Geneva Convention." He pledged that the administration would treat them in a manner "that is reasonably consistent" with the Geneva Conventions but only to the extent that the administration deemed the protocols to be "appropriate."[34]

Compounding the impact of this order was the extraordinarily expansive grounds that the administration proposed for considering a captive to be an unlawful belligerent. The policy applied not only to professed members of terrorist groups but also to anyone who "has engaged in, aided, or abetted, or conspired to commit acts of international terrorism, threatened to cause, or have as their aim to cause injury to or adverse effects on the United States, its citizens, national security, foreign policy, or economy." Thus, while the administration dispensed with the traditional rules of evidence in the military tribunals that would try captives, it also consigned to the jurisdiction of the tribunals anyone whom the president "had reason to believe" meant harm to the United States.[35]

Two overriding concerns seem to have motivated the administration's course. The administration was determined to keep alleged terrorists out of American courts, where it was convinced that activist lawyers, established rules of evidence, and media sensationalism would complicate successful prosecutions. Indeed, as long as captives were outside the civilian justice system and lacked the protections of the Geneva Conventions, the Bush administration could order their detention in perpetuity. The administration also clearly wanted to avoid the legal constraints that international law imposed on the interrogation of prisoners of war. White House legal counsel Alberto Gonzales, in January 2002, endorsed the administration's policies on "unlawful combatants" by confirming that the nation was waging "a new kind of war" that "places a high premium" on the "ability to quickly obtain information from captured terrorists."[36]

A few weeks later, Gonzales made clear the administration's anxiety to minimize the risk of criminal prosecution for conduct that was legally questionable, if not explicitly banned by the Geneva Conventions, the Convention against Torture, and the War Crimes Act. "The new paradigm" of the War on Terror, he asserted, "renders obsolete Geneva's strict limitations on questioning of enemy prisoners and renders quaint some of its provisions." He advised the president to suspend the Geneva Conventions. By doing so, he would "preserve his flexibility" while substantially reducing "the threat of domestic criminal prosecution" for violations of restrictions on interrogating enemy prisoners, especially "outrages of personal dignity" and "inhuman treatment." "It is difficult to predict," Gonzales warned, "the motives of prosecutors and independent counsels who may in the future decide to pursue unwarranted charges" under the War Crimes Act or other legal pretexts.[37]

By the summer of 2002, the Bush administration had thrown off the restraints of federal and international law but had yet to clarify what, if any, constraints it would impose on itself. The question became acute as the number of captured unlawful belligerents in Afghanistan began to grow and interrogators in the field grew impatient to employ the severest possible methods. As early as December 2001, the

General Counsel's Office in the Department of Defense had contacted the military agency that had overseen so-called SERE (Survival Evasion Resistance and Escape) training since the Korean War. Although the expertise of SERE specialists was in training American personnel to resist brainwashing during interrogations, "not in how to conduct interrogations," Rumsfeld and his closest advisers were apparently already interested in interrogation techniques that had hitherto been considered illegal under the Geneva Conventions, such as stripping prisoners of their clothing, placing them in stress positions, putting hoods over their heads, treating them like animals, subjecting them to deafening music and flashing lights, exposing them to extreme temperatures, face and body slaps, and waterboarding. By the time the architects of the War on Terror were codifying plans for harvesting human intelligence, they were looking to apply methods that Americans had denounced when the Chinese had employed them a half century earlier.[38]

Driven by the fear that the nation faced the equivalent of a "ticking bomb" scenario in which unknown fanatical terrorists were poised to launch attacks on the homeland, the inner circle of the Bush administration from the outset of the War on Terror displayed an inclination to interpret the laws constraining the treatment of prisoners as narrowly as possible so that the boundaries could be more effectively stretched, even breached. Seizing on the reservations that President Reagan had voiced regarding the Geneva Conventions almost two decades earlier and ignoring the Conventions' injunction that neither a political crisis nor war justifies the resort to torture, the Bush administration concluded that extant treaty protections for unlawful combatants were limited, especially in the context of counterterrorism and military operations overseas, and did not preclude abusive interrogation techniques, secret detention, or renditions to states that practice torture.[39]

In a crucial legal memo drafted in August 2002, Assistant Attorney General Jay Bybee formulated the administration's guidelines for acceptable interrogation techniques. Bybee's apparent intention was to provide the narrowest possible definition of torture. He focused on two elements of the 1985 Convention against Torture. The intent to inflict severe pain and suffering, he contended, was inherent in torture.

Employing the same line of argument made by military officers during the Philippine Insurrection, Bybee asserted that if an interrogator caused physical or mental pain while seeking information, he had not abused his subject. Bybee left unanswered whether an interrogation could ever devolve into torture because no interrogator was likely to confess to intentionally causing pain. The memo also parsed the types of pain and suffering that constituted torture. The threshold of pain necessary to inflict torture was high, "equivalent in intensity to the pain accompanying serious physical injury, such as organ failure, impairment of bodily function, or even death." "Only extreme acts," in which there was a specific intent to cause pain or enduring mental harm, were prohibited. Significantly, Bybee's interpretation prohibited few of the interrogation techniques that the CIA had honed during the Cold War.[40]

The Bybee memo provided a "golden shield" to interrogators against possible prosecution. Assistant Attorney General Jack Goldsmith would later summarize the glib reasoning evident in the memo: "Violent acts aren't necessarily torture; if you do torture, you probably have a defense; and even if you don't have a defense, the torture law doesn't apply if you act under the color of presidential authority."[41] Yet even while the architects of the policy provided legal cover for "enhanced interrogation," they simultaneously displayed concern that the approved methods remain hidden from prying eyes. The staff judge advocate for the joint task force that conducted interrogations in Guantánamo warned interrogators there that they "might need to curb the harsher operations" whenever members of the International Committee of the Red Cross were present. It was, she counseled, "better not to expose them to any controversial techniques" that might "draw a lot of negative attention."[42]

Questions about the appropriate severity of interrogation techniques persisted even after the approval of "enhanced interrogation" methods. The Bybee memo had granted interrogators wide latitude without clarifying the precise limits of "enhanced interrogation." During the summer and fall of 2002 the foot soldiers of the War on Terror received clear recommendations to interpret broadly their authority to use severe methods. At a strategy meeting for interrogators at Guantánamo in October 2002, Jonathan Fredman, chief counsel for the CIA Counterterrorism Center, suggested that interrogators should exploit the vagueness of the guidelines. Torture, he explained, "is basically subject to perception. If the detainee dies you're doing it wrong."[43] Apparently, any technique that did not conclude in the death of the prisoner was acceptable.

With the CIA taking the lead in interrogating unlawful combatants at Guantánamo and elsewhere, the techniques that the FBI had previously used to interrogate alleged terrorists, which emphasized nurturing rapport between the interrogator and the prisoner, fell into disfavor. CIA operatives and consultants hired by the agency instead "reengineered" the techniques used to train American soldiers to resist torture that originated during the Korean War. Many of the techniques were lifted almost verbatim from a 1957 Air Force study of Chinese techniques to obtain false confessions from American prisoners during the Korean War. The apparent attraction of these techniques was that they were aggressive, seemingly promised swift results, and accorded with the prevailing assumptions that the prisoners were hardened fanatics who would resist less aggressive methods of interrogation. Furthermore, in the perennial competition between the various national security agencies, the CIA was keen to restore its reputation by getting quick results by whatever means necessary.[44]

During the fall of 2002 the CIA began in earnest to interrogate the thousands of prisoners who were flowing into American hands, in no small part because the CIA offered cash "bounties" for captured alleged terrorists. Some who were captured in Afghanistan were shunted to so-called "black sites" in Thailand, Iraq, Africa, and East Europe and were subjected to "enhanced interrogation" by CIA agents. For instance, Abd al-Rahim al-Nashiri, a Saudi Arabian citizen alleged to be the mastermind of several terrorist attacks before his capture in Dubai in 2002, was held for four years in "black sites" in Afghanistan, Thailand, Poland, Morocco, and Romania. In Thailand, Deputy Group Chief Gina Haspel oversaw al-Nasahri's interrogation, which exceeded even those "enhanced interrogation" techniques approved by the Bush administration. After years of interrogation and torture, al-Nashari joined other detainees in Guantánamo, where the CIA further refined its interrogation methods. Yet other captives were "rendered" to Egypt, Syria, Jordan, Morocco, and Uzbekistan, where they were interrogated and tortured by local security agents in collusion with the CIA. Probably at no previous moment in American history were so many American agents across the globe simultaneously engaged in so many practices that flouted both international law and professed American principles.[45]

Almost immediately, the adoption of "enhanced interrogation" techniques aroused concern in the FBI and among military and international law specialists within the Pentagon. The common thread in the dissent was that many of the interrogation techniques could place interrogators and their superiors at risk of criminal prosecution at home and abroad, that they were ineffective, that they could "poison" future attempts to prosecute detainees on the basis of extorted confessions, and that they would leave American personnel vulnerable to retaliation if they were captured.[46] Legal specialists in the Air Force did not mince words; "enhanced interrogation" techniques, they said, "could be construed as torture."[47] A navy specialist agreed, concluding that the techniques "reflect conduct specifically defined as torture" under federal and international law.[48] One army legal adviser declared that he could not approve any interrogation technique that "is predicated upon the principle that all is well if the ends justify the means and others are unaware of how we conduct our business."[49]

Given this opposition, the architects of the War on Terror had ample grounds to reconsider the decision to adopt "enhanced interrogation." The reservations were sufficiently compelling to prompt the legal counsel to the chairman of the Joint Chiefs of Staff to initiate a thorough legal review of the policy. Even before completing the review, the legal team had concluded that the "enhanced interrogation" techniques violated federal law and exposed interrogators to risk of prosecution under the War Crimes Act. Perhaps anticipating the team's conclusions, William J. Haynes, the Pentagon's chief counsel, and Major General Richard Myers, chairman of the Joint Chiefs of Staff, shut it down. Haynes justified the step as a necessary precaution to limit the number of people familiar with the policy. Probably a more important consideration in his decision was the frustration within the president's inner circle over the delays in the resumption of "enhanced interrogation" techniques. Haynes ignored the near unanimous opposition of the legal experts in the Pentagon and in a one-page memo to Secretary of Defense Rumsfeld recommended the approval of fifteen controversial interrogation techniques, ranging from sleep deprivation to waterboarding.[50]

Opposition to "enhanced interrogation," nevertheless, festered in the Pentagon. Navy General Counsel Alberto Mora in particular continued to warn that these interrogation techniques "could rise to the level of torture."[51] In January 2003 he deftly forced another suspension of the policy by threatening to sign a formal memo detailing its potential violations of federal and international law. In a gesture that seemed to acknowledge Mora's concerns, the Department of Defense established a Detainee Working Group to provide a legal analysis of appropriate interrogation methods. But within weeks of its launch, the group was informed that a legal memo by Assistant Attorney General John Yoo, which expanded on Bybee's earlier memo, was authoritative and that any recommendations by the group had to conform with Yoo's conclusions. As one member of the working group later recalled, any report from the group had to be "geared toward a particular conclusion."[52]

Critics of the rationales for "enhanced interrogation" lambasted Bybee, Haynes, Yoo, and the other enablers of the policy for their glaring ignorance of human rights law and for twisting whatever relevant legal precedents they were familiar with to reach preordained conclusions. Given that the architects would brook no obstacles to the adoption of enhanced interrogation, it may appear curious that they went to such lengths to cobble together a legal rationale for it. Yet even they felt a compulsion to square the policy with the laws of the nation and the norms of modern civilization. They were determined that the program would have a patina of legality and would, at least to their satisfaction, fall within the norms of civilized warfare, if only barely.

More important, they could not easily avoid the scrutiny of the legal specialists in international and human rights law in the Pentagon and FBI. However inconsistent American compliance with human rights law had been during the two decades before the War on Terror, clusters of legal experts versed in it had grown within the vast federal bureaucracy. And these specialists, whose careers were not contingent on political winds, had to be either won over or shunted to the side by the advocates of "enhanced interrogation."

By March 2003, the inner circle in the Bush administration had exhausted its patience and elected to override any opposition to its policies within the ranks of the Pentagon and FBI. With the American invasion of Iraq under way by April 2003, the harsh techniques employed by the CIA at Guantánamo and in Afghanistan quickly spread to military intelligence in Iraq. A combination of huge numbers of Iraqi prisoners awaiting interrogation and the worsening insurgency against the American occupation fueled frustration and a sense of urgency to extort more and better intelligence from detainees. In August 2003 Captain William Ponce, a military intelligence officer, vented seemingly widely held sentiments to his peers and subordinates when he wrote, "The gloves are coming off regarding these detainees. . . . We want these individuals broken. Casualties are mounting and we need to start gathering info."[53] Not until five months into the occupation of Iraq did the Department of Defense issue interrogation guidelines for conventional forces, and by then prisoner abuse was so widespread that one commander worried that someone needed "to slam some rules in place" because "a disaster was waiting to happen."[54]

The ratcheting up of the pressure to acquire timely human intelligence in Iraq coincided with the dawning realization in the Bush administration that the weapons of mass destruction that had provided the impetus for the American invasion did not exist. The Bush administration pivoted from justifying the war as a necessary step in the War on Terror to affirming that it had toppled a dictatorial regime that had committed grotesque human rights violations, including torture. Over and over again, President Bush boasted during the fall of 2003 and spring of 2004 that "Iraq is free of rape rooms and torture chambers" and that "there won't be any more mass graves and torture rooms" in Iraq.[55]

The revelations about widespread abuse and torture at Abu Ghraib prison in April 2004 made a mockery of these claims. The Bush administration and its political allies offered vigorous if altogether predictable responses to the mounting evidence of the widespread abuse of detainees. In the immediate aftermath of the publication of images of abuse at the prison, the president explained away the incident, stressing that it had been done by "a small number of American servicemen and women" who had "been given the responsibility of overseeing

FIGURE 8.1. "We Do Not Torture People!" Justin Biliki's 2007 cartoon highlights the rationalizations and euphemisms that characterized the Bush administration's insistence that the United States was complying with international and national laws regarding torture. Included in the cartoon is a visual reference to one of the most notorious images of abuse at the Abu Ghraib prison.

Iraqis in American custody, and doing so in a decent and humane manner, consistent with U.S. law and the Geneva conventions." Parroting the Nixon administration's dismissal of the soldiers responsible for the My Lai Massacre as "a few bad apples," a military investigation promptly assigned blame to "a small group of morally corrupt and unsupervised Soldiers and civilians."[56] This line of argument absolved not only commanding officers but also Bush policy makers of responsibility for the abuse.

Other defenders of the administration denied that detainees at Abu Ghraib or elsewhere had been subjected to torture. The military commander at Guantánamo attested that prisoners there had "not been tortured in any way." General Myers of the Joint Chiefs of Staff agreed, protesting that "we don't think it's torture." Vice President Cheney repeatedly asserted that "waterboarding, the way we did it, was, in fact, not torture." Rush Limbaugh, a conservative talk show host, dismissed the abuse as no different than what happens at college fraternity initiations, and Michael Savage, another radio host, criticized the methods exposed at Abu Ghraib not as cruel and excessive but as too gentle. "We need more of the humiliation tactics, not less," he raged, adding, "I would have liked to have seen dynamite put in their orifices."[57]

Many apologists shifted attention from the alleged atrocities by Americans to the abhorrent character of the enemy. Secretary of Defense Rumsfeld and others routinely referred to the detainees at Guantánamo and Abu Ghraib as the "worst of the worst," with the implication that they were so incorrigible as to be unworthy of pity. General Myers dismissed the prisoners as people who "don't know any moral values," and a chief warrant officer in the 3rd Armored Cavalry Regiment implied that the enemy was too primitive to respond to conventional methods; they only understood "force, not psychological mind games and incentives."[58] John Yoo asserted that "historically there are people so bad that they were not given protection of the laws." In his opinion, clearly, detainees during the War on Terror could be consigned to this reviled group.[59]

The Bush administration also rebutted criticism of its handling of detainees by insisting that it had faced an unprecedented crisis that demanded swift and decisive measures. Only those who had borne a similar burden, apparently, had standing to criticize the president and his advisers. National Security Advisor (and later Secretary of State) Condoleezza Rice proclaimed, "Unless you were there in a position of responsibility after September 11th, you cannot possibly imagine the dilemmas that you faced in trying to protect Americans." "I know a lot of people are second-guessing now," she continued, "but let me tell you what the second-guessing that would really have hurt me—if the second-guessing had been about 3,000 more Americans dying because we didn't do everything we could to protect them."[60] A subsequent military investigation of the handling of detainees displayed unmistakable sympathy for "well intentioned professionals" who, with so much at stake, "found themselves in uncharted ethical ground."[61] By implication, anyone who had been in their circumstances would have made the same choices regarding the treatment of unlawful combatants in the War on Terror.

Following in the tradition of apologists for the occupation of the Philippines and the Vietnam War, allies of the Bush administration

ranted against the misplaced attention devoted to the torture of terrorists and the unfair disparaging of American soldiers. Senator James M.
Inhofe of Oklahoma announced that "we have nothing to be ashamed
of" and protested the repeated "parading [of] these relatively minor infractions before the press and the world." Senator Jeff Sessions of
Alabama mocked the suffering of detainees interrogated at Guantánamo
by asking whether any had "suffered a broken bone or serious permanent injury."[62]

If these justifications failed to persuade, the defenders of "enhanced
interrogation" played their trump; the techniques had extorted information that allegedly protected the lives of nameless Americans from
planned terrorist attacks. Vice President Cheney has been the most tenacious advocate of the effectiveness of "enhanced interrogation."
When the Senate Select Committee on Intelligence released a withering 500-page assessment of the CIA's interrogation and detention
policies, Cheney dismissed its conclusion that "enhanced interrogation" was torture and that it had generated little reliable intelligence.
"It worked," he protested. "It absolutely worked." He acknowledged no
second thoughts about the techniques and vowed that he would "do it
again in a minute." Going even further, he lauded the agency's interrogators for their work: "I'm perfectly comfortable that they should be
praised," he explained. "They should be decorated."[63]

While such claims appeased some Americans, they did not stop the
revelations about torture and abuse at Abu Ghraib and elsewhere during
the War on Terror. Beginning in the summer of 2004, American newspapers finally began to enumerate the consequences of the administration's international campaign against terrorism. By 2005 the Bush administration itself quoted a human rights organization's report that in
Iraq "torture and ill treatment of detainees by police was commonplace," including "beatings with cables and hosepipes, electric shocks
to their earlobes and genitals, food and water deprivation." More than
fourteen thousand Iraqi detainees were crowded for years at a time into
prisons built to hold less than half the number. More than a thousand
of "the worst of the worst" prisoners had been subjected to interrogations at Bagram and Guantánamo. Binyam Mohamed, a British resident seized in Pakistan, for example, was among more than 150 suspects who had been subjected to extralegal renditions to countries that

practiced torture. Before he was released from Guantánamo in 2009, he had been sent to Morocco, where he allegedly was beaten with sticks, whipped with electric cable and rubber whips, sexually humiliated, slashed with a razor, burned with boiling liquid, and deprived of sleep. More than sixty detainees had died under suspicious circumstances, and twenty-six had been murdered while undergoing interrogation.[64]

The ongoing revelations of detainee abuse prompted surprisingly little revision of policy and even less enthusiasm for accountability within the Bush White House. None of the internal investigations undertaken after the revelations enjoyed any significant independence; instead, the military and CIA were charged with investigating themselves. Most important, the investigations failed to examine the role of civilian leaders in crafting and implementing "enhanced interrogation" techniques. More telling, the Bush administration fought a dogged rearguard action to defend controversial techniques. The administration worked strenuously to prevent the passage of the Detainee Treatment Act by Congress in 2005, which required military interrogators to use only techniques approved by the U.S. Army field manual. When the law passed with overwhelming and bipartisan support, the president issued a signing statement asserting that he would disregard the law if he found it impeded the exercise of his powers as commander in chief.[65] Simultaneously, the Department of Justice continued to counsel the CIA that "enhanced interrogation" techniques were legal and to evade any constraints imposed by Congress. In May 2005, a full year after the Abu Ghraib revelations, Deputy Assistant Attorney General Steven G. Bradbury reaffirmed the use of waterboarding, stress positions, striking, extremes of heat and cold, dousing with cold water, and sleep deprivation (for up to seven and a half days) on "high value" detainees. Two years later, Bradbury again had to provide legal authorization because the new law prohibited subjecting any prisoners, including those at Guantánamo, to "cruel, inhuman, or degrading treatment or punishment." The law, however, provided no clear definition of "cruel, inhuman, or degrading treatment," so Bradbury endorsed interrogation methods that contradicted the spirit if not the explicit language of the law, including deprivation of food, sustained sleep deprivation and stress positions for up to four days, and the striking of prisoners.[66]

Frustrated by the administration's tenacious application of "enhanced interrogation" techniques, the Senate in February 2008 passed a bill intended to effectively ban the use of simulated drowning, temperature extremes, and other harsh tactics that the CIA had repeatedly employed during the War on Terror. Less than a month later, President Bush vetoed the bill. During his weekly radio address, the president justified his opposition by claiming that the law "would take away one of the most valuable tools in the war on terror." He swept aside all of the criticism of extreme interrogation methods and detainee abuse by invoking the threat of "hardened terrorists" who were impervious to the methods of interrogation used on conventional combatants. His veto, he reassured Americans, ensured that the nation would not "lose vital information from senior al Qaeda terrorists" that "could cost American lives."[67]

The Bush administration faced sterner challenges from federal judges who began reining in the War on Terror by insisting that it be waged within the confines of conventional law. In June 2004 in *Rasul v. Bush*, the Supreme Court ruled that detainees at Guantánamo could turn to American courts to challenge their confinement. In *Hamdi v. Rumsfeld*, also decided in June 2004, the Court recognized the power of the government to detain unlawful combatants but ruled that detainees must have the ability to challenge their detention before an impartial judge. Though no single opinion of the Court commanded a majority, eight of the nine justices of the Court agreed that the executive branch did not have the power to hold indefinitely an American citizen without basic due process protections enforceable through judicial review. Federal courts subsequently began to extend legal protections to noncitizen detainees as well. In November 2004, a federal court halted the trial of Salim Ahmed Hamdan, who was to be the first Guantánamo detainee brought before a military commission. The district court dismissed the Bush administration's repeated claim that the Geneva Conventions did not apply to unlawful combatants, a position that the Supreme Court confirmed in 2006. As the Bush administration was winding down in June 2008, the Supreme Court ruled, in *Boumediene v. Bush*, that Guantánamo captives were entitled to access the American justice system. By then, much of the legal apparatus of the War on Terror that had been cobbled together in the frenzied months after 9/11 had been dismantled, curtailed, or repudiated by the courts.[68]

The full-throated defense of "enhanced interrogation" by the Bush administration posed a difficult challenge for President Barack Obama. The Bush administration's expansive definition of executive privilege and penchant for secrecy had precluded efforts to trace the origins, use, and effectiveness of "enhanced interrogation." Opponents of the policy believed that in the absence of a full accounting, the American public might again, during some future crisis, be persuaded to endorse these interrogation tactics and other outrages against the law and decency. Defenders of the Bush administration warned that calls for accountability for the excesses during the War on Terror were a thinly veiled campaign for partisan retribution. During his presidential campaign, Obama dwelled on the damage that the War on Terror had done to the nation's international reputation but promised nothing more than a thorough investigation of the use of torture. Once elected he discouraged calls for an independent commission to investigate his predecessor's policies and offered only vague endorsement for prosecution if "somebody has blatantly broken the law." Early in his first term, he appealed for "reflection, not retribution," and urged the nation to look beyond this "dark and painful chapter in our history." "Nothing will be gained," he predicted, "by spending our time and energy laying blame for the past."[69]

Throughout his presidency Obama struggled to reconcile his commitment to acknowledge the historical fact of torture during the War on Terror while avoiding assigning responsibility, much less seeking accountability, for it. Upon taking office he issued an executive order restricting the CIA to interrogation methods outlined in the U.S. Army field manual on interrogations, which was compliant with the Geneva Conventions. This order effectively overturned President Bush's veto of the Senate bill in 2008 and marked the symbolic end of the Bush administration's program of "enhanced interrogation." Yet the question of whether anyone in the previous administration would be prosecuted for the "enhanced interrogation" policies remained unanswered. Since 2005, human rights activists and international law specialists had pressed for criminal investigations of the architects of these interrogation policies. But when Attorney General Eric Holder announced in August 2009 that he had appointed Assistant U.S. Attorney John Durham to conduct a review into possible violations of federal law during the interrogation of detainees, he reassured those who had served in the War on Terror that "the Department of Justice will not prosecute anyone who acted in good faith and within the scope of the legal guidance" given by the Bush administration. Few were surprised two years later when the Department of Justice declined to prosecute anyone for violating the rights of detainees.[70]

Practical political considerations limited the options available to the Obama administration. When the president took office, he confronted a severe economic crisis and had no appetite for arousing the hostility of Republican loyalists at the outset of his presidency. Equally important, his advisers worried that revisiting the War on Terror would provoke an intense backlash within the national security agencies and the military when the administration sought to focus its energies elsewhere. Finally, there was anxiety among the president's advisers that the administration itself might in the future be at risk of politically motivated prosecutions if it took any action against its predecessors.

But more than political expediency lay behind the Obama administration's dogged defense of its predecessors against civil and international prosecution. Leaked diplomatic cables would eventually reveal that administration officials and prominent Republicans worked behind closed doors to persuade Spain and Germany to quash investigations into the American torture of their citizens. When a former detainee brought a case in British courts that risked exposing information about "enhanced interrogation," the Obama administration took the extraordinary step of publicly threatening to stop sharing intelligence with Britain unless the trial was halted. The administration even aggressively invoked national security and immunity doctrines to shield Bush administration officials and private contractors hired during the War on Terror from civil cases brought by torture victims.[71]

While the Obama administration had the will to renounce torture, it had no comparable will to hold anyone accountable for the excesses of the War on Terror. In speeches and executive orders, President Obama reasserted the position that torture is antithetical to American law and principles. Congress and the courts reimposed constraints on how the American military and national security agencies conduct themselves.

But the dispersal of responsibility was so broad and the scale of the violations so vast that any accounting for the excesses of the War on Terror was certain to be inadequate.

Certainly none of the architects of the War on Terror faced meaningful consequences for stretching, overstepping, or outright violating extant laws prohibiting torture. Jay Bybee, whose 2002 legal rationale laid the foundation for the "enhanced interrogation" policy, was appointed to the U.S. Court of Appeals for the Ninth Circuit. John Yoo, whose legal memos fleshed out Bybee's rationale, returned to his endowed professorship in the School of Law at the University of California, Berkeley. William Haynes, who had shepherded "enhanced interrogation" protocols through the thicket of opposition in the Department of Defense, suffered the sting of being denied a federal circuit judgeship but subsequently prospered as the chief legal counsel for two major corporations and garnered an affiliation with the George Mason School of Law. David Addington, who assiduously championed "enhanced interrogation" while serving as legal counsel to Vice President Cheney, landed a lofty policy position in the conservative Heritage Foundation. Steven Bradbury, whose memos sanctioned waterboarding and other "enhanced interrogation" methods between 2005 and 2007, served as an adviser to Republican candidate Mitt Romney in 2012, and in 2017 he was appointed legal counsel for the Department of Transportation. Gina Haspel, who presided over the torture of Abd al-Rahim al-Nashiri in 2002 and in 2005 participated in the clandestine destruction of more than ninety videotapes of enhanced interrogations conducted in a CIA black site in Thailand, became director of the CIA in May 2018.

In the end, policy makers in the Bush administration acted with impunity because they dismissed out of hand the moral and legal logic undergirding the prohibitions against torture. The laws rest on a presumed consensus about the definition of torture and the moral and ethical obligation of those who wield power to refrain from endorsing coercion that approximates torture. During the War on Terror, Bush and his advisers turned these assumptions on their head. Not only did the Bush administration hone its own idiosyncratic (and self-serving) definition of torture, it also undermined the legitimacy of the international law that the United States and other nations had compiled since

World War II. The Geneva Conventions were now obsolete and quaint; executive powers were untrammeled by international law; and the national emergency justified any recourse that the president deemed legitimate. The terrorist threat was portrayed as an unprecedented, catastrophic, and immediate challenge to American values, to the American way of life, and to civilization itself. The portrayal of the scale and nature of the threat and the demonization of the enemy as evil and irrational stirred up fears of a uniquely dangerous menace so extreme that legal and moral considerations could be, and indeed must be, waived. The state of emergency justified the suspension of normal politics as well as preemptive war, the abridgment of the established human rights of terrorist suspects, and the narrowing of civil liberties and basic freedoms. The sheer brazenness and scale of the Bush administration's assaults on the prevailing consensus regarding torture and democratic accountability remain staggering even as the events recede into the past.

Against the backdrop of urban disorder, police repression, and the so-called War on Crime in the last decades of the twentieth century, the violence and torture inflicted by Jon Burge and his accomplices in the Chicago police force was almost invisible. While the use of cattle prods, plastic bags, and crank telephones as tools of the trade may have been uncommon in many police forces, the cresting rhetoric of "law and order" and the national anxiety about urban decay gave license to law officers across the nation to employ methods that otherwise would have been inconceivable and unjustifiable.

With mounting urgency during the 1960s, prominent public leaders fed the pervasive anxiety about worsening urban crime. In 1968 presidential candidate Richard Nixon stoked fears by warning that "the city jungle will cease to be a metaphor" and that "the barbaric reality and the brutal society that now flourishes in the core cities" would soon "annex the affluent suburbs." When elected, Nixon promised to wage war against "the enemy within."[72] Once installed in office, he continued to denounce the "brutal societies in the central cities" and the "criminal species" responsible for them, including inner-city drug dealers who, according to Nixon's head of drug enforcement, were "the very vermin of humanity."[73] Like George Wallace before him, Nixon decried the Supreme Court for elevating the rights of defendants above the rule of law. "Some of our courts have gone too far in their decisions weakening the peace forces," he proclaimed.[74]

"The law's delay," which previously had been a convenient excuse for Americans' resorting to vigilantism and lynching, now was invoked by President Gerald Ford as the principal impediment to the nation's War on Crime. Criminal prosecutions, he complained, had overwhelmed the nation's courts, while lenient plea bargains offered by prosecutors swamped by crushing caseloads allowed chronic offenders to escape punishment. Meanwhile, defense attorneys threw sand into the gears of justice by securing delays and exploiting every loophole. When President Reagan took up the issue, he plowed already deep furrows. "For too many years, the scales of criminal justice were tilted toward protecting rights of criminals," he declared. "How many times," he asked, "have we seen law enforcement officers handcuffed by the maze of technicalities that make collection and presentation of evidence so difficult?"[75]

Politicians drew inspiration for their anti-crime jeremiads from reams of social and behavioral science scholarship funded by government largesse. Just as the behavioral sciences had been crucial to "brain warfare" during the 1950s and 1960s, so too social and behavioral scientists played a central role in legitimizing the War on Crime. Building on a long-established prejudice that black men were peculiarly prone to crime, social scientists identified a "tangle of pathologies," as Assistant Secretary of Labor Daniel Patrick Moynihan put it in 1965, that set young black men on a path to delinquency and crime. A widely touted study of crime in Philadelphia, for example, affirmed the prevailing assumption in the Nixon and Ford administrations that black career criminals were responsible for most urban crime.[76] By the end of the 1970s, the portrait of the principal enemy of law and public order had been precisely drawn; he was a black male youth, untutored in useful skills or values by a failing school, raised in a dysfunctional single-parent home in an inner-city neighborhood, who displayed absolute contempt for authority and a penchant for mindless violence.[77]

During the early 1990s this image of the hyper-violent black male criminal reached its apotheosis in the so-called super-predator. Here was black criminality so depraved as to be beyond any human sympathy. Super-predators were raving beasts marked by "impulsive violence," "vacant stares and smiles," and "remorseless eyes" who had "no respect for human life and no sense of the future." They killed and maimed on impulse, "without any intelligible motive." Incapable of the human emotions that undergirded civilization, they assigned "zero value on the lives of their victims, whom they reflexively dehumanize."[78] These and other contemporary depictions, which seemed indebted more to Victorian melodrama than rigorous science, enjoyed almost universal acceptance across the political spectrum.

Contemporary popular culture amplified these notions of chronic violence, remorseless criminals, and haggard police straitjacketed by excessive legalism. The vigilante movie, exemplified by *Dirty Harry* (1971) and *Death Wish* (1974), enjoyed its heyday during the 1970s and 1980s. In *Dirty Harry*, Clint Eastwood is Harry Callahan, a rogue San Francisco cop who defies protocol, his superiors, and popular opinion to intimidate, threaten, mock, torture, and dispatch punks with his trademark .44 Magnum. *Death Wish* shifts the setting to Manhattan, where Charles Bronson plays a middle-aged Upper West Side architect who takes it on himself to rid the city of the hooligans and riffraff who prey on innocent citizens. Critics like Pauline Kael attacked the new cinema of vigilantism as "fascist medievalism" and a grotesque reactionary fantasy, but the success of the genre testified to the huge numbers of Americans captivated by the fantasy.[79]

The public anxiety about urban crime and extravagant rhetoric justifying the War on Crime encouraged police departments to recalibrate their crime strategies. According to James Q. Wilson, an influential political scientist and adviser to the Nixon administration, the duties of a policeman should "be defined more by his responsibility for maintaining order than by his responsibility for enforcing the law."[80] Translated into day-to-day policing, Wilson's emphasis on order meant a more punitive approach to patrolling, surveillance, and sentencing in urban neighborhoods that fit the profile of high-crime zones. Any accompanying violence by the police was a regrettable by-product of imposing order in areas where only an aggressive police response would suffice. Indeed, some police violence was a necessary complement to the restoration of order.

While the policies and rhetoric of the War on Crime promoted a siege mentality nationally, they exacerbated the long-established propensity of the Chicago police to reflexively employ brute force. Some units within the police, such as the Robbery Unit and the Gang Intelligence Unit, had well-earned reputations for tolerating excessive violence and targeting black and Hispanic youth. During the late 1960s Chicago police had carried undercover counter-radical tactics as far as any police force in the nation, including the outright assassination of Fred Hampton and other Black Panthers in 1969. In addition, the ongoing border wars that flared across the city wherever white residents and the police attempted to restrict the swelling African American population to traditional black enclaves contributed to police truculence. In this milieu, Burge and his fellow police officers on Chicago's South Side had ample inspiration for their campaign to extort confessions from black men who politicians and social scientists had identified as "the enemy within."[81]

Burge had returned to Chicago as a decorated army veteran in 1969 and soon thereafter began his two-decade career as a policeman. The son of blue-collar parents of Norwegian and western European descent, he had been raised on the southeast side of the city. After high school he briefly attended the University of Missouri but lasted only one semester. In 1966 he enlisted in the Army Reserve and began six years of service, including two years of active duty. He received military police training, including in interrogation methods, at Fort Benning, before being stationed in South Korea. In 1968 he volunteered for duty in Vietnam, where he was assigned to the 9th Military Police Company of the 9th Infantry Division. His duties included escorting convoys, providing security for bases, and serving as a provost marshal investigator. He earned high praise from his commanding officers, and by the end of his tour he had earned a Bronze Star, a Purple Heart, the Vietnamese Cross of Gallantry, and two Army Commendation Medals for rescuing wounded men while under fire.[82]

By all outward appearances, Burge was an excellent policeman. In May 1972, he was promoted to detective and assigned to Area 2, near the famed Pullman railroad car factory on the South Side. Subsequently he rose through the ranks, eventually serving as the commander of the Area 2 Violent Crimes Unit from 1981 to 1986. Another promotion placed him in command of the Bomb and Arson Unit, and finally in 1988 he was promoted to Area 3 (Brighton Park) detective command.

Within a year of the start of his police career, he and several other Vietnam veterans on the force began employing torture methods that bore striking similarities to the techniques that had been used in Vietnam. Burge claims to have had no exposure to torture while serving in Vietnam; but those who served with him remember differently, pointing out that he was assigned to a base where both interrogations and torture were commonplace. While serving with the Chicago police, Burge beat prisoners, threatened them with death, and improvised his own version of the "Bell Telephone Hour" interrogation technique widely used in Vietnam by using a crank telephone, with wires attached to suspects' ears, hands, or genitals, to generate intense shocks. To heighten the pain and disorientation, he and his accomplices draped plastic bags over their suspects' heads so that they experienced the sensation of suffocation and electrocution simultaneously. Anthony Holmes, one of their earliest victims, recalled, "When he hit me with the voltage, . . . it [felt] like a thousand needles going through my body. . . . It [felt] like something just burning me from the inside, and, um, I shook, I gritted, I hollered, then I passed out."[83]

Burge and his "Asskickers," as they were known, have never explained why they resorted to torture. They clearly viewed their victims, who were exclusively African American, with utter contempt and no pity. The overtly racial character of this police violence on the South Side was a striking development. Previously, African Americans had been victimized by police brutality in Chicago, but they had not been the exclusive targets of police violence. Now, on the South Side of Chicago, Burge and his accomplices directed their violence solely against the bodies of black men. His African American colleagues viewed Burge as an avowed racist and suspected that he was a Ku Klux Klan member. He displayed his torture mechanism, which he called "the nigger box," on his office desk, took only token precautions to hide torture sessions, and openly discussed the use of plastic bags, telephone books, and the "Vietnamese treatment" to extort confessions. Police officers recalled that Burge's torture device "was running rampantly through the little unit up there" and that anyone who opposed his methods risked threats of violence.[84]

Once Burge and his accomplices began routinely torturing suspects, they must have quickly recognized that they could do so with impunity. The response of city officials to the allegations of the torture of Andrew Wilson in 1982 was a case in point. After two white Chicago gang unit officers were shot and killed on the South Side in February 1982, Police Superintendent Richard Brzeczek and Mayor Jane Byrne placed Burge in charge of a massive manhunt for the killers. Burge and his officers conducted the search with wanton disregard for the fine points of the law, and when they eventually captured Wilson, Burge and his circle beat him, burned him with a cigarette lighter, shackled him to a hot radiator, and repeatedly used Burge's crank telephone to shock his ears, lips, nose, and genitals. The injuries that Wilson sustained before he confessed to the murder were the cause of the doctor's report that landed on a desk in the Office of Police Standards a year later. By that time, the circuitous journey of the doctor's allegations had already confirmed that city officials had no intention of reining in Burge.[85]

Dr. John Raba's letter alleging the torture of Wilson had been sent to Police Superintendent Brzeczek. Perhaps because the superintendent was new to his job and uncommonly young, he forwarded the letter to State's Attorney Richard M. Daley, accompanied with a cover letter confiding that he would not investigate the allegations unless Daley directed him to do so. The superintendent clearly wanted to tread carefully and sought cover for whatever action he took from Daley, the son of one of the city's legendary mayors. Years later, he recalled "the situation was potentially volatile politically over at the State's Attorney Office."[86] Daley consulted with two of his assistants before deciding to ignore the superintendent's request. He initiated no investigation himself and instead publicly commended Burge. Meanwhile, his assistant, who had participated in the decision not to launch an investigation, prosecuted and convicted Wilson on the basis of his extorted confession. Only after these crucial decisions had been made did the doctor's letter wend its way to the OPS, the equivalent of the dead letter file for such allegations.[87]

The OPS itself was a facade to project a semblance of responsiveness to public concerns about police excesses while camouflaging entrenched institutional opposition to any meaningful public oversight of the police. Any oversight would have been thwarted by dense webs of personal, familial, political, and racial loyalties among police and city employees that undercut any obligation to observe notions of abstract human rights or justice. Some of Burge's colleagues felt a tribal loyalty to the force and have steadfastly supported him to the present day. Others may have disapproved of his methods, but they abided by the "code of silence" that prevailed among Chicago police. And others, such as Burge's commanding officer in Area 2, who was an African American, may have ignored Burge's brutality because of a combination of expediency and institutional loyalty.[88] These loyalties ensured that any allegations made by African Americans accused of crimes, including violence against police, were dismissed out of hand. In stark terms, why should the accusations of a black cop killer like Wilson have any standing against the word of a decorated white veteran and policeman like Burge?[89]

The coerced confessions extorted by Burge and his accomplices secured scores of convictions in Chicago courtrooms, but they eventually attracted unwelcome scrutiny from appeals court judges. One of the earliest public acknowledgments of the extent and character of the police torture on the South Side came in response to an appeal by Gregory Banks, a black man convicted of the murder of a drug dealer. In October 1983 Banks had been brought to Area 2 Violent Crimes for interrogation regarding the murder. There, detectives put a gun in his mouth, placed a plastic bag over his head, and beat him while he suffocated. He quickly confessed to the crime and was convicted on the basis of his confession. Six years later, the Illinois Appellate Court reversed his conviction and upbraided the police, the prosecutors, and judges responsible for it. "In our system of government," the court affirmed, "the use of a defendant's coerced confession as substantive evidence of his guilt cannot be considered harmless error." The judges stressed "the grave responsibility that trial judges have and must be willing to exercise when ruling on motions to suppress based on charges of police brutality and racial intimidation." With barely concealed frustration, the court complained that "while we no longer see cases involving the use of the rack and thumbscrew to obtain confessions, we are seeing cases, like the present case, involving punching, kicking and placing a plastic bag over a suspect's head." On remand, the state dismissed the charges against Banks, and he was released after serving seven years in prison.[90]

Lawyers representing Burge's victims gradually began to expose the extent of institutional tolerance for Burge and his methods. Anxious to determine the police department's legal exposure from Burge's transgressions, the OPS in 1990 conducted an investigation of Area 2, which found that suspects held in custody there had been subjected to "systematic" and "methodical" abuse, that the abuse included "planned torture," and that Area 2 command personnel were "aware of the systematic abuse" and encouraged it by "actively participating" or failing to take action to stop it. Police Superintendent LeRoy Martin, who was the city's second African American police chief, suppressed the report, perhaps because he had previously been Burge's commander at Area 2 and had taken no action to curtail his torture. Not until a U.S. district judge ordered its release in February 1992 did the investigation's conclusions become public. Richard M. Daley, who had been elected mayor in 1989, scoffed at the findings as "only allegations . . . rumors, stories, things like that."[91]

This and other small victories over institutional stonewalling proved short-lived. During the early 1990s lawyers for the torture victims began clamoring for the appointment of a special prosecutor to investigate the ever-increasing number of documented torture cases. Their appeals went nowhere until 2002, when Citizens Alert, a small but tenacious police watchdog group, and other grassroots organizations filed a petition before a Cook County Criminal Court judge. Swayed by their plea, the judge appointed two former assistant Cook County state's attorneys, Edward Egan and Robert Boyle, as special prosecutors. Their investigation dragged on for four years and ran up a bill for more than $17 million. When it concluded, the investigators acknowledged Burge's record of torture but returned no indictments. Even worse, they completely absolved Daley and other city officials of any responsibility for Burge's decades-long reign of terror. Yet again, the investigation exposed the loyalties that continued to protect Burge from prosecution. Egan and Boyle had been prominent lieutenants of Mayor Richard J. Daley, the current mayor's father. Egan himself was the son of a police officer and had nine relatives who were Chicago police officers, including one who had served under Burge at Area 2 and had participated in the arrest of Gregory Banks.[92]

Frustrated by the foot-dragging of city officials and disinterest among the city's major media, activists sought to yoke the international crusade against torture and for human rights to their campaign to expose and halt Chicago police torture. In 1989, an alliance of grassroots community organizations and churches had initiated the Coalition to End Police Torture and Brutality and called for the investigation of police torture and the dismissal of Burge and his accomplices. Having made little headway locally, the organization reached out to Amnesty International to investigate police torture in Chicago, and in 1998 it hosted Pierre Sané, the secretary general of Amnesty International, when he visited the city and met with victims of police torture. Amnesty International subsequently released a major report on human rights violations in the United States, with particular attention paid to police torture in Chicago. By 2005, activists and lawyers for Burge's victims drew attention to the impunity that Chicago police enjoyed despite having employed methods of torture similar to those employed at Guantánamo, Abu Ghraib, and elsewhere during the War on Terror. They, along with one of Burge's victims, presented allegations of Chicago police torture before the Inter-American Commission on Human Rights (IACHR) of the Organization of American States, a body that more often heard accusations of human rights violations by juntas and death squads. (At the time, the anti-torture campaigners were unaware that Richard Zurley, a detective on Chicago's North Side and a naval reservist, had applied "enhanced interrogation" methods with a rigor that appalled observers while leading interrogations at Guantánamo in 2003 and was then using similar methods in Chicago.) Anti-torture campaigners also brought their campaign before the United Nations Committee against Torture (CAT), which had been established to enforce the Declaration against Torture. While Mayor Daley dismissed the campaign as grandstanding, it did undercut and embarrass his bid for the city to host the 2016 Summer Olympics, which he hoped would burnish both his legacy and the city's reputation as a global metropolis.[93]

FIGURE 8.2. *Protesters Demand Justice for Victims of Chicago Police Torture*, by Tim Boyle. During a demonstration in Chicago on July 21, 2006, a poster explicitly linked the torture in Chicago with torture during the so-called War on Terror. While some activists drew the connection, few national commentators acknowledged the links, and the torture scandal in Chicago aroused little national comment.

Despite these and other tactics to prod the city to take action, despite abundant evidence of widespread torture, and despite a lengthening list of convictions overturned or remanded because of coerced confessions, Burge and his accomplices escaped punishment for torture. The city did fire Burge in 1993 but continued to pay his pension and to provide him with legal representation. But by the time the Egan investigation concluded in 2006, the statute of limitations had expired for all of the reported instances of torture. When a federal prosecutor finally prosecuted Burge, it was for obstructing justice and perjury and not for his decades-long torture spree. During the perjury trial in 2010, Anthony Holmes, who Burge had tortured thirty-seven years earlier, and other torture victims finally had an opportunity to confront their tormentor. Burge remained unmoved and unrepentant throughout his trial, even allegedly asking a courtroom observer whether he thought the jury would "believe that bunch of niggers." The jury did, and Burge received a sentence of four and a half years. He was released six months early, after which he returned to his retirement in Florida on his police pension.

The costs of police torture in Chicago have been staggering. In the face of mounting civil suits by Burge's victims, Chicago has paid an estimated $64 million in settlements and judgments. So many convictions were tainted by Burge's methods that in 2000 Governor George Ryan of Illinois imposed a moratorium on the death penalty until the guilt of death-row convicts could be confirmed. With the goal of accurately establishing the extent of Burge's depredations, the Illinois General Assembly in 2009 created the Illinois Torture Inquiry and Relief Commission (TIRC). The commission was soon swamped by hundreds of credible but previously unreported allegations of torture committed by Burge and his circle as well as other police officers in Chicago. Finally, in 2015 the City of Chicago acknowledged the complicity of city officials in the torture scandal by establishing a $5.5 million reparations fund to compensate victims of torture, provide psychological counseling for victims and their families, and provide free classes at the city college for children and grandchildren of victims.[94]

The sheer number of torture victims, the length of time that the practice persisted, the extent of institutional complicity, the damage to the lives of torture victims, and the cumulative cost of settlements, legal fees, and reparations, are staggering. When recounting the saga of the Chicago torture scandal, it is hard to discern a silver lining in it, other than in the tenacity of activists and lawyers committed to exposing and stopping the torture. Continuing allegations of torture by police in Chicago indicate that the decades-long campaign to expose and punish Burge and his accomplices failed to discourage some Chicago police from employing torture. The lesson that police who followed the campaign to prosecute Burge may have drawn was that city authorities would go to extraordinary lengths and spend enormous sums of money to defend employees who even the city itself acknowledged had committed torture. John Conroy, a journalist who tirelessly worked for more than a decade to expose police torture in Chicago in the face of popular disinterest and official complacency, observed wryly that "the city lived very comfortably" for years with the open secret that police employed torture.[95] Seemingly too many in Chicago were for too long untroubled that a police badge in Chicago came close to being a license of impunity.

We cannot credibly claim that when other countries torture it reflects their basic character, but when we torture it violates ours. Any claims that Americans are intrinsically moral and that torture is an exceptional aberration whenever we commit it are difficult to reconcile with the history recounted here. America's leaders, or those who act on our behalf, possess no innate moral or ethical lodestar that predisposes them to respect human dignity or rights. To the contrary, the American political system rests on the recognition that Americans, like all other human beings, have the capacity, even the inclination, to abuse power. The oft-repeated claim that the United States is a "nation of laws" is a concise expression of the Founders' aspiration to channel and temper the exercise of power with rules, procedures, and constraints. Equally important, the rule of law presumes that our liberties and rights are most secure when the exercise of power is subject to public scrutiny. The glare of public scrutiny is not an unfailing prophylactic against abuses of power, but power exercised in the absence of scrutiny is certain to foster abuses.

To suggest, however, that torture flourishes only when and where it is hidden is to misinterpret the history recounted here. Admittedly, torture sometimes has festered where public scrutiny is impossible, such as in prisons, at CIA black sites, or on the frontiers of the American empire. In other circumstances, though, many Americans ignored torture that was visible but was comfortably outside their day-to-day experience. It took decades to establish that the third degree was an intolerable threat to the liberties of all citizens. And it took decades in an age of modern mass media and seemingly robust protections of civil rights to expose police torture in Chicago. Exposing torture to the light of day undoubtedly is crucial to any campaign to halt it but we are naive to assume that exposure alone will arouse public outrage.

At other times torture has gone unacknowledged because the victims have been deemed unworthy of sympathy. Abolitionists campaigned for decades to persuade their contemporaries that the violence

inherent in slavery was a grotesque affront to civilized norms. Likewise, it took decades to erode the legitimacy of the spectacle of lynch
mobs brutalizing victims in fetes of bloodlust. The response of many
Americans to the revelations of the abuse of detainees during the War
on Terror is illustrative. Extensive public opinion polling revealed
that although Americans recoiled from and often opposed specific
methods of "enhanced interrogation," such as waterboarding and electric shocks, a majority nevertheless supported using interrogation
methods if they were vaguely described as "severe."[96] Other Americans,
of course, have openly, even enthusiastically endorsed the use of torture. Donald Trump, for example, boasted at a Republican presidential
debate in February 2016 that "I would bring back waterboarding, and I
would bring back a hell of a lot worse than waterboarding."[97]

For most of the nation's history, the prohibition on torture in American law and tradition largely rested on the premise that the civilized
sensibilities of Americans, especially the capacity and even obligation
for empathy for fellow citizens, would make torture unthinkable. But
the nation's boundaries and polyglot population grew faster than did
Americans' capacity to sympathize with all of those with whom they
shared the continent. The extension of rights also lagged, creating
disparities in the protections that law and tradition afforded those who
had been deemed undeserving, unwelcome, and powerless. And during
war, of course, military exigencies and the primal urge for retaliation
attenuated Americans' capacity for sympathy. Thus, those who were
least likely to enjoy the shield of their neighbors' compassion or were
deemed least deserving to be Americans were the most vulnerable to
torture.

The history of torture, above all, reveals the toxic consequences
when rhetoric and policies that dehumanize "the enemy within" or a
foreign foe exploit popular anxiety about security. In 1843, Karl Marx
was prescient when he observed that "security is the highest social concept of civil society, the concept of *police,* expressing the fact that the
whole of society exists only in order to guarantee to each of its members the preservation of his person, his rights, and his property."[98] From
the age of European conquest to the nineteenth century, the expansion
of "civilization" over the continent and its disparate peoples was
inextricably linked to security, at least in the eyes of most white

Americans. Even the much-touted American experiment with the penitentiary during the early republic was as much an expression of the search for security as of the quest for rehabilitative punishment. If anything, the search for security has become even more acute in an age of hyper-technology, weapons of mass destruction, and global mobility. During the past half century, American insecurities have been stoked by the War on Crime, the War on Drugs, and the War on Terror, all of which have been accompanied by frightening images of imminent violence and vicious enemies of civilization.

Appeals to security have been the ultimate excuse for and defense of torture. Over and over again, history reveals that when the preservation of rights is believed to impede or diminish security, then rights are easily jettisoned and even the prohibition of torture becomes conditional. President Trump has acknowledged as much, contending that "if [torture is] so important to the American people, I would go for it. I would be guided by that." The "emergency" measures that the United States has adopted when its security has been threatened have not been outside the law or an abandonment of the rule of law. Rather they have been the means to allow agents of the state to employ violence that otherwise is beyond the "normal" limits of the rule of law. As a result, American torturers have plausibly claimed to act both with popular support and in defense of the nation.

The American tradition discourages any precise assignment of responsibility for acts of torture carried out in the name of the American people. In part, the failure to assign responsibility is inherent in the broad dispersal of power across American institutions. In Chicago, for example, the police department, the mayor's office, the judicial system, and the state's attorney's office all bore responsibility for the persisting scandal of police torture. During the War on Terror, the architects of "enhanced interrogation" were scattered throughout national security agencies, executive departments, the White House, and even independent contractors hired by the CIA and Pentagon. In light of this recent history, the sober wisdom of the philosopher Hannah Arendt is timely. She prophesied in 1969 that "the greater the bureaucratization of public life, the greater will be the attraction of violence." She warned of the dangers of "a tyranny without a tyrant," which would arise when "there is nobody left with whom one could argue, to whom one could present grievances, on whom the pressures of power could be exerted."[99] American democracy has not reached such a dire state, but the opponents of torture during the War on Terror and in Chicago may be excused if they concluded that Arendt's dystopia had arrived and that torturers are indeed above the law.

To know the history of torture in the United States, alas, provides no shield against future torture. But understanding the American tradition does provide precedents with which to anticipate the circumstances in which the nation may next debate torture and how apologists will justify torture. And an understanding of the tradition should inform the inevitable campaign to cleanse the nation of the stain of torture. To observe the subtle work of denial and erasure we need only look to the recent past when American media applied the neologism "enhanced interrogation" to acts performed by Americans that the same media described as "torture" when carried out by other nationalities. Perhaps the most enduring characteristic of the American tradition is the compulsion to restore national innocence so that Americans can once again take comfort that torture is something done by other people elsewhere.

NOTES

ACKNOWLEDGMENTS

ILLUSTRATION CREDITS

INDEX

Notes

INTRODUCTION. A QUESTION OF CIVILIZATION

1. "Torture and Homicide in an American State Prison," *Harper's Weekly* 2 (December 25, 1858): 818.

2. *New York Times*, January 27, 1883, February 23, 1883; *Prison Association of New York* 18 (1890–1891), 50ff.

3. Quoted in David J. Silbey, *A War of Frontier and Empire: The Philippine-American War, 1899–1902* (New York: Hill and Wang, 2007), 164.

4. Matthew Weaver, "CIA Waterboarded al-Qaida Suspects 266 Times," *London Guardian*, April 20, 2009.

5. Quoted in Marguerite Feitlowitz, *Lexicon of Terror: Argentina and the Legacies of Torture*, rev. ed. (New York: Oxford University Press, 2011), 212.

6. "Defiant Spy Calls CIA Heroic in 9/11 Defense," *New York Daily News*, September 27, 2002.

7. Michel de Montaigne, "Of Cannibals," in *Complete Essays of Montaigne* (Palo Alto, Calif.: Stanford University Press, 1965), 152.

8. *Fort Edward (N.Y.) Ledger*, December 14, 1860, 1; *Prisoners Friend* 1 (May 1849): 380; *New York Evangelist* 22 (July 31, 1851): 122.

9. Zebulon Brockway, *Fifty Years of Prison Service: An Autobiography* (New York: Charities Publication Committee, 1912), 258, 314, 356.

10. *Des Moines (IA) Leader*, May 11, 1902, 5.

11. Transcript, *Ahmanpour*, CNN International, January 20, 2010, http://transcripts.cnn.com/TRANSCRIPTS/1001/20/ampr.01.html, accessed October 2, 2017.

12. *United Nations Convention against Torture and Other Cruel, Inhuman or Degrading Treatment or Punishment,* http://www.ohchr.org/EN/Professional Interest/Pages/CAT.aspx, accessed October 2, 2017.

13. Quoted in Moorfield Storey and Julian Codman, *Secretary Root's Record, "Marked Severities" in Philippine Warfare: An Analysis of the Law and Facts Bearing on the Action and Utterances of President Roosevelt and Secretary Root* (Boston: G. H. Ellis, 1902), 3.

14. Richard Sylvester, "A History of the 'Sweat Box' and the Third Degree," *Proceedings of the International Association of Chiefs of Police,* reprinted in John Henry Wigmore, *The Principles of Judicial Proof* (Boston, Mass.: Little, Brown, 1913), 551. See also *New York Times,* April 9, 1910.

15. John Conroy, *Unspeakable Acts, Ordinary People: The Dynamics of Torture* (New York: Knopf, 2000), 76, 160.

16. Dick Cheney, *Meet the Press,* September 16, 2001.

17. "Floor Statement by Senator John McCain on Senate Intelligence Committee Report on CIA Interrogation Methods," December 9, 2014.

18. Quoted in *City and State,* April 9, 1903, 4. James R. Arnold, *The Moro War: How America Battled a Muslim Insurgency in the Philippine Jungle, 1902–1913* (New York: Bloomsbury Press, 2011).

19. Eric Umansky, "Failures of Imagination," *Columbia Journalism Review* 45 (September–October 2006): 17–18.

20. Erving Goffman, "The Characteristics of Total Institutions," in *Asylums: Essays on the Social Situation of Mental Patients and Other Inmates* (Garden City, N.Y.: Anchor Books, 1961); Michel Foucault, *Discipline and Punish: The Birth of the Prison* (New York: Pantheon Books, 1977).

I. THE MANNERS OF BARBARIANS

1. Nose-cropping, curiously, was also a method of dishonoring a captive among the Algonquians; see Brett Rushforth, *Bonds of Alliance: Indigenous and Atlantic Slaveries in New France* (Chapel Hill: University of North Carolina Press, 2012), 43–44, 68–69.

2. Garcilaso Inca de la Vega, "History of the Conquest of Florida," in E. Barnard Shipp, ed., *The History of Hernando de Soto and Florida; or, Record of the Events of Fifty-Six Years, from 1512 to 1568* (Philadelphia: Robert M. Lindsay, 1881), 36–38. See also Charles M. Hudson, *Knights of Spain, Warriors of the Sun: Hernando de Soto and the South's Ancient Chiefdoms* (Athens: University of Georgia Press, 1997).

3. James Axtell, "The Scholastic Philosophy of the Wilderness," *William and Mary Quarterly,* 3rd ser., 29 (July 1972): 340.

4. Nancy Shoemaker, *A Strange Likeness: Becoming Red and White in Eighteenth-Century North America* (New York: Oxford University Press, 2004), 3.

5. The best survey of Indian torture remains Nathaniel Knowles, "The Torture of Captives by the Indians of Eastern North America," *Proceedings of the American Philosophical Society* 82 (1940): 151–225. See also Thomas S. Abler, "Scalping, Torture, and Rape: An Ethnohistorical Analysis of Conflicting Cultural Values of War," *Anthropologica* 34 (1992): 3–20; Douglas B.

Bamforth, "Indigenous People, Indigenous Violence: Precontact Warfare on the North American Great Plains," *Man*, new ser., 29 (March 1994): 95–115; and Jon L. Gibson, "Aboriginal Warfare in the Protohistoric Southeast: An Alternative Perspective," *American Antiquity* 39 (January 1974): 130–133. For more recent work on precontact torture, see Keith P. Jacobi, "Disabling the Dead: Human Trophy Taking in the Prehistoric Southeast," in Richard J. Chacon and David H. Dye, eds., *The Taking and Displaying of Human Body Parts as Trophies by Amerindians* (New York: Springer, 2007), 320–323. For Mississippi, see Nancy Ross-Stallings, "Trophy Taking in the Central and Lower Mississippi Valley," in Chacon and Dye, *Taking and Displaying of Human Body Parts*, 344–346.

6. James Adair, *The History of the American Indians: Particularly Those Nations Adjoining to the Missisippi [sic], East and West Florida, Georgia, South and North Carolina, and Virginia; Containing an Account of Their Origin, Language, Manners, . . . with a New Map of the Country Referred to in the History* (London: Edward and Charles Dilly, 1775), 186.

7. Joseph-François Lafitau, *Customs of the American Indians Compared with the Customs of Primitive Times*, ed. and trans. by William N. Fenton and Elizabeth L. Moore (Toronto: Champlain Society, 1974–1977), 1:490; Richard White, *The Middle Ground: Indians, Empires, and Republics in the Great Lakes Region, 1650–1815* (New York: Cambridge University Press, 1991), 80.

8. William Strachey, *The Historie of Travell into Virginia Britania* (1612; London: Hakluyt Society, 1953), 104.

9. John Lawson, *A New Voyage to Carolina* (1709; Chapel Hill: University of North Carolina Press, 1984), 208.

10. José António Brandão, in *Your Fyre Shall Burn No More: Iroquois Policy towards New France and Its Native Allies to 1701* (Lincoln: University of Nebraska Press, 1997), provides a systematic tabulation of all of the casualties and captives recorded by French Jesuit missionaries to the Huron and Iroquois.

11. Cadwalder Colden, *The History of the Five Indian Nations of Canada: Which Are Dependent on the Province of New-York in America, and Are the Barrier between the English and French in That Part of the World; with Particular Accounts of Their Religion, Manners, Customs . . . to Which Are Added Accounts of the Several Other Nations of Indians in North-America . . . in Two Volumes*, 3rd ed. (London: Lockyer Davis, 1755), 1:10.

12. Bruce G. Trigger, *The Children of Aataentsic: A History of the Huron People to 1660* (Montreal: McGill-Queen's University Press, 1976), 1:70.

13. Louis Armand Lahontan, *New Voyages to North America: Reprinted from the English Ed. of 1703, with Facsims. of Original Title Pages, Maps, and Illus., and the Addition of Introd., Notes, and Index* (Chicago: A. C. McClurg, 1905), 2:80.

14. Daniel K. Richter, "War and Culture: The Iroquois Experience," *William and Mary Quarterly*, 3rd ser., 40 (October 1983): 528–559; James H. Merrill, *The Indians' New World: Catawbas and Their Neighbors from European Contact through the Era of Removal* (New York: W. W. Norton, 1991), 121–122; Ian K. Steele, "Surrendering Rites: Prisoners on Colonial North American

340 NOTES TO PAGES 18–20

Frontiers," in Stephen Taylor, ed., *Hanoverian Britain and Empire: Essays in Memory of Philip Lawson* (Rochester, N.Y.: Boydell Press, 1998), 139; Lafitau, *Customs of the American Indians*, 2:156. The broad participation in and public nature of torture was an extension of clan and tribal affiliations.

15. Brandão, *Your Fyre Shall Burn No More*, 40–41; Adam Stueck, "A Place under Heaven: Amerindian Torture and Cultural Violence in Colonial New France, 1609–1730" (Ph.D. diss., Marquette University, 2012), 158. For children engaging in torture, see Reuben Gold Thwaites, *The Jesuit Relations and Allied Documents: Travels and Explorations of the Jesuit Missionaries in New France, 1610–1791: The Original French, Latin, and Italian Texts, with English Translations and Notes* (Cleveland: Burrows Bros., 1896–1901), 28:125 (hereafter cited as *JR*).

16. *JR*, 23:93.

17. For a subtle interpretation of Indian torture traditions in New France, see Stueck, "Place under Heaven," 63, 96.

18. Stueck, "Place under Heaven," 66–69. Examples of the destruction of the body of enemies abound in reports from New France; see Samuel de Champlain, *Voyages of Samuel de Champlain, 1604–1618* (New York: C. Scribner's Sons, 1907), 97; *JR*, 9:251; 17:63, 71; 22:47, 247; 30:193; 31:19; 46:53.

19. Andrew Lipman, "'A Meanes to Knitt Them Together': The Exchange of Body Parts in the Pequot War," *William and Mary Quarterly*, 3rd ser., 65 (January 2008): 13.

20. Trigger, *Children of Aataentsic*, 1:73.

21. William Douglass, *A Summary, Historical and Political, of the First Planting, Progressive Improvements, and Present State of the British Settlements in North-America* (London: R. and J. Dodsley, 1760), 1:549.

22. Henry Lewis Morgan, *League of the Ho-dé-no-sau-nee or Iroquois*, ed. and annotated by Herbert M. Lloyd (New York: Dodd, Mead, 1901), 1:335.

23. R. Todd Romero, "'Ranging Foresters' and 'Women-Like Men': Physical Accomplishment, Spiritual Power, and Indian Masculinity in Early-Seventeenth-Century New England," *Ethnohistory* 53 (Spring 2006): 292.

24. Emma Helen Blair, *The Indian Tribes of the Upper Mississippi Valley and Region of the Great Lakes as Described by Nicolas Perrot, French Commandant in the Northwest* (Cleveland: Arthur H. Clark, 1911), 1:142–143.

25. Lipman, "Exchange of Body Parts," 11.

26. Philipp Georg Reck, *Von Reck's Voyage: Drawings and Journal of Philipp Georg Friedrich Von Reck*, ed. by Kristian Hvidt, with the assistance of Joseph Ewan, George F. Jones, and William C. Sturtevant (Savannah, Ga.: Beehive Press, 1980), 47.

27. M. Bossu, *Travels in the Interior of North America, 1751–1762*, trans. and ed. Seymour Feiler (Norman: University of Oklahoma Press, 1962). See also Colden, *History of the Five Indian Nations of Canada*, 122. During the 1820s a French traveler in Texas recounted the torture of a Lipan warrior by Tahuacanos. "He heard the sentence with cool indifference and began to sing his death song. He then insulted his executioners, hurling every kind of epithet at them, threatening them, giving them a thousand indications of his

contempt, forgetting no possible means of exciting their ferocity." Jean Louis Berlandier, *The Indians of Texas in 1830* (Washington, D.C.: Smithsonian Institution Press, 1969), 77.

28. Romero, "'Ranging Foresters' and 'Women-Like Men,'" 299. In 1636, Pequot warriors tortured John Tilley, an English trader. They "tied him to a stake, slead his skin off, put hot embers between the flesh and skinne, cut off his fingers and toes, and made hatbands of them." And although they also cut off his hands and feet, he survived for three days; "he was a stout man, because he cried not in his torture." His endurance impressed even his captors. John Underhill, *Nevves from America; or, A New and Experimentall Discoverie of New England* (London: Peter Cole, 1638), 23.

29. See, for example, *JR*, 17:105; 22:247.

30. Wayne E. Lee, "Peace Chiefs and Blood Revenge: Patterns of Restraint in Native American Warfare, 1500–1800," *Journal of Military History* 71 (July 2007): 728.

31. Adam J. Hirsch, "The Collision of Military Cultures in Seventeenth-Century New England," *Journal of American History* 74 (March 1988): 1207.

32. Armstrong Starkey, *European and Native American Warfare, 1675–1815* (Norman: University of Oklahoma Press, 1998), 72, 77.

33. *JR*, 32:185.

34. Allan Greer, "Iroquois Virgin: The Story of Catherine Tekakwitha in New France and New Spain," in Allan Greer and Jodi Bilinkoff, eds., *Colonial Saints: Discovering the Holy in the Americas, 1500–1800* (New York: Routledge, 2003), 235–250.

35. Steuck, "Place under Heaven," 22.

36. Stueck, "Place under Heaven," 132–42. For Father Le Jeune and the Huron, see *JR*, 26:179–181; for tormenting the body and soul, see *JR*, 23:33–35; for Father Brébeuf's torture, see *JR*, 39:253; for the Huron stopping Father Millet from baptizing captives, see *JR*, 54:25.

37. Stueck, "Place under Heaven," 217; Rushforth, *Bonds of Alliance*, 164–165, 193–197; Alan Gallay, *The Indian Slave Trade: The Rise of the English Empire in the American South, 1670–1717* (New Haven, Conn.: Yale University Press, 2002), 298–301; Christina Snyder, *Slavery in Indian Country: The Changing Face of Captivity in Early America* (Cambridge, Mass.: Harvard University Press, 2010), 46–79.

38. Mark F. Boyd, *Here They Once Stood: The Tragic End of the Apalachee Missions* (Gainesville: University of Florida Press, 1951), 31, 35–38.

39. Gail D. Danvers, "Gendered Encounters: Warriors, Women, and William Johnson," *Journal of American Studies* 35 (August 2001): 195.

40. [John Bradstreet], *An Impartial Account of Lieut. Col. Bradstreet's Expedition to Fort Frontenac, 1758* (London: printed for T. Wilcox, et. al., 1759), 38.

41. James Maaschaele, *Jury, State and Society in Medieval England* (New York: Palgrave Macmillan, 2008), 81–89.

42. Edward Peters, *Torture*, exp. ed. (Philadelphia: University of Pennsylvania Press, 1996), 27.

43. Antonia Fraser, *The Gunpowder Plot: Terror and Faith in 1605* (London: Mandarin, 1997), 176–179.

44. Anthony Musson, *Medieval Law in Context: The Growth of Legal Consciousness from Magna Carta to the Peasants' Revolt* (New York: Palgrave, 2001), 231–232.

45. John Bellamy, *The Law of Treason in England in the Later Middle Ages* (Cambridge: Cambridge University Press, 2004), 39. The gruesome spectacle moved Fawkes, who was still weak from the torture he had endured two months prior, to thwart the crown and escape the agony of his execution by jumping from the gallows to his death. Fraser, *Gunpowder Plot*, 230–234; J. A. Sharpe, *Remember, Remember: A Cultural History of Guy Fawkes Day* (Cambridge, Mass.: Belknap Press of Harvard University Press, 2005), 73–77.

46. Peters, *Torture*, 49, 53.

47. Despite the lurid accounts of inquisitorial cruelty that proliferated during the eighteenth and nineteenth centuries, church inquisitions, including the infamous Spanish Inquisition, resorted to torture less often and with greater restraint than secular courts. Recent research suggests that, even in the Spanish Inquisition, torture was used in only a small percentage of cases, and the extravagant sadism of popular lore was rare.

48. Wolfgang Behringer, *Witches and Witch-Hunts: A Global History* (Malden, Mass.: Polity Press, 2004), 92–101, 149–151; Brian Levack, *The Witch Hunt in Early Modern Europe*, 3rd ed. (London: Longman, 2006), 211–212.

49. Camille Naish, *Death Comes to the Maiden: Sex and Execution, 1431–1933* (London: Routledge, 1991), 27–28.

50. Levack, *Witch Hunt*, 23.

51. Peters, *Torture*, 43–44, 46, 69; Robert Bartlett, *Trial by Fire and Water: The Medieval Judicial Ordeal* (New York: Clarendon Press, 1986); Esther Cohen, *The Modulated Scream: Pain in Late Medieval Culture* (Chicago: University of Chicago Press, 2009), 44, 52, 56.

52. Lisa Silverman, *Tortured Subjects: Pain, Truth, and the Body in Early Modern France* (Chicago: University of Chicago Press, 2001), 9.

53. Silverman, *Tortured Subjects*, 74; Donald Mowbray, *Pain and Suffering in Medieval Theology: Academic Debates at the University of Paris in the Thirteenth Century* (Rochester, N.Y.: Boydell Press, 2009), 13–42; Stephen Pender, "Seeing, Feeling, Judging: Pain in the Early Modern Imagination," in Jan Frans van Dijkhuizen and Karl A. E. Enenkel, eds., *The Sense of Suffering: Constructions of Physical Pain in Early Modern Culture* (Boston: Brill, 2009): 469–495.

54. James Q. Whitman, *The Origins of Reasonable Doubt: Theological Roots of the Criminal Trial* (New Haven, Conn.: Yale University Press, 2008), 126–127.

55. Levack, *Witch Hunt*, 100.

56. William Blackstone, *Commentaries on the Laws of England* (Oxford: Clarendon Press, 1765), 4:321.

57. One careful study identified only eighty-one extant warrants. John H. Langbein, *Torture and the Law of Proof* (Chicago: University of Chicago Press, 1977), 81ff.

58. Langbein, *Torture and the Law of Proof,* offers an especially cogent discussion of the differences in the logic behind continental torture and English *peine forte* (p. 184). Andrea McKenzie demonstrates that *peine forte* was applied with some frequency; see "'This Death Some Strong and Stout Hearted Man Doth Choose': The Practice of *Peine Forte et Dure* in Seventeenth- and Eighteenth-Century England," *Law and History Review* 23 (Summer 2005): 279–313.

59. On the English model of empire, see John Darwin, *Unfinished Empire: The Global Expansion of Britain* (London: Allen Lane, 2012), chaps. 1–3.

60. On punishment in colonial Dutch New York, see Keith Scott Christianson, "Criminal Punishment in New Netherlands," in Nancy Anne McClure Zeller, ed., *A Beautiful and Fruitful Place: Selected Rensselaerswijck Seminar Papers* (Albany: New Netherlands Project, 1991): 111–118; and Dennis Sullivan, *The Punishment of Crime in Colonial New York* (New York: Peter Lang, 1997), esp. 73, 74–75, 239–240. The virtual absence of torture against Europeans in New France is discussed in Raymond Boyer, *Les Crimes Et Les Châtiments Au Canada Français Du XVIIe Au XXe Siècle* (Montreal: Cercle du Livre de France, 1966), 254–264; and André Lachance, *La Justice Criminelle Du Roi Au Canada Au XVIIIe Siècle: Tribunaux Et Officiers* (Québec: Presses de l'Université Laval, 1978), 68–73, 79–85. In New Spain, the application of torture was permissible under Spanish law until prohibited by the Constitution of 1812, and therefore it would have been dutifully recorded in the criminal files, as were other judicial actions; Michael C. Scardaville, "Justice by Paperwork: A Day in the Life of a Court Scribe in Bourbon Mexico City," *Journal of Social History* 36 (2003): 1005. See also John F. Chuchiak, *The Inquisition in New Spain, 1536–1820: A Documentary History* (Baltimore: Johns Hopkins University Press, 2012); Colin M. MacLachlan, *Criminal Justice in Eighteenth Century Mexico: A Study of the Tribunal of the Acordada* (Berkeley: University of California Press, 1974), 73; Jose Sanchez-Arcilla Bernal, "La Administracion de Justicia inferior en la Ciudad de Mexico a finales de la Epoca colonial. I. La punicion de la embriaguez en los Libros de Reos (1794–1798)," *Cuadernos de Historia del Derecho* 7 (2000): 371–453; Teresa Lozano Armendares, *La Criminalidad en la Ciudad de Mexico, 1800–1821* (Mexico City, 1987), 185; and Claudio Saunt, "'My Medicine Is Punishment': A Case of Torture in Early California, 1775–1776," *Ethnohistory* 57 (Fall 2010): 679–708.

61. *JR,* 13:75.

62. Jean de Léry, *Histoire d'un Voyage Fait en la Terre du Brésil* (Paris: Le Livre de Poche, 1994), 571.

63. Daniel Baraz, *Medieval Cruelty: Changing Perceptions, Late Antiquity to the Early Modern Period* (Ithaca, N.Y.: Cornell University Press, 2003), 143–145.

64. On Spain's "Black Legend" of cruelty, see Friedrich Edelmayer, "The 'Leyenda Negra' and the Circulation of Anti-Catholic and Anti-Spanish Prejudices," European History Online, published June 29, 2011, http://ieg-ego.eu /en/threads/models-and-stereotypes/the-spanish-century/friedrich-edelmayer -the-leyenda-negra-and-the-circulation-of-anti-catholic-and-anti-spanish -prejudices, accessed October 1, 2012; William S. Maltby, *The Black Legend*

in England (Durham, N.C.: Duke University Press, 1971); and Benjamin Schmidt, *Innocence Abroad: The Dutch Imagination and the New World, 1570-1670* (New York: Cambridge University Press, 2001).

65. Some of the early advocates of colonization viewed the Indians of the New World more positively, but they nevertheless assumed that Indians were primitive savages. See Ethan A. Schmidt, "The Well-Ordered Commonwealth: Humanism, Utopian Perfectionism, and the English Colonization of the Americas," *Atlantic Studies* 7 (2010): 309-328. The concept of the "barren lands" was spelled out by John Locke, who argued that the "wild woods and uncultivated waste of America" were "vacant places" awaiting the steady industry of Europeans to turn them into productive resources. John Locke, *Two Treatises on Government* (Boston: Edes and Gill, 1773), bk. 5, secs. 36, 37.

66. Charter of New England (1620), Avalon Project, Yale Law School, http://avalon.law.yale.edu/17th_century/mass01.asp, accessed October 1, 2012; First Charter of Virginia (1606), Avalon Project, http://avalon.law.yale.edu/17th_century/va01.asp, accessed October 1, 2017.

67. Adam Smith, *The Theory of Moral Sentiments; or, An Essay Towards an Analysis of the Principles by Which Men Naturally Judge concerning the Conduct and Character, First of Their Neighbors, and Afterwards of Themselves* (Dublin: J. Beatty and C. Jackson, 1777), 280-282; Adam Ferguson, *History of Civil Society* (Philadelphia: A. Finley, 1819), for example, 361-363.

68. *JR*, 9:253-257.

69. Alejandro Malaspina, quoted in David J. Weber, *Bárbaros: Spaniards and Their Savages in the Age of Enlightenment* (New Haven, Conn.: Yale University Press, 2005), 40; William Robertson, *The History of America* (Dublin: Messrs. Whitestone, 1777), 269ff.

70. "An Account of the Country, at present the Seat of War in North-America and of the Original Inhabitants of it, generally called Indians," *New Universal Magazine; or, Miscellany of Historical, Philosophical, Political and Polite Literature*, May 20, 1757, 193; Ferguson, *History of Civil Society*, 122.

71. Bellamy, *Law of Treason in England*, 39; John G. Bellamy, *The Tudor Law of Treason: An Introduction* (London: Routledge & K. Paul, 1979), 187.

72. Levack, *Witch Hunt*; Alfred Soman, "The Parlement of Paris and the Great Witch Hunt (1565-1640)," *Sixteenth Century Journal* 9 (July 1978): 30-44; Alfred Soman, "Witch Lynching in Juniville," *Natural History* 95 (1986): 8-15.

73. For cogent surveys of evolving rules of war in Europe, see Robert C. Stacey, "The Age of Chivalry," in Michael Howard, George J. Andreopoulos, and Mark R. Shulman, eds., *The Laws of War: Constraints on Warfare in the Western World* (New Haven, Conn.: Yale University Press, 1994), 27-40; and Geoffrey Parker, "Early Modern Europe," in Howard et al., *Laws of War*, 41-62.

74. Steele, "Surrendering Rites."

75. Baraz, *Medieval Cruelty*, 5, 34, 35. See also Jan Frans van Dijkhuizen, "Partakers of Pain: Religious Meanings of Pain in Early Modern Europe," in van Dijkhuizen and Enenkel, *Sense of Suffering*, 188-219; and Jetze Touber, "Articulating Pain: Martyrology, Torture, and Execution in the Works of Antonio Gallonio," in van Dijkhuizen and Enenkel, *Sense of Suffering*, 59-89.

76. Manuel Solana to Governor Zuñiga, San Luis, July 8, 1704; Testimony of Juan de la Cruz, June 1705; Testimony of Manuel de Quiñones; Testimony of Manuel Solana, in Boyd, *Here They Once Stood*, 53, 75–80.

77. Allan Greer, "Colonial Saints, Gender, Race, and Hagiography in New France," *William and Mary Quarterly*, 3rd ser., 57 (April 2000); 330; Julia Boss, "Writing a Relic: The Uses of Hagiography in New France," in Greer and Bilinkoff, *Colonial Saints*, 214–215.

78. Among the large body of scholarship on captivity narratives, see Tara Fitzpatrick, "The Figure of Captivity: The Cultural Work of the Puritan Captivity Narrative," *American Literary History* 3 (Spring 1991): 1–26; Sheila McIntyre, "'I Heare It So Variously Reported': News-Letters, Newspapers, and the Ministerial Network in New England, 1670–1730," *New England Quarterly* 71 (December 1998): 593–614; and Evan Haefeli and Kevin Sweeney, "'The Redeemed Captive' as Recurrent Seller: Politics and Publication, 1707–1853," *New England Quarterly* 77 (September 2004): 341–367.

79. Christopher Tomlins, "Law's Wilderness: The Discourse of English Colonizing, the Violence of Intrusion, and the Failures of American History," in John Smolenski and Thomas J. Humphrey, eds., *New World Orders: Violence, Sanction, and Authority in the Colonial Americas* (Philadelphia: University of Pennsylvania Press, 2005), 41; *The Law of Nations* (New York: printed for Messrs. Berry and Rogers, 1787), 520; Joyce E. Chaplin, *Subject Matter: Technology, the Body, and Science on the Anglo-American Frontier, 1500–1676* (Cambridge, Mass.: Harvard University Press, 2001), 83.

80. Harold E. Selesky, "Colonial America," in Howard et al., *Laws of War*, 61; Nicholas Canny, *The Elizabethan Conquest of Ireland* (Sussex: Harvester Press, 1976); Nicholas Canny, *Making Ireland British, 1580–1650* (Oxford: Oxford University Press, 2001); Wayne E. Lee, *Barbarians and Brothers: Anglo-American Warfare, 1500–1865* (New York: Oxford University Press, 2011), 15–120.

81. Quoted in Caroline A. Williams, "Resistance and Rebellion on the Spanish Frontier: Native Responses to Colonization in the Colombian Chocó, 1670–1690," *Hispanic American Historical Review* 79 (August 1999): 410.

82. Samuel de Champlain, *Works of Samuel Champlain*, ed. H. P. Biggar (Toronto: Champlain Society, 1936), 3:212; Lafitau, *Customs of the American Indians*, 2:289.

83. Stueck, "Place under Heaven," 111–112; *JR*, 5:27–31, 13:37, 42:97.

84. Stueck, "Place under Heaven," 197. For baptizing the Iroquois, see *JR*, 17:63–65; for stopping the suicide, see *JR*, 17:97–99; for the death of Father Jogues's killer, see *JR*, 32:19–25; for Father Le Jeune, see *JR*, 32:19–25; 43:105.

85. Samuel Penhallow, *The History of the Wars of New-England, with the Eastern Indians; or, A Narrative of Their Continued Perfidy and Cruelty, from the 10th of August, 1703, to the Peace Renewed 13th of July, 1713, and from the 25th of July, 1722, to Their Submission 15th December, 1725, Which Was Ratified August 5th 1726* (Boston: T. Fleet, 1726), 20–23; Steele, "Surrendering Rites," 147; Henry J. Young, "A Note on Scalp Bounties in Pennsylvania," *Pennsylvania History* 24 (July 1957): 207–218; J. F. Lozier, "The Use

of Scalping in New-France: The French Policy of Payment for Scalps," *Revue d' Histoire De L Amerique Francaise* 56 (2003): 513–542.

86. Steuck, "Place under Heaven," 208.

87. Steuck, "Place under Heaven," 198–199. For Bienville on Governor Frontenac, see Dunbar Rowland and A. G. Sanders, eds. and trans., *Mississippi Provincial Archives: French Dominion, 1729–1748*, rev. and ed. Patricia Kay Galloway (Baton Rouge: Louisiana State University Press, 1984), 3:116. For Governor Frontenac's personal and political goals, see W. J. Eccles, *Canada under Louis XIV, 1663–1701* (New York: Oxford University Press, 1964), 196–203. For torture by French soldiers, see *JR*, 65:27.

88. Thomas H. Naylor, *The Presidio and Militia on the Northern Frontier of New Spain: A Documentary History* (Tucson: University of Arizona Press, 1986), 245, 248, 264, 268, 645.

89. Edward Waterhouse, "A Declaration of the State of the Colony and Affaires in Virginia [1622]," in Susan Myra Kingsbury, ed., *The Records of the Virginia Company of London* (Washington, D.C.: U.S. Government Printing Office, 1906–1935), 3:556–557.

90. Reverend Solomon Stoddard to Massachusetts Bay Governor Joseph Dudley, October 22, 1703, *New England Historical and Genealogical Register* 24 (1870): 269–270; *New York Gazette*, quoted in Benjamin Martin, *Miscellaneous Correspondence, Containing a Variety of Subjects, Relative to Natural and Civil History, Geography, Mathematics, Poetry, Memoirs of Monthly Occurrences, Catalogues of New Books, &c.* (London: William Owen, 1759), 2:652.

91. Weber, *Bárbaros*, 267.

92. *JR*, 12:181–183, 13:79.

93. John E. Ferling, *A Wilderness of Miseries: War and Warriors in Early America* (Westport, Conn.: Greenwood Press, 1980), 47.

94. William Henry to John Heckewelder, reprinted in Paul A. Wallace, ed., *The Travels of John Heckewelder in Frontier America* (1958; Pittsburgh, Pa.: University of Pittsburgh Press, 1985), 77.

95. *A Dialogue, between Andrew Trueman, and Thomas Zealot: about the killing the Indians at Cannestogoe and Loncaster* (Philadelphia: [Anthony Armbruster, 1764]), 3. In another pamphlet, a Scotch-Irish character brags, "It gives me Pleasure to think on't, Slaughter'd, kill'd and cut off a whole Tribe! A Nation at once." See *A Dialogue Containing Some Reflections on the Late Declaration and Remonstrance of the Back-Inhabitants of the Province of Pennsylvania* (Philadelphia: [Andrew Stewart], 1764), 4.

96. Benjamin Franklin, *A Narrative of the Late Massacres* (Philadelphia: Franklin and Hall, 1764). The pamphlet war that followed the massacre is surveyed in Alison Olson, "The Pamphlet War over the Paxton Boys," *Pennsylvania Magazine of History and Biography* 123 (January–April 1999): 31–55; Joanna Brooks, "Held Captive by the Irish: Quaker Captivity Narratives in Frontier Pennsylvania," *New Hibernia Review* 8 (Autumn 2004): 31–46; Jeremy Engels, "'Equipped for Murder': The Paxton Boys and 'the Spirit of Killing All Indians' in Pennsylvania, 1763–1764," *Rhetoric and Public Affairs* 8 (Fall 2005): 355–381; and Peter Silver, *Our Savage Neighbors: How Indian War Transformed Early America* (New York: Norton, 2008), 179–203.

97. Ben Franklin to William Johnson, September 12, 1766, in Benjamin Franklin, *The Papers of Benjamin Franklin* (New Haven, Conn.: Yale University Press, 1959), 13:416.

98. Arthur St. Clair, *The St. Clair Papers: The Life and Public Services of Arthur St. Clair: Soldier of the Revolutionary War, President of the Continental Congress; and Governor of the North-Western Territory: With His Correspondence and Other Papers* (Cincinnati: R. Clarke, 1882), 1:301.

99. Louis Antoine de Bougainville, *Adventure in the Wilderness: The American Journals of Louis Antoine de Bougainville, 1756–1760* (Norman: University of Oklahoma Press, 1964), 175.

100. Eliga H. Gould, "Zones of Law, Zones of Violence: The Legal Geography of the British Atlantic, circa 1772," *William and Mary Quarterly*, 3rd ser., 60 (July 2003): 483.

101. The "classic" historical account of Duston's captivity is Robert Boodey Caverly, *Heroism of Hannah Duston, Together with the Indian Wars of New England* (Boston: Russell, 1874), 14–21.

102. Cotton Mather, *Humiliations Follow'd with Deliverances: A Brief Discourse on the Matter and Method, of that Humiliation . . .* (Boston: B. Green and J. Allen for Samuel Phillips, 1697), 46–47.

103. Matthew Smith, *A Declaration and Remonstrance of the Distressed and Bleeding Frontier Inhabitants of the Province of Pennsylvania* (Philadelphia: [William Bradford], 1764), 7–8.

104. "Extract of a Letter from Paxton, in Lancaster County, October 23," *Pennsylvania Gazette*, October 27, 1763, 3.

105. First Charter of Virginia, Avalon Project.

106. Roy Harvey Pearce, *Savagism and Civilization: A Study of the Indian and the American Mind*, rev. ed. (Baltimore: Johns Hopkins University Press, 1967), 4.

2. DISCIPLINE IN A YOUNG DEMOCRACY

1. George Washington Smith, *Description of Eastern State* (Philadelphia, 1829), 7.

2. Thomas B. McElwee, *A Concise History of the Eastern Penitentiary of Pennsylvania: Together with a Detailed Statement of the Proceedings of the Committee, Appointed by the Legislature, December 6th, 1834* (Philadelphia: Neall and Massey, 1835), 17–18, 158–159, 167, 177–179; Michael Meranze, *Laboratories of Virtue: Punishment, Revolution, and Authority in Philadelphia, 1760–1835* (Chapel Hill: University of North Carolina Press, 1996), 305–318.

3. J. M. Beattie, *Crime and the Courts in England, 1660–1800* (Princeton, N.J.: Princeton University Press, 1986), 451–455, 530–538; Frank McLynn, *Crime and Punishment in Eighteenth-Century England* (New York: Routledge, 1989), 242–298.

4. Adam Smith, *The Theory of Moral Sentiments* (Philadelphia: Anthony Finley, 1817), 2; Louis P. Masur, *Rites of Execution: Capital Punishment and the Transformation of American Culture, 1776–1865* (New York: Oxford University Press, 1989), 54–60.

5. Benjamin Rush, *An Enquiry into the Effects of Public Punishments upon Criminals, and upon Society* (Philadelphia: J. James, 1787), 4–8; Richard Clark, *Capital Punishment in Britain* (London: Ian Allan, 2009), 69–105.

6. British Bill of Rights, British Library, https://www.bl.uk/collection-items /the-bill-of-rights, accessed July 24, 2017; William Blackstone, *Commentaries on the Laws of England* (Oxford: Oxford University Press, 2016), 4:293–297.

7. John D. Bessler, *Cruel and Unusual: The American Death Penalty and the Founders' Eighth Amendment* (Boston: Northeastern University Press, 2012), 97–221; Anthony F. Granucci, "'Nor Cruel and Unusual Punishments Inflicted': The Original Meaning," *California Law Review* 57 (October 1969): 839–865; Rebecca M. McLennan, *The Crisis of Imprisonment: Protest, Politics, and the Making of the American Penal State, 1776–1941* (New York: Cambridge University Press, 2008), 20–23.

8. See Chapter 6 for a discussion of the nineteenth-century Supreme Court's limited understanding of the Bill of Rights.

9. Stephen Burroughs, *Memoirs of the Notorious Stephen Burroughs of New Hampshire* (London: Jonathan Cape, 1924).

10. Scott Christianson, *With Liberty for Some: 500 Years of Imprisonment in America* (Boston: Northeastern University Press, 1998), 59–63.

11. Adam J. Hirsch, *The Rise of the Penitentiary: Prisons and Punishment in Early America* (New Haven, Conn.: Yale University Press, 1992), 14–18, 28; Harry E. Barnes, *The Evolution of Penology in Pennsylvania: A Study in American Social History* (Indianapolis: Bobbs-Merrill, 1927), 72–120.

12. Michael Ignatieff, *A Just Measure of Pain: The Penitentiary in the Industrial Revolution, 1750–1850* (New York: Pantheon Books, 1978), 44–113; Meranze, *Laboratories of Virtue,* 140–142.

13. Cesare Beccaria, *On Crimes and Punishments and Other Writings* (Toronto: University of Toronto Press, 2008), 1–86; John D. Bessler, "Revisiting Beccaria's Vision: The Enlightenment, America's Death Penalty, and the Abolition Movement," *Northwestern Journal of Law and Social Policy* 4 (2009): 195–328; Hirsch, *Rise of the Penitentiary,* 26.

14. For reports on the perceived crime wave in New England, see *Connecticut Journal,* April 16, 1784, May 18, 1785, August 20, 1789; *Boston Gazette,* May 24, 1784, January 15, 1787, December 24, 1787, March 10, 1788; *Connecticut Gazette,* July 30, 1784, March 18, 1785, August 21, 1789; *Massachusetts Spy,* May 20, 1785; *Worcester Magazine,* March 19, 1789, October 10, 1789; Linda Kealey, "Crime and Society in Massachusetts in the Second Half of the Eighteenth Century" (Ph.D. diss., University of Toronto, 1981), 142, 199, 366–367, 372, 377, 410. For Pennsylvania, see *Pennsylvania Packet,* August 2, 1785, November 17, 1785; *Pennsylvania Gazette,* November 2, 1785; for Charleston, S.C., see John A. Hall, "'Nefarious Wretches, Insidious Villains, and Evil-Minded Persons': Urban Crime Reported in Charleston's City Gazette in 1788," *South Carolina Historical and Genealogical Magazine* 88 (July 1987): 158.

15. Linda Kealey, "Punishment at Hard Labor: Stephen Burroughs and the Castle Island Prison, 1785–1798," *New England Quarterly* 57 (June 1984): 249–254;

Linda Kealey, "Patterns of Punishment: Massachusetts in the Eighteenth Century," *American Journal of Legal History* 30 (April 1986): 163–186.

16. "Extracts from the Diary of Mrs. Ann Warder," March 30, 1787, *Pennsylvania Magazine of History and Biography* 18 (1894): 61; Meranze, *Laboratories of Virtue*, 78–81.

17. Burroughs, *Memoirs of the Notorious Stephen Burroughs*.

18. *Independent Gazetteer*, January 25, 1787; *Pennsylvania Packet*, October 19, 1786, May 22, 1787, June 26, 1787. See also "Extracts from the Diary of Ann Warder," 61; McLennan, *Crisis of Imprisonment*, 32–35; Meranze, *Laboratories of Virtue*, 91–98; Negley K. Teeters, *Cradle of the Penitentiary: The Walnut Street Jail at Philadelphia, 1773–1835* (Philadelphia: Pennsylvania Prison Society, 1955), 7–28.

19. Meranze, *Laboratories of Virtue*, 91–109; Robert R. Sullivan, "The Birth of the Prison: The Case of Benjamin Rush," *Eighteenth-Century Studies* 31 (Spring 1998): 333–344.

20. Rush, *Enquiry into the Effects of Public Punishments*, 10–13.

21. Meranze, *Laboratories of Virtue*, 137–138.

22. Thomas Eddy, *An Account of the State Prison or Penitentiary House, in the City of New York* (New York: Isaac Collins, 1801); W. David Lewis, *From Newgate to Dannemora: The Rise of the Penitentiary in New York, 1796–1848* (Ithaca, N.Y.: Cornell University Press, 1965), 29–53; Masur, *Rites of Execution*, 71–88; David J. Rothman, *The Discovery of the Asylum: Social Order and Disorder in the New Republic* (Boston: Little, Brown, 1971), 61; Wallace Shugg, *A Monument to Good Intentions: The Story of the Maryland Penitentiary, 1804–1995* (Baltimore: Maryland Historical Society, 2000), 3–28.

23. *Niles Weekly Register* 15 (1818): Supplement, 59; McLennan, *Crisis of Imprisonment*, 44–46, 50–52.

24. McLennan, *Crisis of Imprisonment*, 54–58; Meranze, *Laboratories of Virtue*, 217–251; Rothman, *Discovery of the Asylum*, 82–88.

25. Jennifer Lawrence Janofsky, "Hopelessly Hardened: The Complexities of Penitentiary Discipline at Philadelphia's Eastern State Penitentiary," in Michelle Lise Tarter and Richard Bell, eds., *Buried Lives: Incarcerated in Early America* (Athens: University of Georgia Press, 2012), 106–123; Meranze, *Laboratories of Virtue*, 253–265.

26. "Sketches of Prison Life and Discipline," *National Police Gazette* 1 (March 7, 1846): 26; Lewis, *From Newgate to Dannemora*, 92–93; McLennan, *Crisis of Imprisonment*, 54–58.

27. "Report of the Commissioners to the State Prison at Auburn," *Journal of the Senate of New York* (Albany, 1827), Appendix A, 30; "Rules and Regulations of the Connecticut State Prison," reprinted in Gustave de Beaumont and Alexis de Tocqueville, *On the Penitentiary System in the United States: and Its Application in France; with an Appendix on Penal Colonies, and Also, Statistical Notes* (Philadelphia: Carey, Lea & Blanchard, 1833), 216; *Rules and Regulations for the Government of the Massachusetts State Prison* (Boston: 1829), 102; William Crawford, *Report of William Crawford, Esq., on the Penitentiaries of the United States* (London, 1835), app. 72.

28. Janofsky, "Hopelessly Hardened," 115; Gershom Powers, *A Brief Account of the Construction, Management and Discipline, &c. &c., of the New-York State Prison at Auburn* (Auburn, N.Y. : U. F. Doubleday, 1826), 3, 7; Crawford, *Report of William Crawford*, 10, 16; *Rules and Regulations for the Government of Massachusetts State Prison* (Boston: J. Belcher, 1811), 5–7, 13–15; "System of Discipline of Charlestown Prison," *Annual Register; or, A View of the History, Politics, and Literature of the Year* 6 (1833): 462; Harry Elmer Barnes, *A History of the Penal, Reformatory, and Correctional Institutions of the State of New Jersey* (Trenton, N.J.: MacCrellish and Quigley, 1918), 464; *Report of the Prison Association of New York, 5th Report* (1850), 93, 105; Boston Prison Discipline Society, *Reports of the Boston Prison Discipline Society* 1 (1826): 336–337; "Second Annual Report of the Inspectors of State Prisons," *Documents of the Senate of New York* 16 (1850), 147; Lewis, *From Newgate to Dannemora*, 133.

29. Ignatieff, *Just Measure of Pain*, 198; Boston Prison Discipline Society, *Reports of the Boston Prison Discipline Society* 1 (1826): 39; Jennifer Graber, *The Furnace of Affliction: Prisons and Religion in Antebellum America* (Chapel Hill: University of North Carolina Press, 2011), 47–102.

30. *Documents of the Senate of New York, 62nd Session* 1 (January 1838): 13–16.

31. Crawford, *Report of William Crawford*, 58–59; *Journal of the Assembly of New York* (Albany, 1823), 29; Dorothea Dix, *Remarks on Prisons and Prison Discipline in the United States* (Boston: Munroe and Francis, 1845), 41.

32. Luca Follis, "Democratic Punishment and the Archive of Violence: Punishment, Publicity and Corporal Excess in Antebellum New York," *Journal of Historical Sociology* 29 (June 2016): 1–25.

33. Powers, *Brief Account*, 4, 14; Beaumont and Tocqueville, *Penitentiary System*, 32.

34. Norman Johnston, "Noble Ideas Collide with Reality," *Eastern State Penitentiary: Crucible of Good Intentions* (Philadelphia: Philadelphia Museum of Art, 1994), 8–49. On similarly demoralizing admissions procedures at Sing Sing, see Levi S. Burr, *A Voice from Sing Sing: Giving a General Description of the State Prison* (Albany, 1833), 19.

35. Burr, *Voice from Sing Sing*, 14; John Reynolds, *Recollections of Windsor Prison: Containing Sketches of Its History and Discipline* (Boston: A. Wright, 1834), iii, 16, 39.

36. Quoted in Larry Goldsmith, "Penal Reform, Convict Labor, and Prison Culture in Massachusetts, 1800–1880" (Ph.D. diss., University of Pennsylvania, 1994), 98, 256, 277; Boston Prison Discipline Society, *Reports of the Boston Prison Discipline Society* 2 (1827): 58; Janofsky, "Hopelessly Hardened," 112–113.

37. Goldsmith, "Penal Reform," 274; Barnes, *History*, 408, 410, 418. Regarding prisoner resistance at Eastern State, see Janofsky, "Hopelessly Hardened," 119–120; for conditions at Auburn, see Lewis, *From Newgate to Dannemora*, 60.

38. Boston Prison Discipline Society, *Reports of the Boston Prison Discipline Society* 16 (1841): 39.

39. Quoted in *Report on the Penitentiary System of the United States* (New York: M. Day, 1822), 99.

40. Quoted in Powers, *Brief Account*, 35; Philip Klein, "Prison Methods in New York" (Ph.D. diss., Columbia University, 1920), 203–207.

41. Charles Dickens, *American Notes; and The Uncommercial Traveler* (Philadelphia: T. B. Peterson and Bros., n.d.), 128; Caleb Smith, "Harry Hawser's Fate: Eastern State Penitentiary and the Birth of Prison Literature," in Tarter and Bell, *Buried Lives*, 238–246.

42. *Laws of the State of New York, 1819* (Albany, 1819), 87.

43. Henry Hall, *History of Auburn* (Auburn, N.Y.: Dennis Bros., 1869), 349.

44. Lewis, *From Newgate to Dannemora*, 101–106, 136–138, 206–209.

45. *Documents of the Senate of New York, 57th Session* 1 (1834): 38; Jennifer Graber, *The Furnace of Affliction: Prisons and Religion in Antebellum America* (Chapel Hill: University of North Carolina Press, 2011), 103–134; Lewis, *From Newgate to Dannemora*, 204–206.

46. Eddy, *Account of the State Prison*, 25–26.

47. Boston Prison Discipline Society, *Reports of the Boston Prison Discipline Society* 1 (1827), 18–20; Eddy, *Account of the State Prison*, 25, 26–28; Reynolds, *Recollections of Windsor Prison*, 14, 20, 22–23, 25; W. A. Coffey, *Inside Out; or, An Interior View of the New York State Prison* (New York: printed by author, 1823), 18, 20, 38, 44–46, 78–79, 191; Barnes, *History*, 456, 459.

48. Burr, *Voice from Sing Sing*, 17; James R. Brice, *Secrets of the Mount-Pleasant State Prison, Revealed and Exposed* (Albany, N.Y.: printed by author, 1839), 69; *Hudson River (NY) Chronicle*, April 23, 1839; *Auburn (N.Y.) Journal*, February 4, 1846; see also H. B. C., *A Peep into the State Prison at Auburn, N.Y.* (Auburn, NY: s.n., 1839), 6, 12, 27, 30, 33, 41, 48, 50.

49. *Prisoners Friend* I, May 1849, 376.

50. "Annual Report of the Inspectors of State Prisons," *Documents of the Senate of New York* 30 (1849): 232; *Prisoners Friend* I, May 1849, 379.

51. Lewis, *From Newgate to Dannemora*, 268–270; Barnes, *History*, 133, 411, 519.

52. "Annual Report of the Inspectors of State Prisons," *Documents of the Senate of New York* 9 (1843): 72.

53. *Fort Plain (N.Y.) Mohawk Valley Register*, August 30, 1860, 1; Boston Prison Discipline Society, *Reports of the Boston Prison Discipline Society* (1852): 715–719; Fred A. Packard, *Memorandum on a Late Visit to the Auburn Penitentiary* (Philadelphia: Philadelphia Society for Alleviating the Miseries of Public Prisons, 1842), 4–7; Klein, "Prison Methods," 208–216.

54. Dix, *Remarks on Prisons and Prison Discipline*, 24–25.

55. *Fort Edward (N.Y.) Ledger*, December 14, 1860, 1; *Prisoners Friend* I, May 1849, 380; *New York Evangelist* 22, July 31, 1851, 122.

56. *Plattsburgh (N.Y.) Republican*, August 5, 1848, 2; *Prisoners Friend* I, September 1848, 27; "Torture and Homicide in an American State Prison," *Harper's Weekly* 2, December 25, 1858, 818.

57. *Documents of the Senate of New York, 84th Session* (1861), I, no. 25, 27; "Torture and Homicide," 808–810.

58. Havelock Ellis, preface to *The New York State Reformatory in Elmira*, by Alexander Winter (London: Swan Sonneschein, 1891), viii.
59. Klein, "Prison Methods," 217–221.
60. *New York Times*, January 27, 1883, February 23, 1883.
61. *Prison Association of New York* 18 (1890–1891), 50ff.
62. Zebulon Brockway, *Fifty Years of Prison Service: An Autobiography* (New York: Charities Publication Committee, 1912), 258, 314, 356.
63. The accusations against Brockway are rebutted at length in *The New York State Reformatory at Elmira. Closing Argument of Mr. Wm. M. Ivins, of Counsel for The Defense, in The Action of The New York World Against The Board of Managers* (New York, 1895); for an overview of Brockway's regime, see Alexander W. Pisciotta, *Benevolent Repression: Social Control and the American Reformatory-Prison Movement* (New York: New York University Press, 1994), 34–59.
64. McLennan, *Crisis of Imprisonment*, 301–303.
65. Frederick Powers Wines, *Punishment and Reformation: An Historical Sketch of the Rise of the Penitentiary System* (New York: T. Y. Crowell, 1895), 152.
66. Beaumont and Tocqueville, *On the Penitentiary System in the United States*, 47.
67. Quoted in Wines, *Punishment and Reformation*, 158.

3. CRUELTY AND THE PARADOX OF SLAVE PROPERTY

1. "Shocking Barbarities," *New Orleans Mercantile Advertiser*, April 11, 1834, quoted in La Roy Sunderland, *Anti-Slavery Manual: Containing a Collection of Facts and Arguments on American Slavery* (New York: S. W. Benedict, 1837), 75.
2. The principal contemporary sources for the Lalaurie atrocities are *New Orleans Courier*, April 10–11, 1834; *New Orleans Bee*, April 11–12, 1834; and *New Orleans Mercantile Advertiser*, April 11, 1834. For a recent scholarly account, see Courtney Baker, *Humane Insight: Looking at Images of African American Suffering and Death* (Urbana: University of Illinois Press, 2015), 18–34.
3. *New Orleans Courier*, April 10, 1834; *New Orleans Bee*, April 12, 1834.
4. For international reports, see *London Morning Post*, May 22, 1834, 5; *London Standard*, May 22, 1834, 1; *London Morning Chronicle*, May 23, 1834, 4; *Bristol Mercury*, May 24, 1834, 2; *Bell's Life in London and Sporting Chronicle*, May 25, 1834; *Berrow's Worcester Journal*, May 29, 1834, 2; and *Caledonian Mercury* (Edinburgh), May 29, 1834, 8. Among the published accounts of the Lalaurie scandal, see E. Thomas, *A Concise View of the Slavery of the People of Colour in the United States: Exhibiting Some of the Most Affecting Cases of Cruel and Barbarous Treatment of Slaves* (Philadelphia: E. Thomas, 1834), 33–37; Edward S. Abdy, *Journal of a Residence and Tour in the United States* (London: John Murray, 1835), 392–393; *The Slave's Friend*, 9–10; Sunderland, *Anti-slavery Manual*, 75; Harriet Martineau, *Retrospect of Western Travel* (London: Saunders and Otley, 1838), 263–267; Theodore Dwight Weld, *American Slavery As It Is: Testimony of a Thousand Witnesses* (New York: American Anti-slavery Society, 1839), 91; E. Bunner, *History of Louisiana*

(New York: Harper and Brothers, 1842), 252–254; and Benjamin Lundy and Thomas Earle, *The Life, Travels, and Opinions of Benjamin Lundy: Including His Journeys to Texas and Mexico, with a Sketch of Contemporary Events, and a Notice of the Revolution in Hayti* (Philadelphia: William D. Parrish, 1847), 113.

5. David Walker, *Walker's Appeal, in Four Articles: Together with a Preamble, to the Coloured Citizens of the World, but in Particular, and Very Expressly, to those of the United States of America, Written in Boston, State of Massachusetts, September 28, 1829* (Chapel Hill: University of North Carolina at Chapel Hill Library, 2011), 15–16.

6. Valuable entry points to the vast scholarship on abolitionism are Robin Blackburn, *The American Crucible: Slavery, Emancipation and Human Rights* (London: Verso, 2011), 277–390; David Brion Davis, *Inhuman Bondage: The Rise and Fall of Slavery in the New World* (New York: Oxford University Press, 2006), 175–204, 250–267; and Manisha Sinha, *The Slave's Cause: A History of Abolition* (New Haven, Conn.: Yale University Press, 2016), 97–228.

7. George Bourne, *Picture of Slavery in the United States of America* (Middletown, Conn.: Edwin Hunt, 1834), 14, 33, 104.

8. William Lloyd Garrison, *Thoughts on African Colonization; or, An Impartial Exhibition of the Doctrines, Principles and Purposes of the American Colonization Society: Together with the Resolutions, Addresses and Remonstrances of the Free People of Color* (Boston: Garrison and Knapp, 1832), 79.

9. Elizabeth Cady Stanton and Susan B. Anthony, *Elizabeth Cady Stanton, Susan B. Anthony, Correspondence, Writings, Speeches*, ed. Ellen C. DuBois (New York: Schocken, 1981), 34–35.

10. Abraham Lincoln, "Address at a Sanitary Fair in Baltimore," in Joseph R. Fornieri, ed., *The Language of Liberty: The Political Speeches and Writings of Abraham Lincoln* (New York: Regnery, 2009), 691.

11. Markus Rediker, *The Slave Ship: A Human History* (New York: Viking, 2007), esp. 217–221, 239–244.

12. Adam Smith, *The Theory of Moral Sentiments* (Edinburgh: A. Kincaid and J. Bell, 1759), 2.

13. "William Lloyd Garrison to Ebenezer Dole, July 14, 1830," in Walter M. Merrill, ed., *The Letters of William Lloyd Garrison* (Cambridge, Mass.: Belknap Press of Harvard University Press, 1971), 1:104–106.

14. *Haverhill (Mass.) Gazette*, May 10, 1834.

15. *New Orleans Courier; New Orleans Bee.*

16. *Boston Liberator*, May 3, 1834, 3.

17. Weld, *American Slavery As It Is*, 7.

18. *Ohio Observer* (Hudson), May 15, 1834, 3.

19. *Ohio Observer*, May 15, 1834, 3.

20. John Stuart Mill, "Civilization," *London and Westminster Review* 3 (April 1836): 12.

21. Norman S. Fiering, "Irresistible Compassion: An Aspect of Eighteenth-Century Sympathy and Humanitarianism," *Journal of the History of Ideas* 37 (April–June 1976): 195.

22. Richard Henry Dana, *Two Years before the Mast: A Personal Narrative of Life at Sea* (New York: Harper and Brothers, 1840), 128.

23. Myra C. Glenn, *Campaigns against Corporal Punishment: Prisoners, Sailors, Women, and Children in Antebellum America* (Albany: State University of New York Press, 1984), 92–100; Myra C. Glenn, *Jack Tar's Story: The Autobiographies and Memoirs of Sailors in Antebellum America* (New York: Cambridge University Press, 2010), 112–143.

24. *Boston Liberator*, May 3, 1834. Nearly two decades later, the *Westminster Review* reached the same conclusion while reflecting on the implications of the slave master's prerogatives: "The slave is subject to the will of his master, or mistress, be she a Madame Lalaurie or no." "American Slavery, and Emancipation by the Free States," *Westminster Review* 59 (January 1853): 143.

25. Martineau, *Retrospect of Western Travel*, 264.

26. Judith K. Schafer, "'Details Are of a Most Revolting Character': Cruelty to Slaves as Seen in Appeals to the Supreme Court of Louisiana," *Chicago-Kent Law Review* 68 (1993): 1283–85; Judith K. Schafer, *Slavery, the Civil Law, and the Supreme Court of Louisiana* (Baton Rouge: Louisiana State University Press, 1994), 1–27.

27. Theodore Rosengarten, Thomas Benjamin Chaplin, and Susan W. Walker, *Tombee: Portrait of a Cotton Planter* (New York: Morrow, 1986), 456–458.

28. Martineau, *Retrospect of Western Travel*, 265.

29. Evidence that Mme. Lalaurie still owned slaves after 1834 can be found in *James Burkett and Other v. Robert Layton and Others*, 7 La. 457, 458.

30. *Boston Liberator*, March 1, 1850.

31. "The most salient distinction between the master-slave relationship and other human interactions," one scholar explains, "was the unlimited violence and oppression that the slave master could legitimately inflict upon bondsmen"; Andrew Fede, "Legitimized Violent Slave Abuse in the American South, 1619–1865: A Case Study of Law and Social Change in Six Southern States," *American Journal of Legal History* 29 (April 1985): 94–93, 150. See also Marvin L. Michael Kay and Lorin Lee Cary, "The Planters Suffer Little or Nothing: North Carolina Compensations for Executed Slaves, 1748–1772," *Science and Society* 40 (Fall 1976), 44–74, 357–368.

32. *Gillian v. Senter*, 9 Ala. 395, 396 (1846). See also Jenny Bourne Wahl, "Legal Constraints on Slave Masters: The Problem of Social Cost," *American Journal of Legal History* 41 (1997): 1–24.

33. James H. Hammond, "Negro Slavery in the South," in J. D. B. De Bow, ed., *Industrial Resources, Etc., of Southern and Western States* (New Orleans: De Bow's Review, 1852), 350–354.

34. Fede, "Legitimized Violent Slave Abuse," 93, 113; Donna J. Spindel, "The Administration of Justice in North Carolina, 1720–1740," *American Journal of Legal History* 25 (April 1981): 141–162, 144.

35. *North Carolina v. Mann*, 13 N.C. 263 (N.C. 1830), also known as *State v. Mann*.

36. Samuel E. Cornish, *New York Colored American*, March 4, 1837.

37. Moses Roper, *A Narrative of the Adventures and Escape of Moses Roper, from American Slavery* (Philadelphia: Merrihew and Gunn, 1838), 47ff.

38. John W. Blassingame, *Slave Testimony: Two Centuries of Letters, Speeches, Interviews, and Autobiographies* (Baton Rouge: Louisiana State University Press, 1977), 218, 221.

39. Blassingame, *Slave Testimony*, 280.

40. John Brown, *Slave Life in Georgia: A Narrative of the Life, Sufferings, and Escape of John Brown, a Fugitive Slave, Now in England*, ed. L. A. Chamerovzow (London: W. M. Watts, 1855), 40, 42, 67.

41. "Recollections of Slavery by a Runaway Slave," *Emancipator*, September 20, 1838.

42. Harriet Jacobs, *Incidents from the Life of a Slave Girl* (New York: Cosimo Classics, 2009), 41; Lewis Clarke, *Narratives of the Sufferings of Lewis and Milton Clarke* (Boston: Bela Marsh, 1846), 17.

43. Compensation law ensured planters' cooperation in punishing slaves because it permitted masters to avoid the potential conflict between enforcing discipline and protecting from physical harm a substantial investment in human property. See Kay and Cary, "Planters Suffer Little or Nothing," 290, 292, 299, 301.

44. Marvin L. Michael Kay and Lorin Lee Cary, *Slavery in North Carolina, 1748–1775* (Chapel Hill: University of North Carolina Press, 1995), 81–83; Seth Kotch and Robert P. Mosteller, "The Racial Justice Act and the Long Struggle with Race and the Death Penalty in North Carolina," *North Carolina Law Review* 88 (2010): 2047–2048.

45. Robert L. Paquette, "The Great Louisiana Slave Revolt of 1811 Reconsidered," *Historical Reflections* 35 (Spring 2009): 72–96; Daniel Rasmussen, *American Uprising: The Untold Story of America's Largest Slave Revolt* (New York: Harper, 2011), 147–166. For an account of the brutal white response to an alleged slave insurrection in North Carolina, see Jeffrey J. Crow, "Slave Rebelliousness and Social Conflict in North Carolina, 1775 to 1802," *William and Mary Quarterly* (January 1980): 85, 99, 101.

46. *State v. Tackett*, 8 N.C. 217 (1820); Fede, "Legitimized Violent Slave Abuse," 115. See also Daniel T. Flannigan, "Criminal Procedure in Slave Trials in the Antebellum South," *Journal of Southern History* (February 1974): 147–152.

47. *Caldwell v. Langford*, 1 McMullan 275 (1841).

48. Ariela J. Gross, *Double Character: Slavery and Mastery in the Antebellum Southern Courtroom* (Princeton, N.J.: Princeton University Press, 2000), esp. 108–120.

49. *State v. David*, 49 N.C. 354 (1857).

50. In North Carolina, for example, during the century and a half from the colony's founding to the end of the Civil War, only one white was executed for murdering a black; see Kotch and Mosteller, "Racial Injustice Act," 2049.

51. *Boston Liberator*, May 10, 1834, 3.

52. Frederick Douglass, *Narrative of the Life of Frederick Douglass, an American Slave* (Boston: Anti-slavery Office, 1845), 17.

53. *Boston Liberator*, May 10, 1834, 3.

54. *Ohio Observer* (Hudson), May 15, 1834, 3.

55. Beecher, quoted in David W. Bartlett, *Modern Agitators; or, Pen Portraits of Living American Reformers* (New York: C. M. Saxton, 1859), 20.

56. *Boston Liberator,* July 30, 1831.

57. William J. Anderson, *Life and Narrative of William J. Anderson, Twenty-Four Years a Slave; Sold Eight Times! In Jail Sixty Times!! Whipped Three Hundred Times!!! or The Dark Deeds of American Slavery Revealed. Containing Scriptural Views of the Origin of the Black and of the White Man. Also, a Simple and Easy Plan to Abolish Slavery in the United States. Together with an Account of the Services of Colored Men in the Revolutionary War—Day and Date, and Interesting Facts* (Chicago: Daily Tribune Book and Job Publishing, 1857), 19.

58. Solomon Northup, *Twelve Years a Slave: Narrative of Solomon Northup, a Citizen of New-York, Kidnapped in Washington City in 1841, and Rescued in 1853* (Auburn, N.Y.: Derby and Miller, 1853), 188–189.

59. Jacobs, *Incidents in the Life of a Slave Girl,* 46.

60. *Connecticut Gazette* (New London), May 7, 1834, 2; *Pittsfield (Mass.) Sun,* May 8, 1834, 1; *Boston Liberator,* May 10, 1834, 3; *New York Journal of Commerce,* May 10, 1834, 3; *Haverhill (Mass.) Gazette,* May 10, 1834, 3; *Providence (R.I.) Patriot,* August 2, 1834, 2. For insights into the recourse to violence by plantation mistresses, see Thavolia Glymph, *Out of the House of Bondage: The Transformation of the Plantation Household* (New York: Cambridge University Press, 2008), 5–7, 27–33; for discussions of the complicated status of Mme. Lalaurie and other Creole women in antebellum New Orleans, see Kathy Frances Morlas, *La Madame et la Mademoiselle: Creole Women in Louisiana, 1718–1865* (M.A. thesis, Louisiana State University, 2005), 111–126; and Shirley Elizabeth Thompson, *Exiles at Home: The Struggle to Become American in Creole New Orleans* (Cambridge, Mass.: Harvard University Press, 2009), 164–209.

61. Margaret Nicola Abruzzo, *Polemical Pain: Slavery, Cruelty, and the Rise of Humanitarianism* (Baltimore: Johns Hopkins University Press, 2011), 159–189.

62. Weld, *American Slavery As It Is,* 116–117.

63. "A Professional Planter," *Practical Rules for the Management and Medical Treatment of Negro Slaves, in the Sugar Colonies* (London: J. Barfield, 1803), 233.

64. Benjamin Moseley, *A Treatise on Tropical Diseases on Military Operations, and on the Climate of the West-Indies* (London: Nichols and Son, 1803), 493.

65. John H. Dye, *Illustrated Edition of Painless Childbirth or Healthy Mothers and Healthy Children,* 19th ed. (Buffalo: J. H. Dye Medical Institute, 1912), 32–36. See also Joanna Bourke, "Pain Sensitivity: An Unnatural History from 1800 to 1965," *Journal of Medical Humanities* 35 (September 2014): 303–308.

66. *Charleston Courier,* cited in *Anti-slavery Almanac 1839* (New York: S. W. Benedict, 1839), 32.

67. Glenn, *Campaigns against Corporal Punishment,* 103–126. For an incisive interpretation of the white southern patriarchal ideology, see Stephanie McCurry, *Masters of Small Worlds: Yeoman Households, Gender Relations, and the Political Culture of the Antebellum South Carolina Low Country* (New York: Oxford University Press, 1997), esp. 37–91.

68. Benjamin Rush, *An Inquiry into the Influence of Physical Causes upon the Moral Faculty* (Philadelphia: Haswell, Barrington, and Haswell, 1839), 15.

69. George Tucker, *Valley of Shenandoah; or, Memoirs of the Graysons* (New York: C. Wiley, 1824), 206.

70. WGS [William Gilmore Simms], "Miss Martineau on Slavery," *Southern Literary Messenger* 3 (November 1837): 657, italics in original.

71. *Charleston Courier*, quoted in Lydia Maria Child, *The Patriarchal Institution: As Described by Members of Its Own Family* (New York: American Anti-slavery Society, 1860), 9.

72. Abel Parker Upshur, "Domestic Slavery," *Southern Literary Messenger* 5 (October 1839): 686–687.

73. An Overseer, "On the Conduct and Management of Overseers, Drivers and Slaves," *Southern Agriculturalist* 9 (May 1836): 228.

74. Joseph A. S. Acklen, "Rules in the Management of a Southern Estate," *De Bow's Review* 22 (April 1857): 376, 379.

75. W. W. Hazzard, "On the General Management of a Plantation," *Southern Agriculturalist* 4 (July 1831): 350.

76. Franklin, quoted in James O. Breeden, *Advice among Masters: The Ideal in Slave Management in the Old South* (Westport, Conn.: Greenwood Press, 1980), 82.

77. H. N. McTyeire, "Plantation Life—Duties and Responsibilities," *De Bow's Review* 29 (September 1860): 361.

78. *Congressional Globe*, 30th Congress, 2nd Session (1849), 510.

79. *Congressional Globe*, 32nd Congress, 1st Session (1852), 222.

80. *Congressional Globe*, 32nd Congress, 1st Session (1852), 919.

81. McTyeire, "Plantation Life," 361.

82. *Charleston Mercury*, August 13, 1833.

83. Theodore Clapp, *Slavery: A Sermon* (New Orleans: John Gibson, 1838), 51–52.

84. Z. Kingsley, *A Treatise on the Patriarchal, or Co-operative, System of Society as It Exists in Some Governments, and Colonies in America: And in the United States, under the Name of Slavery, with Its Necessity and Advantages* (n.p., 1829), 3.

85. Eric Foner, *Free Soil, Free Labor, Free Men: The Ideology of the Republican Party before the Civil War* (New York: Oxford University Press, 1970), esp. chap. 8.

86. *Dred Scott v. Sandford*, 60 U.S. 393 (1857).

87. Speech to the U.S. Senate, May 7, 1860, quoted in *Louisville Daily Courier*, June 2, 1860: 1.

88. Frederick Douglass, *Two Speeches by Frederick Douglass; One on West India Emancipation, Delivered at Canandaigua, Aug. 4th, and the Other on the Dred Scott Decision, Delivered in New York, on the Occasion of the Anniversary of the American Abolition Society, May, 1857* (Rochester, N.Y.: C. P. Dewey, 1857), 31.

89. Michael Vorenberg, *Final Freedom: The Civil War, the Abolition of Slavery, and the Thirteenth Amendment* (New York: Cambridge University Press, 2001), 190–191.

90. Hannah Arendt, *The Origins of Totalitarianism* (San Diego: Harcourt, 1994), 294–296.

4. TORTURE IN THE BROTHERS' WAR

1. Court-martial proceedings of Captain Theodore McGowan, Asst. Adjt. Genl., Case file OO1382, Record Group 153, Records of the Office of the Judge Advocate General (Army), National Archives and Records Administration, Washington, D.C. (hereafter cited as McGowan court-martial file).

2. The torture in Washington, D.C., is briefly mentioned in Margaret Leech, *Reveille in Washington, 1860–1865* (New York: Harper and Brothers, 1941; repr., New York: Time, 1962), 94; Mark Neely, *The Fate of Liberty: Abraham Lincoln and Civil Liberties* (New York: Oxford University Press, 1991), 109–112; and Steven J. Ramold, *Baring the Iron Hand: Discipline in the Union Army* (DeKalb: Northern Illinois University Press, 2010), 348.

3. Prussian consul's telegram to the court, August 16, 1865 (document labeled "A"), McGowan court-martial file.

4. John W. Hunt to Governor Vance, March 6, 1863; Jeremiah Phillips to Gov. Vance, April 14, 1863; Gilliam Jones to Z. B. Vance, January 2, 1864, Governors Papers, Zebulon B. Vance, North Carolina State Archives, Raleigh, N.C; Thomas B. Settle to Z. B. Vance, September 21, 1864, October 4, 1864, Thomas B. Settles Letters, North Carolina State Archives, Raleigh, N.C.

5. A useful starting point in the voluminous material on Wirz and Andersonville is Fred R. Ruhlman, *Captain Henry Wirz and Andersonville Prison: A Reappraisal* (Knoxville: University of Tennessee Press, 2006).

6. *New York Tribune* and *New York Times* quoted in Edward Alfred Pollard, *The First Year of the War* (Richmond: West & Johnston, 1863), 70; *New York Evening Post*, April 23, 1861. For northern warmongering, see Russell McClintock, *Lincoln and the Decision for War: The Northern Response to Secession* (Chapel Hill: University of North Carolina Press, 2008), 254–274; and Emory Thomas, *The Dogs of War, 1861* (New York: Oxford University Press, 2011), 1–36.

7. *New York Herald*, January 27, 1861, 4; Lloyd Lewis, *Sherman, Fighting Prophet* (Harcourt, Brace, 1932), 158.

8. Arthur Waldron, "Looking Backward: The People in Arms and the Transformation of War," in Daniel Moran and Arthur Waldron, eds., *The People in Arms: Military Myth and National Mobilization since the French Revolution* (New York: Cambridge University Press, 2003).

9. Luther Giddings, *Sketches of the Campaigns in Northern Mexico, in Eighteen-Hundred Fifty-Six and Seven* (New York: G. P. Putnam, 1853), 280; Charles Winslow Elliott, *Winfield Scott: The Soldier and the Man* (New York: Macmillan, 1937), 448.

10. Walt Whitman, *Drum Taps* (New York: Peter Eckler, 1865), 37; Charles Eliot Norton, *The Soldier of the Good Cause* (Boston: American Unitarian Association, 1861), 5–6.

11. Thomas Wentworth Higginson, *Army Life in a Black Regiment* (New York: Dover, 2002), 170; Carlton McCarthy, *Detailed Minutiæ of Soldier Life in the Army of Northern Virginia, 1861–1865* (Richmond: C. McCarthy, 1882),

208; James Jones White to Mary White, August 14, 1861, James Jones White Papers, Southern Historical Collection, University of North Carolina (hereafter cited as SHC).

12. Julius Murry to his brother, September 24, 1861, Julius A. Murray Papers, Wisconsin Historical Society; Elizabeth Samet, *Willing Obedience: Citizens, Soldiers, and the Progress of Consent in America, 1776–1898* (Stanford, Calif.: Stanford University Press, 2004); Steven J. Ramold, *Baring the Iron Hand: Discipline in the Union Army* (DeKalb: Northern Illinois University Press, 2010), 43–67; Joseph A. Frank, *With Ballot and Bayonet: The Political Socialization of American Civil War Soldiers* (Athens: University of Georgia Press, 1998), 22–25.

13. Clifford Dowdey, ed., *The Wartime Papers of R. E. Lee* (New York: Bramhall House, 1961), 533–534.

14. Henry Livermore Abbott, *Fallen Leaves: The Civil War Letters of Major Henry Livermore Abbott* (Kent, Ohio: Kent State University Press, 1991), 95–96; Ramold, *Baring the Iron Hand*, 66, 356–365; U.S. War Department, *The War of the Rebellion: A Compilation of the Official Records* (hereafter cited as *OR*), 129 vols. (Washington, D.C.,1880–1901), series I, 13:881.

15. Quoted in Samet, *Willing Obedience*, 6.

16. Ella Gertrude Clanton Thomas, *Secret Eye: The Journal of Ella Gertrude Clanton Thomas, 1848–1889*, ed. Virginia Ingraham Burr (Chapel Hill: University of North Carolina Press, 1990), 200.

17. *Huntington (Ind.) Herald*, December 2, 1863, 1.

18. *Nashville Daily Union*, April 21, 1864. See also *Chicago Daily Tribune*, May 15, 1862; *Nashville Daily Union*, May 31, 1864, 1.

19. H. C. Kendrick to his sisters, November 18, 1861, in H. C. Kendrick Letters, SHC; *Richmond Whig*, October 26, 1861.

20. Valuable introductions to the guerrilla warfare of the Civil War include Michael Fellman, *Inside War: The Guerrilla Conflict in Missouri during the American Civil War* (New York: Oxford University Press, 1989); and Daniel E. Sutherland, *A Savage Conflict: The Decisive Role of Guerrillas in the American Civil War* (Chapel Hill: University of North Carolina Press, 2009). For an alternative interpretation of Confederate guerrillas in Missouri, see Joseph M. Beilein Jr., *Bushwhackers: Guerrilla Warfare, Manhood, and the Household in Civil War Missouri* (Kent, Ohio: Kent State University Press, 2016), 165–188.

21. *Jefferson City (Mo.) State Times*, July 25, 1863, 1; *Cleveland Daily Leader*, April 18, 1863.

22. *Pittsburgh Daily Commercial*, November 16, 1864, 1.

23. *OR*, series I, 23:310; *Semi-weekly Wisconsin* (Milwaukee), February 27, 1863, 2; Assistant Adjutant General O. D. Greene, St. Louis, to General Alfred Pleasonton, September 3, 1864, *OR*, 41, 47; *Gettysburg (PA) Adams Sentinel*, April 5, 1864, 1. For an eyewitness account of Unionist exiles from Arkansas, see *Macon (MO) Gazette*, July 1, 1864, 1; for a graphic account of the terrorization of Unionists in Missouri, see *Fremont (OH) Weekly Journal*, November 25, 1864; for depredations of Confederate forces in Louisiana, *OR*, series I, 34:925. For a skillful survey of the guerrilla war in the border

states, see Christopher Phillips, *The Rivers Ran Backward: The Civil War and the Remaking of the American Middle Border* (New York: Oxford University Press, 2016), 236–284.

24. *White Cloud Kansas Chief,* May 19, 1864, 4; *Marysville (Kans.) Big Blue Union,* May 7, 1864.

25. Halleck to T. Ewing, January 1, 1862, *OR,* series II, 1:247; Sherman, quoted in Lewis, *Sherman,* 248; Ramold, *Baring the Iron Hand,* 80–81, 121–122.

26. Haskell to his mother, May 4, May 8, 1861, Haskell Papers, SHC; Henry Ewing to Harry St. John Dixon, May 1, 1861, in Harry St. John Dixon Papers, SHC; Edward O. Guerrant Diary, March 8, 1862, in Edward Owings Guerrant Papers, SHC; William R. Redding to his wife, August 1861, William R. Redding Papers, SHC; "To the Good People of the Counties of Loudoun, Fairfax, and Prince William," June 5, 1861, *OR,* series I, 2:907.

27. *Staunton (Va.) Spectator,* August 11, 1863; *OR,* series I, 32:118.

28. *Richmond Daily Enquirer,* September 29, 1862, 4; *OR,* series II, 6:42–43.

29. *Cleveland Daily Leader,* May 12, 1862.

30. *Cleveland Daily Leader,* April 18, 1863.

31. *Huntington (Ind.) Herald,* December 2, 1863, 1.

32. *Louisville (Ky.) Journal,* quoted in the *Vincennes (Ind.) Gazette,* March 15, 1862, 1.

33. "Atrocities of the Rebellion," *Advocate of Peace* 14 (January/February 1862): 22.

34. *Richmond Dispatch,* April 5, 1864, 4.

35. Walt Whitman, *Walt Whitman's Civil War* (New York: Knopf, 1960), 144.

36. Frances Lieber, *Amendments to the Constitution* (New York: Loyal Publication Society, 1865), 11.

37. Holmes to his mother, December 12, 1862, *Touched with Fire: Civil War Letters and Diary of Oliver Wendell Holmes, Jr.,* ed. Mark De Wolfe Howe (Cambridge, Mass.: Harvard University Press, 1946), 78.

38. Frank McIntosh Myers to "Dear Home Folks," May 16, 1864, Civil War Times Illustrated Collection, Military History Institute, Carlisle, Penn.

39. Moncure Conway, *Golden Hour* (Boston: Ticknor and Fields, 1862), 30–34.

40. Robert McAllister, *The Civil War Letters of General Robert McAllister,* ed. James Robertson Jr. (Baton Rouge: Louisiana State University Press, 1998), 49.

41. Julia B. Whiting to Richard Henry Dulany, July 27, 1864, in Margaret Ann Vogtsberger, *The Dulanys of Welbourne: A Family in Mosby's Confederacy* (Berryville, Va.: Rockbridge, 1995), 188–189.

42. Haskell to his mother, May 22, 1862, Haskell Papers, SHC.

43. H. C. Kendrick to his mother, June 6, 1863, Kendrick Papers, SHC.

44. McAllister, *Civil War Letters,* 558.

45. Gerald F. Linderman, *Embattled Courage: The Experience of Combat in the American Civil War* (New York: Free Press, 1987), 123.

46. James A. Connolly, *Three Years in the Army of the Cumberland: The Letters and Diary of Major James A. Connolly* (Bloomington: Indiana University Press, 1959), 324.

47. R. H. Simpson, quoted in Randall C. Jimerson, *The Private Civil War: Popular Thought during the Sectional Conflict* (Baton Rouge: Louisiana State University Press, 1988), 129.

48. James K. Edmondson to Emma Edmondson, August 7, 1864, in James K. Edmondson, *My Dear Emma: War Letters of Col. James K. Edmondson, 1861–1865* (Verona, Va.: McClure Press, 1978), 131–132. See also Achilles J. Tynes to Harriet Louisa Tynes, July 29, 1864, Achilles J. Tynes Papers, SHC.

49. Emer de Vattel, *The Law of Nations; or, Principles of the Law of Nature, Applied to the Conduct and Affairs of Nations and Sovereigns* (Philadelphia: T. & J. W. Johnson, 1852), bk. III, chap. 8, sec. 138; bk. II, chap. 18, sec. 339.

50. On the legal issues surrounding the Civil War and the codification of the laws of war during the Civil War, see Mark E. Neely, *The Fate of Liberty: Abraham Lincoln and Civil Liberties* (New York: Oxford University Press, 1991); Stephen C. Neff, *Justice in Blue and Gray: A Legal History of the Civil War* (Cambridge, Mass.: Harvard University Press, 2010); and esp. John Fabian Witt, *Lincoln's Code: The Laws of War in American History* (New York: Free Press, 2012).

51. General Order No. 100, sec. I, no. 16, in *OR*, series III, 3:148–164.

52. Quoted in Witt, *Lincoln's* Code, 236.

53. Vattel also condoned retaliation with the aim of "chastising an unjust and barbarous nation" and "checking her brutality."

54. Seddon to Robert Ould, June 24, 1863, repr. in Francis Lieber, *Lieber's Code and the Law of War*, ed. Richard S. Hartigan (Chicago: Precedent, 1983), 123–124.

55. The best history of Civil War prisons remains William B. Hesseltine, *Civil War Prisons: A Study in War Psychology* (1930; repr., Columbus: Ohio State University Press, 1998). A recent valuable contribution is Paul J. Springer, *Transforming Civil War Prisons: Lincoln, Lieber, and the Politics of Captivity* (New York: Routledge, 2015).

56. The exchange policy is succinctly described in Springer, *Transforming Civil War Prisons*, 1–27.

57. Entries for January 2, 4, 12, 15, 17, 1862, Gray Diary, SHC.

58. Charles Mattocks, *Unspoiled Heart: The Journal of Charles Mattocks of the 17th Maine*, ed. by Philip N. Racine (Knoxville: University of Tennessee Press 1994), 156 ; Margaret Peele, *Letter from Libby Prison*, 60; T. H. Mann, "A Yankee in Andersonville," *Century Magazine* 40 (July 1890): 458.

59. Ted Genoways and Hugh H. Genoways, eds., *Perfect Picture of Hell: Eyewitness Accounts by Civil War Prisoners from the 12th Iowa* (Iowa City: University of Iowa Press, 2001), 38–39, 116.

60. James T. Wells, *Southern Historical Society Papers* 8 (July 1879): 324—330.

61. *OR*, series II, 4:195.

62. Charles L. Sambardo, "Incidents of Prison Life, with Causes of Confederate Cruelty," *Glimpses of the Nation's Struggle: Papers Read before the Minnesota Commandery of the Military Order of the Loyal Legion of the United States*, 3rd series (1887), 347–377; Thomas E. Berry, *Confederate Veteran* (February 1912): 65–69.

63. Samuel Fiske, *Dunn Browne in the Army* (Boston: Nichols and Noyes, 1865), 157.

64. Hesseltine, *Civil War Prisons*, 7–34, 67–113; Robert Scott Davis, *Ghosts and Shadows of Andersonville: Essays on the Secret Social Histories of America's Deadliest Prison* (Macon, Ga.: Mercer University Press, 2006), 177; Thomas E. Byrne, *Elmira's Civil War Prison Camp, 1864–65* (Elmira, N.Y.: Chemung County Historical Society, 1989), 592.

65. L. Leon, *Diary of a Tar Heel Confederate Soldier* (Charlotte, N.C.: Stone, 1913), 81.

66. *OR*, series I, 5:455–456, 469–470, 484, 487, 674–679, 844–845, 855, 867, 966–967; 6:34–35, 73, 132, 134, 139–140, 146, 159, 163, 169, 187–188, 523–524, 868, 892–893; Hesseltine, *Civil War Prisons*, 7–13, 67–113, 172–209..

67. Ruhlman, *Captain Henry Wirz*.

68. Samuel S. Boggs, *Eighteen Months a Prisoner under the Rebel Flag: A Condensed Pen-Picture of Belle Isle, Danville, Andersonville, Charleston, Florence and Libby Prisons from Actual Experience* (Lovington, Ill.: S. S. Boggs, 1889), 33.

69. U.S. Sanitary Commission, *Narrative of Privations and Sufferings of United States Officers and Soldiers While Prisoners of War in the Hands of the Rebel Authorities* (Philadelphia: King and Baird, 1864); "Privations and Sufferings of U.S. Soldiers in Rebel Prisons," *Atlantic Monthly* (December 1864): 777–778.

70. Benjamin G. Cloyd, *Haunted by Atrocity: Civil War Prisons in American Memory* (Baton Rouge: Louisiana State University Press, 2010); Ann Fabian, *The Unvarnished Truth: Personal Narratives in Nineteenth-Century America* (Berkeley: University of California Press, 2000), 117–158; M. Keith Harris, *Across the Bloody Chasm: The Culture of Commemoration among Civil War Veterans* (Baton Rouge: Louisiana State University Press, 2014).

71. W. B. Yeats, *Oxford Book of Modern Verse* (New York: Oxford University Press, 1936), xxxiv.

72. Robert H. Kellogg, *Life and Death in Rebel Prisons: Giving a Complete History of the Inhuman and Barbarous Treatment of Our Brave Soldiers by Rebel Authorities, Inflicting Terrible Suffering and Frightful Mortality* (Hartford, Conn.: L. Stebbins, 1867), title page. See 389–390.

73. U.S. Sanitary Commission. *Narrative of Privations and Sufferings*, 31, 48, 156, 500.

74. Lawrence Sangston, *Bastilles of the North* (Baltimore: Kelly, Hedian and Piet, 1863), 129.

75. Joseph Barbière, *Scraps from the Prison Table: At Camp Chase And Johnson's Island* (Doylestown, Pa.: W.W.H. Davis, Printer, 1868).

76. Mann, "Yankee in Andersonville," 449.

77. H. M. Davidson, *Fourteen Months in Southern Prisons; being a Narrative of the Treatment of Federal Prisoners of War in the Rebel Military Prisons of Richmond, Danville, Andersonville, Savannah and Millen* (Milwaukee: Daily Wisconsin Printing House, 1865), 54.

78. *Southern Historical Society Publications*, 1 (April 1876): 281–289.

79. Leon, *Diary of a Tar Heel Confederate Soldier*, 80.

80. John Rufus King, *My Experience in the Confederate Army and in Northern Prisons* (Clarksburg, W.V.: Stonewall Jackson Chapter No. 1333, United Daughters of the Confederacy, 1917), 42.

81. *Confederate Veteran* (March 1898): 121–122; *Confederate Veteran* (June 1912): 294–297; John Dyer, *Reminiscences; or, Four Years in the Confederate Army* (Evansville, Ind.: Keller, 1898), 36–37; Frederick A. Bartleson, *Letters from Libby Prison: Being the Authentic Letters Written While in Confederate Captivity in the Notorious Libby Prison, at Richmond, as Preserved and Edited by Margaret W. Peelle* (New York: Greenwich, 1956), 82–83.

82. Mann, "Yankee in Andersonville," 455.

83. "Deposition of T. D. Henry," *Southern Historical Society Papers* I (March 1876): 276.

84. Boggs, *Eighteen Months*, 76; see also *Confederate Veteran* (November 1896): 387.

85. Ambrose Spencer, *A Narrative of Andersonville, Drawn from the Evidence Elicited on the Trial of Henry Wirz, the Jailer. With the Argument of Col. N. P. Chipman, Judge Advocate* (New York: Harper and Brothers, 1866), 69.

86. Gilbert E. Sabre, *Nineteen Months a Prisoner of War* (New York: American News, 1865), 103; Dorence Atwater, *Report of the Joint Committee on Reconstruction*, 39th Congress, 1st Session, 1866, report no. 30, 283; *Confederate Veteran* (December 1907): 565–566; Mildred Throne, "Iowans in Southern Prisons," *Iowa Journal of History* 54 (January 1956): 67–88; John A. Wilson, *Adventures of Alf. Wilson: A Thrilling Episode of the Dark Days of the Rebellion* (Washington, D.C.: National Tribune, 1897).

87. *Confederate Veteran* (November 1910): 516.

88. *OR*, series II, 5:897.

89. King, *My Experience*, 42.

90. Boggs, *Eighteen Months*, 43. See also Atwater, *Report of the Joint Committee on Reconstruction*, 283; Genoways and Genoways, *Perfect Picture of Hell*, 213, 249.

91. Davidson, *Fourteen Months*, 179.

92. *Confederate Veteran* (March 1898): 121–122.

93. Barbiere, *Scraps from the Prison Table*, 288; Genoways and Genoways, *Perfect Picture of Hell*, 214, 240; Mann, "Yankee in Andersonville," 458.

94. Charles T. Loehr, "Point Lookout," *Southern Historical Society Papers* 18 (1890): 119–120.

95. *Charleston Mercury*, October 29, 1861.

96. *OR*, series I, 8:167.

97. Quoted in Robert Penn Warren, *The Legacy of the Civil War: Meditations on the Centennial* (New York: Random House, 1961), 89.

98. *St. Joseph (Mo.) Morning Herald*, June 5, 1862, 2.

99. Herman Melville, *Battle-Pieces and Aspects of the War* (New York: Harper and Brothers, 1866), 279.

100. *Greensboro New North State*, May 16, 1872, 2; *Raleigh Sentinel*, July 26, 1876; *Greensboro New North State*, August 25, 1876, 3; Jeffrey Crow,

"Thomas Settle Jr., Reconstruction, and the Memory of the Civil War," *Journal of Southern History* 62 (Fall 1996): 689–726; Adam Domby, "War within the States: Loyalty, Dissent, and Conflict in Southern Piedmont Communities, 1860–1876" (Ph.D. diss., University of North Carolina, 2015), esp. 363–370.

101. Mann, "Yankee in Andersonville," 447.

102. Peter Novick, *That Noble Dream: The "Objectivity Question" and the American Historical Profession* (New York: Cambridge University Press, 1988), esp. 41–85.

103. *Andersonville National Historic Site: Long-Range Interpretive Plan* (Washington, D.C.: National Park Service, U.S. Department of the Interior, 2010), 2.

104. Cloyd, *Haunted by Atrocity*, 164–179.

5. IMPERIALIST EXCESSES

1. Court-martial of Captain George W. Brandle, #19802, Record Group 153, National Archives, Washington, D.C. The best survey of the prosecution of American servicemen for atrocities in the Philippines is Christopher J. Einolf, *America in the Philippines, 1899–1902: The First Torture Scandal* (New York: Palgrave Macmillan, 2014).

2. Kenneth Ray Young, *The General's General: The Life and Times of Arthur MacArthur* (Boulder, Colo.: Westview Press, 1994), 119–214.

3. Court-martial of Captain George W. Brandle.

4. Court-martial of Captain George W. Brandle.

5. *Chicago Tribune*, September 29, 1900, 9. Brandle's career can be traced in *National Tribune* (Washington, D.C.), June 2, 1898, 3; *Brooklyn Daily Eagle*, June 6, 1901, 2; *Louisville Courier-Journal*, April 17, 1902, 4; *Charlotte Observer*, April 16, 1903, 7; *Evening Star* (Washington, D.C.), January 7, 1904, 5, July 19, 1904, 3, October 30, 1905, 7.

6. "Review of a Discourse Delivered at Plymouth, December 22, 1820 by Daniel Webster," *North American Review* 14 (July 1822): 21; "A Salmagundi," *United States Democratic Review* 38 (December 1836): 411.

7. Louis A. Pérez, *The War of 1898: The United States and Cuba in History and Historiography* (Chapel Hill: University of North Carolina Press, 1998), 1–23; Louis A. Pérez, *Cuba in the American Imagination: Metaphor and the Imperial Ethos* (Chapel Hill: University of North Carolina Press, 2008), esp. 1–12.

8. For cogent and concise introductions to the origins of the conflict, see Douglas Carl Peifer. *Choosing War: Presidential Decisions in the Maine, Lusitania, and Panay Incidents* (New York: Oxford University Press, 2016), 15–66.

9. For the opening of American involvement in the Philippines, see Brian McAllister Linn, *The Philippine War, 1899–1902* (Lawrence: University Press of Kansas, 2000), 3–21; David A. Silbey, *War of Frontier and Empire: The Philippine-American War, 1899–1902* (New York: Hill and Wang, 2007), 3–29.

10. Teodoro A. Agoncillo, *The Revolt of the Masses: The Story of Bonifacio and the Katipunan* (Quezon City: University of the Philippines Press, 1956); Teodoro A. Agoncillo, *Malolos: Crisis of the Republic* (Quezon City: University of the Philippines Press, 1960); Renato Constantino, *A History of the Philippines: From the Spanish Colonization to the Second World War* (New York: Monthly Review Press, 1975), 81–197; Reynaldo Clemeña Ileto, *Pasyon and Revolution: Popular Movements in the Philippines, 1840–1910* (Quezon City: Ateneo de Manila University Press, 1979); Reynaldo Clemeña Ileto, *Filipinos and Their Revolution: Event, Discourse, and Historiography* (Quezon City: Ateneo de Manila University Press, 1998), 1–116; Teodoro M. Kalaw, *The Philippine Revolution* (Mandaluyong: Jorge B. Vargas Filipiana Foundation, 1969); Paul A. Kramer, *The Blood of Government: Race, Empire, the United States, and the Philippines* (Chapel Hill: University of North Carolina Press, 2006), 35–82; Benito J. Legarda, *After the Galleons: Foreign Trade, Economic Change and Entrepreneurship in the Nineteenth Century Philippines* (Quezon City: Ateneo de Manila University Press, 1999).

11. The early American military campaigns are expertly recounted in Kramer, *Blood of Government*, 87–111; and Linn, *Philippine War*, 22–159.

12. James F. Rusling, "Interview with President McKinley," *Christian Advocate* 78 (January 22, 1903): 137–138.

13. *A Compilation of the Messages and Papers of the Presidents: Prepared under the Direction of the Joint Committee on Printing, of the House and Senate* (Washington, D.C.: U.S. Government Printing Office, 1900), XIV, 6392; *Congressional Record: Proceedings and Debates of the Fifty-Fifth Congress, Third Session* (Washington, D.C.: U.S. Government Printing Office, 1899), 838.

14. "Speech of George F. Hoar before the Republicans of Worchester, November 1, 1898," in *Political Speeches of Hon. George F. Hoar* (Washington, D.C.: n.p., [1904?]), 66.

15. Linn, *Philippine War*, 174–176.

16. John R. M. Taylor, *The Philippine Insurrection against the United States: A Compilation of Documents with Notes and Introduction* (Pasay City, Philippines: Eugenio Lopez Foundation, 1971); Leonard Y. Andaya, "Ethnicity in the Philippine Revolution," in *The Philippine Revolution of 1896: Ordinary Lives in Extraordinary Times*, ed. Florentino Rodao Garcia and Felice Noelle Rodriquez (Manila: Ateneo de Manila University Press, 2001), 49–82; Kramer, *Blood of Government*, 130–133.

17. Resil B. Mojares, *The War against the Americans: Resistance and Collaboration in Cebu, 1899–1906* (Quezon City: Ateneo de Manila University Press, 1999), 41–42, 80; Linn, *Philippine War*, 185, 194–196; Frederick Funston, *Memories of Two Wars: Cuban and Philippine Experiences* (New York: C. Scribner's Sons, 1911), 375; *Charges of Cruelty, Etc., to the Natives of the Philippines*, 57th Congress, First Session (1902), Senate Document 205.

18. "Speech at Dinner of the Home Market Club, Boston, February 16, 1899," *Speeches and Addresses of William McKinley, from March 1, 1897 to May 30, 1900* (New York: Doubleday and McClure, 1900), 189; Elihu Root, *The Military and Colonial Policy of the United States: Addresses and*

Reports, ed. Robert Bacon and James Brown Scott (Cambridge, Mass.: Harvard University Press, 1916), 31.

19. John M. Gates, *Schoolbooks and Krags: The United States Army in the Philippines, 1898–1902* (Westport, Conn.: Greenwood Press, 1973), 3–155; Glenn A. May, *Social Engineering in the Philippines: The Aims, Execution, and Impact of American Colonial Policy, 1900–1913* (Westport, Conn.: Greenwood Press, 1980), 77–96.

20. Brian McAllister Linn, *The U.S. Army and Counterinsurgency in the Philippine War, 1899–1902* (Chapel Hill: University of North Carolina Press, 1989), 63–162; Glenn Anthony May, *Battle for Batangas: A Philippine Province at War* (New Haven, Conn.: Yale University Press, 1991), 131–210; Mojares, *War against the Americans,* 37–116; William Henry Scott, *Ilocano Responses to American Aggression, 1900–1901* (Quezon City, Philippines: New Day, 1986), 44–144.

21. Moorfield Storey and Julian Codman, *Secretary Root's Record, "Marked Severities" in Philippine Warfare: An Analysis of the Law and Facts Bearing on the Action and Utterances of President Roosevelt and Secretary Root* (Boston: G. H. Ellis Co., 1902), 64; *The Philippine Situation: Testimony and Statements of Witnesses, American and Foreign* (Washington, D.C.: U.S. Government Printing Office, 1902), 22; Kramer, *Blood of Government,* 116–124.

22. Storey and Codman, *Secretary Root's Record,* 55–59, 65, 67; *Washington Times,* May 11, 1902. On Filipino auxiliaries, see Dennis Edward Flake, *Loyal Macabebes: How the Americans Used the Macabebe Scouts in the Annexation of the Philippines* (Angeles City, Philippines: Juan D. Nepomuceno Center for Kapampangan Studies, Holy Angel University, 2009), 33–84; Kramer, *Blood of Government,* 113–114; Clayton Laurie, "The Philippine Scouts: America's Colonial Army, 1899–1913," *Philippine Studies* 37 (Second Quarter 1989): 174–185; Linn, *U.S. Army and Counterinsurgency,* 44–45, 81, 83, 128–129, 203, 260.

23. U.S. Congress, Committee on the Philippines, *Affairs in the Philippine Islands: Hearings before the Committee on the Philippines,* Part 2 (Washington, D.C.: U.S. Government Printing Office, 1902), 1609.

24. U.S. Congress, *Affairs in the Philippine Islands,* Part 2, 1572; Storey and Codman, *Secretary Root's Record,* 68, 71, 75, 76.

25. *San Francisco Call,* September 30, 1901: 1; Storey and Codman, *Secretary Root's Record,* 28, 73; *American Occupation of the Philippines: Historical Record from the Date of the Capitulation of Manila to Admiral Dewey and the United States Navy* 19 (1904), 109.

26. Quoted in Linn, *Philippine War,* 211; Linn, *U.S. Army and Counterinsurgency,* 23. See also Anne Paulet, "The Only Good Indian Is a Dead Indian: The Use of United States Indian Policy as a Guide for the Conquest and Occupation of the Philippines, 1898–1905" (Ph.D. diss., Rutgers University, 1995).

27. Brian McAllister Linn, "The Long Twilight of the Frontier Army," *Western Historical Quarterly* 27 (Summer 1996): 159.

28. U.S. Congress, *Affairs in the Philippine Islands*, Part 2, 1572; David L. Fritz, "Before the 'Howling Wilderness': The Military Career of Jacob Hurd Smith, 1862–1902," *Military Affairs* 43 (December 1979): 187–188.

29. Quoted in *Hartford Courant*, April 18, 1902, 9.

30. Linn, *Philippine War*, 210–216; John Fabian Witt, *Lincoln's Code: The Laws of War in American History* (New York: Free Press, 2012).

31. Storey and Codman, *Secretary Root's Record*, 38; *Reports of Lieutenant-General Nelson A. Miles* (Boston: Anti-Imperialist League, 1909), 6.

32. Storey and Codman, *Secretary Root's Record*, 10, 15, 19, 38; *Boston Transcript*, March 10, 1902.

33. Linn, *Philippine War*, 222; Mojares, *War against the Americans*, 140–141; Storey and Codman, *Secretary Root's Record*, 25.

34. Storey and Codman, *Secretary Root's Record*, 46.

35. U.S. Congress, *Affairs in the Philippines*, Part 2, 1766–1767. Wire services carried summaries of Flint's testimony, and it was published coast to coast; for one example, see *Akron (Ohio) Daily Democrat*, April 21, 1902, 1.

36. *New York Evening Post*, April 8, 1902.

37. *Omaha World-Herald*, May 13, 1900.

38. *Annual Reports of the War Department*, 1901 (Washington, D.C.: U.S. Government Printing Office, 1902), IV:93094, 251–252.

39. Linn, *Philippine War*, 173–174.

40. Charles J. Crane, "Paragraphs 93, 97, and 88, of General Orders 100," *Journal of the Military Services Institution* 32 (March–April 1903), 254.

41. Funston, *Memories of Two Wars*, 333.

42. Quoted in Linn, *Philippine War*, 212.

43. "Certain Information Regarding the Issuance of Certain Orders in the Philippines," 57th Congress, 1st Session (1902), Senate Document 347.

44. *New York Sun*, March 10, 1902.

45. *San Francisco Call*, November 14, 1902, 2.

46. U.S. Congress, *Affairs in the Philippines*, Part 1, 559.

47. *Congressional Record*, 56th Congress, 1st Session (1899): 704–712.

48. Tisa J. Wenger, *Religious Freedom: The Contested History of an American Ideal* (Chapel Hill: The University of North Carolina Press, 2017), 54–99.

49. *Philadelphia Ledger*, November 11, 1900; Frederick Palmer, "White Man and Brown Man in the Philippines," *Scribner's Magazine* 27 (January 1900): 81.

50. Willard B. Gatewood, *"Smoked Yankees" and the Struggle for Empire: Letters from Negro Soldiers, 1898–1902* (Urbana: University of Illinois Press, 1971), 243, 280; Kramer, *Blood of Government*, 128–130, 139–144.

51. U.S. Congress, *Affairs in the Philippines*, Part 2, 950.

52. U.S. Adjutant-General's Office, *Correspondence Relating to the War with Spain, 1898–1902* (Washington, D.C.: U.S. Government Printing Office, 1902), 1329.

53. *Congressional Record*, 57th Congress, 1st Session (1902), 950.

54. *Atlanta Constitution*, April 25, 1902, 2.

55. Donald W. Disbrow, "Herbert Welsh, Editor of City and State, 1895–1904," *Pennsylvania Magazine of History and Biography* 94 (January 1970): 62–74;

William T. Hagan, *The Indian Rights Association: The Herbert Welsh Years, 1882–1904* (Tucson: University of Arizona Press, 1985), 1–19.

56. Hagan, *Indian Rights Association*, 65–189.

57. Michael Patrick Cullinane, *Liberty and American Anti-imperialism, 1898–1909* (New York: Palgrave Macmillan, 2012), 116–117; Fabian Hilfrich, *Debating American Exceptionalism: Empire and Democracy in the Wake of the Spanish-American War* (New York: Palgrave Macmillan, 2012), 101–102; E. Berkeley Tompkins, *Anti-imperialism in the United States: The Great Debate, 1890–1920* (Philadelphia: University of Pennsylvania Press, 1970), 140–160.

58. The best collective portrait of the anti-imperialists remains Robert L. Beisner, *Twelve against Empire: The Anti-imperialists, 1898–1900* (New York: McGraw-Hill, 1968).

59. *Army and Navy Journal*, quoted in *City and State*, April 24, 1902, 266.

60. Carl Schurz to William McKinley, May 9, 1898, in *Speeches, Correspondence and Political Papers of Carl Schurz*, ed. Frederic Bancroft (New York: G. P. Putnam's Sons, 1913), 5:465–466.

61. *City and State*, August 4, 1898, 70–71; see also Hilfrich, *Debating American Exceptionalism*, 168–171.

62. *City and State*, February 23, 1899, 125.

63. *City and State*, March 1, 1900, 135; see also Cullinane, *Liberty and American Anti-imperialism*, 51–74.

64. Cullinane, *Liberty and American Anti-imperialism*, 93–114; James Edward Kerr, *The Insular Cases: The Role of the Judiciary in American Expansionism* (Port Washington, N.Y.: Kennikat Press, 1982); Lanny Thompson, *Imperial Archipelago: Representation and Rule in the Insular Territories under U.S. Dominion after 1898* (Honolulu: University of Hawai'i Press, 2010).

65. *City and State*, May 29, 1902, 341.

66. *City and State*, August 31, 1899, 134; November 23, 1899, 330; January 4, 1900, 9. On slavery in the Philippines, see Michael Salman, *The Embarrassment of Slavery: Controversies over Bondage and Nationalism in the American Colonial Philippines* (Berkeley: University of California Press, 2001), esp. 71–121.

67. *City and State*, July 11, 1901, 24.

68. *City and State*, December 1, 1898, 345; February 5, 1899, 74–75. See also Hilfrich, *Debating American Exceptionalism*, 31–34.

69. Quoted in *Springfield Republican*, January 26, 1902. See also Hilfrich, *Debating American Exceptionalism*, 168–171.

70. *City and State*, November 24, 1898, 323.

71. *City and State*, September 15, 1898, 165.

72. *City and State*, April 13, 1899, 244.

73. *City and State*, February 27, 1902. Bolton Hall, et al., "Why I Oppose Imperialism: A Symposium," *Arena*, 28 (July 1902): 6; Stuart Creighton Miller, *"Benevolent Assimilation": The American Conquest of the Philippines, 1899–1903* (New Haven, Conn.: Yale University Press, 1982), 82–87, 164–166; Hilfrich, *Debating American Exceptionalism*, 178–179.

74. *City and State*, June 22, 1899, 403; July 20, 1899, 35; July 27, 1899, 53–55; September 21, 1899, 183–184; July 5, 1900, 5.

75. *City and State*, April 17, 1902, 248.

76. *City and State*, February 13, 1902, 103.

77. *City and State*, November 30, 1899, 346.

78. *City and State*, April 20, 1899, 261; May 4, 1899, 292–293.

79. George Kennan, "The Philippines: Present Conditions and Possible Courses," *Outlook* 67 (1901): 576–584.

80. Quoted in *City and State*, November 19, 1900.

81. *Congressional Record*, 57th Congress, 1st Session (1901), 597, 649–651; Cullinane, *Liberty and American Anti-imperialism*, 124–125; Miller, *Benevolent Assimilation*, 212.

82. *City and State*, April 10, 1902, 230.

83. Box 82, Folders 1–10, Herbert Welsh collection (Collection 702), The Historical Society of Pennsylvania, Philadelphia, PA.

84. New accounts of Taft's testimony; Gregg R. Jones, *Honor in the Dust: Theodore Roosevelt, War in the Philippines, and the Rise and Fall of America's Imperial Dream* (New York: New American Library, 2012), 272–273.

85. Riley's testimony was republished in newspapers across the country; for examples, see *Philadelphia Times*, April 15, 1902, 1; *Washington Evening Times*, April 14, 1902, 1; *Des Moines (Iowa) Leader*, April 15, 1902, 1.

86. For a sampling of denials by soldiers and politicos, see *Baltimore Sun*, February 22, 1902; *Detroit Free Press*, February 22, 1902; *Nashville Tennessean*, March 6, 1902; *New Orleans Times-Democrat*, March 12, 1902; *Fort Wayne (Ind.) News*, June 25, 1902; *Indianapolis Journal*, April 23, 1902; *Washington Times*, May 16, 1902; *Atlanta Constitution*, June 4, 1902; *Washington Evening Star*, June 6, 1902. See also Kramer, *Blood of Government*, 146–151.

87. Cullinane, *Liberty and American Anti-imperialism*, 129–130; Jones, *Honor in the Dust*, 274–275, 296–304.

88. Court-martial of Edwin F. Glenn, #30755, Record Group 153, National Archives, Washington, D.C. Valuable contemporary news accounts include *Washington Times*, April 18, 1902; *San Francisco Chronicle*, May 2, 1902; and *Indianapolis Journal*, July 24, 1902. See also Einolf, *America in the Philippines*, 159–168; and Witt, *Lincoln's Code*, 327–365. For an extended analysis of the court-martial testimony, see Louise Barnett, *Atrocity and American Military Justice in Southeast Asia* (New York: Routledge, 2010), 9–120.

89. Court-martial of First Lieutenant Julien E. Gaujot, 10th Cavalry, #30756, Record Group 153, National Archives, Washington, D.C.

90. Court-martial of James A. Ryan, #31443, Record Group 153, National Archives, Washington, D.C.; *Washington Evening Times*, May 8, 1902; *Boston Post*, July 7, 1902; *Topeka (Kans.) Daily Capital*, July 12, 1902; *Oakland (Calif.) Tribune*, July 18, 1902; James A. Ryan, "The Defense of Captain J. A. Ryan, Fifteenth U.S. Cavalry," *Journal of the United States Cavalry Association* 15 (1902): 185–193.

91. On the Samar campaigns, see Linn, *Philippine War*, 306–321; Miller, *Benevolent Assimilation*, 219–252; and Joseph L. Schott, *The Ordeal of Samar* (Indianapolis: Bobbs-Merrill, 1964), 59–150.

92. Jones, *Honor in the Dust*, 344–350; Kramer, *Blood of Government*, 154–157.

93. James R. Arnold, *The Moro War: How America Battled a Muslim Insurgency in the Philippine Jungle, 1902–1913* (New York: Bloomsbury Press, 2011).

94. Mojares, *War against the Americans*, 173; Thomas Reppetto, *American Police: The Blue Parade, 1845–1945* (New York: Enigma Press, 2011), 129–131.

95. Jeremy Kuzmarov, *Modernizing Repression: Police Training and Nation Building in the American Century* (Amherst: University of Massachusetts Press, 2012), 21–36; Alfred W. McCoy, *Policing America's Empire: The United States, the Philippines, and the Rise of the Surveillance State* (Madison: University of Wisconsin Press, 2009), 59–268.

96. *City and State*, March 5, 1903, 186–189.

97. The murder of Father Augustine had previously received periodic coverage; see *Atlanta Constitution*, April 24, 1902; *Minneapolis Journal*, November 8, 1902; and *New York Tribune*, November 20, 1902.

98. Quoted in *City and State*, April 9, 1903, 4. Arnold, *Moro War*.

99. Cullinane, *Liberty and American Anti-imperialism*, 149–176; Hagan, *Indian Rights Association*, 228–254.

100. *Brooklyn Daily Eagle*, June 10, 1902.

101. War Department, Office of the Chief of Staff, *Rules of Land Warfare* (Washington D. C.: Government Printing Office, 1914).

102. Harold H. Utley, "An Introduction to the Tactics and Technique of Small Wars," *Marine Corps Gazette* 15 (May 1931): 50–54.

103. Michael Cullinane, *Ilustrado Politics: Filipino Elite Responses to American Rule, 1898–1908* (Quezon City: Ateneo de Manila University Press, 2003), 49–72, 102–111, 274–303; Paul D. Hutchcroft, "Colonial Masters, National Politicos, and Provincial Lords: Central Authority and Local Autonomy in the American Philippines, 1900–1913," *Journal of Asian Studies* 59 (May 2000): 284–294.

6. POLICE STATION TRESPASSES

1. *Buffalo (N.Y.) Commercial*, September 5, 1901, 1.

2. *Minneapolis Journal*, September 12, 1901, 3.

3. Sidney Fine, "Anarchism and the Assassination of McKinley," *American Historical Review* 60 (July 1955): 781–783.

4. The wire services carried several accounts of Czolgosz's torture; *Rochester (N.Y.) Democrat and Chronicle*, September 10, 1901, 1; *Honolulu Hawaiian Star*, September 19, 1901, 1; *Winston-Salem (N.C.) Union Republican*, September 26, 1901, 1. His torture is mentioned in Emma Goldman, *Living My Life* (New York: Cosimo, 2011), 316. See also Eric Rauchway, *Murdering McKinley: The Making of Theodore Roosevelt's America* (New York: Hill and Wang, 2003), 29–30, 217.

5. *Chicago Daily Tribune*, August 15, 1902, 12. See also *Washington Post*, February 5, 1901, 4; and *Chicago Inter-Ocean*, March 9, 1902, 8.

6. For the early history of American police, see Bruce Chadwick, *Law and Disorder: The Chaotic Birth of the NYPD* (New York: St. Martin's Press, 2017); Sam Mitrani, *The Rise of the Chicago Police Department: Class and Conflict, 1850–1894* (Urbana: University of Illinois Press, 2013); Thomas Reppetto, *American Police: The Blue Parade, 1845–1945* (New

York: Enigma Books, 2011), 40–223; and Allen Steinberg, *The Transformation of Criminal Justice, Philadelphia, 1800–1880* (Chapel Hill: University of North Carolina Press, 1989), 117–196.

7. Jeffrey S. Adler, "Shoot to Kill: The Use of Deadly Force by the Chicago Police, 1875–1920," *Journal of Interdisciplinary History* 38 (Autumn 2007): 238, 250; Jeffrey S. Adler, "'The Killer behind the Badge': Race and Police Homicide in New Orleans, 1925–1945," *Law and History Review* 30 (May 2012): 498, 504; Mark H. Haller, "Historical Roots of Police Behavior: Chicago, 1890–1925," *Law and History Review* 10 (Winter 1976): 303–323; Marilynn S. Johnson, *Street Justice: A History of Police Violence in New York City* (Boston: Beacon Press, 2003): 12–56; Dennis C, Rousey, *Policing the Southern City: New Orleans, 1805–1889* (Baton Rouge: Louisiana University Press, 1996): 80–90, 174; Marcy S. Sacks, "'To Show Who Was in Charge': Police Repression of New York City's Black Population at the Turn of the Twentieth Century," *Journal of Urban History* 31 (September 2005): esp. 805–806; Christopher Thale, "The Informal World of Police Patrol: New York City in the Early Twentieth Century," *Journal of Urban History* 33 (January 2007): 184.

8. Paul O'Hara, *Inventing the Pinkertons; or, Spies, Sleuths, Mercenaries, and Thugs: Being a Story of the Nation's Most Famous (and Infamous) Detective Agency* (Baltimore: Johns Hopkins University Press, 2016), 71–90.

9. Adler, "Shoot to Kill," 251; Lawrence Friedman, *Crime and Punishment in American History* (New York: Basic Books, 1993), 108; Richard A. Leo, *Police Interrogation and American Justice* (Cambridge, Mass.: Harvard University Press, 2008), 66–69; Steven Penney, "Theories of Confession Admissibility: A Historical View," *American Journal of Criminal Law* 25 (Spring 1998): 323–325; Samuel Walker, *Popular Justice: A History of American Criminal Justice* (New York: Oxford University Press, 1980).

10. Steinberg, *Transformation of Criminal Justice*, 117–150.

11. George Fisher, "Plea Bargaining's Triumph," *Yale Law Journal* 109 (March 2000): 893–935; Robert A. Kagan, *Adversarial Legalism: The American Way of Law* (Cambridge, Mass.: Harvard University Press, 2001), 83–95; John H. Langbein, "Torture and Plea Bargaining," *University of Chicago Law Review* 46 (January 1978): 2–22; and Leo, *Police Interrogation*, 29–33.

12. Lucian E. Dervan and Vanessa A. Edkins, "The Innocent Defendant's Dilemma: An Innovative Empirical Study of Plea Bargaining's Innocence Problem," *Journal of Criminal Law and Criminology 103*, no. 1 (Winter 2013): 7; Fisher, "Plea Bargaining's Triumph," 984–1063; Raymond Moley, "The Vanishing Jury," *Southern California Law Review* 2 (1928): 97, 105; Jay Wishingrad, "The Plea Bargain in Historical Perspective," *Buffalo Law Review* 23 (Winter 1974): 499.

13. Nigel McCrery, *Silent Witnesses: The Often Gruesome but Always Fascinating History of Forensic Science* (Chicago: Chicago Review Press, 2014); Reppetto, *American Police*, 43, 242–248.

14. *New York Times*, August 5, 1907, 6.

15. Oswald Garrison Villard, "Official Lawlessness: The Third Degree and the Crime Wave," *Harper's Magazine* 155 (October 1, 1927): 607; Leo, *Police Interrogation*, 58.

16. George Walling, *Recollections of a New York Chief of Police* (New York: Caxton Book Concern, 1887), 189–190.

17. *New York Times*, October 6, 1901.

18. *Chicago Tribune*, December 18, 1910, 2.

19. "Voluntary Confessions," *Michigan Law Review* 2 (February 1904): 401–402; "The 'Third Degree'—Its Origins and History," *Bench and Bar* 18 (July 1909): 9–15; "The 'Third Degree' in Its Constitutional Aspects," *National Corporation Lawyer* 38 (July 22, 1909): 789; *Wilkes Barre Record*, February 10, 1910, 14; *Cincinnati Enquirer*, May 20, 1910, 1; *Chicago Inter-Ocean*, March 16, 1911, 12; *Washington Post*, June 30, 1915, 6.

20. *Washington Post*, April 19, 1905, 6.

21. *Rochester (N.Y.) Democrat and Chronicle*, May 21, 1908, 6. For similar coerced confessions, see *Brooklyn Daily Eagle*, January 31, 1887, 2; *Springfield (Mo.) Leader Democrat*, June 24, 1898, 1; *Baltimore Sun*, June 30, 1906, 8; *Los Angeles Times*, May 25, 1907, 3; *St. Louis Post-Dispatch*, February 4, 1909, 1; *Oakland Tribune*, February 23, 1909, 3; *New Castle (Pa.) Herald*, September 18, 1909, 1; and *Binghamton (N.Y.) Press and Sun-Bulletin*, November 15, 1910, 6. On premodern ideas about involuntary physical manifestations of guilt, see Geoffrey C. Bunn, *The Truth Machine: A Social History of the Lie Detector* (Baltimore: Johns Hopkins University Press, 2012), 7–9.

22. *New York Times*, October 6 1901, SM 12; British readers received a historical survey of the American practice of the third degree in the *London Spectator*, July 10, 1909, 47–48.

23. *Louisville Courier-Journal*, October 6, 1889, 20; *Atlanta Constitution*, September 29, 1894, 2. On Byrnes, see also *New York Times*, February 4, 1887, 8; May 31, 1895, 9; *Chicago Daily Inter-Ocean*, September 23, 1889, 4; *Baltimore Sun*, May 8, 1901, 11; Frank Marshall White, "Inspector Byrnes and the Third Degree," *Harper's Weekly* 54 (June 18, 1910): 16–17; "Thomas Byrnes and the 'Third Degree,'" *Bench and Bar* 2 (June 1910): 91–93; Daniel J. Czitrom, *New York Exposed: The Gilded Age Police Scandal That Launched the Progressive Era* (New York: Oxford University Press, 2016), 36–44; Reppetto, *American Police*, 54–56.

24. *Chicago Tribune*, November 28, 1897, 3.

25. *Chicago Tribune*, February 18, 1906, 10.

26. For examples, see *Chicago Tribune*, August 15, 1902, 12; *Louisville Courier-Journal*, October 22, 1905, 3; *Washington Post*, March 12, 1906, 3; and *Baltimore Sun*, August 15, 1908, 14.

27. Ray L. Chesebro, "The Third Degree Illegal," *Lawyer and Banker* 4 (February 1911): 6.

28. Harry Eugene Kelly, "Third Degree Outrages," *Lawyer and Banker* 5 (October 1912): 301.

29. William T. Root, *A Psychological and Educational Survey of 1916 Prisoners in the Western Penitentiary of Pennsylvania* ([Pittsburgh]: Board of Trustees of the Western Penitentiary, 1927), 209.

30. National Commission on Law Observance and Enforcement, *Report on Lawlessness in Law Enforcement* (Washington, D.C.: Government Printing

Office, 1931), 158; for discussions of race and police torture, see *Chicago Defender*, March 29, 1924, 5; July 23, 1927, A2; February 2, 1929, A2.

31. *Tacoma (Wash.) Times*, November 3, 1909, 2; *Chicago Inter-Ocean*, November 10, 1912, 5, March 5, 1913, 16; *Great Falls (Mont.) Tribune*, January 26, 1914, 1; *Leavenworth (Kans.) Weekly Times*, July 8, 1915, 2; *Akron (Ohio) Beacon Journal*, August 10, 1921, 2.

32. *Chicago Tribune*, May 26, 1895, 7; March 4, 1913, 8; October 28, 1919, 1. For other examples, see *Allentown (Pa.) Leader*, July 3, 1897, 3; *Brooklyn (N.Y.) Daily Eagle*, February 19, 1902, 4; *New York Times*, May 31, 1904, 8; *Alexandria (Va.) Gazette*, August 12, 1904, 1; *Philadelphia Inquirer*, June 21, 1906; *Altoona (Pa.) Tribune*, February 3, 1909, 1; and *Fort Wayne (Ind.) Daily News*, September 8, 1913, 14.

33. *Louisville (Ky.) Courier Journal*, October 22, 1905, 3; *Washington Post*, March 12, 1906, 3.

34. *Baltimore Sun*, June 27, 1910, 5.

35. William F. Baker, "The Sweating or Third Degree System," *Annals of the American Academy of Political and Social Science* 36 (July 1910): 9. See also *Philadelphia Inquirer*, April 30, 1904, 1, for commentary mocking editorialist for exaggerating the severity of the third degree.

36. Richard Sylvester, "The Treatment of the Accused," *Annals of the American Academy of Political and Social Science* 36 (July 1910): 18.

37. Richard Sylvester, "A History of the 'Sweat Box' and 'the Third Degree,'" *Proceedings of the International Association of Chiefs of Police*, repr. in John Henry Wigmore, *The Principles of Judicial Proof* (Boston: Little, Brown, 1913), 551. See also *New York Times*, April 9, 1910.

38. *Chicago Tribune*, November 27, 1910, B4.

39. *Chicago Tribune*, December 6, 1896, 25.

40. *Chicago Tribune*, January 13, 1907, 5.

41. Baker, "Sweating or Third Degree System," 10.

42. Sylvester, "Treatment of the Accused," 16.

43. Arthur Train, *Courts, Criminals, and the Camorra* (New York: Charles Scribner's Sons, 1912), 22.

44. *Chicago Tribune*, April 13, 1919, 13.

45. *The Muncie (Ind.) Star Express*, June 14, 1913, 1.

46. Theodore A. Bingham, "The Treatment of the Accused and the Offender," *Annals of the American Academy of Political and Social Science* 36 (July 1910): 12. In 1887, one editor complained that the Texas Court of Appeals "seems to have been organized to overrule and reverse. At least, since its organization that has been its chief employment." "Overruled Their Judicial Superiors," *American Law Review* 21 (September–October 1887): 610.

47. Henry C. Spurr, "The Third Degree," *Case and Comment* 16 (May 1910): 370–374; Lewis Hochheimer, "The Third Degree—An Illegal Procedure," *Central Law Journal* 71 (July 1910): 24–26; Edwin R. Keedy, "'The Third Degree' and the Position of the Trial Judge in Illinois," *Illinois Law Review* 7 (December 1912): 303–310; Edwin R. Keedy, "The 'Third Degree' and Trial by Newspapers," *Journal of the American Institute of Criminal Law and Criminology* 3 (November 1912): 502–505; "Confessions," *California Law Review* 2

(March 1914): 241–243; Victor Rousseau, "Bargaining with Criminals," *Harper's Weekly* 53 (February 13, 1909): 13.

48. Bunn, *Truth Machine*, 7–51.

49. Elaine S. Abelson, *When Ladies Go A-thieving: Middle-Class Shoplifters in the Victorian Department Store* (New York: Oxford University Press, 1989); Edward J. Balleisen, *Fraud: An American History from Barnum to Madoff* (Princeton, N.J.: Princeton University Press, 2017), 107–244.

50. Page DuBois, *Torture and Truth* (New York: Routledge, 1991), especially 9–68.

51. James Q. Whitman, *The Origins of Reasonable Doubt: Theological Roots of the Criminal Trial* (New Haven, Conn.: Yale University Press, 2008). As Peter Brooks has pointed out, "Only when the culpable avow themselves as culpable, verbally assume their guilt, can there be purgation." See Brooks, *Troubling Confessions: Speaking Guilt in Law and Literature* (Chicago: University of Chicago Press, 2000), 155.

52. Jean Delumeau, *L'aveu et le pardon: Les difficultés de la confession XIII-XVIII siècle* (Paris: Fayard, 1990), 9.

53. Lisa Silverman, *Tortured Subjects: Pain, Truth, and the Body in Early Modern France* (Chicago: University of Chicago Press, 2001), 9.

54. Lynn Hunt, *Inventing Human Rights* (New York: Norton, 2007), 70–112; Edward Peters, *Torture* (Philadelphia: University of Pennsylvania Press, 1996), 74–141; Silverman, *Tortured Subjects*, 153–178.

55. Coleman L. Blease, "Duty and Responsibility of the Governor in Dealing with Prisoners," *Proceedings of the Eighth Meeting of the Governors of the States of the Union Held at Boston, Massachusetts August 24–27, 1915* (n.p.: National Governors' Conference, 1915), 161–162; *Wichita (Kans.) Daily Eagle*, August 28, 1915, 4; *Wilmington (N.C.) Dispatch*, September 13, 1915, 4.

56. W. Fitzhugh Brundage, *Lynching in the New South: Georgia and Virginia, 1880–1930* (Urbana: University of Illinois Press, 1993); Michael J. Pfeifer, *Rough Justice: Lynching and American Society, 1874–1947* (Urbana: University of Illinois Press, 2004); Ashraf H. Rushdy, *American Lynching* (New Haven, Conn.: Yale University Press, 2012); Stewart E. Tolnay and E. M. Beck, *A Festival of Violence: An Analysis of Southern Lynchings, 1882–1930* (Urbana: University of Illinois Press, 1995).

57. George C. Wright, *Racial Violence in Kentucky, 1865–1940: Lynchings, Mob Rule, and "Legal Lynchings"* (Baton Rouge: Louisiana State University Press, 1990), 251–305.

58. *Dade County (Ga.) Weekly Times*, March 16, 1888; *Wilmington (Del.) Evening Journal*, June 23, 1903, 1; *Wilmington (Del.) Morning News*, June 23, 1903, 1; Brundage, *Lynching in the New South*, 40–41.

59. Arthur F. Raper, *The Tragedy of Lynching* (Chapel Hill: University of North Carolina Press, 1933), 141–144. See also Brundage, *Lynching in the New South*, 36–45; David Garland, "Penal Excess and Surplus Meaning: Public Torture Lynchings in Twentieth-Century America," *Law and Society Review* 39 (December 2005): 793–834; and Grace Elizabeth Hale, *Making Whiteness: The Culture of Segregation in the South, 1890–1940* (New York: Pantheon Books, 1998), 199–240.

60. *New York Times*, July 20, 1902, 22.

61. *Jewish Exponent*, July 10, 1908, 4.

62. *Oshkosh (Wis.) Northwestern*, September 21, 1901, 4.

63. *Chicago Tribune*, August 19, 1902, 2. See also *Los Angeles Times*, November 8, 1909, 16.

64. *Washington Post*, November 26, 1911, E4. The *Fayetteville (N.C.) Weekly Observer*, September 23, 1909, 1, denounced "false confessions of guilt wrung from them by the thumb-screw or other instrument of torture ruthlessly applied by a dunderhead police official."

65. *Chicago Tribune*, December 6, 1896, 25; Hugh C. Weir, *The World To-day* 18 (February 1910): 171–178.

66. *Louisville Courier-Journal*, January 31, 1907, 4.

67. Charles Klein, *The Third Degree: A Play in Four Acts* (New York: S. French, 1908); Charles Klein and Arthur Hornblow, *The Third Degree: A Narrative of Metropolitan Life* (New York: Grosset and Dunlap, 1909). See also J. Sanderson Christison, *The Tragedy of Chicago—A Study in Hypnotism: How an Innocent Young Man Was Hypnotized to the Gallows, Denouncements by Savants* (Chicago: n.p., 1906); and *Washington Post*, December 27, 1906, 2. The Ivens case can be followed in the *Chicago Tribune*, January 15, 1906, 1; January 20, 1906, 3; January 31, 1906, 1; February 13, 1906, 1; February 23, 1906, 1; March 6, 1906, 3; March 7, 1906, 3; March 8, 1906, 2; March 9, 1906, 3; March 10, 1906, 2; March 11, 1906, 2; March 13, 1906, 6; March 17, 1906, 11; March 20, 1906, 5; March 21, 1906, 11; March 22, 1906, 7; March 23, 1906, 3; March 24, 1906, 3; March 25, 1906, 3; March 27, 1906, 1; March 28, 1906, 5; April 22, 1906, 8; June 21, 1906, 3; June 22, 1906, 1; June 23, 1906, 4. In 1912, prosecutors successfully countered a defendant's accusations of police misconduct by insisting that the third degree was an invention of Charles Klein's play; *Cincinnati Enquirer*, May 20, 1910, 1.

68. *Ammons v. State*, 80 Miss. 592, 595 (Miss. 1902); Christopher Waldrep, *Jury Discrimination: The Supreme Court, Public Opinion, and a Grassroots Fight for Racial Equality in Mississippi* (Athens: University of Georgia Press, 2010), 213–215.

69. *New York Times*, July 20, 1902, 22.

70. *Buffalo (N.Y.) Commercial*, August 6, 1908, 1; October 5, 1908, 7; October 6, 1908, 8. The 1903 episode is traced in *Rochester (N.Y.) Democrat and Chronicle*, March 8, 1903, 6; *St. Louis Post-Dispatch*, March 10, 1903, 16; and *Baltimore Sun*, March 14, 1903, 4.

71. *New York Times*, July 6, 1902, 23; July 20, 1902, 22; *Annual Report of the Colorado Bar Association*, 15 (1912): 93–99; *Baltimore Sun*, December 13, 1911, 14.

72. *St. Louis Post-Dispatch*, August 17, 1913, 10; *Wilmington (N.C.) Morning Star*, September 3, 1913, 1.

73. *Chicago Tribune*, September 28, 1895, 3; *Baltimore Sun*, February 2, 1907, 12; *San Juan (Wash.) Islander*, December 31, 1909, 3; *Chicago Tribune*, December 18, 1910, 2; *Wichita (Kans.) Daily Eagle*, January 23, 1921, 1.

74. *Pittsburgh Daily Post*, September 4, 1908, 5; *Chicago Tribune*, November 28, 1918, 17.

75. Fisher, "Plea Bargaining's Triumph," 989–1000.

76. The evolution of juridical review of confessions can be traced in Paul G. Kauper, "Juridical Examination of the Accused: A Remedy for the Third Degree," *Michigan Law Review* 73 (November 1974): 39–70; Richard Leo, "From Coercion to Deception: The Changing Nature of Police Interrogation in America," *Crime, Law, and Social Change* 18 (September 1992): 35–60; and Penney, "Theories of Confession Admissibility."

77. *Kentucky Statutes* (Louisville: Courier-Journal Job Printing, 1915), 296; *Louisville (Ky.) Courier Journal*, April 27, 1913, A6; *Nashville Tennessean*, December 28, 1917, 8.

78. *Senate Report No. 128*, 62nd Congress, 1st Session, 2; *Los Angeles Times*, April 26, 1910, 14; *Sheboygan Daily Press*, June 27, 1910, 7; *Nashville Tennessean*, July 2, 1910, 10; *Reno Gazette-Journal*, November 23, 1910, 3. For ineffective attempts to ban the third degree, see *Philadelphia Inquirer*, September 29, 1908, 1, 5; *Rolla (Mo.) Sharp Shooter*, February 26, 1909, 2; *Indianapolis Star*, January 10, 1911, 6; *San Juan (Wash.) Islander*, January 13, 1911, 3; *Philadelphia Inquirer*, June 30, 1911, 2; *Oakland (Calif.) Tribune*, April 17, 1915, 8; March 7, 1917, 5; and *Cincinnati Enquirer*, August 22, 1915, 24.

79. *Chicago Tribune*, May 5, 1910, 10.

80. *Official Records of the National Commission on Law Observance and Enforcement* (Washington, D.C.: U.S. Government Printing Office, 1931), 5:201.

81. *Bulletin of the Chicago Crime Commission* 6 (October 1, 1919): 1.

82. Fredrick Law Allen, *Only Yesterday* (New York: Harper and Row, 1931), 82. The best modern study of Prohibition is Lisa McGirr, *The War on Alcohol: Prohibition and the Rise of the American State* (New York: W. W. Norton, 2016).

83. John Kobler, *Ardent Spirits: The Rise and Fall of Prohibition* (New York: G. P. Putnam's Sons, 1973), 248.

84. John F. Padgett, "Plea Bargaining and Prohibition in Federal Courts, 1908–1934," *Law and Society Review* 24 (1990): 413–450.

85. McGirr, *War on Alcohol*, esp. 121–156.

86. "What Prohibition Has Done: Two Viewpoints," *New York Times*, January 27, 1929, section 10, 4.

87. David M. Rabban, *Free Speech in Its Forgotten Years* (New York: Cambridge University Press, 1997), 248–380.

88. *New York Times*, January 17, 1929, 1; Gardner Jackson, "Wickersham and His Commission," *Nation* 132 (January 21, 1931): 64.

89. Herbert Hoover, "President's News Conference of March 8, 1929," *Public Papers of the Presidents of the United States, Herbert Hoover, 1929* (Washington D. C.: U.S. Government Printing Office, 1929): 17. Hoover's innovations in federal crime policy are charted in James D. Calder, *The Origins and Development of Federal Crime Control Policy: Herbert Hoover's Initiatives* (Westport, Conn.: Greenwood, 1993).

90. Hoover, *Public Papers*, 159–160.

91. *Chicago Tribune*, August 12, 1928, 6; Hoover, *Public Papers*, 511.

92. The best extant histories of the commission are Calder, *Origins and Development of Federal Crime Control Policy*, 77–102; and Deok-Ho Kim, "A House Divided: The Wickersham Commission and National Prohibition" (Ph.D. diss., State University of New York at Stony Brook, 1992), 104–221.

93. Wickersham to Felix Frankfurter, June 4, 1929, Felix Frankfurter Papers, Library of Congress, Reel 48.

94. Zechariah Chafee, *Free Speech* (New York: Harcourt, Brace and Howe, 1920). For Chafee's evolution into a civil libertarian, see Donald L. Smith, *Zechariah Chafee, Jr., Defender of Liberty and Law* (Cambridge, Mass.: Harvard University Press, 1986), 58–115.

95. Boxes 114–119, Record Group 10, National Commission on Law Observance and Enforcement, National Archives, College Park, MD.

96. National Commission on Law Observance and Enforcement, *Report on the Enforcement of the Prohibition Laws of the United States* (Washington, D.C.: U.S. Government Printing Office, 1931).

97. For assessments of the commission's significance, see Calder, *Origins and Development of Federal Crime Control Policy*, 95–102; and McGirr, *War on Alcohol*, 225–229.

98. Zechariah Chafee Jr., Walter H. Pollak, and Carl S. Stern, *The Third Degree: Report to the National Commission on Law Observance and Enforcement* (Washington, D.C.: U.S. Government Printing Office, 1931), 191.

99. *Baltimore Sun*, August 26, 1931, 10; August 28, 1931, 2; *Washington Post*, August 27, 1931, 2; September 5, 1931, 6; September 18, 1931, 1; November 20, 1931, 1; November 26, 1931, 1; *New York Times*, September 6, 1931, 2.

100. *Washington Post*, December 26, 1931, 16; see also *Washington Post*, October 26, 1931, 16.

101. *New York Times*, August 11, 1931, 12; August 19, 1931, 44; *Scranton (Pa.) Republican*, August 11, 1931, 2; *Chicago Tribune*, August 11, 1931, 13.

102. Zechariah Chafee Jr., "Remedies for the Third Degree," *Atlantic Monthly* 148 (1931): 621–630.

103. *New York Times*, April 15, 1937, 3; April 16, 1937, 11.

104. Emanuel Henry Lavine, *The Third Degree: A Detailed and Appalling Exposé of Police Brutality* (New York: Vanguard Press, 1930); Ernest Jerome Hopkins, *Our Lawless Police: A Study of the Unlawful Enforcement of the Law* (New York: Viking Press, 1931); Cornelius Willemse, *Behind the Green Lights* (New York: Garden City Publishing, 1931); Cornelius Willemse, *A Cop Remembers* (New York: E. P. Dutton: 1933).

105. Claire Bond Potter, *War on Crime: Bandits, G-Men, and the Politics of Mass Culture* (New Brunswick, N.J.: Rutgers University Press, 1998).

106. *Dunkirk (N.Y.) Evening Observer*, July 22, 1932, 1; *Dixon (Ill.) Evening Telegraph*, July 25, 1932, 1; *Brooklyn Daily Eagle*, July 28, 1932, 5; September 10, 1932, 4; *Alton (Ill.) Evening Telegraph*, August 29, 1932, 1; *Baltimore Sun*, August 30, 1932, 8; *Albuquerque Journal*, September 13, 1932, 1.

107. Gene E. Carte and Elaine H. Carte, *Police Reform in the United States: The Era of August Vollmer, 1905–1932* (Berkeley: University of California Press, 1975); Samuel Walker, *A Critical History of Police Reform: The Emergence of Professionalism* (Lexington, Mass.: Lexington Books, 1977); Bunn, *Truth Machine*, 134–173. On the FBI's promotion of "professionalism," see Matthew Cecil, *Hoover's FBI and the Fourth Estate: The Campaign to Control the Press and the Bureau's Image* (Lawrence: University Press

of Kansas, 2014), 12–100; and Matthew Cecil, *Branding Hoover's FBI: How the Boss's PR Men Sold the Bureau to America* (Lawrence: University Press of Kansas, 2016), esp. 12–73.

108. Penney, "Theories of Confession Admissibility."

109. Dan T. Carter, *Scottsboro: A Tragedy of the American South* (Baton Rouge: Louisiana State University Press, 1969), 160–165.

110. Curt Gentry, *Frame-up; The Incredible Case of Tom Mooney and Warren Billings* (New York: Norton, 1967).

111. Richard C. Cortner, *A "Scottsboro" Case in Mississippi: The Supreme Court and Brown v. Mississippi* (Jackson: University Press of Mississippi, 1986).

112. *Brown v. Mississippi*, 297 U.S. 278 (1936).

113. *Rochin v. California* 342 U.S. 165 (1952).

114. *Miranda v. Arizona*, 384 U.S. 436 (1966).

115. On the early activities of the ACLU, see Robert C. Cottrell, *Roger Nash Baldwin and the Civil Liberties Union* (New York: Columbia University Press, 2000), 218; Samuel Walker, *In Defense of American Liberties: A History of the ACLU*, 2nd ed. (Carbondale: Southern Illinois University Press, 1999), 87–88; and Donald Johnson, "American Civil Liberties Union: Origins, 1914–1924" (Ph.D. diss., Columbia University, 1960).

116. For one of the few accounts of the NAACP's campaign against police brutality before World War II, see Silvan Niedermeir, "Torture and 'Modern Civilization': The NAACP's Fight against Forced Confessions in the American South (1935–1945)," in *Fractured Modernity: America Confronts Modern Times, 1890s to 1940s*, ed. Thomas Welskopp and Alan Lessof (Munich: Oldenbourg Verlag, 2012): 169–189.

117. Stephen Rushin, *Federal Intervention in American Police Departments* (New York: Cambridge University Press, 2017), 9–14.

118. 29 Ill. 2d 97 (1963), 193 N.E. 2d 814, *The People of the State of Illinois, Appellee, v. Roosevelt Scott, Appellant.* No. 36492–3.

119. Simon E. Balto, *Occupied Territory: Policing Black Chicago from Red Summer to Black Power* (Chapel Hill: University of North Carolina Press, 2019), 119–120.

7. COLD WAR BRUTALITY

1. *Life* (May 14, 1951).

2. *New York Times*, June 9, 1951, 6; Robert A. Vogeler, *I Was Stalin's Prisoner* (New York: Harcourt, Brace, 1952); Susan L. Carruthers, *Cold War Captives: Imprisonment, Escape, and Brainwashing* (Berkeley: University of California Press, 2009), 136–173.

3. James Doolittle, "The Report on the Covert Activities of the Central Intelligence Agency" (PDF), 3, https://www.cia.gov/library/readingroom/docs/doolittle_report.pdf, accessed October 2, 2017.

4. Paul Hagenloh, *Stalin's Police: Public Order and Mass Repression in the USSR, 1926–1941* (Washington, D.C.: Johns Hopkins University Press, 2009); Hiroaki Kuromiya, *The Voices of the Dead: Stalin's Great Terror in the 1930s* (New Haven, Conn.: Yale University Press, 2007).

5. *New York Times*, April 23, 1943; October 6, 1943; *Atlanta Constitution*, February 1, 1944; *Washington Post*, February 12, 1944; April 1, 1944; *Los Angeles Times*, April 28, 1945; *Chicago Tribune*, September 3, 1945.

6. John W. Dower, *War without Mercy: Race and Power in the Pacific War* (New York: Pantheon, 1986), 35, 69; Ulrich Straus, *The Anguish of Surrender: Japanese POWs of World War II* (Seattle: University of Washington Press, 2003), 116–117; James J. Weingartner, "Massacre at Biscari: Patton and an American War Crime," *Historian* 52 (1989): 24–39.

7. Among the many works on the massacre, the two best are Steven P. Remy, *The Malmedy Massacre: The War Crimes Trial Controversy* (Cambridge, Mass.: Harvard University Press, 2017); and James J. Weingartner, *Crossroads of Death: The Story of the Malmédy Massacre and Trial* (Berkeley: University of California Press, 1979).

8. Remy, *Malmedy Massacre*, 44–90; James J. Weingartner, *A Peculiar Crusade: Willis M. Everett and the Malmedy Massacre* (New York: New York University Press, 2000), 75–117.

9. Edward L. Van Roden, "American Atrocities in Germany," *Progressive* 13 (February 1949): 21–22; *Chicago Tribune*, March 26, 1949.

10. *Malmedy Massacre Investigation, Hearings before a Subcommittee of the Committee on Armed Services*, U.S. Senate, 81st Congress, 1st Session (Washington, D.C.: U.S. Government Printing Office, 1949), 11.

11. Remy, *Malmedy Massacre*, 230; David Oshinsky, *A Conspiracy So Immense: The World of Joe McCarthy* (New York: Free Press, 1983), 74–80.

12. *Time*, 55 (March 13, 1950): 30.

13. *Corpus Christi (Tex.) Caller-Times*, January 12, 1954, 2.

14. *Los Angeles Times*, October 23, 1952; *Chicago Tribune*, February 24, 1953; Edward Hunter, *Brain-Washing in Red China: The Calculated Destruction of Men's Minds* (New York: Vanguard, 1951); Carruthers, *Cold War Captives*, 174–216; Matthew W. Dunne, *A Cold War State of Mind: Brainwashing and Postwar American Society* (Amherst: University of Massachusetts Press, 2013), 81–115.

15. D. V. Gallery, "We Can Baffle the Brainwashers!" *Saturday Evening Post* 227 (January 22, 1955): 20; Harold H. Martin, "They Tried to Make Our Marines Love Stalin," *Saturday Evening Post* 224 (August 25, 1951): 106–110.

16. Quoted in Alfred W. McCoy, *Torture and Impunity: The U.S. Doctrine of Coercive Interrogation* (Madison: University of Wisconsin Press, 2012), 58.

17. *New York Times*, April 4, 1953; September 13, 1953, 13; *Washington Post*, December 16, 1953.

18. *Ogden (Utah) Standard Examiner*, March 29, 1953; Joost Abraham Meerloo, *The Rape of the Mind: The Psychology of Thought Control, Menticide, and Brainwashing* (Cleveland: World Publishing, 1956); William Sargeant, *Battle for the Mind: A Physiology of Conversion and Brainwashing* (London: Heinemann, 1957).

19. Peter Wyden, "Ordeal in the Desert: Making Tougher Soldiers to Resist Brainwashing," *Newsweek* (September 12, 1955): 33–35; Robert Genter, "Understanding the POW Experience: Stress Research and the Implementation of

the 1955 U.S. Armed Forces Code of Conduct," *Journal of the History of the Behavioral Sciences* 5 (Spring 2015): 154–159.

20. *San Rafael (Calif.) Daily Independent Journal,* September 8, 1955, 1.

21. *Wall Street Journal,* June 24, 1955; *New York Times,* July 10, 1955; *Atlanta Constitution,* July 14, 1955; Dunne, *Cold War State of Mind,* 97–115; Genter, "Understanding the POW Experience," 143–145.

22. Joint Chiefs of Staff, "Review of the Current World Situation and Ability of the Forces Being Maintained to Meet United States Commitments," *Foreign Relations of the United States, 1951* (Washington, D.C.: U.S. Government Printing Office, 1979), 1:74.

23. Ellen Herman, *The Romance of American Psychology: Political Culture in the Age of Experts* (Berkeley: University of California Press, 1995), 82–152; H. E. Page, "The Role of Psychology in the ONR," *American Psychologist* 9 (October 1954): 621–628; Christopher Simpson, *Science of Coercion: Communication Research and Psychological Warfare, 1945–1960* (New York: Oxford University Press, 1994), 31–63; Frank Summers, "Making Sense of the APA: A History of the Relationship between Psychology and the Military," *Psychoanalytic Dialogues* 18 (September–October 2008): 618–624.

24. Dwight D. Eisenhower, "Address at the Columbia University Bicentennial Dinner, New York City, May 31, 1954," *Public Papers of the Presidents of the United States: Dwight D. Eisenhower, 1954* (Washington D.C.: U.S. Government Printing Office, 1955), 518.

25. *Final Report of the Select Committee to Study Governmental Operations with Respect to Intelligence Activities,* Senate Report no. 94–755, 94th Congress, 2nd Session (Washington, D.C.: U.S. Government Printing Office, 1976), 1:393.

26. "Summary of Remarks by Mr. Allen W. Dulles at the National Alumni Conference of the Graduate Council of Princeton University, Hot Springs, Va., April 10, 1953," https://www.cia.gov/library/readingroom/document/cia-rdp80r01731r001700030015-9, accessed May 18, 2018.

27. Quoted in John Marks, *The Search for the "Manchurian Candidate"* (New York: Norton, 1979), 25.

28. Marks, *Search for the "Manchurian Candidate";* Gordon Thomas, *Journey into Madness: The True Story of Secret CIA Mind Control and Medical Abuse* (New York: Bantam Books, 1989).

29. Philip Solomon, Philip Kubzansky, P. Herbert Leiderman Jr., Jack H. Mendelson, Richard Trumbull, and Donald Wexler, eds., *Sensory Deprivation: A Symposium Held at Harvard Medical School* (Cambridge, Mass.: Harvard University Press, 1961), 6.

30. Alfred W. McCoy, *A Question of Torture: CIA Interrogation, from the Cold War to the War on Terror* (New York: Metropolitan Books / Henry Holt, 2006), 32–38.

31. Anne Collins, *In the Sleep Room: The Story of the CIA Brainwashing Experiments in Canada* (Toronto: Lester and Orpen Dennys, 1988); Harvey Weinstein, *Psychiatry and the CIA: Victims of Mind Control* (Washington, D.C.: American Psychiatric Press, 1990).

32. Stanley Milgram, *Obedience to Authority* (New York: Harper and Row, 1974), 189.

33. Milgram, *Obedience to Authority*, xii.

34. Thomas Blass, *The Man Who Shocked the World: The Life and Legacy of Stanley Milgram* (New York: Basic Books, 2004), 100.

35. Victor Marchetti and John Marks, *The CIA and the Cult of Intelligence* (New York: Knopf, 1974).

36. *Neosho (Mo.) Daily News*, September 15, 1955, 1.

37. *Tyrone (Pa.) Daily Herald*, September 12, 1955, 4.

38. *Petersburg (Va.) Progress-Index*, September 9, 1955, 4.

39. *Saturday Review*, September 24, 1955, 22.

40. *Bridgeport (Conn.) Telegram*, September 9, 1955.

41. *Hazleton (Pa.) Plain Speaker*, September 8, 1955, 2; *Washington Post*, September 9, 1955, 1; September 10, 1955, 18; September 14, 1955, 1.

42. *North Adams (Mass.) Transcript*, September 15, 1955, 6.

43. Rowland Brucken, *Most Uncertain Crusade: The United States, the United Nations, and Human Rights, 1941–1953* (DeKalb: Northern Illinois University Press, 2013).

44. Barbara J. Keys, *Reclaiming American Virtue: The Human Rights Revolution of the 1970s* (Cambridge, Mass.: Harvard University Press, 2014), 31.

45. Noam Chomsky, "The Responsibility of Intellectuals," *New York Review of Books*, February 23, 1967.

46. *U.S. Policy toward Asia: Hearings before the United States House Committee on Foreign Affairs*, Subcommittee on the Far East and the Pacific, 89th Congress, 2nd Session (Washington, D.C.: Government Printing Office, 1966).

47. Quoted in Ron Theodore Robin, *The Making of the Cold War Enemy: Culture and Politics in the Military-Intellectual Complex* (Princeton, N.J.: Princeton University Press, 2001), 186.

48. Lesley Gill, *The School of the Americas: Military Training and Political Violence in the Americas* (Durham, N.C.: Duke University Press, 2004), 59–89; Jeremy Kuzmarov, *Modernizing Repression: Police Training and Nation Building in the American Century* (Amherst: University of Massachusetts Press, 2012), esp. 52–152; Alfred W. McCoy, *Policing America's Empire: The United States, the Philippines, and the Rise of the Surveillance State* (Madison: University of Wisconsin Press, 2009), 372–396.

49. *KUBARK Counterintelligence Interrogation*, 90, accessed October 10, 2017, https://nsarchive2.gwu.edu/NSAEBB/NSAEBB122/index.htm#kubark.

50. Darius M. Rejali, *Torture and Democracy* (Princeton, N.J.: Princeton University Press, 2007), 427–429.

51. Edward Miller and Tuong Vu, "The Vietnam War as a Vietnamese War: Agency and Society in the Study of the Second Indochina War," *Journal of Vietnamese Studies*, 4 (Fall 2009): 1–16.

52. Bernd Greiner, *War without Fronts: The USA in Vietnam* (London: Bodley Head, 2009), 30.

53. Joshua Kyle Akers, "Straddling the Threshold of Two Worlds: The Culture of American Soldiers in the Vietnam War, 1965–1973" (Ph.D. Dissertation, University of North Carolina, 2018), 27–68.

54. Stuart I. Rochester and Frederick T. Kiley, *Honor Bound: The History of American Prisoners of War in Southeast Asia, 1961–1973* (Washington, D.C.: Historical Office, Office of the Secretary of Defense, 1998).

55. Quoted in Rochester and Kiley, *Honor Bound,* 12–13.

56. Donald Duncan, "The Whole Thing Was a Lie!" *Ramparts* (February 1966): 14.

57. James William Gibson, *The Perfect War: Technowar in Vietnam* (Boston: Atlantic Monthly Press, 1986), 183.

58. *Report of the Department of the Army Review of the Preliminary Investigations into the My Lai Incident* (Washington, D.C.: U.S. Government Printing Office, 1970), 1:12–29, 12–30, 12–31, accessed October 12, 2017, https://www.loc.gov/rr/frd/Military_Law/pdf/RDAR-Vol-I.pdf.

59. Rejali, *Torture and Democracy,* 172–173, 583.

60. Quoted in Nick Turse and Deborah Nelson, "Civilian Killings Went Unpunished," *Los Angeles Times,* August 6, 2006. See also Deborah Nelson, *The War behind Me: Vietnam Veterans Confront the Truth about U.S. War Crimes* (New York: Basic Books, 2008), esp. 51–71; and Nick Turse, *Kill Anything That Moves: The Real American War in Vietnam* (New York: Metropolitan Books / Henry Holt, 2013).

61. Greiner, *War without Fronts,* 100–101; Rejali, *Torture and Democracy,* 585.

62. Quoted in Turse and Nelson, "Civilian Killings."

63. Marchetti and Marks, *CIA and the Cult of Intelligence,* 206–207.

64. Rejali, *Torture and Democracy,* 170–172; Mark Moyar, *Phoenix and the Birds of Prey: The CIA's Secret Campaign to Destroy the Viet Cong* (Annapolis, Md.: Naval Institute Press, 1997), 90–99.

65. Moyar, *Phoenix and the Birds of Prey,* 90, 99.

66. Moyar, *Phoenix and the Birds of Prey,* 91.

67. Rhodri Jeffreys-Jones, *Peace Now! American Society and the Ending of the Vietnam War* (New Haven, Conn.: Yale University Press, 1999); Melvin Small, *Antiwarriors: The Vietnam War and the Battle for America's Hearts and Minds* (Wilmington, Del.: Scholarly Resources, 2002), 55–74.

68. *New York Times,* February 6, 1966; February 11, 1966; October 23, 1966.

69. Duncan, "Whole Thing Was a Lie," 24.

70. Chomsky, "Responsibility of Intellectuals."

71. Stuart C. Miller, "Our Mylai of 1900: Americans in the Philippine Insurrection," *Trans-Action* 7 (September 1970): 19.

72. Hanson W. Baldwin, *New York Times,* May 29, 1965; Jimmy Breslin, *New York Herald Tribune,* September 29, 1965; "Total, Bloody Mayhem," *New York Herald Tribune,* April 25, 1965; *New Republic,* October 9, 1965; Jack Langguth, *New York Times,* July 7, 1965; "The Best Torture," *Nation,* October 25, 1965; "A Big, Dirty Little War," *New York Times Magazine* (November 28, 1965); "The Cruel War," *London Sunday Mirror,* April 4, 1965; "Obey P.O.W. Code, U.S. Soldiers Told," *New York Times,* December 1, 1965.

73. Chomsky, "Responsibility of Intellectuals."

74. Don Duncan, *The New Legions* (New York: Random House, 1967).

75. Richard Stacewicz, *Winter Soldiers: An Oral History of the Vietnam Veterans against the War* (New York: Prentice Hall International, 1997); Michael Uhl,

Vietnam Awakening: My Journey from Combat to the Citizens' Commission of Inquiry on U.S. War Crimes in Vietnam (Jefferson, N.C.: McFarland, 2007), esp. 117–185.

76. Quoted in Greiner, *War without Fronts*, 241.

77. Quoted in Howard Jones, *My Lai: Vietnam, 1968, and the Descent into Darkness* (New York: Oxford University Press, 2017), 169.

78. Anthony B. Herbert Collection, ms. 3421, Hargrett Rare Book and Manuscript Library, University of Georgia Libraries, Box 10, Folders 1–15; Box 11, Folders 1–4; Box 13, Folders 10–19. Anthony B. Herbert and James T. Wooten, *Soldier* (New York: Holt, Rinehart and Winston, 1973).

79. Two especially good histories of My Lai are Jones, *My Lai*; and Kendrick Oliver, *The My Lai Massacre in American History and Memory* (Manchester, U.K.: Manchester University Press, 2006). On rape and the meaning of the massacre, see Gina Marie Weaver, *Ideologies of Forgetting: Rape in the Vietnam War* (Albany: State University of New York Press, 2010), esp. 72–77.

80. *New York Times*, November 27, 1969, 18.

81. *Time*, April 12, 1971, 15.

82. Herbert C. Kelman and Lee H. Lawrence, "Assignment of Responsibility in the Case of Lt. Calley: Preliminary Report on a National Survey," *Journal of Social Issues* 28 (January 1972): 199.

83. *Time* (January 12, 1970), 10–11.

84. George Gallup, *The Gallup Poll: Public Opinion, 1935–1971*, 3 vols. (New York: Random House, 1972), 3:2296; Kelman and Lawrence, "Assignment of Responsibility in the Case of Lt. Calley," 188, 193, 199.

85. Quoted in Oliver, *My Lai Massacre*, 67.

86. Jones, *My Lai*, 298–304; Oliver, *My Lai Massacre*, 89–96.

87. Ira Glasser, "Judgment at Fort Jackson: The Court-Martial of Howard B. Levy," *Law in Transition Quarterly* 4 (September 1967): 154, 155; Oliver, *My Lai Massacre*, 103.

88. McCoy, *Question of Torture*, 68.

89. Harold P. Ford, "William E. Colby as Director of Central Intelligence," Central Intelligence Agency, CIA History Staff, 1993 (declassified August 10, 2011), 63–159, accessed October 17, 2017, https://nsarchive2.gwu.edu/NSAEBB /NSAEBB362/index.htm; John Prados, *Lost Crusader: The Secret Wars of CIA Director William Colby* (New York: Oxford University Press, 2003), 297–339.

90. *New York Times*, April 4, 1971, 56.

8. THE ENEMY WITHIN

1. Stuart A. Herrington, *Stalking the Vietcong: Inside Operation Phoenix, A Personal Account* (New York: Presidio, 2012); Stuart A. Harrington, "Foreword," in Douglas A. Pryer, *The Fight for the High Ground: The US Army and Interrogation during Operation Iraqi Freedom, May 2003–April 2004* (Fort Leavenworth, Ks.: Command and General Staff College, 2009), xii–xx; "Inquiry into the Treatment of Detainees in U.S. Custody," *Report on Armed Services*, U.S. Senate, 110th Congress, 2nd Session (Washington, D.C.: Government Printing Office 2008); *Washington Post*, December 1, 2004, 216.

2. "Inquiry into the Treatment of Detainees in U.S. Custody," 217–219.

3. The OPS report is reproduced in Edward J. Egan and Robert D. Boyle, "Report of the Special State's Attorney Appointed and Ordered by the Presiding Judge of the Criminal Division of the Circuit Court of Cook County in No. 2001 Misc. 4" (2006), 107–111; John Conroy, *Unspeakable Acts, Ordinary People: The Dynamics of Torture* (New York: Random House, 2000), 83–84.

4. Eric Zorn, "Police Brutality Alleged," *Chicago Tribune,* October 2, 1997, 129.

5. *New York Times,* March 20, 1983.

6. Tom Morganthau et al., "Justice for Louima," *Newsweek* (June 7, 1999): 42.

7. Sarah Liebowitz, Peter Eliasberg, Margaret Winter, and Esther Lim, "Cruel and Usual Punishment: How a Savage Gang of Deputies Controls LA County Jails" (ACLU National Prison Project and the ACLU of Southern California, 2011); Victoria Kim, "Ex-Deputy Details Culture of Abuse in L.A. County Jail," *Los Angeles Times,* June 3, 2014; Ryan Fonseca, "Here's the Fallout from the LA County Sheriff's Department Jail Abuse Scandal," *Los Angeles Daily News,* August 28, 2017.

8. Ronald Reagan, "Message to the Senate Transmitting the Convention against Torture and Inhuman Treatment or Punishment, May 20, 1988," http://www.presidency.ucsb.edu/ws/?pid=35858, accessed January 30, 2018.

9. Deb Riechmann, "Bush Declares: 'We Do Not Torture,'" *Washington Post,* November 7, 2005.

10. Daniel J. Sargent, *A Superpower Transformed: The Remaking of American Foreign Relations in the 1970s* (New York: Oxford University Press, 2015), 201–209.

11. Rose Styron, "Torture," *New Republic,* December 8, 1973; Barbara J. Keys, *Reclaiming American Virtue: The Human Rights Revolution of the 1970s* (Cambridge, Mass.: Harvard University Press, 2014), 185–220; Jonathan Power, *Like Water on Stone: The Story of Amnesty International* (Boston: Northeastern University Press, 2001), 95–142.

12. Samuel Moyn, *The Last Utopia: Human Rights in History* (Cambridge, Mass.: Belknap Press of Harvard University Press, 2010), 129–148.

13. Keys, *Reclaiming American Virtue,* 182–183.

14. Michael Cotey Morgan, *The Final Act: The Helsinki Accords and the Transformation of the Cold War* (Princeton, N.J.: Princeton University Press, 2018); Moyn, *Last Utopia,* 122–124, 148–150; Sargent, *Superpower Transformed,* 209–219.

15. Keys, *Reclaiming American Virtue,* 221–275; Sargent, *Superpower Transformed,* 231–238.

16. Linda Greenhouse, "Human Rights Abuses Worldwide Are Held to Fall under U.S. Courts," *New York Times,* June 30, 2004; William J. Aceves, *The Anatomy of Torture: A Documentary History of Filartiga v. Pena Irala* (New York: Brill, 2007), 17–76. A quarter century later, a unanimous Supreme Court in *Sosa v. Alvarez-Machain* affirmed the interpretation of the statute proposed by the Carter administration and endorsed by the Court of Appeals for the Second Circuit.

17. Sargent, *Superpower Transformed,* 251–258; Lars Schoultz, *Human Rights and United States Policy toward Latin America* (Princeton, N.J.: Princeton University Press, 1981), 109–134; Lars Schoultz, *Beneath the United States:*

A History of U.S. Policy toward Latin America (Cambridge, Mass.: Harvard University Press, 1998), 332–366.

18. *Shreveport (La.) Times*, June 8, 1979, 6.

19. Jeane Kirkpatrick, "Dictatorships and Double Standards," *Commentary Magazine* 68 (November 1979): 34–45; Jesús Velasco Nevado, *Neoconservatives in U.S. Foreign Policy under Ronald Reagan and George W. Bush: Voices behind the Throne* (Washington, D.C.: Johns Hopkins University Press, 2010), 86–110.

20. "Text of the President's Remarks during a Meeting with Cuban-American Leaders, March 19, 1984," *Public Papers of the Presidents of the United States, January 1–June 29, 1984* (Washington, D.C.: Government Printing Office, 1985), 370; "Question-and-Answer Session with Reporters on the President's Trip to Latin America, December 4, 1982," http://www.presidency.ucsb.edu/ws/?pid=42070, accessed January 30, 2018; Susanne Jonas, *The Battle for Guatemala: Rebels, Death Squads, and U.S. Power* (Boulder, Colo.: Westview Press, 1991), 4–158; Stephen M. Streeter, *Managing the Counterrevolution: The United States and Guatemala, 1954–1961* (Athens: Ohio University Center for International Studies, 2000).

21. Bob Woodward, *Veil: The Secret Wars of the CIA, 1981–1987* (New York: Simon and Schuster, 1987).

22. James LeMoyne, "Testifying to Torture," *New York Times*, June 5, 1988.

23. Lesley Gill, *The School of the Americas: Military Training and Political Violence in the Americas* (Durham, N.C.: Duke University Press, 2004), 59–90, 110–197; Jeremy Kuzmarov, *Modernizing Repression: Police Training and Nation Building in the American Century* (Amherst: University of Massachusetts Press, 2012), 208–231.

24. Isaac A. Linnartz, "The Siren Song of Interrogational Torture: Evaluating the U.S. Implementation of the U.N. Convention against Torture," *Duke Law Journal* 57 (March 2008): 1485–1516; Matthew Lippman, "The Development and Drafting of the United Nations Convention against Torture and Other Cruel, Inhuman or Degrading Treatment or Punishment," *Boston College International and Comparative Law Review* 17 (1994): 275–335.

25. Tim Weiner, "U.S. Judge Orders Ex-Guatemala General to Pay $47.5 Million," *New York Times*, April 13, 1995; Robert F. Drinan and Teresa T. Kuo. "Putting the World's Oppressors on Trial: The Torture Victim Protection Act," *Human Rights Quarterly* 15 (August 1993): 605–624; Raúl Molina Mejía, "The Struggle against Impunity in Guatemala," *Social Justice* 26 (Winter 1999): 55–83.

26. R. Jeffrey Smith, "Detainee Abuse Charges Feared: Shield Sought from '96 War Crimes Act," *Washington Post*, July 28, 2006.

27. National Commission on Terrorist Attacks upon the United States, "Final Report of the National Commission on Terrorist Attacks upon the United States, Executive Summary," 1, https://govinfo.library.unt.edu/911/report/911Report_Exec.pdf, accessed January 31, 2018.

28. "Dr. Condoleezza Rice's Opening Remarks to Commission on Terrorist Attacks," April 8, 2004, https://georgewbush-whitehouse.archives.gov/news/releases/2004/04/text/20040408.html, accessed January 31, 2018.

29. Jane Mayer, *Dark Side: The Inside Story of How the War on Terror Turned into a War on American Ideals* (New York: Doubleday, 2008), 1–10; Adam Hodges, *The War on Terror Narrative: Discourse and Intertextuality in the Construction and Contestation of Sociopolitical Reality* (New York: Oxford University Press, 2011), 19–40, 65–82.

30. Richard A. Clarke, *Against All Enemies: Inside America's War on Terror* (New York: Free Press, 2004), 24.

31. John Yoo, "Memorandum from John C. Yoo, Deputy Assistant Attorney Gen., U.S. Dep't of Justice, to the Deputy Counsel to the President, 'The President's Constitutional Authority to Conduct Military Operations against Terrorists and Nations Supporting Them,'" September 25, 2001; Mayer, *Dark Side*, 46–71; Binoy Kampmark, "Apologists for Power: The Yoo Brief, Executive Power and the State of Exception," *Australian Journal of Politics and History* 61 (March 2015): 82–99.

32. Bruce P. Montgomery, *Richard B. Cheney and the Rise of the Imperial Vice Presidency* (Westport, Conn.: Praeger, 2009), 15–100; Shirley Anne Warshaw, *The Co-presidency of Bush and Cheney* (Stanford, Calif.: Stanford Politics and Policy, 2009), 159–177.

33. "Inquiry into the Treatment of Detainees in U.S. Custody," xiii.

34. Katherine Q. Seelye, "A Nation Challenged: The Prisoners; First 'Unlawful Combatants' Seized in Afghanistan Arrive at U.S. Base in Cuba," *New York Times*, January 12, 2002; David P. Forsythe, *The Politics of Prisoner Abuse: The United States and Enemy Prisoners after 9/11* (New York: Cambridge University Press, 2011), 168–179.

35. Office of the Press Secretary, "Military Order—Detention, Treatment, and Trial of Certain Non-citizens in the War against Terrorism; November 13, 2001," http://avalon.law.yale.edu/sept11/mil_ord_001.asp, accessed January 30, 2018.

36. Alberto Gonzales, "Memorandum for the President: Subject: Decision re Application of the Geneva Convention on Prisoners of War to the Conflict with Al Qaeda and the Taliban," in Joshua L. Dratel and Karen J. Greenberg, eds., *The Torture Papers: The Road to Abu Ghraib* (New York: Cambridge University Press, 2005), 118–119.

37. Gonzales, "Memorandum for the President," 120; John Barry, Michael Hirsh, and Michael Isikoff, "The Roots of Torture," *Newsweek* (May 24, 2004).

38. "Inquiry into the Treatment of Detainees in U.S. Custody," 39; James E. Mitchell and Bill Harlow, *Enhanced Interrogation: Inside the Minds and Motives of the Islamic Terrorists Trying to Destroy America* (New York: Crown Forum, 2016), 44–58.

39. "Memorandum for Alberto R. Gonzales Counsel to the President RE: Standards of Conduct for Interrogation, August 1, 2002," in Dratel and Greenberg, *Torture Papers*, 172–222.

40. "Memorandum for Alberto R. Gonzales," 172–222.

41. Jack L. Goldsmith, *The Terror Presidency: Law and Judgment inside the Bush Administration* (New York: W. W. Norton, 2007), 144.

42. "Inquiry into the Treatment of Detainees in U.S. Custody," 55; Mark Fallon, *Unjustifiable Means: The Inside Story of How the CIA, Pentagon, and US Government Conspired to Torture* (New York: Regan Arts, 2017), 82–83.

43. "Treatment of Detainees in U.S. Custody: Hearings before the Committee on Armed Services," U.S. Senate, 110th Congress, 2nd session, 41.

44. Scott Shane, "2 U.S. Architects on Harsh Tactics in 9/11's Wake," *New York Times*, August 12, 2009.

45. Jane Mayer, "Reporter at Large: The Black Sites," *New Yorker* (August 13, 2007); Dana Priest, "CIA Holds Terror Suspects in Secret Prisons," *Washington Post*, November 2, 2005; Forsythe, *Politics of Prisoner Abuse*, 136–161; https://www.nytimes.com/interactive/projects/guantanamo/detainees/10015-abd-al-rahim-al-nashiri/documents/11.

46. "Inquiry into the Treatment of Detainees in U.S. Custody," 86–87.

47. "Inquiry into the Treatment of Detainees in U.S. Custody," 67.

48. "Inquiry into the Treatment of Detainees in U.S. Custody," 119.

49. Major Sam McCahon to CDR CITF, Assessment of JTF-170 Counter-Resistance Strategies and the Potential Impact on CITF Mission and Personnel, November 4, 2002, in L. E. Fletcher and E. Stover, *The Guantánamo Effect: Exposing the Consequences of U.S. Detention and Interrogation Practices* (Berkeley: University of California Press, 2009), 139–142; "Inquiry into the Treatment of Detainees in U.S. Custody," 69–70.

50. "Inquiry into the Treatment of Detainees in U.S. Custody"; Fallon, *Unjustifiable Means*, 118–121; James P. Pfiffner, *Torture as Public Policy: Restoring U.S. Credibility on the World Stage* (Boulder, Colo.: Paradigm, 2010), 13–44.

51. Alberto J. Mora, "Memorandum for Inspector General, Department of the Navy, Subj: Statement for the record: Office of General Counsel Involvement in Interrogation Issues," July 7, 2004, https://en.wikisource.org/wiki/Statement_of_Alberto_J_Mora_on_interrogation_abuse,_July_7,_2004, accessed January 31, 2018.

52. "Inquiry into the Treatment of Detainees in U.S. Custody," 122.

53. "Inquiry into the Treatment of Detainees in U.S. Custody," 168.

54. "Inquiry into the Treatment of Detainees in U.S. Custody," 162.

55. "Remarks at the Republican National Committee Presidential Gala, October 8, 2003," http://www.presidency.ucsb.edu/ws/index.php?pid=64839, accessed January 31, 2018; *Public Papers of the Presidents of the United States: George W. Bush, 2004; Book 1: January 1 to June 30, 2004* (Washington, D.C.: U.S. Government Printing Office, 2007), 49.

56. George R. Fay, "Investigation of Intelligence Activities at Abu Ghraib; Investigation of the Abu Ghraib Detention Facility and 205th Military Intelligence Brigade," 71.

57. Neil A. Lewis, "Red Cross Finds Detainee Abuse in Guantánamo," *New York Times*, November 30, 2004; Neil A. Lewis, "Red Cross President Plans Visit to Washington on Question of Detainees' Treatment," *New York Times*, December 1, 2004; Dick Meyer, "Rush: MPs Just 'Blowing Off Steam,'" *CBS News*, May 6, 2004, https://www.youtube.com/watch?v=2umbVNpn4fA.

58. "Inquiry into the Treatment of Detainees in U.S. Custody," 168; Anna Mulrine, "U.S. Soldiers Deeply Split over Detainee Treatment, Senate Report Reveals," *U.S. News and World Report* (April 22, 2009).

59. Jane Mayer, "Outsourcing Torture: The Secret History of America's 'Extraordinary Rendition' Program," *New Yorker* (February 14, 2005).

60. Annie Lowery, "Passport: Condi Rice Defends Enhanced Interrogation as 'Legal' and 'Right,'" *Foreign Policy* (April 30, 2009).

61. *The Schlesinger Report: An Investigation of Abu Ghraib* (Washington, D.C.: Department of Defense, 2005), 29.

62. Neil A. Lewis, "Report Discredits F.B.I. Claims of Abuse at Guantánamo Bay," *New York Times,* July 14, 2005; "Hearings before the Committee on Armed Services and Subcommittee on Personnel of the Committee on Armed Services," U.S. Senate, 109th Congress, 1st Session, March 10, 2005; July 13, 2005; July 14, 2005, https://www.gpo.gov/fdsys/pkg/CHRG-109shrg28578 /html/CHRG-109shrg28578.htm, accessed January 31, 2018.

63. "Meet the Press Transcript—December 14, 2014," https://www.nbcnews .com/meet-the-press/meet-press-transcript-december-14–2014-n268181, accessed January 31, 2018.

64. Brian Knowlton, "Human Rights Abuses Continued under New Government in Iraq, U.S. Finds," *International Herald Tribune,* March 2, 2005; Edward Wong, "American Jails in Iraq Bursting with Detainees: Number Rises to 8,900 after Policy Changes," *New York Times,* March 4, 2005; "Torture by Proxy," *New York Times,* March 8, 2005; Douglas Jehl and Eric Schmitt, "U.S. Military Says 26 Inmate Deaths May Be Homicide," *New York Times,* March 16, 2005; Eric Schmitt and Thom Shanker, "U.S., Citing Abuse in Iraqi Prisons, Holds Detainees," *New York Times,* December 25, 2005.

65. Josh White, "President Relents, Backs Torture Ban," *Washington Post,* December 16, 2005.

66. Steven G. Bradbury, "Memorandum for John A. Rizzo, re: Application of the War Crimes Act, the Detainee Treatment Act, and Common Article 3 of the Geneva Conventions to Certain Techniques That May Be Used by the CIA in the Interrogation of High Value al Qaeda Detainees, July 20, 2007," https://www.washingtonpost.com/wp-srv/nation/documents/2007_0720 _OLC_memo_warcrimesact.pdf, accessed January 31, 2018; Scott Shane, David Johnson, and James Risen, "Secret Endorsement of Severe Interrogations," *New York Times,* October 4, 2007; Mark Mazzetti and Scott Shane, "Interrogation Memos Detail Harsh Tactics by the C.I.A," *New York Times,* April 16, 2009.

67. Dan Eggen, "Bush Announces Veto of Waterboarding Ban," *Washington Post,* March 8, 2008.

68. Forsythe, *Politics of Prisoner Abuse,* 171–176, 244–245; H. Pohlman, *Terrorism and the Constitution: The Post-9 / 11 Cases* (Lanham, Md.: Rowman and Littlefield, 2008), 76–87, 138–140, 175–177, 252–257.

69. "Statement of President Barack Obama on Release of OLC Memos, April 16, 2009," http://www.washingtonpost.com/wp-dyn/content/article/2009/04/16 /AR2009041602873.html, accessed January 31, 2018.

70. David Johnston and Charlie Savage, "Obama Reluctant to Look into Bush Programs," *New York Times*, January 11, 2009; Forsythe, *Politics of Prisoner Abuse*, 199–201.

71. "Statement of Attorney General Eric Holder on Closure of Investigation into the Interrogation of Certain Detainees, August 30, 2012," https://www.justice .gov/opa/pr/statement-attorney-general-eric-holder-closure-investigation -interrogation-certain-detainees, accessed January 31, 2018; Scott Shaneaug, "No Charges Filed on Harsh Tactics Used by the C.I.A.," *New York Times*, August 30, 2012; Carrie Johnson and Julie Tate, "New Interrogation Details Emerge as Administration Releases Justice Department Memos," *Washington Post*, April 17, 2009; Josh Meyer and Greg Miller, "Holder Opens Investigation into CIA Interrogations," *Los Angeles Times*, August 25, 2009; David M. Herszenhorn and Carl Hulse, "Obama Resisting Push for Interrogation Panel," *New York Times*, April 23, 2009; David Corn, "Obama and GOPers Worked Together to Kill Bush Torture Probe," *Mother Jones*, December 1, 2010; Eli Lake, "Obama Threatens to Limit U.S. Intel with Brits," *Washington Times*, May 12, 2009; Charlie Savage, "Court Dismisses a Case Asserting Torture by C.I.A.," *New York Times*, September 8, 2010; Glenn Greenwald, "Obama's Justice Department Grants Final Immunity to Bush's CIA Torturers," *Guardian*, August 31, 2012.

72. Richard Nixon, "Remarks in New York City: 'Toward Freedom from Fear,' May 8, 1968," http://www.presidency.ucsb.edu/ws/index.php?pid=123915, accessed January 31, 2018; Richard Nixon, "Toward Freedom from Fear (Nixon for President Committee, 1968).

73. *Congressional Record: Proceedings and Debates of the . . . Congress*, 119, Part 13 (Washington, D.C.: U.S. Government Printing Office, 1973), 16865.

74. Quoted in Kevin J. McMahon, *Nixon's Court: His Challenge to Judicial Liberalism and Its Political Consequences* (Chicago: University of Chicago Press, 2011).

75. Ronald Reagan, "Radio Address to the Nation on Proposed Crime Legislation, February 18, 1984," http://www.presidency.ucsb.edu/ws/index.php?pid =39541, accessed January 31, 2018.

76. Daniel P. Moynihan, *The Negro Family: The Case for National Action* (Washington, D.C.: Office of Policy Planning and Research, U.S. Department of Labor, 1965), https://www.dol.gov/oasam/programs/history/webid-meynihan .htm, accessed January 31, 2018; Elizabeth K. Hinton, *From the War on Poverty to the War on Crime: The Making of Mass Incarceration in America* (Cambridge, Mass.: Harvard University Press, 2016), 224–225.

77. Hinton, *From the War on Poverty*, 134–179; Daryl M. Scott, *Contempt and Pity: Social Policy and the Image of the Damaged Black Psyche, 1880–1996* (Chapel Hill: University of North Carolina Press, 1997), 161–202.

78. "Coming of the Super-Predators," John J. Delulio Jr, *Weekly Standard*, November 27, 1995; Matt DeLisi, Brendan D. Dooley, and Kevin M. Beaver, "Super-Predators Revisited," in Karen T. Froeling, ed., *Criminology Research Focus* (New York: Nova Science Publishers, 2007), 21–30.

79. Pauline Kael, "Dirty Harry: Saint Cop," *New Yorker*, January 15, 1972.

80. James Q. Wilson, *Varieties of Police Behavior: The Management of Law and Order in Eight Communities* (Cambridge, Mass.: Harvard University Press, 1968), 16.

81. Elizabeth Dale, *Robert Nixon and Police Torture in Chicago, 1871–1971* (DeKalb: Northern Illinois University Press, 2016), 102–120; Andrew J. Diamond, *Chicago on the Make: Power and Inequality in a Modern City* (Oakland: University of California Press, 2017), 183–184, 212–217; Simon Balto, *Occupied Territory: Policing Black Chicago from Red Summer to Black Power* (Chapel Hill: University of North Carolina Press, 2019), Chapter Five.

82. John Conroy, "Tools of the Trade," *Chicago Reader*, February 3, 2005; Conroy, *Unspeakable Acts, Ordinary People*, 61–62.

83. Matthew Wallberg, "Federal Trial of Burges Opens with Torture Allegations," *Chicago Tribune*, May 26, 2010.

84. G. Flint Taylor, "The Chicago Police Torture Scandal: A Legal and Political History," *CUNY Law Review* (Summer 2014): 355.

85. "Cops Accused of Brutality," *Chicago Tribune*, February 18, 1982; Chinta Strausberg, "Police, Bar Group Ask 'Manhunt' Probe," *Chicago Defender*, February 18, 1982; Egan and Boyle, "Report of the Special State's Attorney," 43–168; John Conroy, "House of Screams," *Chicago Reader*, January 25, 1990.

86. Egan and Boyle, "Report of the Special State's Attorney," 79.

87. Egan and Boyle, "Report of the Special State's Attorney," 79, 87–89, 107–111, 125–126, 131.

88. Egan and Boyle, "Report of the Special State's Attorney," 144–148.

89. United States Department of Justice Civil Rights Division and United States Attorney's Office Northern District of Illinois, "Investigation of the Chicago Police Department" (2017), esp. 74–79.

90. *People v. Banks*, 549 N.E. 2nd, 770, 771; Taylor, "Chicago Police Torture Scandal," 344–345.

91. Michael Goldston, "Chicago Police Department Office of Professional Standards, History of Allegations of Misconduct by Area Two Personnel" (November 2, 1990), 3; David Jackson, "13 Years of Cop Torture Alleged, Daley, Martin, Rip Internal Police Reports," *Chicago Tribune*, February 8, 1992.

92. "Report Near on Alleged '70s Police Torture," *Chicago Sun-Times*, April 28, 2006; Abdon M. Pallasch and Frank Main, "Did Leaders of Burge Inquiry Favor City Hall? Email Show Top Daley Lawyer Pleased with Their Selection," *Chicago Sun-Times*, July 31, 2006; Abdon M. Pallasch and Frank Main, "Torture Report and Family Ties: Top Investigator Had Nephew on Burge's Staff," *Chicago Sun-Times*, August 6, 2006; Andrea J. Ritchie and Joey L. Mogul, "Report on the Failure of Special Prosecutors Edward J. Egan and Robert D. Boyle to Fairly Investigate Systemic Police Torture in Chicago," April 24, 2007, https://www.nlg-npap.org/reports/report-failure-special-pro secutors-edward-j-egan-and-robert-d-boyle-fairly-investigate; "New Report Blasts Probe into Cop Torture," *Chicago Tribune*, April 25, 2007.

93. Ray Long, "Police Torture Probe Sought Here," *Chicago Sun-Times*, January 28, 1991; "Brutality Probe Haunts City, Cops Go Unpunished Despite OPS Findings Suspects Were Tortured," *Chicago Tribune*, February 23,

1999; Dennis Conrad, "Panel Hears Claims of Anti-Black Cop Brutality Here," *Chicago Sun-Times*, October 15, 2005; United Nations Commission against Torture, "Consideration of Reports Submitted by States Parties under Article 19 of the Convention, Conclusions and Recommendations of the Committee against Torture," May 16, 2006; B. Jarovsky, "Can Shame Stop the Games?" *Chicago Reader*, March 23, 2007; "Chicago Must SAY NO to Daley's Olympics," *Chicago Defender*, March 15, 2007; Diamond, *Chicago on the Make*, 260–292.

94. G. Flint Taylor, "The Long Path to Reparations for the Survivors of Chicago Police Torture," *Northwestern Journal of Law and Social Policy* 11 (2016): 330–353.

95. *Columbia Journalism Review*, May 11, 2015.

96. Daniel R. Ames and Alice J. Lee, "Tortured Beliefs: How and When Prior Support for Torture Skews the Perceived Value of Coerced Information," *Journal of Experimental Social Psychology* 60 (2015): 86–92; Courtenay R. Conrad et al., "Threat Perception and American Support for Torture," *Political Behavior* 10 (2017), doi: 10.1007/s11109-017-9433-5; Paul Gronke et al., "U.S. Public Opinion on Torture, 2001–2009," *PS: Political Science and Politics* 43 (July 2010): 437–444; Jeremy D. Mayer and David J. Armor, "Support for Torture over Time: Interrogating the American Public about Coercive Tactics," *Social Science Journal* 49 (2012): 439–446; and Mark Tarrant et al., "Social Identity and Perceptions of Torture: It's Moral When We Do It," *Journal of Experimental Social Psychology* 48 (2012): 513–518.

97. Clark Mindock, "Donald Trump Wants to Bring Back Waterboarding and 'A Hell of a Lot Worse' Interrogation Tactics," *International Business Times*, February 6, 2017.

98. Karl Marx, "On the Jewish Question," 1843, https://www.marxists.org/archive/marx/works/1844/jewish-question, accessed January 31, 2018.

99. Hannah Arendt, "Reflections on Violence," *New York Review of Books*, February 27, 1969.

Acknowledgments

This book had its origins during the strenuous public debate over "enhanced interrogation" in 2004. During the intervening years, I have accumulated a long list of debts. Research for this book was liberally funded by the Guggenheim Foundation and the University of North Carolina. Their timely and generous support expedited the completion of my work.

I owe a particular obligation to scholars who investigated some of the topics addressed herein. The notes in this book convey only a small measure of the inspiration that I have derived from the pioneering work of many authors, including: on the colonial era, Lisa Silverman, Wayne E. Lee, and Christina Snyder; on punishment during the early republic, Michael Meranze, Michael Ignatieff, and W. David Lewis; on cruelty and slavery in antebellum United States, Margaret N. Abruzzo and Myra C. Glenn; on the Civil War era, John Fabian Witt, Harry Stout, and D. H. Dilbeck; on torture in the age of empire, Brian McA. Linn, Christopher J. Einolf, Michael Patrick Cullinane, Fabian Hilfrich, and Paul A. Kramer; on police interrogation and the "third degree," Richard A. Leo, David Garland, and Elizabeth Dale; on the Cold War era, Susan L. Carruthers, Alfred W. McCoy, and Kendrick Oliver; and on the recent past, John Conroy, Jane Mayer, Barbara Keyes, and Samuel Moyn. Finally, the works of Michel Foucault, Darius Regali, Edward Peters, and Elaine Scarry have been my constant companions.

To my friends and colleagues who have listened to me discuss the chilling subject of this book for the past decade, I am sincerely grateful. John Fabian Witt and Amy Wood deserve special mention for their trenchant and enormously helpful comments on the manuscript. I have also had the great privilege of sharing my work with audiences at the Triangle Early American History Seminar, Tulane University, the University of Pittsburgh, the University of Melbourne, Monash University, LaTrobe University, the University of Sydney, the University of Glasgow, the University of Edinburgh, the University of Newcastle, and the University of Oxford. I am indebted to my hosts at each institution and hope to have the opportunity in the future to begin to repay their hospitality and kindness.

Over the years, Anndal G. Narayanan and Joshua Akers proved to be tireless and valued research assistants. Josh, in particular, displayed some of the most enviable research skills I have encountered.

During the past decade and a half, I have had the extraordinary pleasure of working with Joyce Seltzer. Any conversations with her about history, contemporary events, art, literature, music, my own work, or virtually anything have been occasions to relish and savor.

Nor could I not have asked for better care and guidance from Kate Brick and Angela Piliouras. Together they have done superb work transforming my manuscript into the beautifully produced book upon which your eyes currently rest.

Finally, A. T. M. has literally grown up while I have worked on this book. We now spar over historical matters, and I have the great pleasure of being schooled by my son. And words utterly fail to express my gratitude to and love for S. E. J. This book is most certainly not the book she would have had me write, but her support for me has never waned. A day never passes that I don't feel blessed to travel the waters of time in her company.

Illustration Credits

5.2. *Those Pious Yanks Can't Throw Stones at Us Anymore. Life,* May 22, 1902. University Libraries, University of North Carolina, Chapel Hill

6.1. "Well, Captain, the Prisoner Has Confessed to Murder!" "O.K. Hold Him till There Is a Murder!" Caroline and Erwin Swann Collection, Library of Congress.

6.2. *President Herbert Hoover Meeting with the Wickersham Commission, May 1929.* Library of Congress, LC-USZ62–97325

7.1. "The Evidence Is Piling Up." Library of Congress, DLC / PP-1953:R22.8

7.2. *Soldiers Torturing Viet Cong Suspect.* Getty Images/Bettmann/515099564

8.1. "We Do Not Torture People!" CartoonStock

8.2. *Protestors Demand Justice for Victims of Chicago Police Torture.* Getty Images/71496768

Index